# 中学英语
# 联动教研行动研究

张志梅　著

ZHONGXUE YINGYU LIANDONG JIAOYAN XINGODNG YANJIU

中山大學出版社
SUN YAT-SEN UNIVERSITY PRESS
·广州·

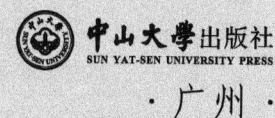

版权所有　翻印必究

**图书在版编目（CIP）数据**

中学英语联动教研行动研究/张志梅著.—广州：中山大学出版社，2023.12

ISBN 978-7-306-07988-6

Ⅰ.①中…　Ⅱ.①张…　Ⅲ.①英语课—教学研究—中学　Ⅳ.①G633.412

中国国家版本馆 CIP 数据核字（2023）第 246045 号

| | |
|---|---|
| 出 版 人： | 王天琪 |
| 策划编辑： | 熊锡源 |
| 责任编辑： | 熊锡源 |
| 封面设计： | 林绵华 |
| 责任校对： | 刘　婷 |
| 责任技编： | 靳晓虹 |
| 出版发行： | 中山大学出版社 |
| 电　　话： | 编辑部 020 - 84110771，84110283，84111997，84110779 |
| | 发行部 020 - 84111998，84111981，84111160 |
| 地　　址： | 广州市新港西路 135 号 |
| 邮　　编： | 510275　传　真：020 - 84036565 |
| 网　　址： | http://www.zsup.com.cn　E - mail：zdcbs@ mail.sysu.edu.cn |
| 印 刷 者： | 广东虎彩云印刷有限公司 |
| 规　　格： | 787mm×1092mm　1/16　20.75 印张　386 千字 |
| 版次印次： | 2023 年 12 月第 1 版　2023 年 12 月第 1 次印刷 |
| 定　　价： | 68.00 元 |

如发现本书因印装质量影响阅读，请与出版社发行部联系调换

# Preface:
# English Teaching and Research as a Harmonious Linkage of Life

    Everyone who comes into this world harbors aspirations and pursuits of life. I, on the other hand, have chosen to embark on the path of teaching and researching English and I am convinced that it is a wonderful harmonious linkage in life.

    It is only by entering into life that we can respect life as it is, and only then can there be a harmonious linkage between life and life. Education is a linked process in which "one soul awakens another". The goal of education should be human-centered. The aim of education is to achieve free, comprehensive and harmonious development of human beings through knowledge learning and practical realization. Education should not only enable people to master knowledge in order to transform the objective world, but also enable them to better adapt to the environment and society, help them understand the world, explore the unknown, and make life better, more balanced and harmonious. The process of education should move with the law. Education is a dynamic and ever-changing process, which requires educators to flexibly adjust the content and methods of teaching according to the learning status and needs of students, so as to make them more in line with the actual needs, and to encourage students to take an active part in educational activities, thus creating a situation of positive interaction between educators and students. Education is a process that can stimulate students' interests and allow them to participate and experience, which requires educators to change the traditional teaching methods and content to adapt to the needs of students and changes in society. The process of education should focus on inquiry, practice and experience, so that students learn in a dynamic, lively and diversified context, not only master the subject knowledge, but also master the subject thinking and methodology, and be able to comprehensively apply the knowledge to solve problems encountered in real life and form a positive way of life. Therefore, "linkage" is a law that should be followed in the process of education, and it is a law that is expressed in the movement of life. By understanding and applying these laws, we can achieve better educational results and a harmonious state of life.

In the process of implementing English linkage teaching and research, I have actively organized and participated in various training and seminar activities with teachers to learn the new curriculum standards and the latest education and teaching concepts, and to gain a deeper understanding and application of advanced teaching strategies. Through activities such as theoretical learning, teaching design, teaching implementation, classroom observation, lesson sharing, mutual evaluation, expert guidance, reflection and enhancement, and subject research, a vigorous learning momentum has been created. During the periods of exchange, sharing and cooperation, we have broadened our professional vision, abandoned the inherent patterns of teaching, built a new model of Planning-Teaching-Observation-Reflection-Evaluation-Creation (PTOREC) teaching and research, made English as the working language, bravely stepped out of the comfort zone to try to innovate, continuously elevating teaching and research to new heights. Under the guidance of the teachers, the students have constantly surpassed themselves, not only learn the use of language skills, but also develop the ability to think and solve problems on their own initiative. They have abandoned their passive receptive roles and demonstrated a confident, active and exploratory attitude towards learning. They become more and more independent and autonomous, and grow into more well-rounded young people. All these are the valuable gifts that the English Linkage Teaching and Research has brought to teachers and students, and inspire us to continue to take more solid steps along this path. I believe that through our joint efforts and unremitting exploration, our students will become talents with a sense of family and country, an international outlook and innovative thinking. They will be able to navigate the globalized world and realize their talents and potential.

Looking back on the past years, I have seen the growing steps of many students and teachers around me, and I have also seen myself gradually changing from a tender teacher to an experienced researcher. In this process of growth, English teaching and research has played a crucial role. English linkage teaching and research is not just a method of teaching and research, but also a resonance of spirit. It made me understand the significance of cooperation and communication among teachers. Through interaction and exchange with experts as well as peers, I have gained a constant stream of inspiration and enlightenment, and I have benefited greatly from their clash of ideas and sharing of experience. It is this harmonious and linked atmosphere that makes the teaching level of the region continuously improve, and makes teachers enjoy the happiness and satisfaction brought by teaching and research even more. In the family of English teaching and research linkage, teachers continue to reap the benefits of professional development, and students take steps toward growth. Together, we are drawing the blueprint of education and injecting infinite hope and strength into the cause of education.

  This is a journey of love and growth, and the starting point of a dream. Here, the seeds of education have taken root and gradually blossomed, and will sow the seeds of hope for the world of the future. I would like to express my heartfelt thanks to the leaders, experts and teachers who have been supporting and encouraging me, it is your love and support that make me keep in mind my initial resolve and forge ahead. At the same time, I would also like to thank my students, it is your efforts and dedication that make me deeply feel the significance of teaching and research. Let's go forward hand in hand and create a brighter future together!

# 自序：
# 英语教研是生命的和谐联动

每一个来到这个世界的人，都怀揣着对生活的向往和追求。而我，选择了走上英语教研的道路，并深信这是生命中一段美好的和谐联动。

走进生命才会尊重生命本来的样子，生命与生命之间才会产生和谐的联动。教育是"一个灵魂唤醒另一个灵魂"，是一个联动的过程。教育的目的是通过知识的学习和实践体悟，实现人的自由、全面、和谐的发展。教育不只是让人掌握知识以改造客观世界，也应该让人更好地适应环境、适应社会、探索未知，让生活变得更加美好、平衡、和谐。教育是一个动态的、不断变化的过程，它要求教育者根据学生的学习状态和需求，灵活调整教学内容和方法，使之更加符合学生的实际需求，并且鼓励学生积极参与到教育活动中，形成教育者和学生良性互动的局面。教育是一个能够激发学生兴趣、让学生参与和体验的过程，这就要求教育者改变传统的教学方法和内容，以适应学生的需求和社会的变化。教育过程应该注重探究性、实践性、体验性，让学生在动态、活泼、多元的情境中学习，从而使学生不仅掌握学科知识，而且掌握学科思想方法，能综合应用知识解决实际生活中遇到的问题并塑造积极的生活方式。所以说"联动"是教育过程中应遵循的规律，是生命运动中表现出来的规律。了解和应用这些规律，才能达到更好的教育效果和生命的和谐状态。

在实施英语联动教研的过程中，我和老师们一起学习新课标和最新的教育教学理念，深入了解和应用先进的教学策略。通过课题研究、理论学习、教学设计、教学实施、观摩课堂、课例分享、相互评议、专家指导、反思提升等活动，形成蓬勃向上的学习动力。在一次次的交流分享和合作中，特别是近年来不断深入研究新课程，实施单元整体教学，我们拓宽了专业视野，摒弃了固有的教学模式，构建了 Planning-Teaching-Observation-Reflection-Evaluation-Creation（PTOREC）教研新模式，勇敢地走出舒适区去尝试创新，实现了把英语作为教研的工作语言，不断将教学教研提升到新的高度。学生们在老师的引领下，不断超越自己，不仅学会了语言技能的运用，而且形成了主动思考和解决问题的能力。他们摒弃了被动接受的角色，展现出自信、积极探索的学习态度。他们变得越来越独立和自主，成长为全面发展的青少年。而这一切正是联动教研带给师生的宝贵礼物，也鼓舞我们继续沿着这条道路迈出更加坚实的步伐。相信通过我们的共同努力和不懈探索，我们的学生将成为具有家国情怀、国际视野和创新思维的人才，能够在全球化的世界中游刃有余。

  回首过去的岁月，我看到了身边许许多多的学生和老师在不断成长，也看到了自己从一个稚嫩的新教师逐渐成为经验丰富的教研员。在这个成长的过程中，英语教研起到了至关重要的作用。英语联动教研不仅仅是一种教研方法，更是一种精神的共鸣。它让我明白了教师之间的合作和交流对于教育的意义。通过与专家以及同行们的互动和交流，我收获了源源不断的灵感和启发，他们的思想碰撞和经验分享让我受益匪浅。正是这种和谐联动的氛围，使得区域的教学水平不断提高，也让老师们更加享受到了教研带来的快乐与满足。我们共同擘画着教育的蓝图，为教育事业注入无穷的希望和力量。

  这是一段关于爱与成长的旅程，也是一个梦想的起航点。在这里，教育的种子已经扎根，不断开花结果。我要衷心感谢那些一直支持和鼓励我的领导们、专家们和老师们，是你们的关爱和支持让我不忘初心，砥砺前行。同时也要感谢我的学生们，是你们的努力和付出，让我深感教研的意义所在。让我们一起携手前行，共同创造更加美好的未来！

**2023 年 8 月 16 日于广州**

# 目 录

## 第一篇 课题引领

第一章 "聚焦单元整体教学的中学英语联动教研行动研究"开题报告 ………………………………………………………………… 2

第二章 "聚焦单元整体教学的中学英语联动教研行动研究"阶段性报告 ………………………………………………………… 14

第三章 "聚焦单元整体教学的中学英语联动教研行动研究"结题报告 …………………………………………………………… 19

## 第二篇 设计先行

第一章 广州共享课堂与国家课程资源
——沪教版七年级模块教学设计 …………… 34

 设计一 Module 3 Travels Unit 5 Visiting the Moon, Grade 7A Extensive Reading …………………………………… 34

 设计二 Module 3 Travels Unit 6 Travelling around the World, Grade 7A Writing ……………………………………… 41

 设计三 Module 3 Travels Grade 7A Module 3 Revision …… 44

第二章 广州共享课堂精品课
——人教版高三年级项目教学设计 …………… 47

 设计四 高中英语选修二 Unit 1 Relationships Project ……… 47

第三章 沪教版八年级单元整体教学设计 ……………………… 54

 设计五 八年级上册 Module 4 School life Unit 8 English Week …… 54

1

设计六　八年级下册 Module 3 Animals Unit 5 Save the Endangered Animals
………………………………………………………………………… 62

## 第四章　人教版八年级课时教学设计………………………………… 71

设计七　八年级下册 Unit 5 What Were You Doing When the Rainstorm Came?
Listening & Speaking ……………………………………………… 71

设计八　八年级下册 Unit 5 What Were You Doing When the Rainstorm Came?
Grammar …………………………………………………………… 74

设计九　八年级下册 Unit 5 What Were You Doing When the Rainstorm Came?
Reading …………………………………………………………… 77

## 第五章　高中英语读后续写区域集体备课作业设计 ……………… 80

设计十　运用"TEAMS"策略提升读后续写作业设计 ……………… 80

# 第三篇　课堂联动

## 第一章　广州市黄埔区与海珠区联动教研 ………………………… 88

课例一　沪教版七年级下册 Unit 7 Poems 英汉诗歌对比阅读课 ……… 88

## 第二章　"云端送教，粤黔共研"海珠瓮安联动教研 ……………… 97

课例二　沪教版八年级上册 Module 4 School Life Unit 8 English Week
阅读课 ……………………………………………………………… 97

## 第三章　广州市初二英语市区联动教研 …………………………… 104

课例三　沪教版八年级下册 Module 1 Social Communication Unit 1 Helping
Those in Need 单元整体复习课 ………………………………… 104

## 第四章　广州市海珠区与湖南省新化县区校联动教研 …………… 119

课例四　运用要素分析和"TEAMS"框架突破高考英语读后续写写作课 … 119

## 第五章　广州市海珠区初三英语教研
　　　　　——中考备考专题 ………………………………………… 126

课例五　课标话题之 Topic 16 Entertainment and Sports 听说课 ……… 126

## 第六章　广州市海珠区区校联动教研 ……………………………… 134

课例六　广州版初中英语 Success with English Book 6A Unit 5 It's Film
Week *Harry Potter* 电影欣赏课 ………………………………… 134

第七章　广州市海珠区集团学校联动教研 …………………… 150
　　课例七　沪教版八年级下册 Unit 6 Pets Grammar 语法课 …… 150
第八章　广州市"百千万人才培养工程"第二批"中学名教师"培养项目
　　　　跟岗活动 ……………………………………………… 156
　　课例八　How to Write a Survey 应用文写作课 ……………… 156
第九章　广州市"百千万人才培养工程"第二批"中学名教师"培养项目
　　　　跟岗以及海珠区高二英语教研活动 ………………… 164
　　课例九　Topic 10—Festivals, Holidays and Celebrations 课标话题写作课
　　　　　　………………………………………………………… 164
第十章　广州市第四批初中英语骨干教师第六组跟岗活动 …… 171
　　课例十　上教社 Going on Safari 整本书阅读示范课 ………… 171

# 第四篇　成果推广

第一章　育人蓝图引领的初中英语单元整体教学
　　　　——以牛津沪教版八年级下册 Unit 1 Helping Those in Need
　　　　单元复习课为例 …………………………………… 180
第二章　基于单元整体教学的初中英语作业设计研究 ………… 188
第三章　"双新"背景下高中英语视频教学中培养学生文化意识的研究
　　　　——以人教版选择性必修三 Unit 1 Art Video Time《清明上河图》
　　　　为例 ………………………………………………… 194
第四章　读后续写的文化转向与运用"TEAMS"框架提升学生文化意识初探
　　　　——以 2023 年新高考英语全国 I 卷为例 ……………… 209
第五章　基于学业水平监测的读后续写分析与"TEAMS"讲评研究
　　　　——以 2023 年 6 月广州市高二英语八区联考读后续写试题为例
　　　　………………………………………………………… 221
第六章　基于核心素养和学生说题的高中英语写作教学课例研究 …… 233
第七章　"主题—探究—评价"活动课教学模式 ……………… 245
　　第一节　建模的背景和意义 ………………………………… 245
　　第二节　对"主题—探究—评价"英语活动课教学模式的基本认识 …… 248

第三节　模式的实施过程及课例点评……………………………………253
　　第四节　英语活动课教学模式点评……………………………262
第八章　"自主、互动、创造"的英语课堂教学模式的实验研究…………263
　　第一节　研究问题的提出……………………………………………263
　　第二节　"自主、互动、创造"的英语课堂教学模式探索……………266
　　第三节　"自主、互动、创造"的英语课堂教学模式的实验……………276
第九章　学习·收获·反思·感悟
　　　　——漫谈赴英国伯明翰大学的"Teacher-Training"……………290
第十章　2023年广州市初中学业水平考试英语试题评析及教学启示……307
第十一章　"实施过程性评价，发展英语核心素养"广州市高一英语市区
　　　　　联动教研活动简报……………………………………………310
第十二章　用英语推进中西文化交流互鉴
　　　　　——广州市海珠区初二英语教研活动简报……………………314
Epilogue………………………………………………………………………317
后　　记………………………………………………………………………318

# 第一篇 课题引领

本篇以笔者主持的广东省课题研究为载体,从开题报告、阶段性报告到结题报告,比较完整地呈现了如何整合区域内外的教研力量、构建联动教研共同体、聚焦英语教学的真问题,以朴素的方式和融入常规工作的思路,从主持上级部门的课题到指导一线教师开展教育教学微课题,从教师教育与教学管理的双重视野来开展研究,直到达成研究预期目标。特别是课题研究提升了教研骨干小组的研究能力,提高了全体教师的研究意识,树立了"教师成为研究者"的理念,同时构建了 Planning-Teaching-Observation-Reflection-Evaluation-Creation(PTOREC)教研新模式,引领课堂教学改进,拓展了区教研活动的深度、广度和关联度,提高了教学教研工作的系统性、针对性和有效性。

# 第一章 "聚焦单元整体教学的中学英语联动教研行动研究"开题报告

## 一、课题名称

本课题为广东省教育研究院2022年中小学英语教育专项研究课题"聚焦单元整体教学的中学英语联动教研行动研究"（课题编号：GDJY-2022-A-yyb33）。课题组成员如表1所示。

表1 课题组成员

| 姓名 | 单位 | 学段 |
| --- | --- | --- |
| 张志梅 | 广州市海珠区教育发展研究院 | 初高中英语，主持人 |
| 王昕 | 华南师范大学附属中学 | 初中英语 |
| 罗曼容 | 广州市第五中学 | 初中英语 |
| 李静 | 广州市海珠区华海双语学校 | 初中英语 |
| 黎绮华 | 广州市第五中学 | 初中英语 |
| 黄凤妹 | 广州市海珠外国语实验中学 | 高中英语 |
| 王迪雅 | 广州市南武中学 | 初中英语 |
| 卢兰芬 | 广州市南武中学 | 初中英语 |
| 张梅花 | 湖南省新化县第二中学 | 高中英语 |
| 张颖 | 中山大学附属中学 | 高中英语 |
| 黄雨 | 广州市第五中学 | 高中英语 |
| 蔡雯莹 | 广州市育才中学 | 高中英语 |
| 魏燕 | 广州市南武实验学校 | 初中英语 |
| 梁楚晖 | 广州市南武中学岭南画派纪念校区 | 高中英语 |
| 周燕梨 | 广州市第九十七中学 | 高中英语 |
| 韦微 | 广州市为明学校 | 高中英语 |

续上表

| 姓名 | 单位 | 学段 |
|------|------|------|
| 陈家宜 | 广州市南武中学 | 高中英语 |
| 林映 | 广州市江南外国语学校 | 初中英语 |
| 梁蕴娜 | 广州市海珠外国语实验学校附属中学 | 初中英语 |
| 庄茹慧 | 广州市绿翠现代实验学校 | 初中英语 |
| 刘志刚 | 广州市为明学校 | 初中英语 |
| 刘德君 | 华南师范大学附属黄埔实验学校 | 初中英语 |
| 曾小倩 | 广州市执信琶洲实验学校 | 初中英语 |
| 黎敏 | 广州市景中实验学校 | 初中英语 |
| 何穗珊 | 广州市劬劳中学 | 初中英语 |
| 关慧思 | 广州市第四十一中学 | 高中英语 |
| 张莉 | 广州市培才高级中学 | 高中英语 |
| 张红艳 | 广州市海珠中学 | 高中英语 |
| 王丽 | 广州市第五中学 | 高中英语 |
| 梁家昕 | 广州市第九十七中学 | 初中英语 |
| 谭珊 | 广州市江南外国语学校 | 初中英语 |
| 陈颖 | 广州市江南外国语学校 | 初中英语 |
| 钟玉华 | 贵州省瓮安六中支教 | 初中英语 |
| 冯国威 | 广州市第六中学 | 初中英语 |
| 姜媛媛 | 广州市海珠区六中珠江中学 | 初中语文 |
| Lukas | 广州市海珠区华海双语学校外教 | 初高中英语 |

## 二、课题研究的背景

《义务教育英语课程标准（2022年版）》（以下简称《新课标》）指出：教学研究与教师培训要着力引导教师准确、深刻领会课程理念、目标和要求，并转化为切实有效的教学实践，不断提升教师的专业素养，全面促成学生核心素养的形成与发展。有条件的地区还可以建立不同区域间和不同学校间教师学习、研究的共同体，帮助教师增进学术交流，拓宽专业视野，提高教学水平。① 由此可见，《新课标》明确了教研团队建设的重要性和努力的方向。

数字时代信息技术的高速发展以及近年疫情防控形势下线上教研的常态化，使得各级各类的联动教研方式得到推广。广东省教育研究院和广州市教育研究院不断深入开展的市区联动教研活动，为跨市跨区联动、城乡联动提供了理论指导和实践平台。海珠区也积极响应广州市教研院的号召，比如：2022年3月31日在高一年级进行了"聚焦核心素养和过程性评价"的市区联动教研；2022年4月7日在初一年级与黄埔区联合进行了"基于主题意义的单元整体教学跨区联动教研活动"；2022年9月29日在初一年级进行了"广州市初中英语单元整体教学·市区联动系列教研活动（海珠专场）"；2022年10月13日在高二年级开展了海珠、越秀联动教研活动，聚焦单元整体教学；2022年10月20日在初二年级进行了"云端送教，粤黔共研——中学英语八年级基于主题意义的单元整体教学设计与实施展示与交流活动"。这类活动深受师生欢迎，也大大地促进了教师专业化水平的提升。在这种新教研模式的带动下，作为一个跨初中和高中学段的教研员，对于区域的教研活动应如何立足区情，有针对性地设计、组织、实施和评价本区的教研活动，进一步深化省市教研成果，为广大师生服务和减负增效呢？本课题"聚焦单元整体教学的中学英语联动教研行动研究"旨在以常规的区教研活动为平台，以全区老师为主体，以全员单元整体集备、校区市公开课、专题研讨为抓手，以课题组老师、中心组老师为示范引领，以信息技术为支持，加强市区校联动教研，调动老师们参与教研的积极性，发挥集体智慧，切实减负增效，提高教学质量，提升核心素养。

## 三、课题的核心概念及其界定

### （一）单元整体教学

单元是学习内容的序列化、结构化、具体化呈现，它以语境为依托，以语篇为载体，是落实课程标准和培养学生核心素养的基本单位。单元整体教学要求从单元视角分析教材教法，确定单元教学目标，设计单元学习活动、作业、评价、资源等。与传统的分段教学方法相比，单元整体教学的优势在于有助于系统的知识训练和整体内容的把握，形成大观念，发展核心素养。

---

① 中华人民共和国教育部：《义务教育英语课程标准（2022年版）》，北京师范大学出版社2022年版，第51页。

## (二) 大观念

大观念是上位观念的一种重要形式。[①]

大：具有生活的价值和很强的迁移价值。

生活价值（lifeworthy）：对学习者的生活有意义的知识才可能具有长久的生命力。

大观念可以理解为从零散概念中统整或提炼出来的上位观念，将有限的、深层次的重要观念进行有意义的联结，共同构成学科的连贯整体。大观念集中体现学科本质性的思维方式和关键观点，是"学生深入挖掘学科内核的概念锚点"[②]。

## (三) 英语教育大观念

英语教育的大观念是语言相关的大观念和内容相关的大观念的有机结合。

语言相关的大观念：从学科角度看，与语言相关的大观念面向英语学科的本体知识，指的是学生在学习和使用语言的过程中感知和体验到的关于如何理解和表达语言的结构、策略和理念的知识。它有助于培养学生的语言能力。

内容相关的大观念：从跨学科的角度看，与内容相关的大观念为学生通过语言学习获得渗透着情感、态度和价值观的跨文化理解提供了语境，使他们能够构建和生成新的知识结构，在对意义的主题探索中发展具有正确价值判断的解决问题的能力，从而培养跨文化理解能力和文化自信。

## (四) 行动研究

考瑞（Stephen M. Corey）在1953年出版的《改进学校实践的行动研究》中，率先把行动研究引入到教育研究中，认为只有教师、学生、管理人员、家长以及其他相关人员不断地探讨学校教育的改进并付诸行动，学校才会有效地发展。此后，行动研究在教育领域流行。20世纪70年代，"教师即研究者"成为教育中的重要概念。

卡尔与凯米斯（Carr & Kemmis）在1985年对行动研究做了比较权威的界

---

[①] David Ausubel. *Cognitive Psychology: A Self-Instructional Approach*. Holt, Rinehart & Winston, 1960.

[②] 王蔷、孙万磊、赵连杰：《大观念对英语学科落实育人导向课程目标的意义与价值》，载《教学月刊》2022年第4期。

定：行动研究是在社会情境（包括教育情境）中，自我反省探究的一种形式，参与者包括教师、学生、校长等人，其目的在于促发社会的或教育实践的合理性及正义性、帮助研究者了解实践工作的相关情景，使实践工作能够付之于实践而有成效。[①]

教师的根本任务是教学，而不是研究，但教学工作是一项高智慧的创新活动，而不是工匠的活动，所以，教师需要在教学中研究，在研究中教学。教学是一种活动或行动，所以，行动研究（action research）是教师研究的重要方法，是其专业发展的重要途径。

### （五）联动教研

教研是基础教育工作的重要组成部分，是解决教学中的疑难困惑、促进教师专业发展的关键途径。教研活动的有效性在于"吸引力"和"参与度"："吸引力"得力于优质研修项目的选择；联动教研则有助于拓宽活动的"参与度"，也就是说能拓展区教研活动的深度、广度和关联度，构成区域内乃至区域外联动教研的新格局。单元是落实课程标准和培养学生核心素养的基本单位，通过联动教研聚焦单元整体教学，将创造平等互动的多元研究氛围，发挥研究共同体的优势，汇集全体老师的力量，进一步明确单元教学目标、明晰教学主线，设计教学活动，开展教学实践，从而大大加强单元教学的整体性、关联性、主题性，有效减轻教师备课负担和学生的学习负担，提高教学效率，助推英语教学质量进一步提高，提升师生的核心素养。教学工作是创造性的，行动研究可以提高教师探究的热情和愿望，增强教师对工作的热爱，提高教师的工作效能。

## 四、本课题国内研究现状述评

核心素养、大观念、单元整体教学和联动教研都是当前英语教学研究的热点。在中国知网数据库以上述4个关键词为主题词进行检索，限定学科为"中学英语"，截止时间为2022年10月7日，共获得中文文献4462篇，其中有关"核心素养"的为4221篇，"中学英语单元整体教学"212篇，"联动教研"54篇，发表时间比较集中在2020—2022年，但是没有关于"中学英语联动教研活动"与"聚焦单元整体教学的中学英语联动教研活动"的文章。目前检索到的研究文献在宏观上主要集中在对核心素养、单元整体教学有关理论和政

---

① Kemmis, S. "Action research as a practice-based practice". *Educational Action Research*, 13 (3), pp. 513–525.

策的解读以及对联动教研范式的研究,微观上多以基于单元整体教学与教、学、评一体化的实施,如何优化作业设计与多样化资源供给等方面的研究为主,而且研究的视角集中在学校的课堂教学和教师层面,对如何通过区域教研活动提升核心素养的实践研究还相对匮乏。经过精读筛选后,选取4篇对本课题研究针对性强的文章,挖掘其中涉及的中学英语单元整体教学实施的方法和策略。

王德美通过设计问卷,调查了教师开展高中英语单元整体教学的现状。调查结果表明,教师对大概念视角下开展高中英语单元整体教学在了解、认知和实践等方面存在不足,提出了教师要学习专业文献,了解最新研究成果与动态;要参加专题培训,更新教学观念;要参与集体备课,提高单元教学设计的实践能力;要参与课例研究,提升课堂教学能力等对策。[①]

李宝荣、国红延认为单元整体教学是落实高中英语课程改革理念、促进学生发展核心素养的有效途径。他们结合具体案例以学习小单元为载体,围绕课程内容六要素分析、整合和利用单元语篇;依据教、学、评一体化理念,设计贯穿于单元的学习活动与评价活动,比较深入探讨了中学英语单元整体教学设计与实施路径。[②]

陈芳、蒋京丽认为基于英语学科大观念的初中英语单元整体教学设计可从"依据课程标准,分析单元内容,梳理各语篇主题意义""基于单元学习内容和语篇主题意义,建构单元大观念""基于单元大、小观念和学情,制订单元与课时教学目标"和"践行英语学习活动观,推进'教—学—评'一体化设计"四个方面展开,真正落实英语课程要培养的核心素养。[③]

王蔷、孙万磊等提出以语言学习为导向的英语学科本体的语言大观念和以学科育人为导向的跨学科主题大观念,探析大观念与英语教育的思辨关系,挖掘大观念对整合课程内容、促进语言学习与主题意义探究相融合、落实英语学科育人整体观的意义与价值,为深化中国基础教育英语课程改革、促进学生核心素养发展提供启示。[④]

---

① 王德美:《大概念视角下高中英语单元整体教学的现状及对策》,载《安徽教育科研》2022年第5期。
② 李宝荣、国红延:《中学英语单元整体教学设计与实施路径——以北师大版高中〈英语〉(2019年版)选择性必修一 Unit 3 Conservation 为例》,载《英语学习》2022年第5期。
③ 陈芳、蒋京丽:《基于英语学科大观念的初中英语单元整体教学设计》,载《教学月刊》2022年第5期。
④ 王蔷、孙万磊、赵连杰:《大观念对英语学科落实育人导向课程目标的意义与价值》,载《教学月刊》2022年第4期。

## 五、本课题国外研究现状述评和理论基础

### (一) 奥苏伯尔理论

奥苏伯尔认为,学生在有意义的接受学习的过程中,并不是将现成知识简单地"登记"到原有认知结构中去,而要经过一系列积极的思维活动,因此,有意义的接受学习是一个主动的过程。

### (二) 建构主义学习理论

建构主义(constructivism),亦称"建构观""认识建构观",它的产生和发展有两条脉络:一条源于哲学,主要受到波普尔、图尔敏、拉卡托斯、库恩的科学哲学思想、新进化论、后现代哲学的影响;另一条源于心理学,是行为主义发展到了认知主义后的进一步发展。

### (三) 深度学习理论

深度学习理论的四个视角如下。

视角一:认知理论。深度学习是高认知水平的学习活动,强调知识的理解、应用与迁移,促进学生高阶思维和复杂技能的发展。

视角二:学习观。深度学习是以学生的理解为基础,对知识意义的主动探寻,而不是灌输。

视角三:信息加工理论。深度学习是学习者全身心投入的过程,综合学习的认知与情感因素、个人与社会因素,强调学习的整体性。

视角四:社会文化理论。深度学习是个体外部环境与内部环境共同作用的结果,强调社会互动,产生于与他人的交往当中,是一个对话的过程。深度学习的意义不仅在于知识内容的建构,更重要的是利用蕴含在社会人际网络中的集体智慧,形成丰富的社会知识网络。

### (四)《义务教育英语课程标准(2022年版)》

《新课标》指出:英语课程内容的组织以主题为引领,以不同类型的语篇为依托,融入语言知识、文化知识、语言技能和学习策略等学习要求,以单元形式呈现。①

---

① 中华人民共和国教育部:《义务教育英语课程标准(2022年版)》,北京师范大学出版社2022年版,第51页。

## 六、研究的目标、内容（或子课题设计）与重点

### （一）研究目标

（1）通过联动教研方式探索深度教研路径，拓展区教研活动的深度、广度和关联度，构建 Planning-Teaching-Observation-Reflection-Evaluation-Creation（PTOREC）教研模式；

（2）在核心素养的统领下，以单元整体教学为突破口，以课例研究为载体，促进教、学、评一体化和教师专业化发展；

（3）发挥集团学校中龙头学校的优势和课题组骨干老师的示范引领作用，开展片区教研和集团学校联动教研，指导薄弱学校校本教研以提高实效，助力教师专业成长，推动教学质量的均衡发展；

（4）以问题为导向开展行动研究，在不断反思改进和解决复杂问题的过程中开发资源，提炼成果并进行推广，加强学科建设，提高核心素养。

### （二）研究内容

本课题将采取分学段（初中、高中）的形式，基本流程如下。

（1）成立联动教研共同体即课题组（如图 1-1 所示），选好片区联动学校的片长、集团学校的团长，构建联动教研机制，探索深度教研路径；

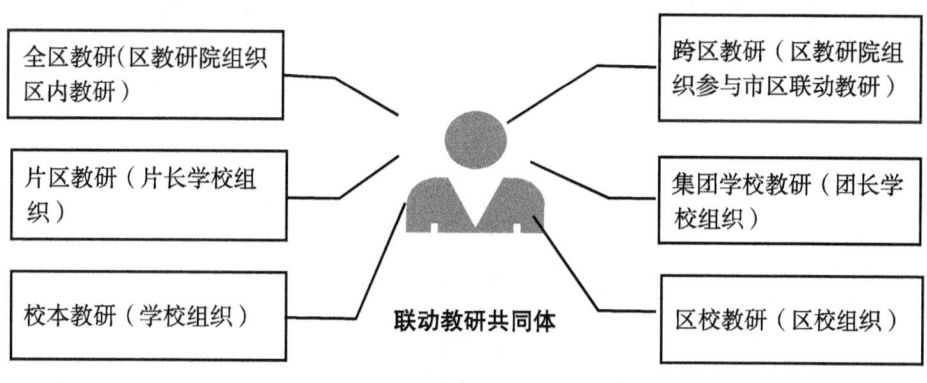

图 1-1　联动教研共同体

（2）开展理论学习和邀请专家指导，内容包括核心素养、单元整体教学设计、素养导向的教学评价、信息技术赋能、课堂观察、联动教研等的理论学习培训和实践指导；

（3）课题组分工合作，分学段先示范一个单元整体教学设计的案例，然后带领全区老师参与集体备课，分单元进行整体教学设计，内容包括单元主

题、单元内容分析、单元教学目标与评价、课时分配与任务安排、分课时教学设计与学案、课件、课外作业等，在全区共享资源，课题组开展行动研究（如图1-2所示）；

（4）在区教研活动中，课题组及区内外骨干老师分单元进行公开课例展示，分课型进行同课同构、同课异构、异课同构等，尝试Planning-Teaching-Observation-Reflection-Evaluation-Creation（PTOREC）教研模式（如图1-3所示），规范区教研活动的内容与形式，提高实效性；

（5）开展专题研讨会和主题论坛，邀请专家指导，课题组交流经验，并经过行动研究—理论提升—实践验证—理论完善的过程，力求有所突破，有所创新，提炼成果推广（重点）；

（6）进行评价工具的研发，比如过程性评价表、常规听评课表、跟踪式评课记录表、学生听说读写能力评价表、学习兴趣评价量表等（难点）。

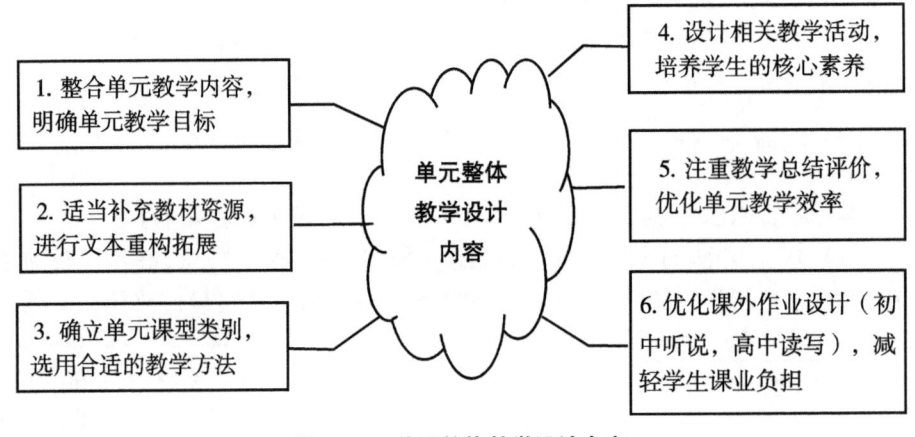

图1-2 单元整体教学设计内容

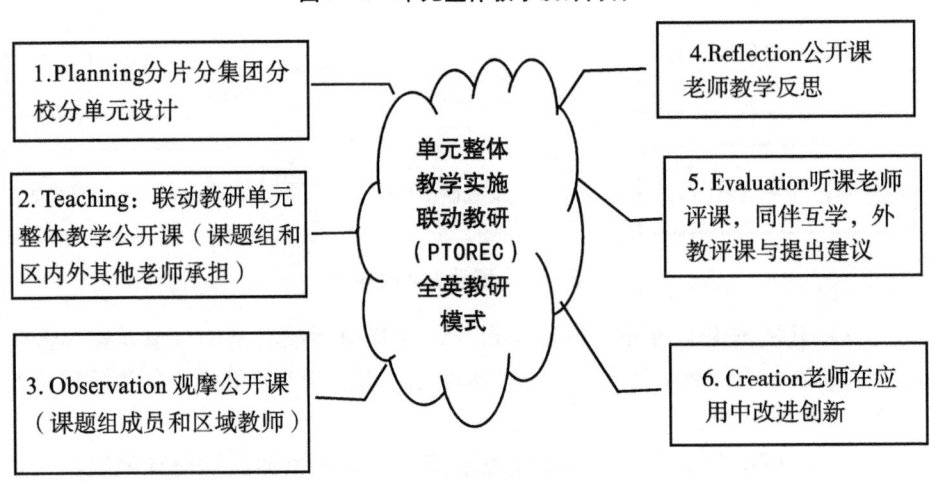

图1-3 单元整体教学实施

## 七、本课题研究的主要方法

### （一）行动研究法

行动研究是把研究原理运用于实践的过程（如图 1-4 所示），以促进教育工作者改进日复一日的实践工作。本课题将通过行动研究获得各种不同的资料和数据，包括学校和教师的记录，学生的作业、文档、录音、录像、日志、观察等，数据调查形式如测验、问卷、访谈、座谈等；辅之以观察法、文献法、调查法等方法。实施的关键在于促进老师们对单元整体教学设计的实践、反思、改进和提高。

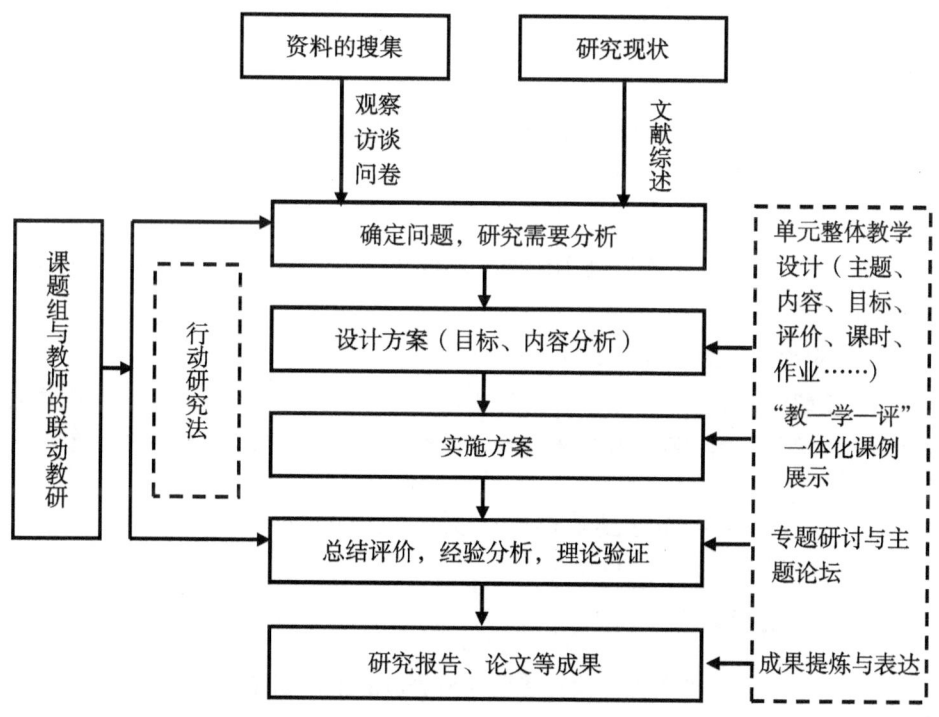

图 1-4　行动研究法

### （二）实验研究法

本课题组将在实验学校广州市第五中学初二年级进行"基于智能交互技术提升初中生英语听说准确性的实验研究"，尝试运用课题组的听说课外作业，增加学生的语言实践机会。利用翼课网、智学网、希沃互动教学平台等辅助批改作业，在引导学生训练听说能力的同时，激发他们学习英语的兴趣，培养综合运用英语的能力和敢于创新的自信心和能力。

1. 被试的选取

被试初步选定为广州市第五中学初二两个平行班，两班学生人数相同。其中一个班为实验班，另一个班为对照班。

2. 实验因子（自变量）

实验班采取相关实验措施，对照班采取常规的教学方法。

3. 因变量

（1）实验过程中，观察两个班英语学习的动态，并以常规的测验为基础，考查两个班的学习情况。

（2）一个学年结束后，两个班接受同一份区统一的听说测试以及英语学习兴趣水平的测试，将这些成绩（得分）进行比较。

4. 设计方法

实验采取的是省去前测的等组实验设计。实验设计解释为：

被试1（实验班）→水平1→后测1

被试2（对照班）→水平2→后测2

水平1、水平2即实验因子的两个不同水平，后测1、后测2即对因变量的检测。

5. 实验结果的分析

实验期满，根据实验要求，对实验班和对照班进行了全面测查，测查内容包含英语学习兴趣水平、常规听说考试成绩情况和动态学习状况三个方面。

## 八、本课题的理论创新程度、实际应用价值

### （一）创新之处

首先，本课题研究结合教研转型和教研员的工作职能，以课题研究的方式开展联动教研活动，以解决教育教学中所面临的共性问题和师生的实际需要为研究目标，整合区域教研力量，构建以实践为导向的学习和研究共同体，合力应对课程改革不断向纵深发展所带来的挑战，使各级各类教研活动在内涵与外延上都具有延续性和系统性。其次，课题组示范带领全区老师参与集体备课，分单元进行整体教学设计，引导教师在读书、学习、思考和研讨过程中，通过倾听与对话、分享与碰撞，激发研究热情，相互取长补短，围绕立德树人根本任务，立足课程，聚焦课堂，分析学生，研读教材，落实目标，优化教学方式

和学习方式，进行评价工具的研发，研究实施教学重点，突破教学难点，也在一定程度上带动全区教学研究实现均衡发展，创新构建区域联动教研的有效模式（PTOREC）。此外，我们长期坚持使用英语作为教研活动的工作语言，由教研员带头，鼓励老师们一起用英语评课、主持、发言、展示才艺，邀请外教参与评课交流，用双语写教学日记与活动总结等，提高语言能力和跨文化交流能力。

（二）实际应用价值

本研究项目的特色是扎根海珠热土，研究真问题，解决师生需求，实现减负增效。研究项目的应用成果具有普适性和可操作性强的特点，可以帮助广大英语教师力求通过整体教学设计实现高效的教学，切实减轻学生的学业负担，从而寻求学校可持续发展的途径，有着很大的实用价值。首先，完整配套的初二单元整体教学设计资源包，包括教学设计、学案和课件，将使全区每一个老师受益，大大减少备课的时间。其次是与单元配套的课外作业优化设计将以学生为本，初中以听说作业为主，高中以读后续写为重点，初中和高中互相衔接，促进学生自主学习，构建师生"学习共同体"，打造和谐共赢的生态课堂，助力国家"双减"政策稳妥实施。最后，课题实施过程中的行动研究要求教师积极转变教学观念，由课程计划的执行者转变为课程的建构者，从而形成优秀教学案例，大力促进校本行动研究，形成丰富的校本课程文化资源库，使教师由纯粹的教书匠向研究型教育工作者转变。其中，部分老师脱颖而出，成为联动教研的中坚力量，推动区域教研工作的创新。区校联动教研也为市区联动教研提供范例。

# 第二章 "聚焦单元整体教学的中学英语联动教研行动研究"阶段性报告*

## 一、课题前期工作回顾

表1 课题前期主要工作一览表

| 时间 | 形式 | 内容 |
| --- | --- | --- |
| 2021年8月—2023年6月 | 广州共享课堂+国家课程资源 | 沪教版七上 M3 U5—6 Lesson 1—13 单元整体教学设计、作业设计和电视课堂 |
| 2022年3月31日 | 广州市高一英语市区联动教研 | 人教版必修三 U3 Diverse Cultures 听说、语法公开课 |
| 2022年4月7日 | 黄埔区、海珠区初一英语教研 | 沪教版七下 M4 U7 Poems 单元整体教学设计及听说、语法、英汉诗歌对比阅读公开课 |
| 2022年9月29日 | 广州市初一英语市区联动教研 | 沪教版 M3 U6 Travel around Asia 词汇、阅读、听力、语法、口语、写作、拓展阅读教学专题发言 |
| 2022年10月13日 | 海珠区、越秀区高二英语联动教研活动 | 人教版选必一 U5 Working the Land 和选必二 U2 Bridging Cultures 单元整体教学设计 |
| 2022年10月20日 | "云端送教,粤黔共研"支教贵州瓮安活动 | 沪教版 M4 U8 English Week 单元整体设计、词汇、阅读公开课 |

---

\* 本报告撰写人:广州市海珠区教育发展研究院张志梅、广州市第五中学罗曼容、广州市海珠外国语实验中学附属学校梁蕴娜、广州市劬劳中学何穗珊。本文获2023年广州市"深度教学"课堂改革试验阶段性成果二等奖。

续上表

| 时间 | 形式 | 内容 |
|---|---|---|
| 2023年3月23日 | 海珠区、番禺区初二英语教研 | 沪教版"中华传统文化"主题听说、阅读、拓展阅读、写作公开课 |
| 2023年3月24日 | 广州市第6批高中英语骨干教师培训班 | 人教版高中英语单元整体教学设计与实施讲座 |

如表1所示，前期系列联动教研开展了单元整体教学的设计以及包括语音、词汇、语法和听、说、读、看、写能力培养在内的各种课例研究，有待探讨的是单元整体复习课。

## 二、研究问题与假设

问题：新课标背景下的"单元整体复习课"是怎样的？

复习课的特点：

终结性：位置是一个单元最后的一课，需对整个单元进行总结、盘点，承上启下。

开放性：没有固定的教学内容，教师有更大的空间去处理教材。

评价性：功能；对学生的学习结果、成果进行评价。

假设：新课标背景下的"复习课"应体现主题意义与语言形式融合。设计一脉相承，蕴含主题意义、实现学习活动难度递进的情境，在有意义的场景中使用语言知识，通过与他人（同伴、老师）的意义协商，促成应用迁移的语言能力，发展思维能力、学习能力，强化主题意义的育人功能。

## 三、研究背景与目标

广州市海珠区教育发展研究院与区内外学校共建共享"深教研"平台，组织"聚焦新课标"系列教学展示活动。活动以广州市五中教育东晓学校为样本学校，由驻点调研、教研员/特约教研员的课例展示（现场直播）、教研沙龙、专题报告和市区联动教研、高校专家指导等组成。本次报告基于在广州市开展的单元整体教学设计与复习公开课课例展示（牛津沪教版八下 Unit 1 Helping those in need 和 Unit 3 Traditional skills），探讨初中英语单元整体教学的联动教研区域实践。

## 四、研究过程与方法

### 1. 基于学业质量监测诊断，研究真问题

广州市五中东晓学校八年级共有 156 名学生参加了 2023 年 3 月海珠区学业质量监测，诊断结果如表 2、图 1 所示。

表 2  学业质量监测诊断结果

| 能力考查 | 实考人数 | 及格人数 | 及格率 | 优秀人数 | 优秀率 | 难度 | 最低分 | 最高分 |
|---|---|---|---|---|---|---|---|---|
| 语法选择 | 156 | 70 | 44.87% | 44 | 28.21% | 0.55 | 1 | 15 |
| 完形填空 | 156 | 56 | 35.90% | 34 | 21.79% | 0.46 | 0 | 10 |
| 阅读理解 | 156 | 64 | 41.03% | 36 | 23.08% | 0.52 | 4 | 30 |
| 阅读填空 | 156 | 47 | 30.13% | 28 | 17.95% | 0.40 | 0 | 5 |
| 语篇填词 | 156 | 57 | 36.54% | 25 | 16.03% | 0.39 | 0 | 5 |
| 完成句子 | 156 | 45 | 28.85% | 26 | 16.67% | 0.37 | 0 | 9.5 |
| 写作 | 156 | 48 | 30.77% | 17 | 10.90% | 0.34 | 0 | 14 |
| 五中东晓学校 | 156 | 51 | 32.69% | 24 | 15.38% | 0.46 | 11 | 87.5 |
| 全区 | 11106 | 5586 | 50.30% | 2599 | 23.40% | 0.60 | 10 | 90 |

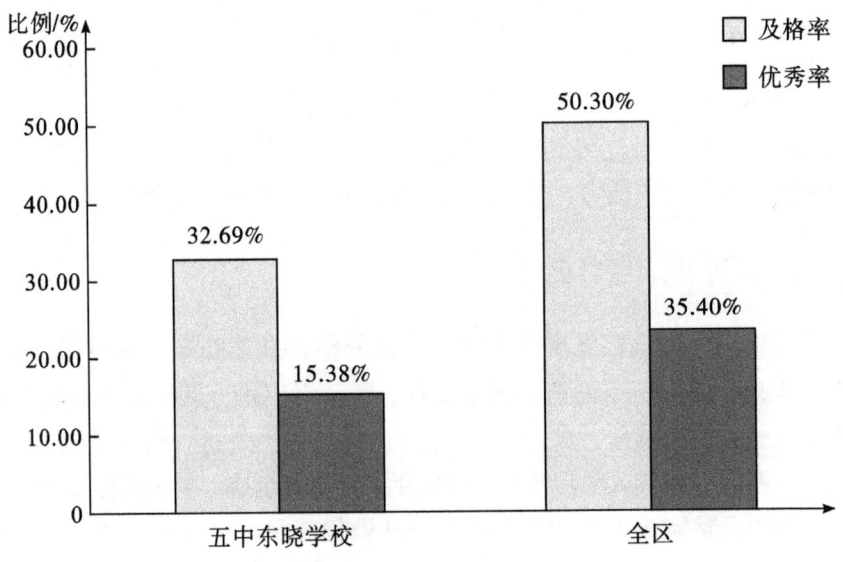

图 1  学业质量监测诊断结果

从答题的情况看，该年级学生得分率达 0.5 以上的板块有语法选择和阅读理解，得分率低于 0.5 的板块有完形填空、阅读填空、语篇填词、完成句子和写作。初二 1 班共 39 名学生，该班的英语水平属于五中东晓学校的中等偏上层次，该班学生阅读填空、语篇填词、完成句子和写作得分率都比较低，也就说明写作能力是该班学生的短板。任课老师反映主要原因是线上教学时间长，对学生的学习状态无法掌控，有学生甚至在疫情期间出现了比较严重的心理问题，大部分学生对熟悉的词汇和语法在语境中不会灵活运用。该班成绩较好的学生上英语课的积极性比较高，但是注意力不集中；学困生则迫切需要通过老师的引导和同学的鼓励来建立自信心。基于以上分析，采用以下教学改进策略：

（1）针对大部分学生对熟悉的词汇在语境中不会灵活运用的问题，引导学生在生活化的情景和多模态语篇中理解和运用单元核心词汇，领悟词汇的基本含义，以及其在特定语境和语篇中的意义、词性和功能；

（2）针对如何灵活运用单元重点语法项目动词不定式作状语和宾语的问题，要帮助学生初步意识到语言使用中的语法知识是"形式－意义－使用"的统一体，明确学习语法的目的是在语境中运用语法知识理解和表达意义；

（3）针对学生写作能力比较弱、注意力不够集中的问题，鼓励学生在主题意义的引领下以参与听、说、读、看活动为主，在课后参与写作活动；

（4）针对学困生自信心和学习动机不足的问题，给他们搭好"脚手架"，鼓励他们在小组合作学习中努力尝试完成难度低的任务，最大程度扩大其参与面，调动其积极性。

## 2. 赋能新课堂，共研新方向

2023 年 5 月 4 日，广州市初中英语单元整体教学市区联动系列教研活动海珠专场在广州市第五中学进行，教研主题为八年级下学期 Unit 1 和 Unit 3 单元整体教学设计与复习公开课。

首先，梁蕴娜老师针对 Unit 1 单元整体教学设计进行分享。梁老师从主题语境、语篇分析和单元主题观念分析、单元整体教学目标分析、单元教学重点和难点、单元教学课时安排、单元评价措施以及单元教学资源七个方面展开对第一单元的整体教学分析。

接着，张志梅老师上了 Unit 1 单元复习与评价公开课。张老师以一曲轻快活泼的 *Count on Me* 开启课堂，学生从最初理解"帮助需要帮助的朋友"，到后面"帮助儿童、老人、动物，乃至社区、世界"，对志愿服务工作有了从表层到深层的理解，体现了思维深度和广度的递进性，联通了课堂与课外、国内与国外、虚拟与现实。

紧接着，何穗珊老师带来 Unit 3 的单元整体教学设计。该单元教材内容处理的难点是内容较散。何老师富有创造性的教学设计促使学生有效整合语言知识、文化知识，提高理解和表达能力，实现思维品质和文化意识的发展。

然后，罗曼容老师进行了 Unit 3 单元复习与评价课例展示。罗老师的课堂注重情境的创设，丰富的场景与活动的设计均与学生真实生活紧密关联，共同围绕一个主题意义推进、拓展，实现课堂上语言与意义融合的学习任务难度递进，充分体现了教学设计的连续性、递进性、丰富性。

本次活动的高潮是专家的点评[①]。专家充分肯定了四位老师的教学设计与课堂教学，认为高效的语言实践活动让学生在玩中学、读中思、学而乐、乐而获，欣喜地看到还原的真实课堂，课堂让不同层次的学生有所成长。老师们基于问题导向，以学业质量评价为依据，实施精准的教学改进，提高了教学实效，促进了教育均衡发展。专家充分肯定了"聚焦新课标，共享深教研"的主题活动发挥了研究共同体的优势，教研员带领一线老师上公开课有助于践行新课标理念，切实指导区域的课堂教学改革，形成"理论—实践—反思"的教师学习发展新模式。专家建议基于学情，精选任务，给学生更多时间去消化、理解、协商、解决问题，使课堂更具过程感，实现深度参与、深度学习。

## 五、反思与展望

新课标背景下的"复习课"体现主题意义与语言形式融合。如何引导学生深度学习？如何对学生的学习结果、成果进行评价？我们需要进行深入的研究。本次教研是师生共同经历的高阶思维的智慧之旅，让我们更加坚定以单元整体教学理念来落实英语学科核心素养培养的信心，让更多的老师获得专业成长，最终让更多学生从优质均衡的教育中受益！

---

① *点评专家：广东外语外贸大学吕琳琼教授。*

# 第三章 "聚焦单元整体教学的中学英语联动教研行动研究"结题报告[*]

## 一、课题简介

### (一) 研究的背景

《义务教育英语课程标准（2022年版）》指出：教学研究与教师培训要着力引导教师准确、深刻领会课程理念、目标和要求，并转化为切实有效的教学实践，不断提升教师的专业素养，全面促成学生核心素养的形成与发展。有条件的地区还可以建立不同区域间和不同学校间教师学习、研究的共同体，帮助教师增进学术交流，拓宽专业视野，提高教学水平。[①]由此可见，《新课标》明确了教研团队建设的重要性和努力的方向。

数字时代信息技术的高速发展以及近年疫情防控形势下线上教研的常态化，使得各级各类的联动教研方式得到推广。广东省教育研究院和广州市教育研究院不断深入开展的市区联动教研活动，为跨市跨区联动、城乡联动提供了理论指导和实践平台。作为一个跨初中和高中学段的教研员，对于区域的教研活动应如何立足区情，有针对性地设计、组织、实施和评价本区的教研活动，进一步深化省市教研成果，为广大师生服务和减负增效呢？本课题"聚焦单元整体教学的中学英语联动教研行动研究"旨在以常规的区教研活动为平台，以全区老师为主体，以全员单元整体集体备课、校区市公开课、专题研讨为抓手，以课题组老师、中心组老师为示范引领，以信息技术为支持，加强市区校联动教研，调动老师们参与教研的积极性，发挥集体智慧，切实减负增效，提高教学质量，提升核心素养。

---

[*] 本课题经专家鉴定为优秀课题。
[①] 中华人民共和国教育部：《义务教育英语课程标准（2022年版)》，北京师范大学出版社2022年版，第51页。

## （二）研究意义

核心素养、大观念、单元整体教学和联动教研都是当前英语教学研究的热点。但目前检索到的研究文献在宏观上主要集中在对核心素养、单元整体教学有关理论和政策的解读以及对联动教研范式的研究，微观上多以基于单元整体教学与"教—学—评"一体化的实施，如何优化作业设计与多样化资源供给等方面的研究为主，而且研究的视角集中在学校的课堂教学和教师层面，对如何通过区域教研活动提升核心素养的实践研究还相对匮乏。经过精读筛选后，选取4篇对本课题研究针对性强的文章，挖掘其中涉及的中学英语单元整体教学实施的方法和策略。

王德美通过设计问卷，调查了教师开展高中英语单元整体教学的现状。调查结果表明，教师对大概念视角下开展高中英语单元整体教学在了解、认知和实践等方面存在不足，提出了教师要学习专业文献，了解最新研究成果与动态；要参加专题培训，更新教学观念；要参与集体备课，提高单元教学设计的实践能力；要参与课例研究，提升课堂教学能力等对策。[①]

李宝荣、国红延等认为单元整体教学是落实高中英语课程改革理念、促进学生发展核心素养的有效途径。他们结合具体案例，以学习小单元为载体，围绕课程内容六要素分析、整合和利用单元语篇；依据教、学、评一体化理念，设计贯穿于单元的学习活动与评价活动，比较深入地探讨了中学英语单元整体教学设计与实施路径。[②]

陈芳、蒋京丽等认为基于英语学科大观念的初中英语单元整体教学设计可从"依据课程标准，分析单元内容，梳理各语篇主题意义""基于单元学习内容和语篇主题意义，建构单元大观念""基于单元大、小观念和学情，制订单元与课时教学目标"和"践行英语学习活动观，推进'教—学—评'一体化设计"四个方面展开，真正落实英语课程要培养的核心素养。[③]

王蔷、孙万磊等提出以语言学习为导向的英语学科本体的语言大观念和以学科育人为导向的跨学科主题大观念，探析大观念与英语教育的思辨关系，挖

---

① 王德美：《大概念视角下高中英语单元整体教学的现状及对策》，载《安徽教育科研》2022年第5期。
② 李宝荣、国红延：《中学英语单元整体教学设计与实施路径——以北师大版高中〈英语〉(2019年版)选择性必修一 Unit 3 Conservation 为例》，载《英语学习》2022年第5期。
③ 陈芳、蒋京丽：《基于英语学科大观念的初中英语单元整体教学设计》，载《教学月刊》2022年第5期。

掘大观念对整合课程内容、促进语言学习与主题意义探究相融合、落实英语学科育人整体观的意义与价值,为深化中国基础教育英语课程改革、促进学生核心素养发展提供启示。①

综上所述,目前国内基础教育研究聚焦单元整体教学的中学英语联动教研的论文很少,进行的课题研究更少,所以,本课题的研究是一种有益的尝试。它倡导以学生为中心的教学模式,强调教学内容的整体性和连贯性,通过整合和优化教学内容,使学生在掌握知识的同时,能够提高语言运用能力,实现学以致用。同时,该研究还强调了教师之间的联动教研,通过分享教学经验和策略,提升教学质量,促进教师专业发展。此外,这种研究也有助于推动教育改革,实现教育教学的创新和发展,具有深远的教育价值和意义。

### (三)理论依据

**1. 深度学习理论**

深度学习理论有四个视角:

视角一:认知理论。深度学习是高认知水平的学习活动,强调知识的理解、应用与迁移,促进学生高阶思维和复杂技能的发展。

视角二:学习观。深度学习是以学生的理解为基础,对知识意义的主动探寻,而不是灌输。

视角三:信息加工理论。深度学习是学习者全身心投入的过程,综合学习的认知与情感因素、个人与社会因素、强调学习的整体性。

视角四:社会文化理论。深度学习是个体外部环境与内部环境共同作用的结果,强调社会互动,产生于与他人的交往当中,是一个对话的过程。深度学习的意义不仅在于知识内容的建构,更重要的是利用蕴含在社会人际网络中的集体智慧,形成丰富的社会知识网络。②

**2. 建构主义学习理论**

建构主义(constructivism),亦称"建构观""认识建构观",它的产生和发展有两条脉络:一条源于哲学,主要受到波普尔、图尔敏、拉卡托斯、库恩

---

① 王蔷、孙万磊、赵连杰:《大观念对英语学科落实育人导向课程目标的意义与价值》,载《教学月刊》2022年第4期。
② 张春莉、王艳芝:《深度学习视域下的课堂教学过程研究》,载《课程·教材·教法》2021年第6期。

的科学哲学思想、新进化论、后现代哲学的影响；另一条源于心理学，是行为主义发展到了认知主义后的进一步发展。

**3. 《义务教育英语课程标准（2022年版）》和《普通高中英语课程标准（2017年版，2020年修订）》**

（1）核心素养：课程标准强调发展学生的核心素养，包括语言能力、文化意识、思维品质和学习能力。① 这些素养的培养是单元整体教学设计的重要依据，有助于实现课程目标。

（2）主题意义：课程内容选取注重时代特征和现实生活联系，以人与自我、人与社会和人与自然为主题范畴。英语课程内容的组织以主题为引领，以不同类型的语篇为依托，融入语言知识、文化知识、语言技能和学习策略等学习要求，以单元形式呈现。② 这为单元整体教学提供了明确的课程内容方向，有助于提高教学的针对性和实效性。

（3）学习活动观：课程标准强调通过综合性、关联性和实践性的英语学习活动③，帮助学生提高英语学习能力和运用能力。这为单元整体教学中的教学活动设计提供了指导，有助于激发学生的学习兴趣和动机。

（4）教学评价：课程标准提倡形成性评价和终结性评价相结合④，既关注学生的学习过程，又关注学生的学习结果。这为单元整体教学的评价提供了依据，有助于提高教学质量和效果。

可见，两个课标为本课题提供了指南，内容包括核心素养培养、主题意义、课程组织、学习活动设计和教学评价等方面，有助于本研究在实践层面上提高中学英语教学的质量和效果。

综上所述，深度学习理论主张学生通过深入理解和应用知识来实现真正的学习；建构主义学习理论认为学习是学生主动构建知识的过程，教师的作用是引导和支持。这些理论共同构成了本课题研究的理论基础。《义务教育英语课程标准》为本研究提供了教学目标和内容的标准，切实指导着教师聚焦单元整体教学进行联动教研。

---

①② 中华人民共和国教育部：《义务教育英语课程标准（2022版）》，北京师范大学出版社2022年版，第2-3页。

③④ 中华人民共和国教育部：《普通高中英语课程标准（2017年版2020年修订）》，人民教育出版社2022年版，第2-3页。

## （四）研究目标

通过课题研究，课题组将达到以下目标：

（1）通过联动教研方式探索深度教研路径，拓展区教研活动的深度、广度和关联度，构建 Planning-Teaching-Observation-Reflection-Evaluation-Creation（PTOREC）教研模式；

（2）在核心素养的统领下，以单元整体教学为突破口，以课例研究为载体，促进教学评一体化和教师专业化发展；

（3）发挥集团学校中龙头学校的优势和课题组骨干老师的示范引领作用，开展片区教研和集团学校联动教研，指导薄弱学校校本教研提高实效，助力教师专业成长，推动教学质量的均衡发展；

（4）以问题为导向开展行动研究，不断反思改进和解决复杂问题的过程中开发资源，提炼成果并进行推广，加强学科建设，提高核心素养。

## （五）研究内容

本课题分学段（初中、高中）展开，基本流程如图1所示。

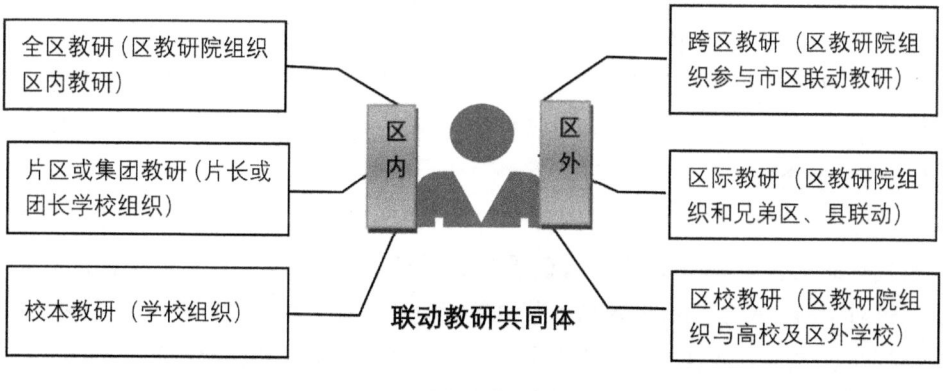

图1 联动教研共同体

（1）建立和壮大区内外联动教研共同体即课题组，选好片区联动学校的片长、集团学校的团长，构建联动教研机制，探索深度教研路径；

（2）开展理论学习和邀请专家指导，包括核心素养、单元整体教学设计、素养导向的教学评价、信息技术赋能、课堂观察、联动教研等的理论学习培训和实践指导；

（3）课题组分工合作，分学段先示范一个单元整体教学设计的案例，然后带领全区老师参与集备，分单元整体教学设计，包括单元主题、单元内容分析、单元教学目标与评价、课时分配与任务安排、分课时教学设计与学案、课件、课外作业等，在全区共享资源，课题组开始进行行动研究；

（4）在区教研活动中，课题组及区内外骨干老师分单元进行公开课例展示，分课型进行同课同构、同课异构、异课同构等，尝试 Planning-Teaching-Observation-Reflection-Evaluation-Creation（PTOREC）教研模式，规范区教研活动的内容与形式，提高实效性；

（5）开展专题研讨会和主题论坛，邀请专家指导，课题组交流经验，并经过行动研究—理论提升—实践验证—理论完善的过程，力求有所突破，有所创新，提炼成果推广（重点）；

（6）进行评价工具，比如过程性评价表、常规听评课表、跟踪式评课记录表、学生听说读写能力评价表、学习兴趣评价量表等的研发（难点）。

（六）研究方法

### 1. 行动研究法

行动研究是把研究原理运用于实践的过程，以促进教育工作者改进日复一日的实践工作。[①] 本课题将通过行动研究获得各种不同的资料和数据，包括学校和教师的记录，学生的作业、文档、录音、录像、日志、观察等，数据调查形式如测验、问卷、访谈、座谈等，辅之以观察法、文献法、调查法等方法。实施的关键在于促进老师们对单元整体教学设计的实践、反思、改进和提高。

### 2. 调查法

已经在海珠区高中年级进行的"广州市海珠区高中英语单元学业水平考试现状的调查研究"[②]，依据《新课标》关于高中英语学业质量水平的要求，通过对实验学校使用海珠区高中英语单元学业水平考试的调查研究，了解当前学校在校内高中英语单元学业水平考试这一环节中的运作情况，旨在发现存在的问题，同时收集教师和学生对考试改革的建议，以便为下一步海珠区高中英语单元学业水平考试的改进提供依据。

### 3. 实验研究法

本课题组将在实验学校广州市第五中学初二年级进行"基于智能交互技

---

① McMillan, J. H. & Schumacher, J. *Action Research: A Guide to Planning and Implementing Participatory Action Research*. Sage Publications，2008.

② "广州市海珠区高中英语单元学业水平考试现状的调查研究"获2023年广东省中小学外语教育论文评选一等奖。

术提升初中生英语听说准确性的实验研究"①，尝试运用课题组的听说课外作业，增加学生进行语言实践的机会。利用翼课网、智学网、希沃互动教学平台等辅助批改作业，引导学生训练听说能力的同时，激发学生学习英语的兴趣，培养学生综合运用英语的能力和敢于创新的自信心和能力。

（1）被试的选取。被试初步选定为广州市第五中学初二两个平行班，两班学生人数相同。其中一个班为实验班，另一个班为对照班。

实验因子（自变量）：实验班采取相关实验措施，对照班采取常规的教学方法。

因变量：实验过程中，观察两个班英语学习的动态，并以常规的测验为基础，考查两个班学习情况。

一个学年结束后，两个班接受同一份区统一的听说测试以及含英语学习兴趣水平两方面的测试，将这些成绩（得分）进行比较。

（2）设计方法。实验采取的是省去前测的等组实验设计。实验设计解释为：

被试 1（实验班）→水平 1→后测 1

被试 2（对照班）→水平 2→后测 2

水平 1、水平 2 即实验因子的两个不同水平，后测 1、后测 2 即对因变量的检测。

（3）实验结果的分析。实验期满，根据实验要求，对实验班和对照班进行了全面测查，包含英语学习兴趣水平、常规听说考试成绩情况和动态学习状况方面。

### 4．文献法

文献法是指搜集、鉴别、整理文献，并通过对文献的研究形成对事实的科学认识的方法。它所要解决的是如何在浩如烟海的文献中选取适用于课题的资料，并对这些资料做出恰当分析与使用的问题。在研究初期，借助中国知网及教育类杂志、书籍等途径收集文献资料，并进行归类整理，梳理已有研究成果，以指导后期的研究。文献法贯穿研究全过程。

### 5．个案法

个案法以典型的课题研究模式为依托，以创新的理念探索灵活多样的课堂教学模式和社会实践活动，通过不同学科案例的收集、展示、分析、研究和概括，验证课题研究假设，提炼总结规律。

---

① 本研究为广东省中小学教师信息技术应用能力提升办公室课题（编号：TSGCKT2022014）已于 2023 年 10 月结题。

## 二、研究过程

本研究从 2020 年 11 月开始筹备,至 2023 年 11 月完成预期研究任务,研究历时三年,课题组所做工作如表 1 所示。

表 1　课题研究阶段

| 序号 | 研究阶段<br>(起止时间) | 阶段成果名称 | 成果形式 |
|---|---|---|---|
| 1 | 2020 年 11 月—2022 年 2 月<br>准备启动阶段(Planning, Teaching & Observation) | 课题组成员的组织、培训与学习 | 完成第二阶段广州市共享课堂七年级上册 M3 U5—6 模块设计 |
| 2 | 2022 年 3 月—2022 年 5 月<br>理论学习阶段(Reflection & Evaluation) | 课题组成员培训和学习 | 1. 专题讲座;<br>2. 单元整体教学设计;<br>3. 研究论文、课题申报书的编写 |
| 3 | 2022 年 5 月—2023 年 5 月<br>实践阶段(Planning, Teaching & Observation) | 教学设计、教学课件、导学案、课外作业、教学案例、教学反思、实验 | 教学设计集、学案集、课件集、听说作业集、读后续写作业集、优秀课例集、研究论文、校本教材 |
| 4 | 2023 年 5 月—2023 年 8 月<br>反思提升阶段(Reflection & Evaluation) | 分析典型案例,整理研究资料,总结研究成果与结论 | 优秀课例集、研究论文、校本教材 |
| 5 | 2023 年 8 月—2023 年 11 月<br>形成成果阶段<br>(Evaluation & Creation) | 完成课题研究报告;编辑《海珠区中学英语单元整体教学设计、优秀教学案例、优秀作业设计》;<br>向学校推广课题的成果 | 结题报告:<br>1.《聚焦单元整体教学的中学英语联动教研行动研究》成果集;<br>2.《基于智能交互技术提升初中生英语听说准确性的行动研究》。<br>3. 著作:《中学英语联动教研行动研究》 |

## （一）准备与启动阶段（2020年11月—2022年2月）

2020年11月，海珠区教育发展研究院接到广州市"共享课堂"录制任务之后，张志梅老师很快就组建了录课团队。在广州市教育研究院中学英语科何琳老师和海珠区教育发展研究院初中部袁泽姬部长的带领下，海珠区录课审核组和参与录课的初中英语老师们承担了广州市共享课堂英语七年级上册（简称"七上"）U5、U6线上课程资源的研发。这是我们课题研究的美好开端，也是联动教研研究共同体构建的基础。

团队分工明确，每位老师负责相应的课型。具体分工如表2所示。

表2　广州市共享课堂英语七上U5、U6资源开发分工

| 课型 | 七上 U5<br>Visiting the Moon | 七上 U6<br>Travelling around Asia |
| --- | --- | --- |
| Lesson 1 Vocabulary & Pre-reading | 张炜麟<br>广州市五中附属初级中学 | 谭珊<br>广州市江南外国语学校 |
| Lesson 2 Reading | 周永恩<br>广州市第六中学 | 林映<br>广州市江南外国语学校 |
| Lesson 3 Listening and Speaking | 高梦瑶<br>广州市海珠区六中珠江中学 | 谢春草<br>广州市江南外国语学校 |
| Lesson 4 Grammar | 安颖欣<br>广州市南武中学 | 卢喜亮<br>广州市江南外国语学校 |
| Lesson 5 Writing | 周彦睿<br>广州市南武实验学校 | 黎绮华<br>广州市第五中学 |
| Lesson 6 Extensive Reading | 熊佳<br>广州市第五中学 | 彭荧<br>广州市江南外国语学校 |
| Module 3 Revision | 梁家昕<br>广州市第九十七中学 | |
| 教研指导与审课专家 | 张志梅<br>广州市海珠区教育发展研究院 | |

13位老师承担了英语七上Module 3 Travels中U5、U6共13节共享线上课程的研发。在温暖的大家庭里，负责相同课型的2位老师、同一单元的7位老师紧密合作，深入研读文本，教学上相互呼应，使两个单元的教学形成一个有机高效的整体，然后整合模块的主题和教学总目标，再细分模块内不同单元的

教学目标，最后落实同一单元内不同课型的教学。在市区教研院和各学校支持下，团队多次开展线上、线下专题研讨，老师们精诚合作，不忘教育初心，精雕细琢，深入研读，反复打磨课件、学案、逐字稿、脚本稿、PPT底板颜色、字体大小、视频音乐等，不断推倒重来，第一稿、第二稿、第三稿，直到第十稿甚至更多，白天挤出课余时间试讲彩排，深夜云集群课堂、云会议，开展说课、评课、录播，同心协力，不断进步。特别感谢给予我们指导，且在百忙中抽空为我们审阅全部资源包和提供技术支持的广州市教育研究院教研员何琳老师、海珠区教育发展研究院初中部袁泽姬部长，衷心感谢越秀区教研员曾苗青老师、黄埔区教研员符丽雪老师、番禺区教研员冯页老师的无私帮助和经验分享，感谢团队每一位成员的不懈努力和携手度过的难忘时光！

（二）理论学习阶段（2022年3月—2022年5月）

在理论学习环节，我们深入探讨了单元整体教学的理念、原则、方法和评价等内容，为实践教学提供了理论支持，邀请了教育专家和一线教师做专题讲座，分享经验和案例，帮助老师们更好地理解和应用单元整体教学策略。在单元整体教学设计方面，我们以课程标准和教材为依据，结合学生的实际需求，对教学内容进行了整合和优化，设计出符合学生认知规律和语言发展特点的教学方案，同时通过实证研究、案例分析和比较研究等方法，探讨了单元整体教学在提高学生英语能力、激发学生学习兴趣和培养学生综合素质等方面的作用，开发了评价量表。在此基础上，准备了课题申报书，在申报书中详细阐述了研究背景、目的、内容、方法和预期成果等内容，为整个研究过程提供了清晰的计划和蓝图。

（三）实践阶段（2022年5月—2023年5月）

在实践阶段，我们以教学设计和教学实践为核心，旨在探讨单元整体教学策略在中学英语教学中的应用。通过联动教研行动，优化教学方法，提高教学质量。在教学设计环节，我们遵循《新课标》的指引和学生的认知规律，对教材内容进行整合和优化，注重培养学生的听、说、读、看、写基本技能，并强调学习策略、文化意识和情感态度的培养，发展学生核心素养。在教学实践环节，我们采用单元整体教学策略，通过任务型教学、情境教学、合作学习等多种教学方法，激发学生的学习兴趣，提高学生的英语能力，同时，在实践中不断反思和调整教学策略，以期实现教学目标。通过研究、实验和实践，我们对单元整体教学策略有了更深入的理解和把握，提升了教学效果。同时，学生们在参与有趣、有挑战的教学活动中，英语能力得到了提高，学习兴趣得到了激发；教师在实施单元整体教学过程中，拓宽了专业视野，摒弃教学的固有模式，构建 Planning-Teaching-Observation-Reflection-Evaluation-Creation（PTOREC）教研新模式，勇敢地走出舒适区去尝试创新，把英语作为教研的工作语言，不断将教学教研提升到新的高度。

### （四）反思提升阶段（2023年6月—2023年8月）

在反思提升阶段，我们对教学设计和教学实践进行了深入的回顾与分析。通过对教学过程中的优点和不足进行全面的总结，进一步明确了单元整体教学策略实施的优势和适用性，如提高学生英语能力、激发学生学习兴趣等，同时也发现了存在的问题和不足，如教学资源整合不够充分、部分教学方法不够灵活等。针对这些问题和不足，我们进行了深入的讨论和研究，提出了一系列的改进措施。例如，加强课程资源的整合，充分利用网络资源和课外教材，丰富教学内容；调整教学方法，加强教学评价，注重学生的主体地位，引导学生主动参与、自主探究；加强对教师的培训和指导，提高教师的教学水平，转变教师教育观念等。通过反思提升阶段的探讨和实践，我们对单元整体教学以及教学实施过程中的问题和挑战有了更加清晰的认识，这不仅有助于提高教学质量和提升学生的学习效果，也为今后的教学改革提供了有力的支撑。总之，反思提升阶段对于课题研究的深化和教学实践的改进具有重要的意义。

### （五）形成成果阶段（2023年5月—2023年11月）

在形成成果阶段，我们进行理论学习，全面整理和分析研究材料，完善和提升研究经验，收集典型教学案例，分析、提炼课题成果，撰写发表论文。其中包括课题研究过程中提炼的论文，案例如信息技术赋能语言教学案例、语言与文化的融合教学案例、双语教学案例，最新中考、高考试题评析，区域学业水平监测质量分析和媒体报道等。这些成果是通过对常规教研工作进行深入研究和实践而不断摸索和总结得来的，它们包含了我们对于特定问题的想法和解决方案。另外，我们也精选了课题立项前积累起来的论文、课例、实验报告、考察报告、教学模式研究等，它们是课题研究宝贵的基础。正是前前后后的积累让我们的教研更富有深度和内涵，也为我们提供了更多解决问题和创新的可能性。通过对这些成果的审视和思考，我们能够从中发现教育工作的真谛和意义，以及我们在其中扮演的角色和承担的使命，激励我们在研究过程中不仅要关注提炼课题成果，还应注重学会反思和学会生活，成为具备丰富经验和智慧的教育者，为学生们提供更优质的服务，推动教育事业的可持续发展。我们也希望通过分享在教研中的创新思维和实践经验，为同行提供参考和借鉴。

## 三、研究成果及分析

### （一）课题成果

#### 1. 阶段性报告

聚焦新课标、赋能新课堂、共研新方向。"聚焦单元整体教学的中学英语联动教研行动研究"阶段性报告获广州市深度教学课堂改革实验阶段性成果阶段性研究报告类二等奖。

#### 2. 教学设计

我们团队分初中和高中学段、分模块、分单元、分课时、分项目、分作业形成比较全面系统的教学设计案例，包括沪教版七年级上册模块三完整的模块教学设计，精选沪教版和人教版八年级的单元整体教学设计和分课时课型的教学设计，人教版高中英语选修第二册第一单元项目教学设计，以及初中、高中的作业设计。我们在市区校联动教研活动中对单元整体教学设计、分课时课型的教学设计，以及初中高中的作业设计进行交流分享。这些有代表性和实用性的优秀设计案例对广大一线老师起到了示范引领的作用，带动老师们积极参与区域集体备课，投身到以素养为导向的单元整体教学设计、教学评价、信息技术赋能、作业设计等研究活动中，提高了区域教学的系统性和针对性，为优化教学过程和提升教学效果奠定了基础。

#### 3. 教学案例

以课例研究的方式优化课堂教学，提升教研品质是教师最重要的行动研究。我们分学段、分单元、分课型的课例研究，涵盖听、说、读、看、写在内的语言技能，以及语音、词汇、语法、英汉诗歌对比阅读，单元复习，中高考话题复习，电影欣赏，整本书阅读等热点课型。

#### 4. 论文与报告

课题研究成果包括论文、案例（如信息技术赋能语言教学案例、语言与文化的融合教学案例、双语教学案例）、最新中考与高考试题评析，区域学业水平监测质量分析、实验报告、考察报告、教学模式研究和媒体报道等。这些成果是通过对常规教研工作进行深入研究和实践不断摸索和总结得来的，它们包含了我们对于特定问题的想法和解决方案，是课题研究不断走向深入的宝贵参考和支持。

**5.《聚焦单元整体教学的中学英语联动教研行动研究》成果集**

包括 2 个开题报告、1 个阶段性报告、25 个有代表性的教学设计、17 个课例研究、18 个教学成果等。主要内容是在课题的统领下，聚焦课堂教学，提供了包括词汇、语法、阅读、写作、复习、英汉诗歌对比阅读、读后续写、中华传统文化、整本书阅读、双师课堂、跨学科课堂、项目式课堂等不同领域的教学案例以及教学论文、媒体报道等。

**6. 著作《中学英语联动教研行动研究》**

该书为广东省教育研究院 2022 年中小学英语教育专项研究课题"聚焦单元整体教学的中学英语联动教研行动研究"（课题编号：GDJY – 2022 – A – yyb33）的重要研究成果。

### （二）成果的应用

课题研究的成果极大地丰富了课题的内涵，拓展了研究的思路。更重要的是，我们的教师也和课题一起成长。

本课题研究结合教研转型和教研员的工作职能，以课题研究的方式开展联动教研行动研究，以解决教育教学中所面临的共性问题和师生的实际需要为研究目标，整合区域教研力量，构建以实践为导向的学习和研究共同体，合力应对课程改革不断向纵深发展所面临的挑战，使各级各类教研活动在内涵与外延上都具有延续性、系统性和创新性。

### （三）成果的推广

课题组示范带领全区老师参与集备，分单元进行整体教学设计，引导教师在读书、学习、思考和研讨过程中，通过倾听与对话、分享与碰撞，激发研究热情，相互取长补短，围绕立德树人根本任务，立足课程，聚焦课堂，分析学生，研读教材，落实目标，优化教学方式和学习方式，进行评价工具的研发，研究实施教学重点，突破教学难点，也带动区域教学研究均衡发展，创新构建区域联动教研的有效模式（PTOREC）。教学成果涵盖了教学设计、论文、案例研究、调查研究、实验研究、行动研究、教学模式、信息技术赋能、作业研究等多种形式，可以为广大一线教师和教研员开展课题研究和指导教学教研提供借鉴。

## 四、问题与展望

问题：

（1）如何有效整合和共享教育资源，为不同层次的学校提供丰富的教学资源支持，是我们需要进一步研究和解决的问题。

（2）在实施单元整体教学的过程中，我们意识到现有的评价机制并不能全面客观地反映学生的学习成果。如何优化区域联动教研的模式（PTOREC），建立与之相匹配的评价体系，以便更好地激励学生学习、促进师生核心素养的提升，需要深入研究和探讨。

（3）我们的实验数据分析不够充分，结果的科学性仍然可以进一步提高。

展望：

在英语联动教研的路上，我们深感一个朴素而伟大的真理：独行速，众行远。当我们汇聚智慧和力量，共同追求教育的宏伟目标时，每个人都成了一座灯塔，在黑暗中闪耀着光芒。我们相信，教育的力量不仅来自课堂和书本，更源自合作与分享。当我们将经验、智慧和创意交织在一起时，那些平凡的瞬间便化作了神奇的火花。团队合作让我们拥有了无限的可能性，因为每个人的贡献都如同一颗星星，点亮了未知的前方。

让我们一起继续前行，在英语联动教研的舞台上翩然起舞，用智慧的旋律奏响和谐幸福的乐章。让我们永远保持着开放的心态，乐享其中，与他人共同分享这份生命的融合之美。让我们铭记共同的使命，不断提升自己的精神境界，戮力同心，勇于担当，不负韶华，携手共进，倾心守护这片教育教研热土，将爱和智慧注入每一个课堂、每一次教研，点燃每个学生心中的火花，让他们品味语言的美妙，发展多元思维，具备全球视野和跨文化交流的能力，走向更宽广的世界！

## 五、致谢

这是一段关于爱与成长的旅程，也是一个梦想的起航点。课题组成员经过3年多的努力终于申请结题，这期间得到了广州市教育研究院镇祝桂老师、何琳老师、陈浩曦老师、劳晓静老师的悉心指导，黄埔区教研员符丽雪老师、番禺区教研员冯页老师、越秀区教研员曾苗青老师的无私帮助和所在区骨干老师的传经送宝，广东外语外贸大学吕琳琼教授、郑杰教授，华南师范大学谷红丽教授、徐曼菲教授、黄丽燕教授、许悦婷教授、刘晓斌教授、金檀教授等专家的指导，海珠区教育发展研究院领导和同事的支持帮助，同时也得到了各级领导、各学校科组老师、英语教学同仁、中心组成员的大力支持、通力协作与无私奉献。在这里，谨代表课题组成员向各位专家及同仁一并表示衷心的感谢，也衷心感谢课题组小伙伴们的团结协作和辛勤付出。由于本人水平有限，其中提到的观点，难免存在不足不当之处，恳请专家、同行不吝赐教，批评指正！

# 第二篇　设计先行

本篇精选笔者全程指导和设计的分初中与高中学段、分模块、分单元、分课时、分项目、分作业的比较系统的教学设计案例，包括沪教版七年级上册模块三的教学设计，精选沪教版和人教版八年级的单元整体教学设计和分课时课型的教学设计，人教版高中英语选修第二册第一单元项目教学设计以及读后续写全区集体备课的作业设计。每一份教学设计都凝聚着老师个人和教研团队的心血和智慧。比如，沪教版七年级上册模块三13份教学设计从2020年11月课题组接到课程研发任务，到2021年8月到广州电视台录制教学视频，再到2022年12月打造成国家资源，历时两年多。在广州市教育研究院何琳老师的全程指导下，我们团队分工明确，市区联动，整体规划，分段推进。疫情期间，老师们不忘教育初心，精雕细琢，深入研读，反复打磨课件、学案、逐字稿、脚本稿、PPT底板颜色、字体大小、视频音乐等，不断推倒重来，每一位老师演绎的时候，其他成员都会仔细聆听并记录修改意见，及时反馈，即时落实。我们从团队中汲取力量，同心协力，最终自信地走到电视台录制课程。正是团队老师们精诚合作，不断完善，才最终把我们的课程打造成国家资源！我们在市区校联动教研活动中交流分享了单元整体教学设计、分课时课型的教学设计，以及初中高中的作业设计，这些有代表性和实用性的优秀设计案例对广大一线老师起到了示范引领的作用，带动老师们积极参与区域集体备课，投身到以素养为导向的单元整体教学设计、教学评价、信息技术赋能、作业设计等研究活动中，提高了区域教学的系统性和针对性，为优化教学过程和提升教学效果奠定了基础。

# 第一章 广州共享课堂与国家课程资源*
## ——沪教版七年级模块教学设计

**设计一** Module 3 Travels Unit 5 Visiting the Moon,Grade 7A Extensive Reading**

### 一、教材解读

主题语境:人与自然(月球旅行)
课程类型:单元拓展阅读课

### 二、教学内容分析

(Why)本单元出自上海教育出版社沪教版《英语(七年级上册)》第五单元,围绕"月球旅行"这一话题展开。【Reading】板块以男孩 Jerry 的一篇日记为载体,介绍了有关太空旅行和月球漫步的科学常识及相关表达,帮助学生初步了解一般将来时的用法;【Listening】板块通过机器人对太空旅馆的介绍,培养学生在听力训练时记录关键信息的能力;【Grammar】板块教授了一般将来时的用法:"will + 动词原形"表达未来可能发生的事,"be going to + 动词原形"表达某人的计划或打算;【Speaking】板块让学生尝试运用一般将来时介绍参观太空博物馆的计划;【Writing】板块引导学生合理运用已有信息制订一份入住太空旅馆的首日计划表,并在此基础上完成一份参观计划书。【More practice】板块延续了主阅读篇章的话题,文章主要以一般将来时展开叙述,对未来月球上可能出现的旅馆进行了描述。文章没有生词,对大部分经过了小学 6 年英语学习的广州市初一学生而言,课文内容比较简单,需要适当拓展补充更具挑战性的材料,以提升词汇量及阅读能力和思考能力。

(What)本节课是在单元以上内容学习的基础上,选用 National Geographic

---

\* 教研指导和审课专家:广州市教育研究院何琳、广州市海珠区教育发展研究院张志梅。
\*\* 设计者:广州市第五中学熊佳。

Learning 和 Cengage Learning 联合出品的分级系列读物 *Reading Explorer* 中 Level 1 第 4 单元第 2 篇文章为材料，拓展阅读与本单元主题相关的文章，以此帮助学生巩固阅读技能、丰富拓展词汇、发展批判性思维及提升观点表达的条理性。

（How）通过对本单元【Reading】内容的回顾，调动学生已有的与单元主题相关的词汇和背景知识；通过快速浏览，了解各段主要内容，训练学生的阅读技能；帮助学生学会运用思维导图理清段落要点，并运用这种方法组织自己的观点；通过阅读，让学生对探索太空形成更全面的认识，发展批判性思维；使学生在阅读的过程中初步接触、了解更丰富的词汇，拓展词汇量。

## 三、教学对象分析

就认知水平而言，七年级的学生正处于认知能力迅速发展的阶段，对于宇宙探索方面的话题普遍比较感兴趣，并且积累了一定的话题背景知识。他们对此有一定的认识，有自己的想法，但存在因对客观知识了解不够全面而导致观点比较片面的问题。

就语言水平而言，七年级的学生在小学阶段接触到的关于科技和宇宙探索方面的词汇非常有限，不习惯阅读稍微长、难、复杂的文章，观点表达的条理性也比较薄弱，需要在老师的指导下阅读有一定挑战性的文章以提升能力。

## 四、教学目标

通过本节课的学习，学生能够达到如下目标：
（1）运用阅读技能，快速浏览，了解各段主要内容。
（2）在思维导图的帮助下，理清段落要点及组织自己的观点。
（3）在阅读中形成对探索太空更全面的认识，发展批判性思维。
（4）在阅读中掌握以下单词，拓充词汇量：establish, independent, settlement, neighbor, rocket, environment, advance, medicine, benefit, mission, surface, concern, culture。

## 五、教学重难点

重点：运用阅读技能，快速浏览，了解各段主要内容，形成对探索太空更全面的认识。

难点：通过思维导图，理清段落要点，并运用这种方法组织自己的观点。

前置任务：
（1）熟读 Reading，能复述本单元课文。
（2）打印本节课的阅读材料和学案备用。

## 六、教学过程

| 步骤 | 设计意图 | 教师活动 | 学生活动 |
| --- | --- | --- | --- |
| 1. Leading-in | 明确本节课学习目标。 | Present the learning objectives of this lesson to the students. | Learn about the learning objectives of this lesson. |
| 2. Revision | 引导学生通过对本单元【Reading】内容的回顾，调动已有的与单元主题相关的词汇和背景知识。 | Show students some pictures and ask them to go over Jerry's trip to space by describing the pictures. | Go over Jerry's trip to space by describing the pictures. |
| 3. Extending | 通过快速浏览，了解各段的主要内容，训练学生的阅读技能；帮助学生学会运用思维导图理清段落要点，并运用这种方法组织自己的观点；通过阅读，对探索太空形成更全面的认识，发展批判性思维；在阅读的过程中初步接触、了解更丰富的词汇，拓展词汇量。 | Pre-reading<br>1. Help Ss understand some new words to prepare for the reading.<br>2. Make Ss complete the sentence "Sending humans into space to live *is/is not* a good idea because…"<br>While-reading<br>1. Make Ss read the passage and match each paragraph with its main idea.<br>2. Make Ss complete the mind map to analyze the reasons listed in Paragraph E.<br>Post-reading<br>1. Ask Ss if they agree with Elon Musk and then use the mind map to organize their reasons to develop their critical thinking.<br>2. Make them compare their reasons with their answer to the question before reading the passage. | Pre-reading<br>1. Read the definitions. Then complete the paragraph with the correct form of the words in bold.<br>2. Read the sentence. Circle their answer and complete the sentence. Later, compare their ideas with those in the passage. "Sending humans into space to live *is/is not* a good idea because…"<br>While-reading<br>1. Read the passage. Then match each paragraph with its main idea.<br>2. Read Paragraph E again. Then complete the mind map below by writing the reasons in the boxes.<br>Post-reading<br>1. Think and tell if they agree with Elon Musk, and then use the mind map to organize their reasons.<br>2. Compare their reasons with their answer to the question before reading the passage. |

续上表

| 步骤 | 设计意图 | 教师活动 | 学生活动 |
| --- | --- | --- | --- |
| 4. Summary | 回顾本节课的学习要点。 | Lead Ss to go over the keys of this period. | Go over the keys of this period with T. |
| 5. Homework | 通过课后练习，巩固词汇和阅读。 | Give Ss some exercises as homework to consolidate what they've learned in this class. | Complete the homework. |
| 6. Self-assessment | 培养学生的自主学习能力。 | Lead Ss to do a self-assessment about the reading skills used in today's class to improve their learning ability. | Ss do a self-assessment to see how well they can use the reading skills for in today's class. |

## 七、作业设计

| 作业类型 | 作业内容 | 设计意图 |
| --- | --- | --- |
| 前置作业 | 熟读 Reading，复述课文内容。 | 帮助学生巩固课文内容和主题词汇，为拓展阅读做准备。 |
| 基础性练习 | 根据划线单词的意思，选择正确答案补全句子。<br>1. An <u>independent</u> country is under _____ control.<br>　　a. its own　　　b. other country's<br>2. A <u>neighbor</u> is a person who lives _____ you.<br>　　a. near　　　　b. far from<br>3. If we make <u>advances</u> in science or technology, we _____ in those areas.<br>　　a. do worse　　b. improve<br>4. A student of <u>medicine</u> probably wants to be a(n) _____.<br>　　a. doctor　　　b. astronaut | |

续上表

| 作业类型 | 作业内容 | 设计意图 |
|---|---|---|
| 基础性练习 | 根据划线单词的意思，选择正确答案补全句子。<br>5. If something <u>benefits</u> you, it _____ you.<br>　　a. helps　　　　b. hurts<br>6. The <u>surface</u> of a planet is the _____ layer of it.<br>　　a. inside　　　　b. outside<br>7. A <u>concern</u> is a fact or situation that _____ you.<br>　　a. surprises　　　b. worries<br>8. A person's <u>culture</u> includes _____.<br>　　a. their way of life　　b. how they breathe<br>根据阅读内容选择最佳答案。<br>1. What is the main purpose of this passage?<br>　　a. Give reasons for and against establishing settlements in space.<br>　　b. Describe what life would be like on the moon.<br>　　c. Explain the history of human space travel.<br>　　d. Compare the environments of Mars and the moon.<br>2. What does "*our*" in Stephen Hawking's quote（引言）"*our future should be safe*"（line 4）refer to?<br>　　a. Hawking's family's　b. scientists'<br>　　c. humans'　d. astronauts'<br>3. Between 2020 and 2030, some countries plan to send astronauts to _____.<br>　　a. Mars　　　　　b. other Earthlike planets<br>　　c. the moon　　　d. another solar system<br>4. Why are some countries planning to create lunar space stations?<br>　　a. To know more about the moon's surface.<br>　　b. To lower Earth's population.<br>　　c. To grow food for humans on Earth.<br>　　d. To prepare humans to live on other planets.<br>5. Which reason for living in space is NOT mentioned?<br>　　a. We can learn if humans can live in a very different environment.<br>　　b. We can create human societies on other planets.<br>　　c. We can search for life on other planets.<br>　　d. We can benefit from scientific advances. | 巩固阅读技能，并加深对拓展阅读文章的理解。 |

续上表

| 作业类型 | 作业内容 | 设计意图 |
| --- | --- | --- |
| 基础性练习 | 6. What does "*First stop: the moon*" mean in the last line?<br>a. Everybody wants to go to the moon first.<br>b. Mars's moon is the best place to have a human settlement.<br>c. All spaceships to other planets will stop at the moon first.<br>d. The first human settlement in space will likely be on the moon. | 巩固阅读技能，并加深对拓展阅读文章的理解。 |
| 拓展性练习 | 完成课本68页的阅读练习。 | 在课后阅读中激发学生进行更多关于探索月球的思考。 |

## 附：七年级上册英语 Unit 5 Extensive Reading 阅读材料
### LIVING IN SPACE

Stephen Hawking, one of the world's most famous scientists, believed that to survive, humans will one day have to move into space. "Once we spread out into space and establish independent settlements, our future should be safe," he said.

Today, the United States, Europe, Russia, China and Japan are all planning to send astronauts back to Earth's closest neighbor: the moon. Some of these countries want to create space stations there within the next 10 years. These stations will prepare humans to visit and later live on Mars or other Earthlike planets.

Robert Zubrin, a rocket scientist, thinks humans should move into space. He wants to start with Mars. Why? He thinks sending people to Mars will allow us to learn a lot of things—for example, the ability of humans to live in a very different environment. Eventually, we could create new human societies on other planets. In addition, any advances we make in the fields of science, technology, medicine, and health will benefit people here on Earth.

SpaceX is a company that builds rockets. Its founder and CEO, Elon Musk, also believes we should move into Mars. He doesn't want to send just "one little mission" though. His long-term goal is to put one million people on the planet in case something bad happens to us here on Earth.

Not everyone thinks sending humans into space is a smart idea. Many say it's too expensive. Also, most space trips are not short. A one-way trip to Mars, for example, would take at least six months. People travelling this kind of distance could face many health problems. In addition, these first people would find life extremely difficult in space. On the moon's surface, for example, the sun's rays① are very dangerous. People would have to stay indoors most of the time.

Despite these concerns, sending people into space seems certain. In the future, we might see lunar② cities or even new human cultures on other planets. First stop: the moon.

注释: ①The sun's rays are narrow beams of light from the sun.

②Lunar means "related to the moon".

文章来源: 美国国家地理和 Cengage Learning 联合出版的 *Reading Explorer*, Level 1 之 4b 文本及部分练习。

## 设计二　Module 3 Travels Unit 6 Travelling around the World，Grade 7A Writing*

### 一、教材解读

主题语境：模块三主题为"旅行"，第五单元话题为"月球旅行"，第六单元话题为"走遍亚洲"。

语篇类型：旅游指南（travel guide）。

### 二、教学内容分析

本单元为沪教版《英语（七年级上册）》第六单元，以"走遍亚洲"为话题，以介绍城市为主线。单元的各个模块均涉及亚洲大城市旅游的介绍，其中包括主阅读模块中上海的城市风光介绍，听力模块中三座亚洲城市北京、东京、曼谷的城市名片，还有补充阅读模块中的香港旅游介绍。

（What is in the text？）本节课是单元写作课第 5 课时。写作 A 要求学生阅读第 81 页的上海旅游信息，然后以讨论的方式，思考如何将所给的信息分类。写作 B 要求学生在学习主阅读、听力文本和写作板块的旅游指南采用的方法后，介绍自己所在城市的旅游资源。

（How is the text organized？）本节课从复习主阅读和听力文本入手，逐步引导学生思考如何构思创作一份旅游指南，并在写作中运用条件状语从句"If you…，you can/will…"。

（Why is the text written？）通过旅游指南写作，让学生有更清晰的框架结构和思路，同时引导学生懂得欣赏身边的美，激发对自己所在地域文化的兴趣，热爱家乡，热爱祖国。

### 三、教学对象分析

（1）年龄特征：学生多为十二三岁，刚从小学六年级升入初中一年级，正处于学习过渡期和适应期，还保留着小学生的学习特征，对色彩、图片、音

---

\* 设计者：广州市第五中学黎绮华。

频、视频等直观事物更感兴趣。语言与认知水平：初一学生有一定的英语基础且对英语学习有兴趣，但学生还未开始学习沪教版《英语（七年级上册）》中"走遍亚洲"的话题，背景知识积累较少。本节课的专有名词比较多，学生尽管能用中文描述景点，但是对相关的英语表达了解甚少，这构成本节课的难点。学生经过前面4个课时的学习，对本单元的主题比较熟悉，但是对于旅游指南的框架结构和如何构思还比较陌生，这是本节课需要帮学生突破的重点。

（2）学习动机：学生喜欢旅游，非常渴望表达与自己所在城市相关的内容。本课时激发学生的学习动力，培养学生对自己所在城市的文化、风土人情的兴趣，尤其要丰富和激发其对广州的认识与热爱。

## 四、教学目标

（1）学生通过仿写，了解制作上海旅游指南的特征，提高语言能力。

（2）学生通过讨论和"蛛网图"学会将景点分类，同时通过在语境中运用条件状语从句提高句子写作能力。

（3）学生通过解读主阅读语篇的结构，了解旅游指南的基本构成，达成思维能力的提升。

（4）学生能进一步了解亚洲大城市上海的民俗风情、地域文化；能懂得发现并欣赏身边的美，激发对自己的家乡——广州的热爱。

## 五、教学重点和难点

重点：掌握旅游指南的文体特征并巩固对条件状语从句的运用；
难点：综合运用本单元所学内容以编写旅游指南。

## 六、教学过程

| 教学环节 | 教学活动 | 设计意图 |
| --- | --- | --- |
| Step 1<br>Pre-writing<br>（5 mins） | 1. T introduces Peter who has travelled around Shanghai.<br>2. T shows the map of Peter's bus tour, ask Ss to find out where he has been. Ss need to write down the names of the places.<br>3. T introduces Sarah to the whole class. She wants to know what to do if she goes to Shanghai.<br>4. Ss are asked to introduce Shanghai by using "if-clause" orally. | 1. To go over what the Ss have learned in this unit.<br>2. To encourage Ss to use if-clause, which is the Grammar of unit 6. |

续上表

| 教学环节 | 教学活动 | 设计意图 |
| --- | --- | --- |
| Step 2<br>1st-writing<br>(5 mins) | 1. Task 1: Finish Part A, finish the travel guide according to the given information about Shanghai.<br>2. Task 2: Make a conclusion about how to make a good travel guide. | Based on the Ss' understanding of the main reading material, help Ss to think about some important elements of making a good travel guide. |
| Step 3<br>2nd-writing<br>(8 mins) | T creates a real situation. Suppose Peter will go to another city—Guangzhou in China.<br>T encourages Ss to tell something about places of interest, food and things to buy in Guangzhou.<br>T plays a video about Guangzhou to arouse Ss' background knowledge.<br>Ss need to finish three tasks.<br>Task 1: Ss are asked to sort out the places in the spider gram.<br>Task 2: Ss will read a short passage about Chen Clan Academy and find out the missing words.<br>Task 3: Ss try to write a travel guide about Guangzhou alone or in a group of three.<br>T helps Ss to assess their travel guide by using the Self-evaluation form. | 1. To arouse Ss' interest in the topic.<br>2. To use the structure of a travel guide.<br>3. To train Ss' writing skills. |
| Step 4<br>Summary<br>(1 min) | Guide Ss to summarize what they have learnt. | To encourage Ss to consolidate what they've learnt. |
| Homework<br>(1 min) | | To polish their travel guide and learn to share with others. |

## 设计三 Module 3 Travels Grade 7A Module 3 Revision *

## 一、教材解读

主题语境：七年级上册 Module 3 的主题是"旅游（Travel）"，主题语境为"人与社会（Man and society）、人与自然（Man and nature）"，包含 Unit 5 和 Unit 6 两个单元。

模块概览：

**Module 3 Travel（旅游）**

Unit 5 Visiting the Moon（探访月球）

| Reading | Jerry 的日记，记述了 Jerry 出发去月球前的心情和对月球旅行的了解。 |
|---|---|
| Listening | 一段关于太空旅馆设施的介绍。 |
| Grammar | 学习一般将来时的两种结构。 |
| Speaking | 运用一般将来时讨论参观太空博物馆的计划。 |
| Writing | 完成入住太空旅馆后首日的活动计划表，然后使用一般将来时完成一份参观计划书。 |
| More Practice | 关于月球旅馆的文章。 |
| Study Skills | 学习如何绘制"蛛网图"。 |
| Culture Corner | 了解中国的航天梦。 |

Unit 6 Travelling around Asia（走遍亚洲）

| Reading | 上海旅游指南，介绍了人民广场、外滩和豫园三处景点。 |
|---|---|
| Listening | 介绍三座亚洲城市，捕捉城市特征，将照片和城市配对，补全城市信息卡。 |
| Grammar | 学习 if 引导的条件状语从句。 |
| Speaking | 谈论自己所在城市的著名景点，并进行简单的口头介绍。 |

---

\* 设计者：广州市第九十七中学梁家昕。

续上表

| Writing | 用 if 引导的条件状语从句完成一份自己所在城市的旅游指南。 |
| --- | --- |
| More Practice | 读有关香港旅游的文章，了解介绍景点的表达方法。 |
| Culture Corner | 了解世界遗产的知识。 |
| Project | 制作一份目的地城市两日游的行程表。 |

本课课型为"模块复习课"，将以 Peter 游览世界之窗的故事为主线，整合模块知识，在情境中帮助学生进行复习。

本节课所使用的素材：课本文本（改编）、七年级上册教师用书分课时教案中的文本（改编）、一个音频（文本改编自课文及七年级上册教师用书分课时教案中的文本）以及一个视频（学生自行制作）。

## 二、学情分析

学生在此模块学习中，在阅读板块已初步掌握日记写作与旅游指南的写作特点；在听力和会话板块中已学会听前预测，通过并捕捉记录相关听力信息，能口头讨论旅游计划以及介绍自己所在的城市；在语法板块中能了解一般将来时和 if 引导的条件状语从句的意义、形式和用法；在写作板块中能运用所学，制作活动计划书和旅游指南；在拓展阅读和文化角板块，学生进一步丰富视野，丰富阅读体验。但学生仍需要进一步巩固所学知识，并学会在情境中运用这些知识。

## 三、教学目标

（1）在语篇中巩固本模块的重点词汇和句型。
（2）在语境中巩固及运用本模块中的学习策略以及语法。
（3）制作一份城市旅游指南，并向他人介绍这个城市。

## 四、教学重点、难点

重点：在语篇中巩固本模块的重点词汇和句型。
难点：在语境中巩固和运用本模块中的学习策略以及语法。

## 五、教学过程

| 教学环节 | 教学活动 | 设计意图 |
| --- | --- | --- |
| Step 1 | 1. T greets the Ss and introduces the teaching aims.<br>2. T leads in the lesson. | To introduce the teaching aims and arouse the Ss' interests. |
| Step 2 | 1. Ss review and use the key words and phrases in texts.<br>2. T leads the Ss to consolidate the listening strategies.<br>3. Ss consolidate the grammar rules through tasks. | To consolidate the key words and phrases, strategies and grammar rules in the module. |
| Step 3 | 1. Ss review what make a reasonable travel plan.<br>2. Ss review what make a good travel guide. | To encourage Ss to make full use of the knowledge they've learned. |

## 六、作业设计

请运用所学内容，制作一份城市旅游指南，并向他人介绍这个城市（旅游指南形式不限，可以是介绍稿、海报、音频或者视频）。

# 第二章 广州共享课堂精品课*
## ——人教版高三年级项目教学设计

### 设计四 高中英语选修二 Unit 1 Relationships Project**

课型：Project：Make an inspiring speech about friendship
主题语境：人与社会
语篇类型：新媒体与多模态语篇
授课时长：40 分钟

## 一、教学内容分析

本单元的主题是"人际关系"，属于《普通高中英语课程标准（2017 年版 2020 年修订）》"人与社会"主题语境下"社会服务与人际沟通"主题群中"良好的人际关系与社会交往"的内容。单元各板块围绕这个大主题从不同角度展开，包括朋友关系、亲子关系、恋爱关系、邻里关系、工作或学习中的合作关系、重大事件中国家乃至世界范围的合作关系等。开篇页的主题图展现了一群欢快的年轻人在一起自拍的场景，体现青少年非常重视朋友关系。学生观察图片并思考良好人际关系的意义。Reading and Thinking 是本单元的精读板块，文章剖析真朋友的一些本质特征，如积极向上、关爱他人、值得信赖等，目的是帮助学生识别真正的朋友，交到真朋友，成为别人的真朋友。Language

---

\* 教研指导和审课专家：广州市教育研究院陈皓曦。

\*\* 设计者：广州市海珠区教育发展研究院张志梅；广州市南武中学白进炜；广州市第五中学黄秀慧、王鑫淇、任倩颐；广州市海珠外国语实验学校肖丽琴；广州市为明学校蔡明；广州市第四十一中学赵玉书；广州市第九十七中学周燕梨；广州市培才高级中学谭飞煌；广州市海珠中学黄胜开；广州市南武中学岭南画派纪念校区陈莹莹；广州市海华高级中学周红；湖南师范大学张泽艺；湖南省新化县第二中学张梅花。授课者：广州市海珠区教育发展研究院张志梅。

Focus 1-2 板块分为词汇和语法两个部分，其中词汇部分复习巩固整个单元的核心词汇，语法部分综合训练强调结构以及梳理表语的各种用法；Exploring the Theme 板块分为四个部分：Section A 是关于武汉抗疫的一篇社论，回顾这个可以载入史册的重大事件，让学生深刻意识到，面临重大灾难时，只有团结一心、众志成城，才能取得胜利。Section B 深入探讨学习和工作场景中常见的合作关系，从不同角度分析了合作的重要性。Section C 是一则采访对话，三个受访者回顾父母浓浓的爱，感人至深。Section D 的语篇节选自经典名著《傲慢与偏见》，展示男女主角在寻找真爱路上遭遇的矛盾冲突，让学生思考爱情建立的基础。Expressing Your Ideas 板块让学生充分表达自己的观点，面对交友过程中的两难境地，思考友谊的本质以及什么是真正的朋友。综合来看，本单元的主题内容从"友情"开始，逐步延伸到"博爱""合作""亲情"和"爱情"，所有内容都密切关联学生的实际生活，能引发他们的思考和想象，增强他们对"人际关系"主题的认知和理解。

　　基于单元内容、主题意义和育人价值，本课 Project 的教学围绕 Expressing Your Ideas about Friendship（"关于友谊"的主题表达）展开，设计思路为：首先，观看同学演唱歌曲 *Shining Friends*，引入项目主题 Relationships 并运用构词法构建 word bank；其次，通过翻译单元语篇中出现的名人名言，引导学生感知多种人际关系，加深对建立良好人际关系主题意义的思考；紧接着，进入主题情境，通过项目学习驱动问题链，引导学生阅读 Expressing Your Ideas 板块中一篇青少年网上求助的帖子、三个同龄人的回帖和一个老师的评论，分析发帖人的语言与特质，辩证思考什么是正确的友谊观；然后，引导学生反思出现在自己和朋友之间的两难情境，学生采访并分享他们的朋友如何帮助自己摆脱困境的轶事，将所读内容与自我建立关联，为后续的演讲做准备；之后，指导学生 prepare an inspiring speech，挑选一个展示作品，指导学生掌握演讲稿的体裁、结构、语言和修辞特点，引导学生参照评价表鉴赏学习这个 demo 并做出评价；最后，学生演讲展示与评价，通过相互评价选出最佳演讲者，使学生成为学习活动真正的主体。课后完成项目式作业，为学校的英语节准备多模态语篇，包括必做题 Write a web post about a dilemma, or a reply post, or a comment post.，并发布到班群，为解决更多人际关系困扰支招。选做题：①为 The Proposal 中 Darcy 和 Elizabeth 的对话配音，培养正确的爱情观；②Interview and share your anecdotes about parental love，培养感恩之心；③What is true friendship/love/cooperation? 的配乐演讲，培养正确价值观和合作精神。

## 二、学情分析

本节课面向广州市全体高三学生和所有学有余力的高中生。进入高中之后，学生掌握了较为复杂的语法规则，能运用所学的词汇和学习策略表达与各种主题相关的信息或观点，具备了较强的逻辑思维和分析能力。此外，他们对英语学习的目标和意义有了更为明确的认识，能够根据自己的需求制订学习计划，独立完成学习任务，在课堂上主动参与讨论，提出问题和观点，表现出较高的自主性、积极性和目标导向性。然而，由于时间紧迫和高考的压力，他们在心理情感方面面临各种问题和挑战，如学业压力、社交困难、家庭问题、情感问题等。根据课前对海珠区1480名高中学生的问卷调查（见附表1），他们非常重视人际关系，超过一半的学生希望探讨朋友关系、亲子关系、师生关系等，所以引导学生正确认识和处理各种关系是本单元主题探究的深远意义所在，对促进学生的身心健康具有非常积极的作用。本课学习的内容为选修二第一单元，是应高中英语课程的提高要求而设计的，大部分学生平时没有接触过选修教材，对单元词汇表中的新单词和短语都很陌生，也没有时间系统地学习单元语篇内容，这对探究单元主题意义、完成项目任务带来很大困难和挑战。

为了帮助学生在极为有限的时间内顺利完成Project，本课采用了产出导向法，提高教学的针对性和有效性。首先通过构词法和思维导图梳理有关人际关系的特质和行为表现，建立word bank，搭好项目语言和内容支架，针对没有时间系统学习单元语篇的情况，精选了既短小精悍又与表达性技能密切相关的网帖进行阅读，帮助学生分析网帖的语言特点，形成结构化知识，搭好项目表达支架，其他语篇则作为项目课后作业让有兴趣的学生选择使用。教师鼓励学生运用可视化的结构图，对小组讨论的项目作品进行直观形象的展示。这既符合高中生的身心特点，又为学生学会合理展示思维过程与结果提供了方法指导。在此过程中，"观众"学生需填写项目成果展示表现性评价表（见附表2和附表3），透过作品看到整个探究学习的过程，促进相互学习、共同成长和核心素养的提高。

## 三、教学目标

在本课学习结束时，学生能够：
（1）利用构词法和思维导图构建自己的关于友谊主题的词库；
（2）深入解读关于友谊的名人名言，进一步理解友谊的本质和深刻含义；

(3)分析网帖的语言特点，辩证思考友谊观及采访朋友之间应对困境的故事；

(4)通过引用名言和讲述故事等技巧，发表以"什么是真正的朋友？"为主题的演讲。

## 四、教学重难点

(1)分析网帖的语言特点，辩证思考友谊观及采访朋友之间应对困境的轶事；

(2)通过引用名言和讲述轶事等技巧，发表以"什么是真正的朋友？"为主题的演讲。

## 五、教学资源

教材、多媒体课件、多媒体设备。

## 六、教学过程

| 步骤 | 教学活动 | 设计意图 |
| --- | --- | --- |
| | 学习理解 | |
| Step 1 | 1. T shows a video of Ss' singing the song *Shining Friends* and facilitates Ss to use word-formation rules.<br>2. Ss build their word banks by sorting out traits and behaviours related to interpersonal relationships through word building and mind mapping. | To arouse students' learning interest, to lead in the theme, and to scaffold the language and content of the project. |
| Step 2 | 1. T encourages Ss to read and translate some famous quotes about friendships that appear in the discourse of the unit.<br>2. Ss are guided to perceive thought-provoking quotes and their meanings. | To deepen Ss' thinking about the significance of building good interpersonal relationships. |

续上表

| 步骤 | 教学活动 | 设计意图 |
|---|---|---|
| 应用实践 | | |
| Step 3 | 1. T introduces Rose's post on a website asking for help with her dilemma.<br>2. Ss read Rose's post and think aloud what her dilemma is and what she should do.<br>3. T asks Ss to read three replies, explain whether they agree and disagree with them and evaluate each person's view on friendship.<br>4. Ss read, compare and discuss who is right by analyzing the language of the posts and the characteristics of the web posters. | To enter the thematic contexts and lead in project learning-driven questions.<br>To help Ss to think dialectically about what the right view of friendship is and to learn how to make themselves a true friend to others. |
| Step 4 | 1. T guides Ss to read the comment from a teacher and explain whether they agree with the teacher.<br>2. Ss discuss, sort and analyze the teacher's attitude, guidance and qualities. | To help Ss construct structured knowledge of web posts for writing their own and develop a deeper understanding of friendship. |
| 迁移创新 | | |
| Step 5 | 1. T guides students to think about dilemmas that occur between themselves and their friends and have an interview.<br>2. Ss reflect on similar experiences, interview and share their anecdotes about how their friends help them out of dilemmas in groups. | To connect what Ss learn to life, to have structured discussions, and to prepare content for subsequent presentations. |
| Step 6 | 1. T instructs students to prepare an inspiring speech, selects a demo piece to help students learn the genre, structure, and linguistic and rhetorical features, and explain the evaluation criteria to them.<br>2. Ss make presentations, using body language and quotes to improve communication.<br>3. Ss choose the best group through peer evaluation. | To improve oral expression skills, self-confidence, and teamwork spirit.<br>To promote positive transfer of knowledge, abilities, thinking, attitudes and values. |

续上表

| 步骤 | 教学活动 | 设计意图 |
|---|---|---|
| Step 7 | T provides feedback on Ss' performance and encourages them to build up healthy relationships. | To cultivate empathy and responsibility. |

| Homework： |
|---|
| 必做题：Write a web post about a dilemma, or a reply post, or a comment post.<br>选做题：请为学校的英语节做准备。<br>　　（1）为教材 The Proposal 中 Darcy 和 Elizabeth 的对话配音；<br>　　（2）Interview and share your anecdotes about parental love；<br>　　（3）What is true friendship/love/cooperation? 的配乐演讲。 |

### 附表1　学生探讨人际关系的需求调查统计

| Statement | To a great extent | To some extent | Not sure |
|---|---|---|---|
| I'd like to talk about relationships with friends. | 910/61.49% | 490/33.11% | 80/5.41% |
| I'd like to talk about relationships with classmates. | 540/36.49% | 750/50.68% | 190/12.84% |
| I'd like to talk about relationships with parents. | 520/35.14% | 660/44.59% | 300/20.27% |
| I'd like to talk about relationships with crushes. | 320/21.62% | 560/37.84% | 600/40.54% |
| I'd like to talk about relationships with teachers. | 290/19.59% | 690/46.62% | 500/33.78% |
| I'd like to talk about relationships with neighbors. | 170/11.49% | 470/31.76% | 840/56.76% |

### 附表2　Interview and share anecdotes 表现性评价表

| Peer Assessment Checklist | Comments |
|---|---|
| Is your anecdote clear and to the point? | |
| Does your anecdote highlight a clear theme? | |
| Is there a logical sequence of events? | |

续上表

| Peer Assessment Checklist | Comments |
|---|---|
| Have you incorporated the beginning-development-climax-ending structure? | |
| Is the anecdote interesting, amusing, inspiring, or thought-provoking? | |
| Have you used appropriate adjectives and phrases to bring your anecdote to life? | |

附表3  Making an inspiring speech 表现性评价表

| Peer Assessment Checklist | Your comments |
|---|---|
| Use one theme only. | |
| Support your speech with an engaging story or anecdotes. | |
| Use a conversational tone with short sentences and simple structures. | |
| Include quotes, and rhetorical devices. | |
| Include a dilemma. | |
| Make good use of humour and eye contact. | |

# 第三章 沪教版八年级单元整体教学设计*

## 设计五 八年级上册 Module 4 School life Unit 8 English Week**

### 一、主题语境

第八单元"English Week（以校园英语周活动为主线）"单元主题属于《义务教育英语课程标准（2022 年版）》"人与自我"范畴下的"生活与学习"主题群，子主题内容为"学校、课程，学校生活与个人感受""丰富、充实、积极向上的生活"和"乐学善学，勤于反思，学会学习"。同时，它也属于"人与社会"范畴下的"文学、艺术和体育"主题群，子主题内容为"运动、文艺等社团活动，潜能发掘"和"中外影视、戏剧、音乐、舞蹈、绘画、建筑等艺术形式中的文化价值和作品赏析，优秀的艺术家及其艺术成就"。

### 二、语篇分析和单元主题大观念分析

第八单元由不同类型语篇组成，各语篇内容及其主题意义如表 1 所示。

表 1 单元语篇内容及其主题意义

| 语篇 | 语篇类型 | 语篇主题 | 语篇内容 | 主题意义 |
| --- | --- | --- | --- | --- |
| Getting Ready（GR） | 卡通图片（对话） | 学校、课程，学校生活与个人感受 | 关于 Lo 想写新闻报道的目的。 | 思考新闻报道的目的。 |
| Reading（R）English: fun for life | 新闻报道（应用文） | 学校、课程，学校生活与个人感受 | 介绍有关 Rosie Bridge 学校举办的"英语周"举办的主要活动。 | 了解新闻报道的特征和学校活动特色。 |

---

\* 教研指导和审课专家：广州市海珠区教育发展研究院张志梅。
\*\* 设计者：广州市南武实验学校魏燕。

续上表

| 语篇 | 语篇类型 | 语篇主题 | 语篇内容 | 主题意义 |
|---|---|---|---|---|
| Listening（L）<br>A play for English Week | 戏剧录音节选（剧本） | 文学、艺术和体育。 | 关于罗宾汉的戏剧录音节选。 | 增加对罗宾汉的了解和英语课本剧的兴趣。 |
| Grammar（G）<br>Modal verb:<br>should; had better | 对话 | 乐学善学，勤于反思，学会学习。 | 在对话情境中理解情态动词 should 和短语 had better 的含义和用法。 | 使用 should、had better 讨论义务和职责及提出建议和劝告等。 |
| Speaking（SP）<br>Talk Time:<br>Word linking<br>Speak up:<br>Ways to improve your spoken English | 对话 | 乐学善学，勤于反思，学会学习。 | 朗读技巧训练和"如何提高英语口语"演讲训练。 | 掌握演讲的基本技巧，练习"如何提高英语口语"的演讲。 |
| Writing（WR）<br>A notice for English Week | 宣传通告（应用文） | 丰富、充实、积极向上的生活。 | 宣传"英语周"的通告。 | 使用"蛛网图"构思写作框架，完成宣传"英语周"的通告。 |
| More Practice（MP）<br>Robin Hood and Prince John | 《罗宾汉》的剧本节选（剧本） | 中外影视、戏剧、音乐、舞蹈、绘画、建筑等艺术形式中的文化价值和作品赏析，优秀的艺术家及其艺术成就。 | 是 Listening 的延续，节选剧本，有利于学生进一步了解罗宾汉和英语课本剧。 | 进一步增加学生对英语课本剧的兴趣。 |

续上表

| 语篇 | 语篇类型 | 语篇主题 | 语篇内容 | 主题意义 |
| --- | --- | --- | --- | --- |
| Culture Corner（CC）Crossword puzzles | 简介（说明文） | 乐学善学，勤于反思，学会学习。 | 介绍了英文中常见的纵横填字游戏。 | 了解纵横填字游戏的概念和游戏规则等内容，积累词汇，提高学习英语的兴趣。 |
| Project（PR）A speaking competition during English Week | 演讲稿（应用文） | 乐学善学，勤于反思，学会学习。 | 根据教材八个单元任选一个话题，进行演讲。 | 小组合作，确认主题、制作幻灯片、撰写演讲稿、演讲等。 |

从语篇类型看，本单元由三篇说明文、两篇剧本节选、三组不同话题的对话和一篇说明文组成。

主阅读篇章是以新闻报道的形式呈现，介绍了学校 Rosie Bridge 的 "英语周"活动；

听力板块和补充阅读板块以戏剧剧本的形式介绍了英语课本剧的基本情况；

写作板块和单元课题板块以应用文的形式帮助学生了解演讲稿的基本框架和演讲的技能。

特别值得注意的是，单元课题 Project 部分的演讲稿任务是对写作板块和整本教材的整合，有八个单元供话题选择，由小组分工合作完成。

三组对话的内容和主题意义各不相同，第一组对话是 Getting Ready 部分，谈及 Lo 想要写一篇报道的愿望，激发同学们对 "英语周"活动的兴趣。第二组对话是语法板块，内容是使用 should 讨论义务和职责及提出建议，用 had better 表示竭力劝告。值得注意的是 Grammar 部分的语境可以设计为，为参与"英语周"活动的选手们提供建议，让 Grammar 的教学更加与主题意义融合，同时也引导学生关注语法的语用功能在实际语境中的应用。第三组对话是 Speak up 的会话部分，引导学生掌握演讲的基本技巧，练习 "如何提高英语口语"的演讲，其中，Talk Time 帮助学生训练在演讲中的发音吐词等，可结合演讲稿一起完成。

从主题观念看，本单元的主题大观念是 "丰富、充实、积极向上的生活；

运动、文艺等社团活动，潜能发掘"。该大观念由两个小观念构成，小观念 1 是"学校、课程，学校生活与个人感受"，小观念 2 是"乐学善学，勤于反思，学会学习"。具体分析如表 2 所示：

表 2　单元整体主题大观念分析

| 教材板块 | 语篇 | 主题意义 | 小观念 | 大观念 |
| --- | --- | --- | --- | --- |
| Getting Ready | Getting Ready | 思考新闻报道的目的。 | 丰富、充实、积极向上的生活。 | 丰富、充实、积极向上的生活。乐学善学，勤于反思，学会学习。 |
| Reading | English: fun for life | 了解新闻报道的特征和学校活动特色。 | | |
| More Practice | *Robin Hood and Prince John* | 进一步增加对英语课本剧的兴趣。 | | |
| Listening | A play for English Week | 增加对罗宾汉的了解和对英语课本剧的兴趣。 | | |
| Culture Corner | Crossword puzzles | 了解纵横填字游戏的概念和游戏规则等内容，积累词汇，提高学习英语的兴趣。 | | |
| Grammar | Modal verb: *should*; *had better* | 使用 should、had better 讨论义务和职责及提出建议和劝告等。 | | |
| Speaking | Talk Time: Word linking Speak up: Ways to improve your spoken English | 掌握演讲的基本技巧，练习"如何提高英语口语"的演讲。 | 乐学善学，勤于反思，学会学习。 | 丰富、充实、积极向上的生活。乐学善学，勤于反思，学会学习。 |
| Writing | A notice for English Week | 使用"蛛网图"构思写作框架，完成宣传"英语周"的通告。 | | |
| Project | A speaking competition during English Week | 小组合作，确认主题、制作幻灯片、撰写演讲稿、进行演讲等。 | | |

从分析中可以看到，本单元语篇主要以"英语周"为话题，以"英语周"的各项活动为主线，但对学生在校园活动中的主创性拓展不够。

为了加强与子主题内容"乐学善学，勤于反思，学会学习"的联系，增添 Extensive Reading 部分，输入小观念 3——如何成为一名成功的演讲者，最终形成本单元的单元主题大观念"丰富、充实、积极向上的生活；乐学善学，勤于反思，学会学习"。

具体结构如图 1 所示：

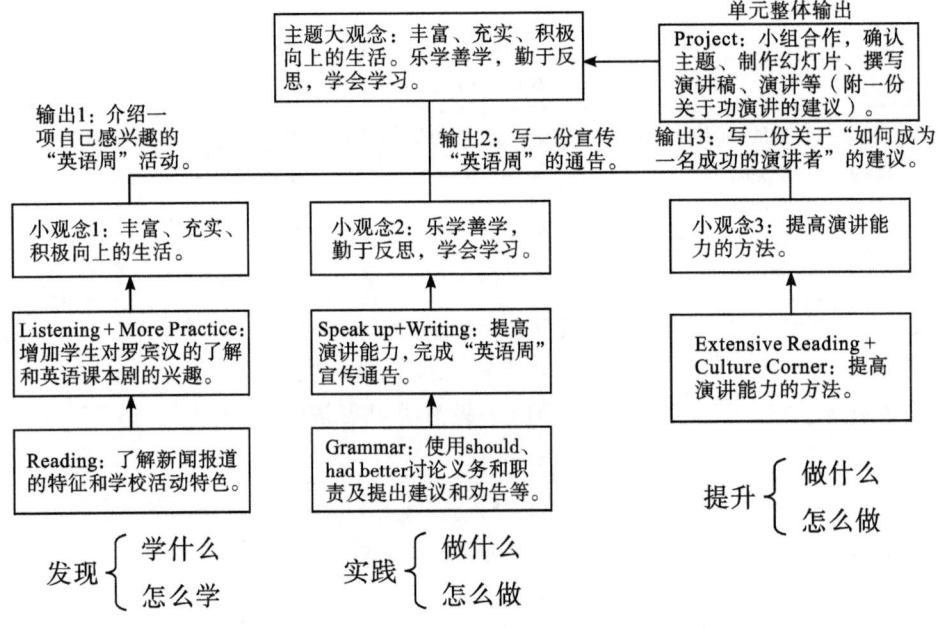

图 1　本单元主题大观念结构

从这个结构图我们可以看到，本单元的大观念生成主要由三个小观念带领的三条主线，归纳为发现、实践、提升。

第一条主线"发现"，是一个从内到外的设计，引导学生发现要"学什么""怎么学"。Reading 展现了校园生活，More Practice 和 Listening 展示国外优秀文艺作品。语篇中出现了大量情态动词的使用，给出各种建议，学生在发现中获得新知。

在第二条主线"实践"中，自然过渡到"做什么""怎么做"。学生通过实践，学习和反思，学会使用正确的方式表达建议，学习写通告，提升语言能力。在此基础上思考，如何使自己成为成功的演讲者。

第三主线"提升"，学生在学习中思考要"做什么""怎么做"，通过小组合作，共同完成一个演讲稿，即根据整本教材的八个单元确认主题，思考如何提高记忆力以及做一名交换生要有哪些准备等。

增加小观念 3——如何成为一名成功的演讲者。学生可以在准备演讲稿的过程中，注意演讲的细节处理和表达方式。各个小观念之间的输出也是相互关联、层层递进的。

首先是小观念 1 的输出，是对校园文化多样化的了解，要求学生能介绍一项自己感兴趣的"英语周"活动。而小观念 2 就进一步提升难度，要求学生能够将自己已知的信息通过通告、演讲的方式表达出来，能够写一份宣传"英语周"的通告。小观念 3 的输出是在同学们合作完成演讲稿的同时，思考如何成为一名成功的演讲者，提升自我修养。小组在合作的过程中，为演讲者写一份小建议。

三个小输出都是为最终的单元整体输出服务的。在 Project 板块，学生需要选择一个单元主题，完成一份演讲稿。在演讲稿中，既要有对已学内容的介绍输出，又要有有益的建议和可行的方法，同时，还要展现学生们在演讲过程中对细节的处理和自身的表达方式，如体态、表情等，是对前面三个任务的综合运用与提升。

## 三、单元整体教学目标分析

本单元整体教学目标如下：

### 1. 语言能力

围绕"英语周"的主题，获取关于校园活动具体内容的信息和了解英语课本剧的内容，能运用所学语言和适当的情态动词提出建议、表达劝告，并能撰写一份宣传"英语周"的通告。

### 2. 学习能力

使用"蛛网图"构思写作框架，完成宣传"英语周"的通告；通过剧本演绎，加深对英语剧本的了解；通过学习连读的朗读技巧和训练肢体语言、表情等，提高演讲的能力；能利用网络资源，了解更多的英语剧本和戏剧表演；能通过合作学习，使用网络媒介，完成一份高质量的演讲稿。

### 3. 文化意识

通过对英语戏剧的学习，了解英语交际中的体态语，如手势、表情等，了解中外戏剧的文化价值和艺术成就，能对优秀作品进行赏析。

### 4. 思维品质

能够运用"蛛网图"建构写作框架，完成宣传通告。理解英语戏剧的台

词表达方式，尝试根据角色身份和特点演绎剧本。能够根据教材八个单元的主题，设计和撰写演讲稿，并能根据演讲内容设计相应的演讲方式，完成一份成功的演讲稿，培养创造性思维品质。

## 四、单元教学重点、难点

单元教学重点：能围绕"英语周"活动的主题，获取校园活动的具体信息；通过与主题相关的语篇材料，了解校园丰富多彩的英语活动，尝试阅读英语戏剧的剧本；学习用"蛛网图"的方式构建写作框架，完成宣传"英语周"的通告；根据所学语言知识，选择主题撰写演讲稿。

单元教学难点：通过了解罗宾汉的故事和英语课本剧，学习阅读英语戏剧剧本，培养对英语戏剧文化的认识，从而了解英语交际中的体态语等。能通过合作学习，运用所学语言，使用"蛛网图"、PPT、视频、搜集信息等多种方式，完成主题内容下的演讲稿。

## 五、单元教学课时安排

本单元的课时安排如下：Reading 在第 1 课时完成，将 Listening 和 More Practice 整合在第 2 和第 3 课时完成，Grammar 是第 4 课时，Speak up 和 Writing 合并为第 5 课时，Extensive Reading 和 Culture Corner 为第 6 课时，Project 是第 7 课时。

## 六、单元评价措施

本单元在教学过程中，评价方式多样。一是充分利用"智慧课堂"评价体系，完成课堂、作业、单元等的精准数据评价，同时，教师也可以预设和设计评价表，在教学任务和教学环节进行评价。作业评价分为课时作业和单元整体作业，单元评价为实现单元小观念和大观念生成和输出做出贡献。二是评价主体多样性，可以采取学生自评、小组成员互评、小组之间互评及教师点评相结合等方式，充分展现学生自主、乐学、善思的主体能动性。

## 七、单元教学资源

本单元的教学资源和手段丰富，充分利用"智慧课堂"和优质网络资源，使课内外学习互为补充、延伸，达到学习效率最大化。

（1）使用真实的语料和网络资源拓展语篇教学，例如，关于英语戏剧剧本的内容可以在网络平台搜索，如推荐网站 kidsinco online recurse（https：//www.kidsinco.com/about/）。戏剧表演融合了语言、文学欣赏、表演等多方面的能力拓展，提升了学生学习的兴趣，开阔了其视野。

（2）利用多种展示手段，完成会话、写作和单元 Project 任务时，可以使用海报、PPT、微视频等多种形式，并在不同网络平台（如微信朋友圈、QQ 班群、QQ 动态、豆瓣网、抖音、小红书等）进行多模态、多媒态展示，并参与互动评奖等。

（3）写作课堂的评价有自评、生生互评和教师点评的方式。在自评阶段，可以让学生在"智慧平台"中进行小组内互评、小组间互评、小组和个人积分等，评出最佳小组和最佳个人。组内外的评价和个人评价结合，既能彰显小组合作的力量，又能展示个人的成就，突出了集体，也表彰了个人，拓展了评价的宽度，提高了评价的质量。

# 设计六　八年级下册 Module 3 Animals Unit 5 Save the Endangered Animals *

## 一、主题语境

英语课本上教版八年级下册第三模块"Animals"第五单元"Save the Endangered Animals（拯救濒危动物）"，单元主题属于《义务教育英语课程标准（2022年版）》"人与自然"范畴下的"环境保护"主题群，它的"子主题内容"为"热爱与敬畏自然，与自然和谐共生"。

## 二、语篇分析

第五单元由不同类型语篇组成，各个语篇内容及其主题意义如表 1 所示。

表 1　单元语篇内容及其主题意义

| 语篇 | 语篇类型 | 语篇内容（what） | 主题意义（why） | 语篇特征（how） |
| --- | --- | --- | --- | --- |
| Reading（R）Giant Panda | 事实档案（说明文） | 介绍大熊猫的数量、分布、外形特征、习性、饮食习惯及面临的困境等基本信息。 | 了解大熊猫的基本情况，思考大熊猫成为濒危动物的原因。 | 介绍大熊猫的说明文：说明对象的图片、从整体到局部的说明顺序、话题相关的小标题、下定义和列数字的说明方法、第三人称及一般现在时和现在进行时展现语篇客观性、准确性。 |

---

\* 设计者：华南师范大学附属中学王昕。

续上表

| 语篇 | 语篇类型 | 语篇内容（what） | 主题意义（why） | 语篇特征（how） |
| --- | --- | --- | --- | --- |
| Listening（L）Endangered animals | 演讲稿（应用文）、对话 | 介绍濒危动物的种类和环保组织，如WWF。 | 增加对濒危动物的了解。 | WWF工作人员演讲：使用第一人称（I, we）和问句、使用if从句及we must等句型展现人类需要为保护濒危动物做什么。 |
| Grammar（G）It's adj for/of + sb + to do It's adj. + enough + to do | 句子、对话 | 在对话情境中学习形容词相关句型It's adj + for/of + sb + to do 以及It's adj. + enough + to do 的含义和用法。 | 使用所学句型谈论人类对动物的某些做法是否正确，以及应该为动物做些什么。 | 结合单元话题，设置目标语法点在具体语境中的使用。 |
| Speaking（S）Talk Time: Talking about obligations Speak up: How can we save endangered animals? | 对话 | 选择听力板块中提到的一种濒危动物，谈论其现状和保护这种濒危动物的措施。 | 能使用should/shouldn't/must/mustn't 来谈论人类对动物的责任，增强学生对保护自然的责任感。 | 表达义务或责任：情态动词。 |
| Writing（W）An endangered animal | 事实档案（说明文） | 介绍一种濒危动物。 | 使用"蛛网图"构思写作框架，完成对一种濒危动物的介绍。 | 介绍一种濒危动物的说明文：使用话题相关的小标题、使用下定义和列数字的说明方法、第三人称及一般现在时和现在进行时等。 |

续上表

| 语篇 | 语篇类型 | 语篇内容（what） | 主题意义（why） | 语篇特征（how） |
| --- | --- | --- | --- | --- |
| More Practice (MP) The story of the red-crowned crane | 故事（记叙文） | 讲述徐秀娟为拯救丹顶鹤而献出生命的故事。 | 了解为保护动物而献出生命的真人事迹，进一步增强学生对保护自然的责任感。 | 徐秀娟的故事：时间顺序、一般过去时、话题相关的图片等。 |
| Culture Corner (CC) WWF | 简介（说明文） | 介绍世界自然基金会的相关信息。 | 了解保护濒危动物的组织——世界自然基金会，并了解保护动物的重要性。 | 介绍世界自然基金会的说明文：说明对象的图片、下定义和列数字的说明方法。 |
| Project (PR) A video about endangered animal protection | 视频（应用文） | 以保护濒危动物为话题，为WWF制作一个宣传片。 | 利用网络资源，小组合作，以视频的形式呈现本单元所学内容。 | 综合单元所学内容，搜索相关视听资料，并运用话题相关词汇、词组、句型等语言知识。 |

  从语篇类型和内容来看，本单元语篇主要以说明文、记叙文、演讲稿、对话的形式出现。主阅读语篇是一篇介绍大熊猫的说明文，对大熊猫的数量、分布、外形、特征、习性、饮食习惯及面临的困境等诸方面的情况做了较为详细的介绍。听力部分的文本是一段由世界自然基金会的工作人员所做的有关濒危动物的演讲。语法板块内有句子、对话等"小语篇"（篇幅较短的语篇），帮助学生掌握和形容词相关的三个句型。会话板块通过对话的形式，展现如何表达义务或责任。学生还需选择听力板块中的一种濒危动物，谈论其现状和保护这种濒危动物的措施。写作板块额外提供了一篇关于亚洲象这一濒危动物的事实档案，并要求学生为学校杂志写一份关于某种濒危动物的事实档案，训练学生在写作任务中使用话题相关词汇和说明文的写作方法。补充阅读篇章讲述了徐秀娟为拯救丹顶鹤而献出生命的故事，文化角板块介绍了世界自然基金会（WWF）的基本信息。单元课题Project以保护濒危动物为话题，为WWF制作

一个宣传片。单元课题的任务情境依托 WWF 这一濒危动物保护组织的相关背景信息，完成本课题还需要对整个单元所学知识和信息进行整合，可由小组分工合作完成。

从语篇的主题意义来看，主阅读语篇让学生了解大熊猫的基本情况，思考大熊猫成为濒危动物的原因。学生通过聆听 WWF 工作人员的讲座，增加了对濒危动物的了解。语法板块让学生在句子和对话中使用所学句型谈论人类对动物的某些做法是否正确，以及应该为动物做些什么。在会话板块中，学生通过阅读三个学生的对话了解如何表达义务或责任，并在关于濒危动物的小组讨论活动中增强对保护濒危动物的责任感。写作板块要求学生自己选择一种濒危动物，完成一篇与主阅读语篇相似的作文。补充阅读篇章通过讲述徐秀娟为保护动物而献出生命的真人事迹，进一步增强了学生对保护自然的责任感。文化角板块让学生在了解 WWF 组织的同时，认识到保护动物的重要性。单元课题 Project 让学生在搜索、整合资料以及小组合作的过程中加深对濒危动物现状的了解，并能以视频的形式呈现相关信息，为保护濒危动物出谋划策。

从以上关于语篇和主题意义的分析可知，本单元原课时安排有以下几点问题：

（1）原相邻课时所学语篇间的内在联系不紧密，主题意义的逻辑线不清晰。例如，Listening 与其相邻的 Reading 和 Grammar 语篇类型相似性不高，主题意义相关性也较低，而与单元结尾 Culture Corner 部分的相关性更高；

（2）完成 Speaking 中的口语练习时，学生缺少相关背景知识，而此板块未提供相关语篇辅助，故需引入有关保护动物的措施的视听资料；

（3）Grammar 部分提供的任务情境与话题关联性较弱，需重设语境；

（4）本单元的写作板块仅与主阅读和听力板块联系较密，需调整顺序，将其作为阶段性的输出任务。

## 三、单元主题大小观念分析与单元教学课时安排

从本单元语篇的主题意义中可以提炼出三个小观念。小观念 1 是了解濒危动物及其保护组织的各种信息；小观念 2 是思考保护濒危动物的重要性，树立保护濒危动物的意识；小观念 3 为思考保护濒危动物的可行方案。这三个小观念共同构成了本单元的主题大观念——了解濒危动物，认识保护濒危动物的重要性，为保护濒危动物出谋划策。

三个小观念及单元主题大观念的关系如图 1 所示：

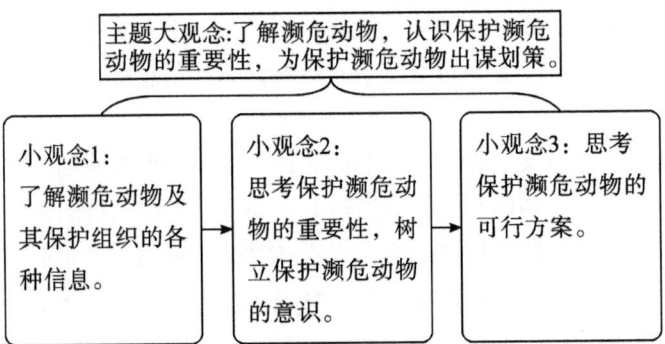

**图 1　单元整体主题大小观念分析**

在分析本单元所有语篇、提炼单元的大小观念后,本单元的课时被重新整合,如表2所示:

**表 2　基于主题大观念重整后的单元课时安排**

| 课时 | 教材板块 | 主题意义 | 小观念 | 大观念 |
| --- | --- | --- | --- | --- |
| Lesson 1 | Listening + Culture Corner | 介绍世界自然基金会的相关信息,增加对濒危动物的了解,并了解保护动物的重要性。 | 了解濒危动物及其保护组织的各种信息。 | 了解濒危动物,认识保护濒危动物的重要性,为保护濒危动物出谋划策。 |
| Lesson 2 & 3 | Reading | 了解大熊猫的基本情况,思考大熊猫成为濒危动物的原因。 | | |
| Lesson 4 | Writing | 使用"思维导图"构思写作框架,完成对一种濒危动物的介绍。 | | |
| Lesson 5 | More Practice | 了解为保护动物而献出生命的真人事迹,进一步增强学生对保护自然的责任感。 | 思考保护濒危动物的重要性,树立保护濒危动物的意识。 | |
| Lesson 6 | Grammar + Speak up | 使用所学句型谈论人类对动物的某些做法是否正确,以及应该为动物做些什么。 | | |
| Lesson 7 | Viewing + Talk Time | 能使用 should/shouldn't/must/mustn't 来谈论人类对动物的责任,增强学生对保护自然的责任感。 | 思考保护濒危动物的可行方案。 | |
| Lesson 8 | Project | 小组合作,确认主题、制作幻灯片、撰写演讲稿、进行演讲等。 | | |

基于主题大观念的单元课时安排具体结构如图2所示：

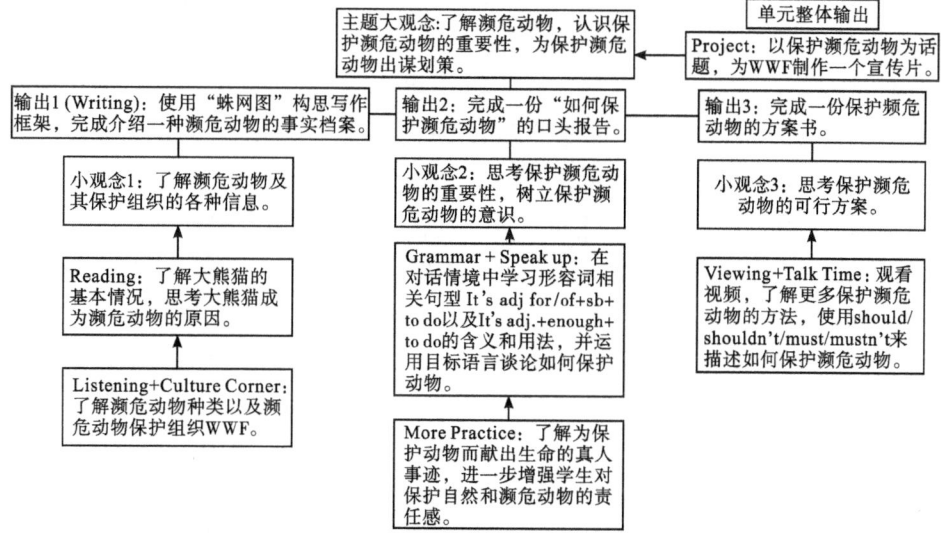

**图2 基于主题大观念重整后的单元课时安排**

图2展示了大小观念与单元课时之间的关系：基于主题大观念重整后，本单元的所有课时被分为三个阶段，每个部分指向一个单元小观念。阶段一由第一课时（Listening + Culture Corner）及第二、第三课时（Reading）组成，学生有关濒危动物的已有知识被激活，同时，能够了解更多濒危动物的种类以及保护濒危动物的组织的相关信息。在阅读语篇中，除了教师输入更多关于大熊猫的基本信息和濒危原因外，学生对于事实档案的语篇特征以及说明方法和说明顺序的学习也为阶段输出任务做铺垫。在第二阶段，补充阅读语篇"The story of the red-crowned crane"讲述了徐秀娟为保护动物而献出生命的真人事迹，让学生在了解濒危动物现状和濒危原因后，增强对保护自然和濒危动物的责任感。第六课时（Grammar + Speak up）输入了 It's adj. for/of + sb + to do 以及 It's adj. + enough + to do 三个与形容词相关的句型，为学生在语境中评价人类对濒危动物的所作所为，在口语活动中表达人类应当如何保护动物搭建了"脚手架"。在本阶段，学生能够进一步认识到人类保护濒危动物的必要性，以及人类作为地球居民与自然、动物和谐共生的重要性，并就帮助已经陷入危机的动物朋友发出自己的声音。由于本单元在如何保护濒危动物的信息和语言方面的输入有限，因此，学生在第二阶段的输出任务中表述会较为雷同。为引导学生意识到不同的动物濒危原因不同，针对不同的濒危原因需要采用不同的保护方式，并帮助学生提出有针对性的可行建议，第七课时（Viewing + Talk

Time）将为学生提供课外的视听资源，提供教材内缺少的相关信息和语言支架，同时让学生在小组讨论中针对保护自己小组负责的濒危动物提出更多行之有效的建议，增强每个学生对于该话题的参与感。小观念不仅为单元课时的划分提供思路，它更是将主题意义串起来的逻辑线，让单元每个课时都能按照指向单元大观念的逻辑排列。每个阶段指向的小观念更是每个阶段的主题意义凝练，它们共同服务于单元大观念的建构。

  本单元共有三个阶段性输出任务，这三个输出任务既是对各小观念的体现，也让学生在完成任务的过程中运用并巩固本阶段所学知识。例如，第一个阶段性输出任务——使用"蛛网图"构思写作框架，完成介绍一种濒危动物的事实档案，即本单元的第四课时（Writing）的要求，学生需要根据第一课时（Listening + Culture Corner）提供的多种濒危动物信息，运用第二课时（Reading）中所习得的写作文的文体特征和说明方法进行相似语篇的写作。这一过程以读促写，同时用写作任务的完成度检测学生关于主阅读语篇的信息获取、语篇分析的情况，体现了"教—学—评"一体化的原则。每个阶段性的输出任务不仅与该阶段的课时内容紧密相关，而且遵照主题意义逻辑线层层递进。第一阶段的输出是让学生以创作事实档案的形式运用已获取的濒危动物的相关信息。第二阶段的输出任务形式则为口头汇报，主题是"如何保护濒危动物"。口头汇报的形式难度高于写作，汇报内容"如何保护濒危动物"也需要学生对某一濒危动物的濒危原因做分析。但在完成此任务前，学生已经在前两个阶段的学习中了解了不同濒危动物的濒危原因，对保护濒危动物的必要性有了更清晰的认识。第六课时（Grammar + Speak up）的语言输入也让学生拥有了输出任务所需的词汇、句型辅助。第三阶段的输出任务是在观看介绍如何保护濒危动物的视频后，完成一份保护濒危动物的方案书。尽管任务形式为撰写一份方案书，但是内容更强调针对某一动物的濒危原因，利用视频资源提供的信息，就如何保护濒危动物提出更多教材以外的建议。三个阶段性输出任务的设计初衷不仅是阶段性学习的总结，或让学生在完成从易到难的任务中循序渐进地理解各语篇内涵的主题意义，而且是让每个输出任务的成果都可以用于完成最终的单元整体输出任务——以保护濒危动物为话题，为WWF制作一个宣传片。宣传片这一形式创造了真实的情境，其内容包括某一濒危动物的基本信息概述、现状介绍、濒危原因、现行保护方式、未来展望等。学生除了要对三个阶段性输出任务的成果进行重新整合、编写，还需要基于口头报告和方案书进行进一步的资料检索和汇总，故这一视频的制作是对前面三个输出任务的进一步提升，也是对本单元所学的真实运用。

## 四、单元整体教学目标分析

本单元整体教学目标如下：

### 1. 语言能力

围绕"保护濒危动物"的话题，在阅读濒危动物的事实档案过程中学会运用扫读的阅读策略，了解说明文的文体特征及写作方法，分析动物濒临灭绝的原因，用目标语法知识在语境中评价人们对濒危动物的所作所为，表述人类保护濒危动物的职责所在，并能运用话题相关词汇和适当的说明方法撰写一个濒危动物的事实档案，最终小组合作完成制作世界自然基金会（WWF）的宣传片。

### 2. 学习能力

通过听力、阅读和观看视频的输入，掌握 WWF 的基本信息，并加深对濒危动物及其濒危原因的了解；利用网络资源，了解更多保护濒危动物的方法，并就不同濒危动物面临的危机提出可行措施；使用"蛛网图"构思濒危动物的事实档案的写作框架和内容；使用网络媒介或图书馆资源，整合单元所学知识，以保护濒危动物为话题，小组合作完成一个 WWF 的宣传片。

### 3. 文化意识

通过阅读为保护动物而献出生命的真人事迹，思考故事主人公的奉献精神，提升学生保护自然和濒危动物的责任感，增强学生作为地球主人翁的社会责任感。

### 4. 思维品质

了解动物濒临灭绝的原因，由此意识到保护动物的重要性并思考如何正确保护它们；能根据本单元主题，小组合作完成一个 WWF 的宣传片，培养小组合作能力和创造性思维品质。

## 五、单元教学重点、难点

### 1. 单元教学重点

在阅读濒危动物的事实档案中学会运用扫读的阅读策略，了解说明文的文体特征及写作方法，分析动物濒临灭绝的原因，用目标语法知识在语境中评价人们对濒危动物的所作所为，表述人类保护濒危动物的职责所在。使用"蛛网图"构思濒危动物的事实档案的写作框架和内容，并能运用话题相关词汇和适当的说明方法撰写一个濒危动物的事实档案。最终整合单元所学知识，以保护濒危动物为话题，小组合作完成一个 WWF 的宣传片。

2. 单元教学难点

在理解关于濒危动物事实档案的基础上，了解说明文的文体特征和写作方法，并在写作任务中恰当运用。通过听力和阅读文本的输入，分析不同濒危动物的濒危原因，并能从拓展视频中获取保护濒危动物的方法。通过徐秀娟的感人故事，提升学生保护自然和濒危动物的责任感。通过合作学习，整合所学知识，运用网络资源，完成一个WWF的宣传片。

## 六、单元评价措施

本单元在教学过程体现了评价方式和主体的多样性。例如，写作课堂上除了有老师提供的学生自评表外，还有写作任务小组合作的形式，小组内、组与组间互评的评价方式同样被用于给予学生及时的反馈。同时，判断是否达成本单元的教学目标，不仅要看学生的随堂练习和课后作业情况，还要考查方案书、口头报告、微视频等多模态形式，因为后者不仅能够给予学生在真实语境中运用所学知识的机会，同时也让教师根据学生完成情况做出教学调整，提供学生所需帮助。

## 七、单元教学资源

本单元的教学使用真实的语料和网络资源拓展语篇教学。例如，浏览WWF官网让学生了解濒危动物保护组织的宗旨以及贡献，补充资料提升了学生对话题的兴趣，开阔了视野。同时，利用学生熟悉的网络信息获取渠道引入双语字幕的视听资源，例如哔哩哔哩和必应等网站提供了优质的话题相关图片和视频，可以被用于辅助各类输出任务的完成。

# 第四章　人教版八年级课时教学设计*

## 设计七　八年级下册 Unit 5 What Were You Doing When the Rainstorm Came? Listening & Speaking**

### 一、Teaching content

八年级下册 Unit 5 What Were You Doing When the Rainstorm Came? Period 1 Listening & Speaking，本节课是 Unit 5 的第一课时。

### 二、Analysis of students

Junior Grade Two students are inquisitive and willing to express their opinions. The students have already studied Unit 1-4 and they have some knowledge of the vocabulary and topics in this unit. However, there is a big difference in the students' English learning level, and some of them have low self-confidence and are afraid to open their mouths to speak English, so some are passive in learning. In order to make students active, diversified learning methods and independent, cooperative, inquiry and personalized learning activities are needed. Teachers need to pay attention to teaching students according to their abilities, adopt different methods for students' characteristics, assign different homework for students at different levels, establish different evaluation standards, and most importantly, stimulate interest in learning and help build self-confidence.

---

\* 教研指导和审课专家：广州市海珠区教育发展研究院张志梅。
\*\* 设计者：广州市海珠区教育发展研究院张志梅。

三、Teaching objectives

(1) Learn the following vocabulary:

核心单词:rainstorm, alarm, heavily, suddenly, strange

核心词组:go off, begin to do sth. , pick up, fall asleep

核心句型:—What were you doing when the rainstorm came? —I was taking a shower.

(2) Apply listening and speaking skills and mini-skills to locate relevant information and use it to express ideas.

(3) Develop a sense of care for animals, take positive and effective measures to overcome natural disasters, and foster confidence, positivity, and an optimistic outlook on life.

四、Teaching focus

Focus:Understand and master the new words and phrases in this section to listen and talk about the passage.

Difficulty:Apply listening and speaking skills to locate relevant information and communicate in class effectively.

五、Procedures

Lead in:Guessing game.

Last night, I went to my mom's house. Please guess what were the animals doing when I arrived?

1. What were the puppies doing when I arrived?

   When I arrived, the puppies were sleeping/fighting.

2. What were the goats doing when I arrived?

   When I arrived, the goats were eating grass/corns (玉米).

3. What was the cat doing when I arrived?

   When I arrived, the cat was sitting/sleeping in a toy car.

Purpose:The cute animals will help to stimulate students' enthusiasm to express themselves in English and also naturally introduce the core sentence pattern:What were they doing when…

Task 1: Listen for key information

Purpose: Apply listening and speaking skills and mini-skills to locate relevant information.

Exercise 1 b Listen to the TV report and circle the correct responses.

a. doing my homework / studying　　b. playing basketball / reading

c. going to work / waiting for the bus　　d. walking home / shopping

Task 2: Report

Purpose: Students can actively use *was/were doing* to describe what people were doing when the storm happened, and cultivate English thinking ability and independent learning ability.

Exercise 1 c Report what the people were doing at the time of the rainstorm.

Hello, everyone! Let me report what people were doing at the time of the rainstorm.

The person in Picture a/b/c/d was...

a. doing homework　　b. reading　　c. waiting for the bus　　d. walking home

Task 3: Broadcast & Exchange

Purpose: Students learn to work as a broadcaster and exchange the underlined information effectively.

　　An important event that I remember well was Notre Dame Fire. It <u>happened</u> on April 16, 2019 in Paris, France. When this event happened, some people <u>were watching</u> and praying on a ship. Some firefighters <u>were trying</u> to put out the fire. The French president <u>was planning</u> to rebuild the building. This event is very important to me because it was a building <u>with a history of over 800</u> years and lots of <u>priceless art works</u>. I remember this event well because it is not only important for France but also <u>a part of the world</u>. We should <u>protect</u> the world culture.

Task 4: Evaluate: Who is the best broadcaster?

Purpose: Encourage students to peer evaluate and peer learn.

I think A is the best because _____

a. his/her English is clear/wonderful.　　b. he/she is very brave/active/confident.

Assignment:

1. Finish 3c: Make sentences with these words: explain, communicate, refuse, nervous, get on with.

2. Retell the article 2a.

# 设计八　八年级下册 Unit 5 What Were You Doing When the Rainstorm Came? Grammar*

## 一、Teaching content

教学片段标题：八年级下册 Unit 5 What Were You Doing When the Rainstorm Came?

Section A 2d 本节课是 Unit 5 的第二课时。

课型：语法课。

## 二、Objectives

(1) Learn the following vocabularies:

Words: fire, happen, saddest, firemen, mayor, president, protect

Phrases: go off, pick up, fall asleep, die down, have a look

Sentences: —What were people doing when the fire happened?

　　　　　—They were traveling…

(2) Use the conjunctions *when* and *while* correctly, describe the Notre Dame Fire in the past tense and the past continuous tense.

(3) Take the students into the real language environment to speak and communicate more, discover the grammar rules, understand the form and meaning of the past continuous tense, and cultivate ability through role-playing, cooperative learning and inquiry learning.

## 三、Teaching focus

Focus: Use the conjunctions when and while correctly.

Difficulty: Use the past progressive tense to describe the Notre Dame de Paris fire as well as to role play.

---

\* 设计者：广州市海珠区教育发展研究院张志梅。

## 四、Procedures

Lead in: Watch the video and ask questions through the Notre Dame fire in Paris:
Purpose: To recall what students have learned and lead in the grammar form.
May: What <u>were</u> the people <u>doing</u> when the fire <u>happened</u>?
Tom: They were travelling by ship.
May: What <u>were</u> the firemen <u>doing</u> while the fire <u>was burning</u>?
Tom: They <u>were putting out</u> the fire.
Task 1 再读句子，你能发现句中包含的时态吗？
Purpose: Students are further guided to discover the rules of grammar by reading aloud a dialogue about the Notre Dame de Paris fire.
Discovery 1: 红色划线部分用的是<u>过去进行时</u>。蓝色划线部分用的是<u>一般过去时</u>。
Discovery 2: 1) 基本概念，过去进行时表示在过去某一时刻或一段时间内<u>正在进行</u>的动作。这一特定的过去时间除有上下文暗示以外，一般用表示过去某一特定时刻的时间状语如 at seven last night, at that time 等表示。2) 结构 was/were + 动词 – ing。
Discovery 3: 主句和从句的动作在过去的某时刻或某段时间同时发生，而且动作都是持续性的，此时用<u>while</u>引导从句，而且主句和从句都用<u>过去进行时时态</u>。
Task 2: 完成课本 2d 的听以及相关的角色扮演任务，填写关键信息。
Purpose: Students are required to listen and understand what they hear, and at the same time actively use *was/were doing* to describe what people were doing, to develop English thinking, independent learning and cooperative learning abilities.

Mary: What were you doing last night, Linda? I called at seven and you didn't pick up.

Linda: Oh, I was in the kitchen helping my mom.

Mary: I see. I called again at eight and you didn't answer then either.

Linda: What was I doing at eight? Oh, I know. When you called, I was taking a shower.

Mary: But then I called again at nine.

Linda: Oh, I was sleeping at that time.

Mary: So early? That's strange.

Linda: Yeah, I was tired. Why did you call so many times?

Mary: I needed help with my homework. So while you were sleeping, I called Jenny and she helped me.

Task 3: Role play as a news reporter for *China Daily* and complete the latest report on Notre Dame de Paris.

Purpose: Through the Notre Dame fire, through the study of the text and role-playing, cultivate students to care about current affairs, love world culture, take positive and effective measures to overcome natural disasters, and face life with self-confidence, positivity and optimism.

Ladies and gentlemen,

Here is the newest report about the Notre Dame de Paris [ˈnəutri deim dəˈpærɪs].

When the terrible fire <u>began</u>, some workers <u>were repairing</u> the building. Some people <u>were walking</u> in front of it. Some other people <u>were traveling by ship</u> near there. <u>While</u> some firemen were putting out the fire, the Paris mayor [meə] (市长) <u>was ordering</u> people to stay away from the building. The French president <u>was planning</u> to rebuild it. People from other countries <u>were supporting</u> France to save it. We believe this world famous building <u>will show its beauty again</u> in the future.

Summary: Although nature brings all kinds of disasters, we never give up hopes.

Assignment: 1. Read 3a over and over again.
             2. Finish the 4b and 4c exercises in the workbook.

## 设计九　八年级下册 Unit 5 What Were You Doing When the Rainstorm Came? Reading*

### 一、Teaching content

教学片段标题：八年级下册 Unit 5 What Were You Doing When the Rainstorm Came?

Period 3 Reading 3a, Paragraph 1-2 本节课是 Unit 5 的第三课时。

课型：Reading。

### 二、Objectives

(1) Learn the vocabularies：

Words: fire, storm, rainstorm, happen, saddest, firemen, candles, matches, mobile phone, midnight, mayor, president, protect.

Phrases：①感觉像 feel like　②首先 at first　③入睡 fall asleep　④逐渐变弱 die down　⑤确信 make sure　⑥醒来 wake up　⑦一团糟 in a mess　⑧清洁 clean up　⑨互相帮助 help each other　⑩在困难时期 in times of difficulty

Sentences：—What were people doing when the fire happened?
　　　　　　—They were traveling...

(2) Use reading strategies correctly to locate details related to topic keywords, understand the topic sentences of the text and details that reflect the author's intention and point of view. Pay attention to some descriptive adjectives and adverbs such as heart-broken, nervous, afraid, and so on.

(3) Undersand the difference between the past tense and the past continuous tense.

---

\* 设计者：广州市海珠区教育发展研究院张志梅。

## 三、Teaching focus

Focus: Correct use of the conjunctions *when* and *while*; skillful use of the past tense in describing the weather and in role-playing.

Difficulty: The ability to use reading strategies to locate details related to the topic, understand topic sentences and details that reflect the author's intention and point of view.

## 四、Procedures

Lead in: Talk about the weather and guess people's feelings.

Task 1: Describe the weather and guess.

Purpose: Take the students into the real language environment to speak and communicate more.

1. The winds were very _____ outside.
2. Although it was day, it felt like _____.
3. Because _____ were making the sky very _____. The news reported the storm.

Guess how people indoor felt then, nervous, afraid, terrible, heart-broken?

Task 2: Let's read 3a quickly and underline all the weather words.

Purpose: Learn the weather vocabularies and think how to deal with bad weather.

What's a storm? Very bad weather with *strong winds* and *heavy rain*, often with *thunder* and *lightning*.

1. Strong winds  2. Black clouds  3. A heavy rainstorm  4. Rain

Task 3: Group Work: Discuss and present: If your family were in a storm, what things would you prepare?

Purpose: Students talk about pictures and review the words: candles, matches, radio, mobile phone, midnight, etc., and then choose three. This task provides real contexts for students to apply the knowledge and skills they have learned in this lesson to solve problems in real life.

Sample:

If our family were in a storm, we would prepare three important things.

First of all, we would...because...

And then, it would be very necessary for us to...because...

Finally, we would not forget to...because...

Task 4: Assess your progress.

Which group has the best preparation?

I think Group 1/2/3 _____ is the best because _____

A. they choose the most important things

B. their English is wonderful.

C. they are very brave/active/confident.

Summary: If everyone gives a hand in times of difficulty, our world will be safer.

Assignment:

1. Remember the words and phrases in this lesson.

2. Finish the 4b and 4c exercises in the workbook.

# 第五章 高中英语读后续写区域集体备课作业设计*

## 设计十 运用"TEAMS"策略提升读后续写作业设计**

### 一、真题呈现

2021年新高考Ⅰ卷读后续写：阅读下面材料，根据其内容和所给段落开头语续写两段，使之构成一篇完整的短文。

The twins were filled with excitement as they thought of the surprise they were planning for Mother's Day. How pleased and proud mother would be when they brought her breakfast in bed. They planned to make French toast and chicken porridge. They had watched their mother in the kitchen. There was nothing to it. Jenna and Jeff knew exactly what to do.

The big day came at last. The alarm rang at 6 a.m. The pair went down the stairs quietly to the kitchen. They decided to boil the porridge first. They put some rice into a pot of water and left it to boil while they made the French toast. Jeff broke two eggs into a plate and added in some milk. Jenna found the bread and put two slices into the egg mixture. Next, Jeff turned on the second stove burner to heat up the frying pan. Everything was going smoothly until Jeff started frying the bread. The pan was too hot and the bread turned black within seconds. Jenna threw the burnt piece into the sink and put in the other slice of bread. This time, she turned down the fire so it cooked nicely.

Then Jeff noticed steam shooting out of the pot and the lid starting to shake. The next minute, the porridge boiled over and put out the fire. Jenna panicked. Thankfully, Jeff stayed calm and turned off the gas quickly. But the stove was a mess

---

\* 教研指导：广州市海珠区教育发展研究院张志梅。

\*\* 设计者：广州市海珠外国语实验中学黄凤妹、中山大学附属中学张颖。

now. Jenna told Jeff to clean it up so they could continue to cook the rest of the porridge. But Jeff's hand touched the hot burner and he gave a cry of pain. Jenna made him put his hand in cold water. Then she caught the smell of burning. Oh dear! The piece of bread in the pan had turned black as well.

注意：
1. 续写词数应为 150 左右；
2. 请按如下格式在答题卡的相应位置作答。

Para 1 *As the twins looked around them in disappointment, their father appeared.*
Para 2 *The twins carried the breakfast upstairs and woke their mother up.*

## 二、运用要素分析梳理原文

Task 1 梳理原文要素

Who: The twins—Jenna and Jeff, mother, their (1) _____

When: (2) _____ Mother's Day

Where: kitchen, upstairs, (brought her breakfast) in (3) _____

How: Twins: filled with (4) _____ → (Jenna) (5) _____ (Jeff) stayed (6) _____ → in (7) _____

What:

The twins, Jenna and Jeff, were very (8) e _____ and planned to bring their mother breakfast in bed on Mother's Day. They (9) p _____ to make French toast and chicken porridge, and they (10) t _____ they knew exactly what to do.

At first, everything went (11) s _____. However, the (12) b _____ turned black within seconds. Jenna had to put in the (13) o _____ slice of bread. Then, the (14) p _____ boiled over and put out the fire. Jenna (15) p _____. Thankfully, Jeff stayed (16) c _____ and turned off the gas quickly. But the stove was a (17) m _____. Next, Jeff's hand get burnt. What's worse, the piece of bread in the pan had turned black as (18) w _____.

The twins were in (19) d _____. Then, their (20) f _____ appeared.

## 三、运用"TEAMS"策略续写

Task 2 运用"TEAMS"策略续写故事

Para 1: *As the twins looked around them in disappointment, their father appeared.*

第一句衔接句承上（衔接首句的内容）：

爸爸的出现对他们来说就像救世主一样。

Father's _____ was like a savior to them.

第二句动作：

在爸爸的指导下，双胞胎快速地采取积极行动清理了厨房并重新准备早餐。

Under the _____ of their father, the twins quickly _____ _____ _____ to _____ _____ the kitchen and start _____ the breakfast again.

第三句动作：

爸爸帮助他们调整火的大小，这是成功的关键。

Father helped them _____ the fire, _____ was the key _____ success.

第四句衔接句承上（衔接上句的内容）：

因此，这次一切都没问题了。

_____, It was all right this time.

第五句动作：

很快，他们完美地做好了面包，粥也准备好了。

Soon, they _____ the bread perfectly and the porridge was also _____.

第六句动作：

小心翼翼地端着早餐盘，加上他们做的一张漂亮的卡片，双胞胎走出了厨房。

_____ the breakfast tray carefully and _____ a beautiful card they had made, the twins _____ _____ _____ _____ the kitchen.

Para 2: *The twins carried the breakfast upstairs and woke their mother up.*

第一句衔接句承上（衔接首句的内容）+对话：

妈妈轻轻睁开朦胧睡眼那一刻，双胞胎就大叫："亲爱的妈妈，母亲节快乐！"

_____ _____ Mom _____ _____ her _____ eyes, the twins _____, "Happy Mother's Day, darling Mummy!"

第二句情感：

妈妈相当惊讶也高兴。

Mom was quite _____ and _____.

第三句动作：

她还来不及跟双胞胎说"谢谢"，床边桌子上放着的装着一叠法式烤面包和一碗粥的餐盘就吸引了她的注意力。

_____ she said "thank you" to the twins, a breakfast tray with a plate of French toast and a bowl of porridge placed on the table beside the bed _____ _____.

第四句对话：

"妈妈，快试一下！" Jeff 立马提议说，"我们给您做的！"

"Mom, have a try!" Jeff _____ immediately, "We made it for you!"

第五句动作+情感：

妈妈瞪大了眼睛，凝视着餐盘，泪光闪烁。

Mom's eyes _____, _____ _____ the breakfast tray, _____ _____.

第六句回归主题，升华感情：

令她感动的不仅是这份礼物，还有孩子们对她的爱。

It was _____ _____ the gift, _____ _____ the love of the children for her _____ moved her very much.

## Task 3 朗读参考范文

Para. 1 *As the twins looked around them in disappointment, their father appeared.* Father's appearing was like a savior to them. Under the guidance of their father, the twins quickly took positive actions to clean up the kitchen and start preparing the breakfast again. Father helped them adjust the fire, which was the key to success. Therefore, It was all right this time. Soon, they made the bread perfectly and the porridge was also ready. Holding the breakfast tray carefully and adding a beautiful card they had made, the twins walked out of the kitchen. (82)

Para. 2 *The twins carried the breakfast upstairs and woke their mother up.* The moment Mom slightly opened her sleepy eyes, the twins yelled, "Happy Mother's Day, darling Mummy!" Mom was quite surprised and happy. Before she said "thank you" to the twins, a breakfast tray with a plate of French toast and a bowl of porridge placed on the table beside the bed caught her attention. "Mom, have a try!" Jeff suggested immediately, "We made it for you!" Mom's eyes widened, staring at the breakfast tray, tears glittering. It was not only the gift, but also the love of the children for her that moved her very much. (97)

Task 4 总结反思评价

Summarize what I have learned:

T：每一段第一句为衔接句，衔接首句的内容；结尾句回归主题（Theme），升华感情。

Emotion: twins: excited—panicked/calm—disappointed—happy

　　　　　Mom: surprised, happy—moved

Action: clean up, prepare, adjust, hold, add, walk, caught, widen, stare, glitter

Dialogue: yell, suggest

Task 5 评价

| 项目 | 评价标准 | 自我评价 | 同伴评价 | 教师评价 |
|---|---|---|---|---|
| I know the five elements of the story. | Excellent. Good. So-So. | | | |
| I can use "TEAMS" strategies. | Excellent. Good. So-So. | | | |

Task 6 好句点评

<u>Under</u> the guidance of their father, the twins <u>quickly took</u> positive actions to <u>clean</u> up the kitchen <u>and start</u> preparing the breakfast again. （under介词短语作状语，并列动词的使用，副词的正确使用）

Father helped them adjust the fire, <u>which</u> was the key to success. （定语从句）

Soon, they made the bread <u>perfectly</u> and the porridge was also ready. （副词的正确使用）

<u>Holding</u> the breakfast tray <u>carefully</u> and <u>adding</u> a <u>beautiful</u> card they had made, the twins walked out of the kitchen. （非谓语动词，副词、形容词的正确使用）

The moment Mom slightly opened her sleepy eyes, the twins yelled, "Happy Mother's Day, darling Mummy!"(the moment 引导状语从句，副词的正确使用)

Before she said "thank you" to the twins, a breakfast tray with a plate of French toast and a bowl of porridge placed on the table beside the bed caught her attention.（before 引导状语从句，catch 的巧用）

"Mom, have a try!" Jeff suggested immediately, "We made it for you!"（副词的正确使用）

Mom's eyes widened, staring at the breakfast tray, tears glittering.（谓语动词，非谓语动词，独立主格的正确运用）

It was not only the gift, but also the love of the children for her that moved her very much.（not only... but also 及强调句的使用）

Keys：
Task 1 梳理原文要素

(1) father      (2) morning     (3) bed            (4) excitement
(5) panicked    (6) calm        (7) disappointment (8) excited
(9) planned     (10) thought    (11) smoothly      (12) bread
(13) other      (14) porridge   (15) panicked      (16) calm
(17) mess       (18) well       (19) disappointment (20) father

Task 2 运用"TEAMS"策略续写故事

Para1: *As the twins looked around them in disappointment, their father appeared.*

第一句衔接句承上（衔接首句的内容）：爸爸的出现对他们来说就像救世主一样。Father's appearing was like a savior to them.

第二句动作：在爸爸的指导下，双胞胎快速地采取积极行动清理了厨房并重新准备早餐。Under the guidance of their father, the twins quickly took positive actions to clean up the kitchen and start preparing the breakfast again.

第三句动作：爸爸帮助他们调整火的大小，这是成功的关键。
Father helped them adjust the fire, which was the key to success.

第四句衔接句承上（衔接上句的内容）：因此，这次一切都没问题了。
Therefore, It was all right this time.

第五句动作：很快，他们完美地做好了面包，粥也准备好了。

Soon, they made the bread perfectly and the porridge was also ready.

第六句动作：小心翼翼地端着早餐盘，加上他们做的一张漂亮的卡片，双胞胎走出了厨房。

Holding the breakfast tray carefully and adding a beautiful card they had made, the twins walked out of the kitchen.

Para 2：*The twins carried the breakfast upstairs and woke their mother up.*

第一句衔接句承上（衔接首句的内容）+对话：妈妈轻轻睁开蒙眬睡眼那一刻，双胞胎就大叫"亲爱的妈妈，母亲节快乐！"

The moment Mom slightly opened her sleepy eyes, the twins yelled, "Happy Mother's Day, darling Mummy！".

第二句情感：妈妈相当惊讶也高兴。

Mom was quite surprised and happy.

第三句动作：她还来不及跟双胞胎说"谢谢"，床边桌子上放着的装着一叠法式烤面包和一碗粥的餐盘就吸引了她的注意力。

Before she said "thank you" to the twins, a breakfast tray with a plate of French toast and a bowl of porridge placed on the table beside the bed caught her attention.

第四句对话："妈妈，快试一下！"Jeff 立马提议说，"我们给您做的！"

"Mom, have a try！" Jeff suggested immediately, "We made it for you！"

第五句动作+Emotion 情感：妈妈瞪大了眼睛，凝视着餐盘，泪光闪烁。

Mom's eyes widened, staring at the breakfast tray, tears glittering.

第六句回归主题，升华感情：令她感动的，不仅是这份礼物，还有孩子们对她的爱。

It was not only the gift, but also the love of the children for her that moved her very much.

# 第三篇 课堂联动

《新课标》指出：教研员是教师专业发展过程中的指导者和合作伙伴。教研员要率先学习课程标准提出的新理念、新要求，深刻理解其内容精髓，主动走进课堂，与教师共同实践，指导教师开展教学研究，不断提升课程育人质量。① 教研员要定期深入基层学校，特别是农村学校和薄弱学校，走进课堂。教研员要带领教师把课程标准中对学生长远的培养目标转化为具体的单元、语篇和课时的教学目标，并与教师合作，开展磨课和试课，在这个过程中观察学生的反应和变化，以及教学对学生学习行为和学习成效的影响，共同反思和总结，持续优化和改进。教研员还要借助基于实证分析和数据分析的教学诊断，携手教师共同研究和解决教学中的问题，带领教师逐步将课程理念转化为具体的课堂教学实践。② 可见教研员带领一线教师以课例研究的方式优化课堂教学、提升教研品质是重要的行动研究，符合《新课标》理念。本篇介绍了笔者分学段、分单元、分课型的 10 个示范课例，涵盖听、说、读、看、写在内的语言技能，以及语音、词汇、语法、英汉诗歌对比阅读、单元复习、中高考话题复习、电影欣赏、整本书阅读等热点课型。在联动教研活动中，教研员和课题组及区内外骨干老师携手进行公开课例展示，分课型进行同课同构、同课异构、异课同构等，尝试 Planning-Teaching-Observation-Reflection-Evaluation-Creation（PTOREC）教研模式。我们坚持使用英语作为工作语言，规范了区教研活动的内容与形式，提高了针对性、实效性和系统性，同时，联动教研平台和研究共同体为英语教研注入了活力，促进了教师间的深度合作和交流，激发了创新思维和教学热情，使我们的课堂充满生命的活力，让我们在教师专业化发展的路上越走越远。

---

①② 中华人民共和国教育部：《义务教育英语课程标准（2022 年版）》，北京师范大学出版社 2022 年版，第 78 页。

# 第一章　广州市黄埔区与海珠区联动教研*

**课例一**　沪教版七年级下册 Unit 7 Poems 英汉诗歌对比阅读课**

## 一、教材分析

The teaching material is taken from Unit 7, Module 4, Oxford English. It is the second period of the reading part. The reading material is two poems about ordinary people. After reading the two poems, students can know the writing methods and the writer's feeling towards the poem. It can let students have a better understanding about the listening part, speaking part and writing part.

## 二、学情分析

As Junior One students, they are presumed to be active and motivate in English classes. They have learnt some basic knowledge about poem, such as "verse, line and rhyme". However, writing methods and the writer's feeling towards the poem remain a little difficult for them.

## 三、教学重点和难点

There are two teaching focuses, one is to know the writer's feeling towards the poems, and the other is to know the writing methods of the poems. So it is important to guide students to have a better understanding by digesting the key information, which is the difficult point.

---

\*　教研指导和审课专家：广州市黄埔区教育研究院符丽雪、广州市海珠区教育发展研究院张志梅。

\*\*　执教：广州市海珠区教育发展研究院张志梅、广州市海珠区六中珠江中学姜媛媛。
　　点评：广州市绿翠现代实验学校　庄茹慧。

## 四、教学目标

At the end of this lesson, students will be able to:

(1) understand the rhymes, verses, comparisons, repetitions and the feelings used in the two poems;

(2) enjoy and share more poems in groups;

(3) peer evaluate their learning by using the peer-evaluation form;

(4) learn to compare Chinese poems with English poems and appreciate the beauty of poems.

## 五、教学方法与媒体

Teaching methods: Communicative Language Teaching (CLT), Task-Based Method, brainstorming approach.

Learning methods: group work, Audio-Lingual Method.

The teaching aids: computer, blackboard, speakers, and handouts.

## 六、教学过程

| Process | Purpose | Teacher's activity | Students' activity |
| --- | --- | --- | --- |
| Step1: Revision | Help students review some features of an English poem. | Show some features of an English poem. | Review the features of an English poem. |
| Step 2: Leading-in | Have a quiz about poems. | Let students tick the boxes to show their opinion. | Students share their opinions about poems. |
| Step 3: Pre-reading | 1. Let students know what the two poems talk about. 2. To find the verse, line and rhymes of the two poems. | Ask some questions about the topic, verses, lines and rhymes of the two poems. | 1. Answer the questions. 2. Understand "Now + all poems must have rhymes." |

续上表

| Process | Purpose | Teacher's activity | Students' activity |
|---|---|---|---|
| Step 4: While-reading | 1. Get the topic of the two poems. 2. Develop the students' abilities to know the writing methods and the writer's feeling towards the poem by looking for the key information. 3. Help students learn something from the poems. | 1. Ask them to listen to the poems one by one and ask students to know the writing methods and the writer's feeling towards the poem by looking for the key information. 2. Guide the students to summarize what they can learn from the poems. 3. Check a quiz about the poems. | 1. Listen to the poems one by one and know the writing methods and the writer's feeling towards the poem by looking for the key information. 2. Summarize what they can learn from the poems. 3. Check a quiz about the poems. |
| Step 5: Post-reading | 1. Let students read and enjoy more poems in groups. 2. Develop students' ability to read poems with feelings. 3. Figure out the beauty of poems. 4. To make peer-evaluation. | 1. Asks them to read and enjoy more poems in groups with feeling and rhymes. 2. Ask students "Do you like English poems or Chinese poems?" 3. To make peer-evaluation. | 1. Read and enjoy more poems in groups with feeling and rhymes. 2. Share their ideas about "Do you like English poems or Chinese poems?" 3. To make peer-evaluation. |
| Step 6: Sum up | Summarize what they have learned in the class. | Ask students to summarize some features of an English poem. | Summarize some features of an English poem. |
| Step 7: Homework | Read and enjoy the poems in groups. | Read and enjoy the poems in groups. | Read and enjoy the poems in groups. |

附诗歌文本

1. The peasants

At noon they hoe [həʊ] up weeds;

Their sweat [swet] drips on the soil [sɔɪl].

Who knows the rice that feeds

Is the fruit of hard toil [tɔɪl]!

Questions:

(1) Some words like weeds, feeds, soil, toil are _____, they usually appear at the end of the _____.

(2) A poem has many parts. They're called _____.

2. My dad

(1) What is Verse1 about?

Verse1 is about his dad at h _____.

(2) What does the writer think of his dad?

He thinks his dad is a b _____ man.

(3) What is Verse2 about?

Verse2 is about his dad at w _____.

(4) Why does the writer think his dad is a superman?

He's high up in the c _____.

Higher than a k _____.

He's walking on a n _____ piece of wood.

Not worried about the h _____.

- Writing methods (方法): Comparison [kəmˈpærɪsn].
- What can you learn from this poem?

Our parents work hard every day. We should u _____ them and r _____ (尊敬) them.

3. The old newspaper seller

Discuss (讨论), ask and answer questions in pairs.

|  | The old newspaper seller | Other people |
|---|---|---|
| Where do they work? | At the newspaper (1) s _____ near the bus (2) s _____. | Other places. |
| What's the weather like? | The Sun is (3) s _____. It is very (4) h _____. |  |

续上表

|  | The old newspaper seller | Other people |
|---|---|---|
| What are they doing? | He is (5) s_____ newspaper. | • They (6) r_____ out of the bus.<br>• They (7) t_____ their papers quickly and (8) p_____ down some money. |
| What does the writer think about them? | He is patient and keeps (9) s_____. | They are all very busy, with (10) t_____ faces. |

Writing methods（方法）：Repetition [ˌrepəˈtɪʃn]（_____）.

What can you learn from this poem? Everyone should be happy and s_____ when there are difficulties.

What do the two poems have in common（共同之处）? They are both about o_____ people who are also great.

4. Work in groups and show your favorite poem in class

(1) Who has the same hobby as me?

Who has the same hobby as me?　　Sometimes I fish in the sea.
Sometimes I play computer games.　　Sometimes I fly model plane.
Sometimes I play with toy cars.　　Sometimes I look at the stars.
But my favourite hobby is to ski.　　Who has the same hobby as me?

(2) Snow on the River

From hill to hill no bird in flight,
From path to path no man in sight.
A lonely fisherman afloat,
Is fishing snow in a lonely boat.

flight [flaɪt] 飞翔　　path [pɑːθ] 道路，小路　　sight [saɪt] 景象
afloat [əˈfləʊt] 漂浮

(3) Spring Morning

This morning of spring in bed I'm lying,
Not to awake till birds are crying.
After one night of wind and showers,
How many are the fallen flowers!

(4) You Are My Special Teacher

I just want you to know

I always had fun in your class.

How the time has flown!

Thank you for helping me

To learn all that I know.

I will always remember you

Even when I'm grown!

I'll miss you as my teacher.

I know the reason why

I am feeling very sad

Because it's time to say goodbye.

## 七、教学评价

Peer-evaluation（互评）：Please write down how many smiles for each poem.

| OK ☺ Good ☺ ☺ Excellent ☺ ☺ ☺ | Rhymes 押韵 | Feelings 感情 | Creation 创意 | Total & Why 总数和理由 |
| --- | --- | --- | --- | --- |
| Poem One | | | | |
| Poem Two | | | | |
| Poem Three | | | | |
| Poem Four | | | | |

## 八、总结

In all, different cultures have different poems. They all express the writer's feelings. Let's enjoy the beauty of different poems.

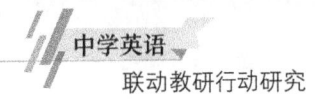

## 九、教学点评

Good afternoon, ladies and gentlemen, I'm 庄茹慧 from Lvcui Modern Experimental School. It is my great honor to share my study notes of Miss Zhang's typical lesson. Many thanks to Miss Zhang for showing all of us an excellent representative model lesson and for giving me this opportunity to speak here.

As the headteacher and English teacher of this class, I felt so lucky to have Miss Zhang directly offer lesson to my students. After the class, they were excited to take a picture with Miss Zhang. These lovely smiles called the success of their love and gratitude toward Miss Zhang.

During this lesson I found that the students were much more engaged than they ordinarily do. I was quite surprised to see their confident answers and good performance, which did rarely appear in the time I spent with them together, nearly one year. So what kind of magic did Miss Zhang apply to them? After that day's on-site learning and repeated research on the video, I found some characters that count for, and I'd like to discuss with all of you.

First of all, the background of students, their English level is irregular. A part of students that learn English very hard, the English level is Low-intermediate, they can't follow the teacher and need others' help to join the class and activities. I'm quite worried about these underachievers. In addition, a part of the students can go to the level of Intermediate, who are active in talking about interesting topics, they also have basic reading ability and willing to express their feelings and opinions on relative topics despite some language mistakes, but they are not so good at expressing their ideas in English exactly. Fortunately, several top-students in my class are willing to show themselves and warmly invite the other students to join into the class activities, so that it makes for coming into being better atmosphere among all the students of learning.

Now, Let's come to my classroom observation. I found that Miss Zhang not only act as the teacher in classroom, but also play a lot of roles during the whole process.

First, she is a great "analyzer" before the class to analyze the value of teaching and education. Take these two fragments as an example. Miss Zhang develops the students' abilities to know the writing methods and the writer's feeling towards the poem and help students learn something from the poems. From this kind of text interpretation, we can find that the teaching objectives and methods are appropriate by her deep analysis.

Next, the second role of Miss Zhang is a good "designer" with reasonable design of class activity to promote students' understanding. Miss Zhang takes the students learning ability into full consideration by designing the appropriate handout paper to help students better understand and follow the teachers leading. It is worth mentioning that Miss Zhang emphasizes phonetic teaching through the whole course, not only in the handout but also in the process of text analysis by writing them on the blackboard with repeat reading to check the master of phonetic. In addition, the whole class has 9 activities. Through these teaching procedures, Miss Zhang leads them to analyze the key information and put forward views to the article. During the teaching process, teacher will build the learning and practicing platform step by step to promote students' comprehension ability.

Then, the third role of Miss Zhang is an excellent "presenter". Miss Zhang serves as a presenter also means a host and a public speaker. She can use accurate, lively and concise teaching language to guide her students to understand the themes, the contents and the authors' feelings towards the poems. As for the warming-up, Miss Zhang uses a chant of a Chinese poem《悯农》to arouse interest of students and make it easier to understand the rhymes, the basic feature of the poem. And the teacher also has rich body language, so that even my students' English level is to an alarming extent, they can still understand the instructions and communication from the teacher. Besides, Miss Zhang always wears a sweet smile with eyes contact to inspire students to express. All of my colleagues were wowed to her perfect performance.

Then, Miss Zhang also serves as a patient "listener" on one hand, she always listens to students and give timely feedback. On the other hand, she plays an important role of "advisor". She focuses on students' question and give timely suggestion to those students who suffer from temporary trouble. To sum up, Miss Zhang is a wise "demonstrator" to show the way as an example so that students can follow it and do the activities.

Last but not least, Miss Zhang plays an important role of "evaluator". She chooses the teaching materials that are close to students' daily lives and provides them with the chances to experience, share and evaluate their learnings. She makes her lesson an integration of teaching-learning-evaluation to organize the latest edition of Compulsory English Curriculum Standard. Peer-evaluation is as encouraging as that of a teacher. Peer-evaluation can also develop students' critical thinking and make them more confident.

In the end, students are the most important part in the class, so Miss Zhang take her teaching atmosphere relaxing and happy to make the students as hosts in the class. I believe there are still many fascinating aspects that we can dig deeper into details.

After the on-site learning from Miss Zhang's typical lesson, I made a profound reflection of my English teaching, both the objectives and strategies. In the future, I will more carefully analyze the value of teaching and education and more reasonably design the class activities by using more activities in the class to finish some tasks such as individual, pair or group work to let students have more chances to organize. I will also listen more patiently and offer the students enough time to think independently and creatively. Pay attention to develop their critical thinking by implementing the students' assessment.

That's all of my sharing today. Many thanks for listening! It will be highly appreciated if you offer any suggestion.

# 第二章 "云端送教,粤黔共研"海珠瓮安联动教研*

**课例二** 沪教版八年级上册 Module 4 School Life Unit 8 English Week 阅读课**

## 一、教材分析

本单元模块为"School Life",话题为"English Week",一共涉及八篇文本。"English: fun for life"是主阅读当中的口号,同时它也是一篇学校新闻报道。它是初中六册英语课本文本当中唯一的一篇新闻报道类型的文章。Reading 部分是关于 Rosie Bridge 学校举办"英语周"的新闻报道,主要介绍"英语周"有哪些活动以及它们对英语学习的帮助。新闻报道里包括了日期、标题、图片、导语。在分析新闻报道时,指出它的文本结构,并且将它与电子邮件、采访进行区分。电子邮件包括 greeting 和 ending,并且 it is online。采访包括了采访人、被采访人,并且以对话形式出现。第一课时 Vocabulary & Pre-reading 里已经介绍过新单词及学习文本 crossword puzzle。结合本节阅读课的英语活动,设定第一个情境,贵州六中将举行"英语周"活动,借此让学生学习英语活动的名称。在课文学习过程中,学生通过问题引导以及收听课文录音,能够感受到参与者的喜悦与期待。邀请学生与老师一起模仿课文对话,给学生一个模仿的例子,鼓励学生模仿对话。模仿的对话内容与文章当中的采访预设基本一致。其中,添加的采访内容是"如果勋劳中学与瓮安六中一样开展'英语周'活动,你会参加哪些英语活动?"通过填空替代形式,训练口语。

---

\* 教研指导和审课专家:广州市海珠区教育发展研究院张志梅。
\*\* 执教:广州市海珠区勋劳中学何穗珊;点评:广州市海珠区教育发展研究院张志梅。

| | |
|---|---|
| What | 在 Unit 8 Vocabulary & Pre-reading 的学习中，学生掌握了 speech, competition, chance, confidently, treasure hunt, in public, put on, in my opinion, above all 等词汇。在前置作业中设置了基础题"依据情境内容填空"，复习已学的单词、短语。提升题"连词成句"帮助学生复习句法。拓展题"crossword puzzle"，主要训练学生通过模拟文化角的英语解析找到线索，回想词汇并加强学生运用英语的能力。这些前置性英语题目为本课 Reading 的展开及学生的活动输出做好铺垫。 |
| Why | 以前置作业复习本单元的词、组、句内容，保证本节课有充足的词语可供学生使用。通过任务型教学，引导学生理解 Reading 内容，感受"英语周"活动的丰富多彩。设计并模仿"英语周"的采访形式，教师引领学生进入情境体验"英语周"活动的多样性，激发学生主动参与英语活动的兴趣。 |
| How | 任务 I 设定第一个情境：贵州六中将举行"英语周"活动。观看图片，图中师生们正在计划一些活动。展示图片，说出英语活动名称，达成学生回想、复习的目的。使用一张思维导图，归纳英语活动的名称，为后续口语活动做铺垫。任务 II 阅读前分析文本体裁的特征，展示新闻报道的特征，点评"它与电子邮件及采访"的区别。任务 III 一边听一边阅读新闻报道的内容，然后通过完成练习熟悉新闻报道的特点。新闻报道具有简洁性，文本表达简单易懂。新闻报道具有真实性，文本采用对话采访形式体现参与者的想法与情感。任务 IV 设定情境二：劭劳中学正准备开展"英语周"活动。我们可以选择像瓮安六中那样的英语活动。老师与同学展示一个对话，要求全班模仿这个对话。通过对话，替换英语活动形式，期望学生对英语活动进行思考，创造性地替换相关内容。举例，第一个空白使用了 singing competition，后面出现了相关的 sing 和 sing confidently。如果学生后续把第一个空白可改成 speaking competition，那么相关的内容就用 speak, speak confidently 进行替换。这一个活动属于输出的活动，也是学生在课程学习思考之后的创造性活动。预设安排（三个）学习小组的竞赛形式，看看哪个小组是最后的获胜者。课程的最后是归纳阅读课的重点并布置作业。 |

## 二、学情分析

学生通过七年级上册 U2 A Day at School 和 U7 The Club Fairs 的学习，掌握了一些描述校园生活主题的英语词汇和句型。通过八年级上册 U2 The King and the Rice 的学习，学生接触过课本剧表演，对 English play 有一定的认识，但对该话题中新出现的一些活动，如 treasure hunt, crossword puzzle 和 book fair 等不太熟悉。Vocabulary & Pre-reading 课型属于第八单元的第一课时。第一课时教授了一种流行的英语游戏字梯,从而对引入英语活动的名称起到支架作用。展示图片,针对高频单词、短语进行教学,对主阅读篇章提出"是否每个学校都要开展'英语周'活动?如果开展'英语周'活动,你最想开展什么样的活动?"的问题。接着,在完成第一课时的教学之后,教师给学生安排了前置作业,为学生能够更好地进入第二课时阅读课做准备。学生的英语水平属于中等偏下,部分学生的英语水平稍好,因此,前置作业分为基础题、提升题及拓展题。前置作业里的基础题是根据课文主要内容的改写,挖空的内容为新单词及短语内容,用以加深学生对新词汇的印象。前置作业里的提升题是连词成句,搭建句子结构,它们分别是 advise sb. to do sth. 以及 be a successful + n. 两种主要句法。拓展题采用了"字梯"游戏形式,让程度高的学生深入学习词汇,锻炼"英英"转换思维。

以上为基础准备,本节课教师通过主阅读关键词的重点展示,为学生搭建文本细节理解任务的支架,促进学生深入了解英语活动的内容及目的,学生能体会到 Henry 和 Amy 的愉快情感。接着为学生搭建替换型口语训练的支架,学生通过思考并参与口语活动,产生参与英语活动的冲动与想法。期待学生"Enjoy learning English!"。

## 三、教学目标

| 第二课时 课型:Reading ||||
|---|---|---|---|
| 学习内容(核心概念)+<br>行为条件+行为内容 | 表现程度 | 作业 ||
| Task Ⅰ: There will be an English week at Wengan No. 6 Middle School, and the teachers and students are planning some activities. Look at the pictures, and speak out the correct names of activities on the pictures. | 熟练 | 基础作业(必做)<br>1. 熟读课文,上传录音,背诵好词好句;<br>2. 认真复习课堂笔记,完成《阳光评价》Reading 部分及课本 117 页;<br>3. 订正前置作业(pre-set homework)。 ||
| Task Ⅱ: Look at the picture, the title and the sub-heading on page 115. Then circle the correct answers. | 理解 |||
| Task Ⅲ: Read the text from paragraph one to seven in details with the recording and then finish the exercises. | 正确选出体裁类型。正确表达"英语周"活动及相关受采访对象的细节。 |||

**续上表**

| 学习内容（核心概念）+ 行为条件+行为内容 | 表现程度 | 作业 |
| --- | --- | --- |
| Task Ⅳ. Situation： Our Qulao Middle School is going to have an English Week. We may choose some interesting activities as Wengan（瓮安）No.6 Middle School. Complete the conversation below with the words from the box. Change their forms if necessary. | 采访（老师与学生做个示范）；小组内同学之间进行对话模仿。 | 拓展作业（选做）：吉姆对英语感兴趣，他想提高英语，请你依据现实情境提出建议或者想法。 |
| Task Ⅴ. Show time | 展示；预设有两到三组学生完成采访对话。 | |

## 四、教学重难点

教学重点：让学生跟着老师的指引，理解课文内容，并对教学情境进行分析。

教学难点：学生如何做好采访？选择自己喜欢的英语活动，合理替换对话的空白处。

Amy：When will this English Week start, Jane?

Jane：It'll start next Monday.

Amy：Will you take part in any activities?

Jane：Yes. I'm going to take part in the (1) _____. It'll be my first (2) _____ to sing in public. I'm really nervous. Do you have any (3) _____ for me?

Amy：Don't worry. Just sing confidently, and you'll be all right. Are there any other activities during the week?

Jane：Yes. On the last day of the week, our head teacher will speak to the (4) _____ school and tell us how to (5) _____ better in English.

Amy：I'm sure your English Week will be a big success.

Jane：Thank you.

## 五、教学流程

| 教学环节 | 学习活动 | 设计意图与评价 |
|---|---|---|
| Task Ⅰ & Ⅱ | 理解加深活动：<br>1. 设置情境一：贵州瓮安六中也开展了"英语周"活动，学习英语活动名称（图片快闪，问题导向）<br>2. 用思维导图归纳英语活动名称。<br>Maybe we have these English activities. | 设计意图：学生回想并使用单词、短语。<br>激发学生学习的兴趣。<br>评价：口头评价 |
| Task Ⅲ & Ⅳ | 应用实践活动：<br>1. Read paragraphs 1-7 and finish the exercises with the help of the recording.<br>2. Complete this notice on page 117. | 设计意图：一边听一边阅读课本，应用课本内容分析课本内容。<br>使用公告形式，归纳 Rosie Bridge School 的"英语周"总体情况。<br>评价：师生互评 |
| Task Ⅴ & Ⅵ | 应用实践活动：采访<br>Our Qulao Middle School is going to have an English Week. We may choose some interesting activities as Wengan No. 6 Middle School.<br>Ms. He sets an example for the whole class with one classmate orally. | 设计意图：以"英语周"活动为主线。把劬劳中学跟贵州瓮安六中联系起来进行英语口语练习。<br>评价：学生他评 |
| | 应用实践活动：采访<br>学生使用 P116 C2 内容进行对话练习，特别提示把第一句改成问句，跟劬劳中学"英语周"活动相结合。When will this English Week start?<br>评出今天的优胜小组，全班学生举手参与投票活动；对于优胜者，全班给予掌声鼓励。 | 设计意图：让学生思考他们喜欢什么样的英语活动？学会合理安排学校生活。<br>评价：学生互评 |
| 小结 | 归纳今天所学知识。 | 评价：师生共评 |

续上表

| 教学环节 | 学习活动 | 设计意图与评价 |
| --- | --- | --- |
| 作业布置 | 基础作业（必做）：1. 熟读课文，上传录音。背诵好词好句。2. 认真复习课堂笔记，完成《阳光评价》Reading 部分及课本 117 页。3. 订正前置作业（Pre-set homework）。<br>拓展作业（选做）：吉姆对英语感兴趣，他想提高英语，请你依据现实情境提出建议或者想法。 | 设计意图：利用信息技术为英语学习赋能，上传课文朗读录音。创设条件让学生完成《学案》等，内化与运用，形成结构化知识。<br>评价：教师评价 |

## 六、教学评价

Peer-assessment（互评）

| Standards | Stars |
| --- | --- |
| Their activities are interesting! | ★★★★★ |
| They can speak clearly. | ★★★★★ |
| They show their confidence. | ★★★★★ |
| | Total：_____ stars |

## 七、教学反思

本次公开课最大的感悟就是团队协作尤其重要。感谢海珠区教育发展研究院张老师、英语中心组的老师们及学校备课小组的同仁们。在试教过程中，每次的修改都得益于团队老师的及时互动。本教学设计许多想法来源于《义务教育英语课程标准（2022 年版）》，标准强调了英语活动的重要性与必要性。"School Life" 主题来源于学生的生活，是学生十分熟悉的话题。设计"如果劬劳中学也展开'英语周'的真实场境"，结合学生实际对话，以"真问题"导向学生思考问题，锻炼了学生的思维，培养学生在解决真实问题中逐渐养成思维品质。以学生为中心的英语对话活动，增强了课堂的互动性，体现了"做中学"的理念。小组之间的比赛增加了趣味性，将来可以继续使用。其次，今后需要改进的方向就是做好英语前置作业设计，在课前把单词、词组及句子的支架搭建好，这样课堂上学生们更加容易"动"起来，实现"用英语做事"的目标。接着,老师要注意观察"待优生"的细微变化,课堂活动先聚焦训练这部分学生,把难度控制在他们努力一下就能达到的范围。"值日生报告"活动在七年级学习阶段培养了学生的口头表达能力;到了八年级,口语替换活动及小组 PK 活动可以优先在"待优生"团体中开展,在课程中段时间展开,助力班级中等层次的学生成长。期待英语学习在"教—学—评"一体化中渐渐形成良性的循环。

## 八、教学点评

何老师的这节课通过任务链的设计,5 个教学活动很好地把教学目标和教学资源整合起来。课堂氛围和谐,教学效果良好,所以这是一节朴实高效的课例展示。具体表现在:①体现了单元整体教学视角下素养导向的阅读目标;②围绕教学目标设计任务链,学生的听、说、读、写、看多种技能都得到培养;③践行学用结合,将学生可以学的瓮安六中的活动转化为学生能参与的劭劳中学的活动,并且通过小组合作展示的方式提升学生在活动中的参与度;④制定了简洁的互评表,及时提供来自学生和教师的有效反馈;⑤何老师全英教学,教态自然亲切,为学生创造了英语学习的良好氛围;⑥值得一提的是,劭劳中学的英语科组老师们团结互助,有非常好的团队合作精神,受到老师们的一致好评。

建议:①加强生生互动,在读前利用图片对瓮安六中进行简介,让学生了解背景知识,产生亲切感,阅读过程中给学生更多的时间和机会思考、讨论和交流,进一步落实学生的主体地位;②加强教学评价,在学生展示之前提供评价表,让学生可利用评价表指导小组对话,同时更有针对性地开展自评和他评活动。

# 第三章 广州市初二英语市区联动教研

## 课例三 沪教版八年级下册 Module 1 Social Communication Unit 1 Helping Those in Need 单元整体复习课*

### 一、单元整体教学目标分析

牛津沪教版八年级下册 Unit 1 Helping Those in Need 单元主题属于《义务教育英语课程标准（2022年版）》"人与社会"范畴下的"社会服务与人际沟通"主题群，子主题内容为"志愿服务与公共服务"。本单元各个语篇主要以"帮助有困难的人"为话题，以志愿服务为主线，三个小观念围绕着大观念，大观念指挥着三个小观念。本单元的大观念主要由三个小观念带领的三条主线生成，分别为学习理解、应用实践、迁移创新。第一条主线是一个从内到外的设计，Reading 介绍了三位在校学生在假期做志愿者的经历，Listening 介绍了被采访的学生所在班级组织的筹款活动的大致情况，而 More Practice 与 Culture Corner 则介绍了"春蕾计划"这个爱心工程与联合国儿童基金会这个志愿组织。学生通过语篇的学习可以多方面认识志愿组织与志愿活动。在第二条主线中，学生在对志愿服务有一定认识的基础上，学会表达参与志愿活动的意愿，学习书写申请组织志愿活动的请求信，提升语言表达能力。而在第三条主线中，学生通过认识"饼图"的形式与作用，学会用"饼图"来表示比例。最后，单元的整体输出为完成一份志愿活动的组织方案以作为大单元的产出，助力实现单元育人目标：将志愿活动和人间大爱进行到底。

通过单元学习，学生将能够达成以下学习目标。

（1）了解志愿服务的目的、主要形式、内容和意义；听有关筹款活动的电台采访录音，巩固提取和记录关键信息的倾听技巧；掌握动词不定式作状语和宾语的用法，通过小组活动，谈论自己打算参加的志愿服务活动。

---

\* 执教：广州市海珠区教育发展研究院张志梅；点评：广州市第六中学吕苏玲，广州市五中东晓学校李翠柳、杨旗，广州市第九十七中学李锦云，广州市海珠区华海双语学校 Lukas。

（2）了解不同的志愿组织，理解志愿服务的重要性；建立良好的道德风尚，培养奉献精神和社会责任感。

（3）从文本中提取关键信息和要点；利用"蛛网图"构建写作框架并完成一封给校长的筹款活动申请书；有逻辑、有创意地表达自己的想法。

（4）在学习活动中积极与他人合作，共同完成自己的志愿工作计划和评价同学的计划，并且尝试用不同的策略来解决语言学习中的问题。

## 二、基于海珠区学业质量监测诊断结果与学情分析的单元整体教学改进策略

广州市五中东晓学校八年级共有 156 名学生参加了 2023 年 3 月的海珠区学业质量监测。从答题的情况看，该年级学生得分率达 0.5 以上的板块有语法选择和阅读理解，这些都是基础语法和中低难度的阅读题。得分率低于 0.5 的板块有完形填空、阅读填空、语篇填词、完成句子和书面表达。该年级学生各项技能都显著低于区平均水平。初二 1 班共 39 名学生，该班的英语水平属于五中东晓学校的中等偏上层次，该班学生阅读填空、语篇填词、完成句子和书面表达得分率都比较低，也就说明写的能力是该班学生的短板。任课老师反映主要原因是线上教学时间长，无法掌控学生的学习状态，有学生甚至在疫情期间出现了比较严重的心理问题。虽然开学初用了两周来复习，但对部分学生来说如同上新课，大部分学生不会在语境中灵活运用熟悉的词汇和语法。该班听、说、读能力较好的学生上英语课的积极性比较高，但是注意力不够集中，教师在课堂上要重点激发兴趣，强化他们学习英语的内驱力，让他们更好地融入到学习中，同时带动其他同学参与学习。英语水平一般的学生和学困生则迫切需要通过老师的引导和同学的鼓励以建立自信心，才能大胆地在老师和全班同学面前进行表达和展示。

基于以上学生的能力水平以及学习动机、态度和特点分析，在单元整体复习教学活动中采用了以下教学改进策略。

（1）针对大部分学生不会在语境中灵活运用熟悉的词汇的问题，引导学生在生活化的情景和多模态语篇中理解和运用单元核心词汇，领悟词汇的基本含义，以及在特定语境和语篇中的意义、词性和功能，这也是《新课标》中关于词汇知识的三级内容要求。

（2）针对单元重点语法项目——动词不定式作状语和宾语时如何灵活运用的问题，要帮助学生初步意识到语言使用中的语法知识是"形式-意义-使用"的统一体，明确学习语法的目的是在语境中运用语法知识理解和表达意义。

（3）针对学生写作能力比较弱、注意力不够集中的问题，按照学生的认知特点和能力水平，鼓励学生在主题意义的引领下以参与听、说、读、看活动为主，写的活动安排在课后作业中，这样可以由浅入深，循序渐进。

（4）针对学困生自信心和学习动机不足的问题，给他们搭好"脚手架"，鼓励他们在小组合作学习中努力尝试完成难度低的任务，最大程度扩大学生的参与面，调动其积极性，也力求把快乐、勇气和自信心带给他们。

## 三、单元整体复习教学设计与实施

### （一）教学内容设计

本课例是牛津沪教版八年级下册 Unit 1 Helping Those in Need 的单元整体复习与评价课，也就是本单元的最后一节课。单元的整体输出为完成一份志愿活动的组织方案，让学生学以致用，将志愿活动付诸行动，助力推进我们的单元主题：将"Helping those in need"进行到底，实现单元育人蓝图。

为了让五中东晓学校初二1班的学生顺利完成任务，本课采用产出导向法（Production-Oriented Approach，POA），即以输出驱动、输入促成假设为核心，教师为媒介，使输入性学习与产出性运用紧密结合，有机互动，形成有真实学习发生的课堂教学。

What：使用主题链的形式，选取对单元主题意义有建构的真正能够打动学生心灵的多模态语篇，包括：①歌曲 Count on Me，学生通过介绍这首歌复习巩固本单元话题词汇的意义、词性和功能。②观看关于 C21 Volunteers 的视频，背景音乐还是 Count on Me，但是内容为 C21 International School 的志愿者帮助儿童的情景。直观生动的视频复现了单元核心词汇，同时帮助学生理解志愿服务的目的、形式、内容和意义等，拓宽学生的国际视野。③Jiang Xu's plan 是广州市第六中学姜旭同学写的志愿工作计划的录音。把学生从国外拉进现实生活，引导学生听读并且完成阅读语篇的"鱼骨图"，包括组织者、受惠者、目的、时间、地点、形式和预期结果等，同时让学生评价 Jiang Xu's plan，让学生清楚完整的计划包含的要素以及对好计划的标准心中有数。④在 Dongxiao show time 活动中，给出四个真实的情景供学生选择，包括南华西敬老院、和谐动物收容所、东晓校园、彩虹社区，小组讨论合作完成自己的志愿工作计划。在学生展示之前，老师把 Jiang Xu's plan 改编为小组介绍的语篇，让学生先合作示范，然后模仿进行小组展示，最后评选出最佳志愿活动计划。⑤在 Poem time，介绍一首教师自创的关怀世界的诗歌，引导学生思考要帮助的

those 可以是人（儿童、老人、病人），还可以是动物、身边的朋友，甚至大自然等，一起努力，让世界更美丽！使学生逐步建构起对单元主题的完整认知，促进其形成正确态度和价值观。

How：以英语教学活动观为依据，教师主导，师生共建，以优化学习过程，促进学生广泛参与、有效互动、思维表达、乐于合作分享，师生过程性评价贯穿始终等作为标准。学生最初从歌曲中理解"帮助需要帮助的朋友"，到后面"帮助需要帮助的儿童、老人、动物，乃至社区、社会、世界"，学生对志愿服务工作的理解由近及远、从表层到深层，体现了思维深度和广度的递进性。最终认识到，我们可以在"Helping those in need"方面有更多作为。这样的结尾既留白，也让人充满美好的期待。

Why：在努力为学生减负的基础上，让他们学得更加开心有效，增强成就感和自信心。

（二）课时教学目标

本课将达成单元整体教学的目标4：在学习活动中积极与他人合作，共同完成自己的志愿工作计划和评价同学的计划，并且尝试用不同的策略来解决语言学习中的问题。

通过本课的学习，学生将能够达成以下学习目标：

（1）Review the words and expressions of Unit 1.

（2）Understand the meaning of the voluntary work.

（3）Learn to make plans to help those in need and share them in groups.

（4）Peer assess（互评）the learning.

（三）教学评价设计

坚持按照《新课标》要求以评促学、以评促教。教师的即时评价、学生自评和同学互评贯穿教与学的全过程。为了激励学生发挥主观能动性并自觉运用评价结果以改进学习，特别针对本课的志愿活动计划进行学生互评，并且设计了具体可操作的评价表。

| 序号 | 标准 | Peer-assessment 互评 |
| --- | --- | --- |
| 1 | Introduce oneself confidently.<br>自信地介绍自己。 | |
| 2 | Use "(in order) to do" to express purpose ['pɜːpəs].<br>使用"(in order) to do"不定式表达目的。 | |

续上表

| 序号 | 标准 | Peer-assessment 互评 |
|---|---|---|
| 3 | Know whom/when/where to help.<br>知道何时何地帮助谁。 | 👍👍👍 |
| 4 | Use "plan/decide/offer/would love to…"<br>使用 "plan/decide/offer/would love to…" 不定式作宾语。 | 👍👍👍 |
| 5 | Use "wish to do" to express expected result.<br>使用 "wish to do" 表达预期效果。 | 👍 |

## （四）"教—学—评"一体化实施过程

| Teaching stages | Students' activities | Teacher's activities | Purpose | Effect evaluation |
|---|---|---|---|---|
| Stage 1.<br>Song time<br>(Listening & Speaking)<br>(4 mins) | Share their feelings and introduce the main idea of the song. | Encourage students to talk about the song. | To review the key-words, expressions and structures of the whole unit in a relaxing way. | Students can use the key words, expressions and structures of the whole unit in the new context. |
| Stage 2.<br>Video time<br>(Watching & Interviewing)<br>(2 mins) | Watch a short video with the above song as the background and interview what they can see and feel after watching. | Guide students to interview, share opinions about the target topic-volunteers and voluntary work. | To create a lively classroom atmosphere and help students to think the meaning of voluntary work. | Students can talk about C21 School volunteers and understand helping others is happiness. |
| Stage 3.<br>Sharing time<br>(Listening & Writing)<br>(6 mins) | Listen to Jiang Xu's plan and finish the mind map. And then show it on projector. Finally peer assess: Is Jiang Xu's plan a good one? | Encourage students to use study skills to comb key factors of Jiang Xu's plan and make comments about it. | To introduce a voluntary work plan from peers around and encourage students to make comments about Jiang Xu's plan, which is scaffolding for their own plan. | Students can make comments about No. 6 Middle School volunteers according to the assessment form. |

续上表

| Teaching stages | Students' activities | Teacher's activities | Purpose | Effect evaluation |
|---|---|---|---|---|
| Stage 4. Show time (Speaking & assessing) (8 mins) | Discuss and brainstorm ideas and present their plans in groups; use self-assessment and peer assessment to select the best volunteers. | Encourage students to use problem-solving strategies to complete their group plans and to self-evaluate and peer-evaluate. | To help students fully reflect and improve their learning progress. | Students can make Dongxiao School voluntary work plans and make comments according to the evaluation form. Teacher can give students positive feedback timely. |
| Stage 5. Poem time (Reading & (2 mins) | Read a poem created called "Helping those in need" and understand the thematic meaning. | Encourage students to enjoy and be inspired by the beauty of the poem. | Understand the importance of helping those in need and increase students' sense of social responsibility. | Students and teacher can read the poem emotionally in groups and chorus. |
| Stage 6. Summary | Use a flow chart to recall the learning trip together. | | | |
| Assignment (1 min) | Must-do（必做）<br>Choose voluntary work you like and write a plan.<br>选择你喜欢的志愿工作，并写一个计划。<br>Optional（选做）<br>Write a diary about "An interesting English lesson".<br>写一篇关于"一节有趣的英语课"的日记。<br>If you have time, work as a volunteer at weekend.<br>如果你有时间，在周末做志愿者。 | | | |

## 四、导学案

Handout for Grade 8 U1 Helping Those in Need

Class _____ Name _____ No. _____

Task 1: Could you please introduce the song in Chinese and English（双语）?

*Count on Me*（《依靠我》）是一首著名的美国歌曲，描述的是（1）friendship _____.

在你身边，有没有这样的朋友？

当你（2）in need _____的时候，

当你（3）feel lonely _____的时候，

当你（4）suffer from illness and pain _____的时候，

（5）in order to _____帮助你，

他们会游遍世界（6）to find you _____;

他们会成为光（7）to guide you _____;

他们会（8）raise your spirits _____;

他们会教会你战胜（9）difficulty _____……

他们会带给你（10）joy, peace and courage _____。

正如谚语所说：A friend in need is a friend indeed. 患难见真情。

*Tip*: You can use the words and expressions in Unit 1 on p. 129.

可以使用第129页第一单元的词汇表作为参考。

Task 2: Interview your partner and talk about the video

1. What are the teenagers ['tiːneidʒəz] doing?

They are doing v_____ work to help children.

2. How do the children feel?

They are very h_____ to stay with volunteers.

3. Why are volunteers [vɒlən'tiəz] so happy?

Because they share hope, love and dream together and helping others is h_____.

Task 3: Read Jiang Xu's plan and finish the fish-bone map.

Hello, boys and girls.

My name is Jiang Xu. I am a Grade 8 student from No. 6 Middle School of Guangzhou. Now I want to tell you about our voluntary work plan.

In order to help old people who suffer from illness and pain, the volunteer club will <u>organize</u> a voluntary activity this Saturday. Volunteers are going to Sunshine Old People's Home. Four groups will take part in this activity.

The first group plans to clean the room and take out the rubbish. The second group decides to put up some beautiful pictures on the walls and some flowers in the rooms. The third group will offer to wash the clothes for the old people. The fourth group would love to sing and dance to make the old people happy.

I believe that we can make the old people's home look more beautiful. More importantly, we wish to bring joy, hope, peace and courage to the old people.

Welcome to join us! That's all. Thank you!

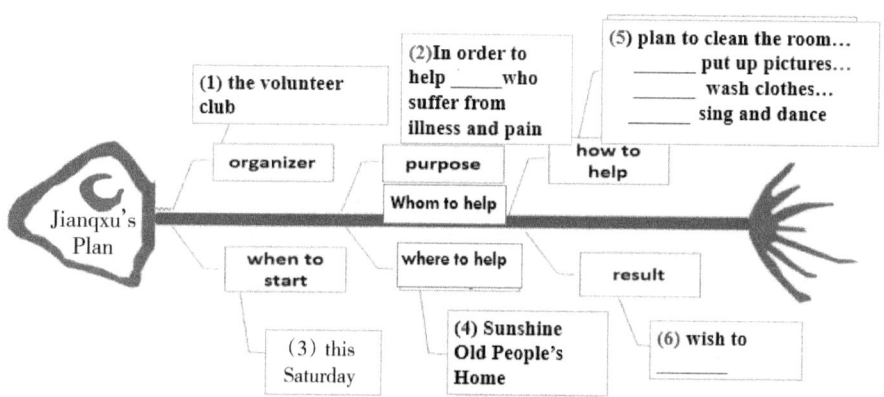

*Study Skill*：我们经常在 plan, decide, would love/like, offer, choose, hope, want, learn, wish 等动词后面 + to do 作宾语；

e. g. The first group <u>plans to clean the room and take out the rubbish</u>.

Task 4：Evaluate（评价）Jiang Xu's plan.

Is Jiang Xu's plan good? How many likes will you give him?

Task 5：Make your plan in groups and give likes to each other.

| 计划一 | 计划二 |
| --- | --- |
| 时间：星期六上午 | 时间：星期六下午 |
| 地点：南华西敬老院 | 地点：和谐动物收容所 |
| (Nanhuaxi Old People's Home) | (Hexie Animal Shelter) |
| 活动：1. 陪老人聊天 | 活动：1. 帮动物洗澡 |
|    2. 照顾老人 |    2. 给动物买食物 |
|    3.（请你补充） |    3.（请你补充） |
| 希望：带给老人快乐、宁静和勇气 | 希望：保护动物 |

| 计划三 | 计划四 |
| --- | --- |
| 时间：星期天上午 | 时间：星期天下午 |
| 地点：东晓校园（Dongxiao School） | 地点：彩虹社区（Rainbow Community） |
| 活动：1. 打扫校园<br>　　　2. 清除垃圾<br>　　　3. （请你补充） | 活动：1. 帮贫困孩子筹款<br>　　　2. 组织书市<br>　　　3. （请你补充） |
| 希望：使校园更加美丽 | 希望：带给贫困孩子爱、快乐和希望 |

Tip：You can walk over to ask teachers for help. 你们可以走过去请教老师们。

| | |
| --- | --- |
| Plan 1 南华西敬老院 | (Nanhuaxi Old People's Home) |
| Plan 2 和谐动物收容所 | (Hexie Animal shelter) |
| Plan 3 东晓学校 | (Dongxiao School) |
| Plan 4 彩虹社区 | (Rainbow Community) |

| 自我介绍 | Good afternoon, boys and girls. I am ＿＿＿＿＿＿. | 自评 | 互评 |
| --- | --- | --- | --- |
| Purpose<br>（目的） | Student 1：In order to help ＿＿＿＿＿＿＿＿＿,<br>we are going to ＿＿＿＿＿＿＿＿＿＿＿. | | |
| How to help | Student 2：First, we plan to ＿＿＿＿＿＿＿＿.<br>Student 3：Next, we decide to ＿＿＿＿＿＿＿.<br>Student 4：Finally, we would like to ＿＿＿＿＿. | | |
| Result/Hope | We wish to ＿＿＿＿＿＿＿＿＿＿＿＿＿＿.<br>Welcome to join us! That's all, thank you! | | |

e. g.

Together：Hello, boys and girls. My name is…

Student 1：In order to help <u>the old people</u>, we are going to <u>Sunshine Old People's Home this Saturday</u>.

Student 2：First, we plan to <u>clean the room and take out rubbish</u>.

Student 3：Next, we decide to <u>put up some beautiful pictures</u>.

Student 4：Finally, we would love to <u>sing beautiful songs to make them happy</u>.

Together：We wish to <u>bring joy, peace and courage to the old people</u>.

Welcome to join us! That's all. Thank you!

Task 6: Read the poem emotionally. （有感情地朗读诗歌）

Helping those in need

Robot: Help those in need, lend a hand,

Make them smile, help them stand.

Students: With love and care in our heart,

Let us do our part, each day to start.

Together: The world is more beautiful because of you and me!

## 五、老师评课

广州市第六中学吕苏玲老师：张老师的设计主线 song time—video time—reading time—show time—poem time 立体、丰富而富有趣味性，"人间有真情"的大爱精神贯穿始终。每一个活动都围绕着这个单元的重点词汇、句型、语法来展开，学生非常自然流畅地达到了复习的效果呢！张老师处处都为学生搭建"脚手架"，让学生有例可循、有话可说、有话敢说。

好开心听到 Count on Me 这首歌，这是我们年级学生在英文歌手比赛中全级大合唱的歌曲，充满正能量；更高兴的是看到我的学生姜旭的作品出现在张老师的课堂上，big surprise!

谢谢张老师为我们带来这样一节示范引领课！

五中东晓学校初二1班英语科任李翠柳老师：张老师的课有以下优点：第一，本班学生基础一般，两头分化较大，有小部分学生英语基础相当薄弱，教师在教学活动的难度把握上有梯度，也能顾及到这批学生的接受能力。第二，与主题紧密关联的丰富的教学资源，如歌曲、视频、录音、诗歌等契合学生的年龄特点，与学生生活息息相关，很好地激发了学生的学习兴趣。第三，教师语言清晰准确，教态亲切自然，始终和颜悦色，营造了轻松愉快的课堂氛围，能与学生很好地互动，充分鼓励学生参与活动，给予学生积极及时的反馈，就连基础薄弱的学生也能积极举手回答问题。第四，教师能给学生搭建足够的"脚手架"，降低教学活动的难度。比如引导学生听读来自同龄学生的志愿服务计划为后面的活动"学生小组分享志愿服务计划"以及"评价优秀小组计划"提供了很好的范本，学生能踊跃参与活动，比较轻松地完成了任务。第五，教师真正做到以"以学生为主体"，为了给更多有参与欲望的孩子提供展现的机会，在后面时间较紧的情况下灵活调整教学计划，满足了更多学生的需求。

两点教学建议：板书设计可以使用不同颜色的笔，更有区分度；教学节奏可以前面稍微加快一些，后面能满足更多孩子的展示需求。

五中东晓学校英语科长杨旗老师：张老师用思维导图的形式，诠释了"Helping those in need"中的 those 指代谁，这也是学生输出的重要组成部分。这一思维导图的设计真是意外，令人惊喜和有所收获。在黑板右边，词汇银行板块书写了高频词 voluntary、volunteer，还标注了音标，有关计划的高频词汇 plan to do, offer to do, decide to do 词组，主题意义探究方面书写了 bring joy, peace and courage to people。张老师突出重点，展示精华，雁过留痕，是我们的学习榜样。

张老师全英组织教学，教学基本功扎实。她语气温婉、语速适中、气定神闲，娓娓道来，整个教学过程都轻松、自在，尤其是她不漏痕迹地表扬学生，相信学生，在学生需要帮助的时候走近学生，在刚好抽中班里最薄弱的一组学生展示分工安排的困境中，不是立马放弃这组学生，而是耐心引导学生、鼓励学生，帮助薄弱生顺利完成任务。这种爱生无痕的鼓励、有教无类的品质，真是令人折服。

广州市第 97 中学英语科长李锦云老师：真的非常欣赏和佩服教研员张老师，她有勇气且成功地给我们展示了一节好课。她提出新理念，引领新"潮流"（方向），带出新方法，体现了新课标所倡导的单元整体教学、"教—学—评"一体化的理念，致力培养学生英语学科素养，培养学生全人的发展。

从这节课，我清晰地看到：张老师是一个以学生为中心，善于观察、关注学生反应，擅于赞美、鼓励学生的好老师。面对着第一次见面的学生，且在学生整体英语水平不太高的情况下，张老师都出尽"法宝"地鼓励学生开口，向众人表现自己。见面打招呼的融冰阶段，张老师就对孩子们说"Miss Li Cuiliu（原英语老师）told me Class One are very friendly…I wish to make friends with you. I wish to share joy, courage and confidence with you… "。鼓励学生回答问题，张老师会说"I want to hear your lovely voice and beautiful words."。回应学生的回答，张老师会说"Good job. /Big hands. /Amazing. /Great. /I like this. / Similar. Big hands to her."。老师真正给学生播撒了甜蜜、快乐和勇敢的种子。

张老师对学生的反应真正诠释了什么是"要研究学情，以生为本"，这样的课才会有效，而且把学习变得有意义、可持续。因此，我非常能理解到课程的后面学生会踊跃举手要上台呈现小组的作品，以及下课后很主动跟第一次来授课的张老师合照的学生的心情。这是因为老师给予学生发自内心的力量和支持。

对这节课的思考：对于 Revision（复习），我觉得这节课达到了对教材主阅读篇章的词汇知识、本单元主题及意义、本单元语法（不定式）进行重现和复习的目标。但是对于张老师所设计的 Assessment（评价）这部分，我觉得自己还没有理解得很透彻，也期待张老师的进一步指导。

华海双语学校外教 Lukas：The overall structure is logical and cohesive. First, "Helping those in need" is an interesting and engaging topic. Second, the intro song is a good idea because it prompts the students that the lesson will be exciting and interesting. Third, the video is useful, it's informative and the students can begin to see the connection between the music and the message behind it. Fourth, in order to fulfill the lesson requirements, it's really worth spending time to clarify what an infinitive is and how it functions grammatically. Fifth, the activities for Dongxiao School are engaging. They help reinforce the connection between abstract and reality, and the lesson progresses coherently.

Personally, the poem idea is interesting and useful as it uses simple direct language which actually may be beneficial to the students at the beginning of the lesson, this will be an easy task for them to point out "helpful" topic related words and give them an idea what to expect from the lesson.

可见外教对课程结构的整体性、合理性、活动的关联性和效果都很肯定，这与《新课标》的理念不谋而合，也提出了具体的改进建议。

## 六、学生反馈

全班39人课后有28人写了关于英语课的日记，用英语写的有8篇，有20篇是用中文写的，下面分享5个学生的感想。

学生1：Reading Time 印象深。

学生2：小组展示赞。

学生3：会语法啦。

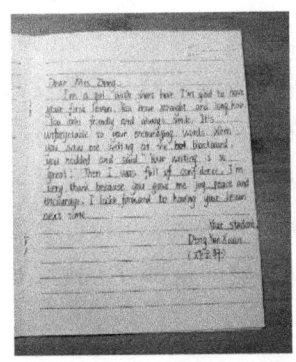

学生4：感受音乐和友谊的力量。歌曲真的令我印象深刻，MV中女孩和朋友玩乐时发自内心的开心的笑和愉悦有韵律的歌曲，看着听着，我的心情也轻松愉悦起来。有一句歌词我觉得它真的很美好，"You can count on me like 123. I'll be there. And I know when need it I can count on you like 432. And you'll be there."。因为在现在这个竞争强烈的社会中，每个人都在想着办法提升自我，而不是花更多时间去陪伴、关心朋友，去感受生活中的美好。

学生5：意犹未尽……

老师您好，我是来自初二一班的吴桐好，我曾在您的课上与另一位同学进行英语对话。上完您的课后，我受益匪浅。课堂不仅让我巩固了第一单元的知识，加深了印象，还令我学会了如何介绍志愿工作，对我的英语学习很有帮助。我对您的印象十分深刻，因为您上课风趣幽默，把生涩难懂的知识变得简单易懂，让人情不自禁地就沉浸在知识的海洋中。当我们小组有不会的单词时，您也耐心解答。下课后，我们都还意犹未尽，想再上一节。期待以后还能有机会上您的课！

## 七、教学反思

第一，收获。

（1）这是一节"零试讲"的既真实又朴实的课，师生第一次合作，但是基于对学生的学业水平和能力诊断，以及和学校科组老师的共同把脉，教师对学情分析精准到位。因而教学目标设定合理，直接指向学生的提升点，教师在真实情景中把单元核心知识与技能融入寓教于乐的主题活动。从课程录像中可以看到，全班39人，举手回答问题和在讲台合作展示的共有32人，教师把学生的积极性调动起来了，培养了学生合作精神的同时，还增强了学生的自信心、成就感和积极参与志愿活动的热情，目标达成度比较高。

（2）作为一名教研员，通过课例展示的方式研究、尝试和实践新课标理念，基于问题导向，以学业质量评价为支撑，实施精准的教学改进，提高了教学实效。更重要的是，研究过程促进教研员深入一线，更好地理解一线教师，更多地关爱学生，坚持下去，必将有助于在今后的工作中更好地指导老师践行《新课标》理念，切实指导区域的课堂教学改革。

（3）单元整体教学活动设计与实施是提升教学质量的抓手，也是老师们的困惑所在，所以很有吸引力；"聚焦新课标，共享深教研"的主题活动则创建了平等互动的多元研究氛围，发挥了研究共同体的优势，进一步明确了单元教学目标，明晰了教学主线，设计教学活动、开展教学实践，也激发了老师们研究的热情。在中心组老师带领下，本学期我们已经完成了八年级所有单元的整体教学设计，并且将其分享给了全区老师，从而加强了单元教学整体性、关联性、主题性，有效减轻了教师备课负担和学生的学习负担。

（4）本课例将"教—学—评"一体化贯穿始终，关注学生的兴趣、需求和能力水平，教师及时进行表现性评价并且鼓励学生尝试了相互评价。一方面使用主题链的形式、多模态的语篇和听说读看写多种活动开展单元核心单词、短语、语法应用的复习，将这些零散的语言知识串联在一系列真实的语境中进行复现，学生易于理解，印象深刻，提升了复习效果；同时，引导学生思考要帮助的 those 不仅仅是人（朋友、儿童、老人、病人），还可以是动物、社区、大自然，甚至整个世界。最后有三组学生分享了志愿服务计划，并且选出了最佳志愿小组，还有学生意犹未尽，跃跃欲试，实现了积极参与志愿活动的育人目标。从学生提交的 28 份感想中发现，歌曲打动了孩子们的心，本课给他们留下了深刻的印象，他们很开心参与其中，学到了知识和技能，希望老师有机会再给他们上课。这是对课程和老师最朴实动人的评价，一张张灿烂的笑脸，都是教育温暖的阳光照耀下开出的花朵。

（5）一节课能够解决的问题毕竟很有限，学生的语言生成也非常简单。但正因为课堂真实，所以更触发了老师们对薄弱学校，特别是学困生的广泛关注。听课的老师们关注到了学生的能力水平；关注到了单词不会读、自信心不足的学生如何在老师的鼓励下登台展示；关注到了从语言信息输入到最后呈现完整的语篇，这个过程中学生的学习到底是如何真实发生的；关注到教研员教学理念的不同……听课老师结合自己的教学实践，生成了很多新思想，特别是"Helping those in need"实际上也包括需要帮助的学生！实现教育均衡也是"双减"的治本之策！这是展示课例最大的意义所在：当老师认真关注学生的学习，就会认真考虑学生未来的发展！老师们在百忙之中写下了 30 多篇评课感想，每一句都是真情实感，融入了对《新课标》的理解、对课例的感悟以及对教育和学生的热爱。老师们如此用心记录,并提出了宝贵的建议,这个"课例"就变得立体起来了,这一课堂的光阴就因此凝固在课例中并留存下来,成为生命中美好的记忆。"水尝无华,相荡乃成涟漪;石本无火,相击而发灵光。"相信播下美好希望,必能收获累累硕果。

第二,教学改进。

(1) 教师主导的部分还是比较多,学生自由探讨和展示的机会被压缩。

(2) 小组开展评价之前,教师先示范评价,教会学生评价方法,课后重点关注作业完成情况并给予个性化评价,给学生关爱、信任和鼓励,体现评价的发展性。

# 第四章　广州市海珠区与湖南省新化县区校联动教研*

## 课例四　运用要素分析和 TEAM 框架突破高考英语读后续写写作课**

### 一、读后续写考察能力分析

基于《普通高中英语课程标准（2017年版2020年修订）》对学业质量水平二级的要求，读后续写考察能力包括：

| | | 考查的认知能力 |
|---|---|---|
| 读后续写 | 阅读能力 | 能理解原文内容；<br>能准确理解原文的篇章结构和关键信息；<br>能深入理解原文的内容要素、内容发展、逻辑关系、语言特点等。 |
| | 写作能力 | 1. 内容产出<br>● 能在原文基础上创造新的内容。<br>● 能与原文内容保持融洽、形成有效协同。<br>2. 语言运用<br>● 能使用丰富的词汇和句子结构并且使用准确、恰当。<br>● 与原文的词汇和句子结构甚至语言风格协同（较高要求）。<br>3. 篇章结构<br>● 能与原文合理衔接。<br>● 能使用恰当的连接手段使续写完整、连贯。 |
| | 思维能力 | 能在根据原文进行续写时体现出创造性。 |
| | 学习能力 | 能通过读后续写学习原文作者的语言特点和写作方式。 |

---

\* 教研指导：广州市海珠区教育发展研究院张志梅。
\*\* 执教：湖南省新化县第二中学张梅花；点评：广州市海珠区教育发展研究院张志梅。

## 二、读后续写的选材原则

### 1. 语篇适当原则

语篇适当原则指语篇长度必须符合高考英语的考查要求，既不能过分冗长，也不能非常简约，词数不够。按照目前高考读后续写语篇长度，以 350 字以内为宜。

### 2. 主题适当原则

主题适当原则是指读后续写的命题应通过各种情节起伏凸显积极向上的主题，从而达到启迪学生、培养学生积极进取的世界观、人生观和价值观的目标。

### 3. 语言适当原则

语言适当原则是指高考英语读后续写题所选用语篇的语言应符合各地区高中学生的实际语言水平。词汇、句式等的难度既不能远远超过学生的实际掌握水平，也不能过分降低考查难度，以致难以反映学生的实际语言水平。

## 三、学情分析

本课的教学对象是高二学生，学生在语言知识方面有一定的基础，他们的认知能力有了进一步的发展，也具备一定的获取信息的能力和写作能力，但是对于读后续写的方法策略还比较模糊，特别是如何准确把握阅读文本的关键信息和语言特点的能力，所续写的短文要具有较丰富的内容，包含详细和生动的情景、态度和情感描写等方面有待提高。

## 四、教学内容分析

（2022 广东省模拟题）阅读下面材料，根据其内容和所给段落开头语续写两段，使之构成一篇完整的短文。

I was sitting at my desk surrounded by New Year gifts, feeling happy that I had managed to buy some hard-to-find items. These were for Kids Need More, a charitable organization offering services to socially <u>disadvantaged</u> children. One of its most popular events is the Holiday Cheer Bus. The organization always fills the buses with donated gifts for the families on the Cheer Bus routes. Each bus is <u>manned</u> by a team of volunteers. My family had been volunteers for years. I had a list of the families on our route.

Just as I was packing up the items with my husband and my son, I received a call from the director of the organization. She asked if I could add a family to my route — here was a young mother, Leanne, and her son.

I called Leanne and told her that a Holiday Cheer Bus would be visiting her family. Leanne seemed really excited and began to cry. I comforted her, "The Holiday Cheer Bus is really going to come. Is there something special that your child would like?" "My son is three. All he wants is a pair of Spider-Man snow boots so that he can play outside in the snow."

I asked about her son's shoe size. She told me the size and I promised I would have Spider-Man snow boots in size 9 for her son.

After I said goodbye and ended the call, panic set in. It was two days before the Holiday Cheer Bus was going on its run, less than a week before New Year. I was going to need a holiday miracle to find Spider-Man snow boots in size 9.

"We have to go shopping!" I called out to my husband and son. They were surprised but still we set off. We went to a few department stores and the shoe departments, without success. We were tired and hungry. We were becoming disheartened. My son suggested giving Leanne a gift card so she could get the boots herself. But I didn't want to give up. I promised we would bring boots.

注意：

1. 续写词数应为 150 左右；
2. 请按如下格式在答题卡的相应位置作答。

At our final stop, expecting defeat, we entered the shoe department. _____

Two days later, we arrived at the young mom's home. _____

"我"和丈夫、儿子在一家慈善组织 Holiday Cheer Bus 做志愿者多年，给那些弱势群体的孩子送上新年礼物。有一个年轻的母亲希望得到组织的帮助，为她三岁的孩子准备一双9码的蜘蛛侠雪地靴作为新年礼物。离新年还有不到一星期了，"我"去过很多商店寻找这特别的雪地靴但都没有找到。

原文材料为记叙文，主题语境属于"人与自我/社会"，是关注做人与做事、社会服务与人际沟通的题材。故事以第一人称视角进行叙述，代入感更强。情节环环相扣，衔接流畅。文本语料地道，语言平实，冷僻词少，但注重对人物动作、心理、环境等方面的描写，颇具感染力。

## 五、教学目标

（1）通过梳理原文五要素，即 Who、When、Where、How、What 来确定文章的主题大意，了解原文中的人物、时间、地点、主要人物的情感变化等。

（2）通过运用操作性强的"TEAMS"框架来完成续写，可以写出与原文衔接合理、语意连贯、逻辑相符的续文。T 指 Transitional sentence（衔接句）或 Theme（主题句）；E 指 Emotion or Environment（心理描写/环境描写）；A 指 Action（动作）；M 指 Monologue or Conversation（独白/对话）；其中，Emotion or Environment、Action、Monologue or Conversation 的写作顺序和次数可根据故事情节的需要作适当调整。

（3）运用 Assess your progress 进行自评和互评。

（4）提高学生助人为乐、服务他人和社会的意识。

## 六、教学过程

在读的阶段，引导学生关注故事的五个要素，理清原文主旨大意；

在写的阶段，提供"TEAMS"写作框架，让学生聚焦"TEAMS"的具体内容完成写作任务；

在评的阶段，引导学生关注语言改进、编辑、互评、分享、教师反馈等。

| 教学环节及时长 | 教学活动 | | 设计意图 |
| --- | --- | --- | --- |
| | 教师 | 学生 | |
| Leading-in（3 mins） | 询问学生收到礼物的经历。Have you ever received any valuable gifts? How did you feel back then? 老师把学生收到的礼物和感受板书。 | Brainstorm descriptive expressions. | 元认知策略：有意识地积累生活中所使用的英语；认知策略：在新旧语言知识之间建立有机联系；情感策略：主动参加学习和运用语言的实践活动。 |

续上表

| 教学环节及时长 | 教学活动 | | 设计意图 |
|---|---|---|---|
| | 教师 | 学生 | |
| 1st Reading<br>(3 mins) | Ask Ss to read one paragraph after another emotionally, and ask them to vote the best reader. | Students raise their hands to read the paragraphs one by one. Students choose the best reader. | 认知策略：通过有感情地朗读理解篇章大意；通过扫读获取篇章具体信息；通过比较、分析和评价等手段，评出最好的朗读者。<br>情感策略：主动参加学习和运用语言的实践活动。 |
| 2nd Reading<br>(5 mins) | Give students the structure of story and ask them to complete it. | In 3 groups, discuss the story reasonably, then fill in the blanks on the worksheet and share with the class later. The group leader report in class. | 认知策略：<br>1. 通过扫读获取篇章具体信息；利用图表收集、整理信息，并预测篇章的主要内容。<br>2. 根据主题表达的需要填出主要信息；小组长组织基本信息向全班汇报。<br>情感策略：培养自主学习和合作学习的能力。 |
| Writing<br>(18 mins) | 1. Provide students TEAM strategies.<br>2. Encourage students to use these strategies in writing. | In 6 groups, students discuss and finish writing. Share the answers on the blackboard and peer evaluate if they are reasonable. | 元认知策略：评价和反思认知策略的学习和使用，总结经验，并根据需要进行调整。<br>认知策略：利用构思、谋篇布局、起草、修改等手段创建和完善文本。<br>情感策略：主动参加学习和运用语言的实践活动。有自主学习和合作学习的能力。 |

续上表

| 教学环节及时长 | 教学活动 | | 设计意图 |
|---|---|---|---|
| | 教师 | 学生 | |
| Summary, assessment and homework (4 mins) | Summarize the strengths and weaknesses of Students' extended writing. | Students sum up, self-assess, and peer assess their learning. Homework: Rewrite the two continued paragraphs on the exercise book creatively. | 元认知策略：完成理解表达任务后，反思、评价和巩固所使用的有效理解和表达的策略，提高学习效率。 |

## 七、板书设计

故事的五要素：Who, When, Where, How, What。

"TEAMS" 写作框架：

T 指 Transitional sentence（衔接句）或 Theme（主题句）；

E 指 Emotion or Environment（心理描写/环境描写）；

A 指 Action（动作）；

M 指 Monologue or Conversation（独白/对话）；

S 指 Style（风格）。

## 八、评估

| 项目 | 评价标准 | 自我评价 | 同伴评价 | 教师评价 |
|---|---|---|---|---|
| I know the five elements of the story. | A. Excellent.<br>B. Good.<br>C. So-So. | | | |
| I can use "TEAMS" strategies. | A. Excellent.<br>B. Good.<br>C. So-So. | | | |
| I want to use "TEAMS" strategies later. | Yes.<br>No. | | | |

Moral Lesson: The roses in her hand, the flavor in mine. 赠人玫瑰，手有余香。

## 九、教学点评

　　教师通过对读后续写题的考查能力、选材原则进行分析，尝试运用操作性强的"TEAMS"框架帮助学生准确把握阅读文本的关键信息和语言特点，有针对性地渗透元认知策略、认知策略和情感策略，帮助学生丰富所续写的短文内容，培养学生正确的态度和积极的价值观。学生参与面广，不同层次的学生有不同收获，教学效果良好。建议进一步对学生的作文进行个性化的讲评，深化写作技能。

# 第五章　广州市海珠区初三英语教研
## ——中考备考专题

**课例五**　课标话题之 Topic 16 Entertainment and Sports 听说课*

## 一、教学背景

活动对象：广州市海珠区全体初三英语老师和广州市景中实验中学初三学生。

活动形式：中考听说考试备考与课标话题视听说教学。

时间：2016 年 4 月 21 日。

地点：广州市景中实验中学。

## 二、教学目标

（1）To open mouths bravely, use English actively, enjoy communication and share positive energy.

（2）To read the words correctly with the help of English phonetics.

（3）To use general questions and special questions to ask classmates or teachers for information about the movie.

（4）To report the information with the help of characters' profile.

（5）To read the theme song correctly and emotionally.

（6）To rethink the learning objectives, evaluate and share with classmates.

---

\*　执教：广州市海珠区教育发展中心张志梅；点评：广州市景中实验中学谢素娟。

## 三、教学过程

Activity I Class Game（全班游戏）

Game Rules：

■ Watch a movie and listen to its introduction.

■ Don't sit down until you hear the word on your small paper.

■ The students will be chosen to read aloud the following phonetics and words.

Ex. 1 Read aloud and spell the words.

1)【ˈhjuːmənz】_____  2)【ˈmɔːdən】_____

3)【ˈsivəlaɪzd】civilized  4)【ˈænɪməl】_____

5)【fiːt】_____  6)【ˈkləʊðɪŋ】_____

7)【tekˈnɒlədʒi】_____  8)【ˈenɪmiz】_____

9)【zuːˈtəʊpiə】Zootopia  10)【ˈəʊlɑː】Ou La (Spanish)

Activity II  Question freely（自由提问）

Ex. 2 Please ask Rainbow a general or special question about the movie, listen to your classmates, note down interesting questions and collect them in the question bank.（请准备1个一般疑问句或者1个特殊疑问句向Rainbow提问，听同学提问，记下有趣的问题并且收藏在问题库里。）

**Question Bank 1**

| General Questions | Special Questions |
| --- | --- |
| e. g. Do you like animals? | e. g. What is your favourite animal? |
| 1. Do/Did you…? | 1. Who/Whom/Whose…? |
| 2. Are/Were you…? | 2. What/Which…? |
| 3. Will /Would you…? | 3. When/Where/Why…? |
| 4. Can/Could you…? | 4. How…? |
| 5. Have/Had you…? | 5. How old/many/much/long/wide/tall/high/big…? |
| 6. Must/May/Should you…? | 6. How often/soon/far…? |

Warm Tips：读一般疑问句用升调，特殊疑问句用降调。回答问题一般使用降调，但是当需要表达惊讶、高兴等感情时也可以用升调。

Activity Ⅲ  Go close to the main characters

Ex. 3  Talk about the characters, make conversations or report using the information.

### Judy's Profile (档案)

| 1 | Animal Name | rabbit/bunny |
|---|---|---|
| | Appearance | round face, purple eyes, long ears, small mouth, grey fur… |
| | Family | Parents' job: grow carrots |
| | Hobbies | explore adventures, detect cases |
| | Dream | a policewoman |
| | Character | easy-going, honest, brave, smart, emotional… |

### Nick's Profile (档案)

| 2 | Animal Name | fox |
|---|---|---|
| | Appearance | short face, bright eyes, sharp ears, big mouth, red fur… |
| | Family | make bad popsicle (冰棒) |
| | Hobbies | hustle (诈骗) others, help Judy find out the truth… |
| | Dream | Judy's husband |
| | Character | foxy (狡猾的), proud, skillful, helpful, wise, gentle… |

### Flash's Profile (档案)

| 3 | Animal Name | sloth (树獭) |
|---|---|---|
| | Appearance | round face, big eyes, long nose, small mouth, brown fur… |
| | Family | live in jungles (丛林), sleep on trees |
| | Hobbies | like joyride (开快车, 兜风), chat with girl friend, show off cool (炫酷) … |
| | Job | officer of DMV (车管所) |
| | Character | very slow, polite, friendly, funny, cute… |

Question Bank 2

| Items（项目） | Questions | Answers |
|---|---|---|
| Name | What's…name? | |
| Appearance | What do/does…look like? How tall/heavy…? | |
| Family | What's…job? What do/does…do? | |
| Hobbies | What do/does…like? How often do you go to cinema? What's your favourite sport/movie/music/food/color/book/novel…? | |
| Dream | What's…dream/ambition? | |
| Character | What kind of person is he? Outgoing/polite/helpful/funny/humorous/brave/honest/kind/energetic… | |

You may begin with a conversation like：

Rainbow：Hello, Bob. What's the name of the animal?

Bob：Bunny.

Rainbow：What does it look like?

Bob：It has a round face….

You may begin with a report like：

Hello, everyone. I'd like to tell you something about my favourite character, Judy. She….

Ex. 4 Watch your classmates' performance and evaluate it with the help of the form. Either English or Chinese is OK. 观看同学的表演，按照评价表进行点评。中英文点评都可以。

| Performers | Shining Points（闪光点） | Tips（建议） |
|---|---|---|
| Pair 1 | | |
| Pair 2 | | |
| Reporter 1 | | |
| Reporter 2 | | |

Activity Ⅳ Enjoy the theme song

Ex. 5 Listen to the song, fill in the blanks and read the lyrics aloud in groups of 4.

Tips：When reading, please pay attention to the speed（语速），linking（连读），stress（重音），intonation（语调）and pauses（停顿）.

I messed up tonight, I lost a _____ (1) fight. 今夜我搞砸了 又一次落败

I still mess up but I'll just start again. 深陷困境但我依然会重新开始

I keep falling down, I keep on hitting the g _____ (2). 我总是失败 总是跌倒

I always get up now to see what's next. 而我总能重新站起 迎接崭新的未来

Birds don't just fly, they fall down and get up. 鸟儿无法振翅高飞 跌落天际却重新展翅

N _____ (3) learns without getting it won. 不经历失败怎会懂成功的喜悦

I won't give up, no I won't give in. 我绝不会屈服 绝不会放弃

Till I reach the end and then I'll s _____ (4) again. 直到我抵达终点 我会重新出发

No I won't leave, I wanna try everything. 不 我不会放弃 我只想竭尽全力

I wanna try even though I could fail. 即便我注定失败我也想要竭尽全力

I won't give up, no I won't give in. 我绝不会屈服 绝不会放弃

Till I r _____ (5) the end and then I'll start again. 直到我抵达终点 我会重新出发

No. I won't leave, I wanna try everything. 不 我不会放弃 我只想竭尽全力

I wanna try even though I could fail. 即便我注定失败我也想要竭尽全力

Try everything 竭尽全力

Look at how far you've come. 坚持了多久

You filled your h _____ (6) with love. 看看满怀着爱的你

Baby you've done enough that cut your breath. 你已经受够了白费力气

Don't beat yourself up, don't need to run so f _____ (7). 请不要自暴自弃 也不必太快抽离

Sometimes we come last but we did our best. 有时我们终能实现梦想只要我们竭尽全力

I won't give up, no I won't give in. 我绝不会屈服 绝不会放弃

Till I reach the end and then I'll start again. 直到我抵达终点 我会重新出发

No I won't leave, I wanna try e _____ (8). 不 我不会放弃 我只想竭尽全力

I wanna try even though I could fail. 即便我注定失败我也想要竭尽全力

I won't give up, no I won't give in. 我绝不会屈服 绝不会放弃

Till I reach the end and then I'll start again. 直到我抵达终点 我会重新出发

No I won't leave, I wanna try everything. 不 我不会放弃 我只想竭尽全力

I wanna try even though I could fail. 即便我注定失败我也想要竭尽全力

I'll keep on m_____ (9) those new mistakes. 我也会固执地坚持犯错

I'll keep on making them every day. 每一天都不会放弃

T_____ (10) new mistakes. 固执地坚持犯错

Try everything. 竭尽全力

Ex. 6 Watch your classmates' performance and evaluate it with the help of the form. Either English or Chinese is OK. 观看同学的表演，按照评价表进行点评。中英文点评都可以。

| Performers | Shining Points（闪光点） | Tips（建议） |
|---|---|---|
| Group 1 | | |
| Group 2 | | |
| Group 3 | | |

Activity Ⅳ Rethink and improve（反思与提高）

Ex. 7 Rethink the learning objectives and share with your classmates what you have learned in this class. 反思本节课的学习目标并与同学分享你所得到的收获。中英文都可以。

| Learning Objectives<br>（学习目标） | You have achieved<br>（收获） | You need to do<br>（努力方向） |
|---|---|---|
| 1. I am able to open mouth bravely, use English actively, enjoy making heartwarming communication, share positive energy. 大胆开口说，积极用英语做事情，享受真心的交流，分享正能量。 | | |
| 2. I am able to read the words correctly with the help of English phonetics. 能够借助音标正确地朗读单词。 | | |

续上表

| Learning Objectives（学习目标） | You have achieved（收获） | You need to do（努力方向） |
| --- | --- | --- |
| 3. I am able to use general questions and special questions to ask for information. 能使用一般疑问句和特殊疑问句询问信息。 | | |
| 4. I am able to report the information with the help of characters' profile. 能使用电影角色的档案转述信息。 | | |
| 5. I am able to read the theme song correctly and emotionally. 能够正确地有感情地朗读主题曲。 | | |
| 6. I am able to rethink the learning objectives, evaluate and share with classmates. 反思评价学习目标并与同学分享。 | | |
| 7. 其他体会：confident/interested/happy/enjoyable… | | |

Homework：Introduce your idol in 1-4 paragraphs. 用1～4段话介绍你的偶像。

| | |
| --- | --- |
| Para. 1 | Describe her/him<br>Who…?<br>Where…born?<br>How old/tall/heavy…?<br>What does…look like? |
| Para. 2 | Family and home<br>Where does…live?<br>How many people…<br>What does…do?<br>What pets… |
| Para. 3 | School or work<br>Where is…school/company?<br>What is it like?<br>What's…dream? |
| Para. 4 | Hobbies and characters<br>What are…hobbies?<br>What kind of person is he/she? |

## 四、教学点评

《疯狂动物城》是一部非常受学生欢迎的英语动画电影，张老师将这样的资源引入到课堂教学中，为学生提供了一个有趣、互动和有效的学习环境，而且巧妙地把中考听说考试的技能融入寓教于乐的活动中。电影片段为英文原声，学生通过聆听和理解这些内容来锻炼自己的听力技巧。同时，通过观看电影中的场景和动作，学生也进一步培养了视觉感知能力。观看电影后，学生通过游戏、自由提问等复述电影的剧情，自然复习了中考听说考试的询问信息题型。与同学讨论自己喜欢的角色，并且使用思维导图介绍自己的偶像等活动，既可以锻炼他们的信息转述能力和口语表达能力，又能提高他们在使用英语时的流利度和准确性。通过主题曲填词的活动，一方面复习了课标里的话题词汇，另一方面学生通过跟唱主题曲完善了他们的发音和语调，激发了学生的学习兴趣和积极性，也给即将中考的学生鼓舞士气，起到了情感的激励作用。美中不足的是，参与的学生有200多人，会议室比较拥挤，给小组活动的开展带来了不便，导致部分学生的发言听不到。

# 第六章　广州市海珠区区校联动教研

## 课例六　广州版初中英语 Success with English Book 6A Unit 5 It's Film Week *Harry Potter* 电影欣赏课*

## 一、教材分析

**教材依据**：广州版初中英语 Success with English Book 6A Unit 5 It's Film Week

**教学内容**：Unit 12 Art & Literature

### PRE-READING

Discuss these questions with your partner.

(1) Have you read any of the *Harry Potter* books or watched the films?

(2) Harry Potter has magical powers. Do you know of any other heroes who have strange powers?

(3) Do you like to watch magic tricks? Have you ever tried doing a magic trick?

### READING

### HARRY POTTER

Welcome to the world of J K Rowling! It is a world of magic and wonders, a world where anything can happen. Many of the creatures in Rowling's world are not real, and much of what happens is strange. J K Rowling has written a series of books about Harry Potter, a boy with a scar on his forehead and a secret past. The books are about magic and strange creatures, but they still tell us something about the real world.

---

\* 执教：广州市第五中学张志梅；点评：广州市育才中学蔡雯莹。本课例被广东省教育厅教研室采纳，收入广东省义务教育新课程实验研修手册《初中新课程英语优秀教学设计与案例——文化意识》(ISBN 7-5361-3294-8，广东高等教育出版社2006年版)。

In the first book about Harry Potter, we meet Harry before he knows anything about magic. Harry seems like a normal boy, but his life is miserable. His parents are dead and he lives with a family that treat him badly. Harry is very unhappy and does not know what to do about his life. His life changes when a bird tells him to go to Hogwarts and become a student of witchcraft and wizardry.

Hogwarts is an unusual school where the students learn about magic. But for Harry, the most important lesson is about real life, friendship and how to be brave. Harry learns more than magic at Hogwarts. He makes new friends and learns how important and difficult it is to be a good friend. His friends help him when he is in trouble, but he must also be strong and help them when they need him. Harry also learns to be brave and to do things he used to be afraid of. He learns the truth about his past, a dark secret that will make his life and his choices more difficult. At Hogwarts, Harry also learns about the power of love. The magic, many strange creatures and the adventures Harry comes across at Hogwarts help him understand the real world.

Harry has to fight against bad wizards and do the right things. Together with his friends, Harry learns that it is not always easy to do what is right. You must believe in what you do and who you are if you want to succeed in the world—the magical world of Hogwarts and the real world. Where someone is born and what a person looks like is not as important as what he or she grows up to be. Two people may speak different languages, have different habits or even come from two different worlds, but they can still be friends if they share the same goals, hopes and dreams. It is not enough to be strong in heart and mind; we must also believe in ourselves and help others if we want to be happy and live a good life.

## POST-READING

EX. 1 Answer the questions below:
(1) Why is Harry's life miserable before he goes to Hogwarts?
(2) What does Harry learn about himself at Hogwarts?
(3) Why does Rowling use strange creatures in her books?
(4) Do you think that we can learn about the real world by reading novels?

EX. 2 The sentences below summarize the article. Read them and decide if they are true or false. Write the letter "T" if the sentence is true. Write "F" if it is false, and then correct the error and give the right information.

(1) Harry Potter is a world-famous writer.
(2) Harry Potter was born in a rich family.
(3) Harry Potter is a boy with a scar on his forehead.
(4) Harry Potter goes to an ordinary school.
(5) Harry Potter learns a lot about the real world at Hogwarts.
(6) Harry Potter discovers that it is easy to do the right thing.

## 二、教材处理

本单元的中心话题是"艺术与文学",具体涉及绘画、电影戏剧、音乐会、小说等内容,语言知识教学和语言技能训练都是围绕这些话题展开的。在本节阅读课前,学生通过从 Warming up、Listening 到 Speaking 课程的学习已经积累了与电影有关的词汇和句型,对定语从句及情态动词等的用法也进行了分析和归纳。为了进一步指导学生在不同语境中正确、恰当地使用语言表达方式和进行人文教育,本课将电影欣赏与单元教学内容有机整合,通过制定电影院规则复习情态动词,通过文化背景介绍练习定语从句的使用,通过欣赏 Harry Potter 剧本片断呈现课文内容,同时根据学生的认知水平对教材中阅读前和阅读后的问题进行了调整和补充。例如,考虑到学生对 Harry Potter 已有一定了解,把 Post-reading 中的第二题放在观看影片前,把其余的问题穿插在观看影片中。通过问题讨论、故事内容概括、听力理解、影片评论、现场采访等形式讲授英语视、听、说、读、写的技巧和电影文化知识,以及电影艺术审美的要领,从而帮助学生将看到的电影内容进行提炼和提升,理解课文的深层含义——从 Harry Potter 身上学会如何面对困难、坚定信念,最终战胜困难。

## 三、教学原则

本节课使用到的教学原则有整合原则、为交际服务原则、通过多样化手段导入文化内容原则、人性教育原则、比较教育原则、人文关怀原则、弘扬民族文化原则。

## 四、教学分析

My students are about 14 or 15 years of age. They have the advantage of being great mimics, are often energetic and are usually prepared to enjoy the activities the teacher has prepared for them. On the other hand, they will not respond well to an activity that they perceive as childish, or well below their intellectual level. They are easily lose confidence in the face of difficulties. Therefore the teaching activities should be within their abilities and developmental stage but at the same time sufficiently stimulating for them to feel satisfied with their work.

The theoretical basis guiding this teaching design is the theory of task-based teaching. By full use of a multiple-media computer, I set up varied scenes to involve my students in lively and interesting situations and activate the teaching content. I assign students different tasks at different stages so they can acquire and learn English by meaningful and communicative activities. In the long run, I hope what I teach today will have something to do with cultivating students cultural sense, promoting students' consciousness of being the subjects of life, and enhancing their all-round qualities.

## 五、教学目标

1. **Linguistic**

(1) New words and expressions.

e. g. wonder, miserable, magic and trick, a series of, come across, believe, believe in…

(2) Grammar.

Review the modal verbs, the restrictive and non-restrictive attributive clause, the past tense and the conjunction *if*.

(3) To have a good understanding of the film: a. To comprehend dialogue, narrative; b. To comprehend the actors, actresses, including their gestures and body language; c. To comprehend the image.

(4) To improve the students' abilities of listening, speaking, reading and writing.

(5) Creative use of English language.

2. **Cultural**

(1) To develop a sense of culture, to enjoy the film, to give the students a chance to relax.

(2) To understand foreign people, their customs and behaviours, values and beliefs, hopes and dreams, loves and hates, ways of thinking and daily activities.

(3) To develop our Chinese traditional virtue.

(4) To encourage co-operation between the students.

(5) To instruct them to realize the real world in a suitable way.

(6) To develop their ability of appreciating art and literature.

(7) To learn English and culture, as one global entity thus cope with the opportunities and challenges.

(8) To improve the students' understanding and aesthetic judgement of motion pictures thus enhancing their enjoyment.

## 六、教学活动

| Pre-task One | Making rules for the cinema |
|---|---|
| Task One | Meet the writer & the child actors |
| Task Two | Film appreciation |
| Task Three | Interview the audiences |
| Task Four | Internet assessment |

## 七、教学评价

### Assessment Criteria

Name: _____    Date: _____    Grade: _____

| 活动项目 | 评价方式 | 评价标准 | 得分 |
|---|---|---|---|
| Pre-task One<br>Making rules for the cinema | Group-assessment | 1. Can he/she apply modal verbs in the real situation?<br>2. Does he/she know how to behave in public? | |
| Task One<br>Meet the writer & the child actors | Self-assessment | 1. I understand some cultural background knowledge of the film, including the writer/director/actors/actress…<br>2. I can use attributive clauses to describe a person or a thing. | |
| Task Two<br>Film appreciation | Self-assessment | I am interested in the film.<br>I comprehend the dialogue, narrative, image and the theme.<br>I can use the past tense to retell the story.<br>I state my opinion clearly. | |

续上表

| 活动项目 | 评价方式 | 评价标准 | 得分 |
|---|---|---|---|
| Task Three<br>Interview the audiences | Peer-assessment | Does he/she cooperate with others?<br>Does he/she speak & act properly?<br>Does he listen to others carefully? | |
| Task Four<br>Internet assessment | Teacher-assessment | 1. He/She finishes the form clearly and completely. | |
| 合计得分 | | | |

说明：1. 每个选项得分值分别为：4（Excellent）、3（Good）、2（So-so）、1（Need improvement）

2. 总分36～48（Excellent）、24～35（Good）、12～23（So-so）、≤12（Need improvement）

## 八、教学评析

Step 1 Pre-task One

| Making rules for the cinema | | |
|---|---|---|
| Teacher's Activities | Students Activities | Purposes |
| To create a real situation for the students to use modal verbs. | To work in groups and work out rules by using modal verbs. To report the rules in class. | To apply modal verbs in the real situation.<br>To think about behavior in public places. |

In class：

Teacher：We have talked a lot about films. Do you want to watch a real English film?

Students：Yes.

Teacher：Ok, I promise you. But before we watch the film, I'd like to ask you to make your own rules for the cinema so that you will behave yourselves. I hope you'll work in groups and work out your rules by using modal verbs. For example, you can say, we should keep quiet in the cinema and so on. After two minutes, you'll report your own rules in class. Are you clear?

Students: Yes.

(*The students are eager to finish the task in order to watch the mysterious film. They make many useful rules. E. g. We mustn't spit/shout/fight/push...; We must keep the cinema clean/tidy...; We may eat candies; We needn't wear uniforms and so on. This activity keep the children interested and excited.*)

Step 2 Task One

| Meet the writer & the child actors | | |
| --- | --- | --- |
| Teacher's Activities | Students' Activities | Purposes |
| Offer a multiple-media computer to the students. | Introduce the writer—J. K. Rowling, the child actors and actresses. Play a piece of light music. | To understand the cultural background knowledge of the film. To use attributive clauses to describe a person/thing... |

In class:

The students are very happy to see the lively pictures and hear the music.

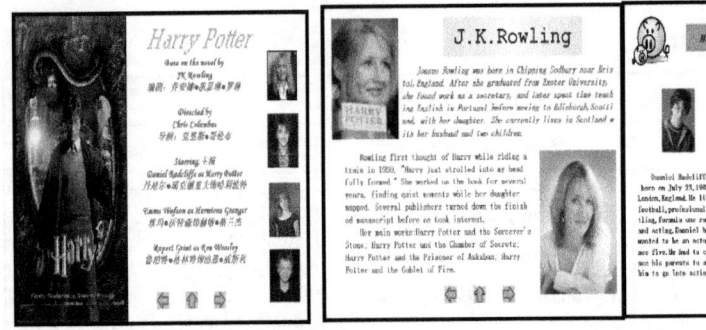

Step 3 Task Two

| Film appreciation | | | |
| --- | --- | --- | --- |
| Steps | Teacher's Activities | Students' Activities | Purposes |
| Judge Watch & Answer | a. Show T-F exercises. b. Play 1st part of the film. c. Ask the students to think and compare. | a. Watch the film carefully. b. Finish the exercises. | To give students confidence. To comprehend the dialogue, narrative. To keep up the Chinese traditional moral excellence. |

续上表

| Steps | Teacher's Activities | Students' Activities | Purposes |
|---|---|---|---|
| Watch Ask & Answer | a. Show the students Wh-questions.<br>b. Play Part 2 & 3 of the film.<br>C. Help the students in need. | Read the questions before watching.<br>Ask and answer the questions in pairs.<br>Ask the teacher questions.<br>Discuss the difficult questions. | To comprehend the image.<br>To get a deeper understanding of the film.<br>To understand the real world in a suitable way. |
| Listen Retell & Discuss | a. Show the students pictures and the prompt.<br>b. Play the tape to let the students listen to the brief story of *Harry Potter*.<br>c. Encourage the students to think and speak. | Listen to the tape.<br>Retell the whole story according to the pictures and the prompt.<br>Finish the short passage.<br>Discuss the theme of the film. | To use the new words and expressions in the right situation.<br>To get a full understanding of the film.<br>To use the past tense & the conjunction *if*.<br>To comprehend the theme of the film.<br>e. To improve the students' understanding and aesthetic judgment of motion pictures thus enhancing their enjoyment. |

In class:

The teacher shows the three parts of the film one by one and helps the students to understand each part of the film. The students are very excited to see the lively motion pictures. They are eager to ask and answer questions. It is surprising they absorb unconsciously very much.

Part 1: Harry Potter's childhood

Teacher: J. K. Rowling has written a series of books about Harry Potter. E. g. *Harry Potter and the Sorcerer's Stone*, *Harry Potter and the Ghamber of Secrets*, *Harry Potter and the Prisoner of Azkaban*, *Harry Potter and the Goblet of fire*. So a series of books means a lot of books in order about the same people or topic. Can you guess the meaning of "series"?

Teacher: Now we are going to watch *Harry Potter and the Sorcerer's Stone*. Have you ever read the book or seen the film?

Students: Some students say "yes", while some of them say "no".

Teacher: Ok, before I play the film, I'd like to test how much have you learned about Harry Potter. Please decide if these statements are "yes" or "no".

a. Harry Potter is a world-famous writer.

b. Harry Potter was born in a rich family.

c. Harry Potter is a boy with a scar on his forehead.

d. Harry Potter goes to an ordinary school.

e. Harry Potter learns a lot about the real world at Hogwarts.

f. Harry Potter discovers that it is easy to do the right thing.

(*These questions are easy. The students are very confident and vie with each other in answering.*)

Teacher: Excellent. Now please watch the first part of the film carefully and try to hear every word clearly. Later I will ask you questions in detail, Ok?

Students: Ok.

(*The teacher plays the film for the students.*)

Teacher: How many people does Harry Potter live with? Who are they?

Students: Three. They are Harry Potter's uncle, aunt, and cousin.

Teacher: What is the name of Harry's cousin?

Students: Dudley.

Teacher: What does Dudley say and do to Harry?

Students: He says, "Who wants to make friends with you?" Then he hits Harry.

Teacher: Why is Harry's life miserable or terrible?

Students: Because his parents are dead and his uncle's family treats him badly.

Teacher: Good.

Part 2: Hogwarts School & magic

(*In this part, the teacher shows some questions to the students before watching the film. Then they ask and answer the questions in pairs.*)

Student 1: What have you seen?

Student 2: A cage, a man and a building.

Student 3: What's in the cage?

Student 4: Some strange animals.

Student 5: What does the man deal with the strange animals in the cage?

Student 6: He lets them out.

Student 7: How are the children feeling?

Students: Very terrible/frightened/afraid/scared…

Student 9: Is the building a King's palace?

Student 10: No, it is the school building of Hogwarts.

Student 11: Why is Hogwarts a very unusual school?

Student 12: Because the students learn about magic and they have strange powers.

Student 13: What else does Harry learn besides magic at Hogwarts?

Students: He learns to be brave/the truth about his past/about the power of love/the importance of friendship…

Part 3: Harry Potter fights against bad wizards

(*The teacher and the students ask each other questions.*)

Teacher: Ok, I have asked you many questions. Now it's your turn to ask me questions. Are you brave enough to challenge me?

Students: Sure.

(*The students are eager to show off themselves.*)

Student 1: Is Harry afraid when he is fighting against the big snake?

Teacher: No, he isn't.

Student 2: How does Harry kill the big snake?

Teacher: He kills the poisonous snake with his sharp sword.

Student 3: What's the name of the bad wizard?

Teacher: Ridel.

Student 4: What does Ridel say to Harry when Harry falls to the ground?

Teacher: He says, "I guess you have only one minute to live. You'll see your dead mud blood mother soon."

Student 5: What does "mud blood" mean? Can you explain it?

Teacher: Well, mud means wet earth, and blood usually means red liquid flowing throughout our bodies, but here it means relationships of a family. In Chinese, it means "血统". Ridel uses mud blood to laugh at Harry's secret past. Are you clear now?

Student 5: Yes.

Student 6: Would you please repeat that 咒语?

Teacher: First I'd like to tell you the English for 咒语 is "incantation". I hear the bad wizard say 佩思奇皮衣佩思特咯米, but I don't know how to write them in English.

(*The students laugh happily.*)

Listen, retell & discuss

*Listen to the recorder and then try to fill in the blanks with the words from the listening material.*

J. K. Rowling has written a _____ of books about Harry, a boy with a _____ on his forehead and a _____ past.

Harry seems _____ a normal boy, but his life is _____. His parents are dead and he is badly _____ by his overbearing Aunt, Uncle and Cousin. Harry's life changes when he goes to Hogwarts—an unusual school for the students to learn about magic.

At Hogwarts, Harry learns _____ _____ magic. For example, he fights _____ bad wizards. He tries to help friends who are _____ _____. What's _____, Harry realizes that if we want to _____ a happy life, we must _____ _____ ourselves and help others.

Retell the story by using the past tense.

Discussion: What is the theme of *Harry Potter*?

1) *Harry Potter* is mainly about _____.

A. Love & hate    B. Friendship & happiness    C. The right & the evil (邪恶)

2) What must we do if we want to be successful in the real world?

If we want to be successful, we must: a) _____; b) _____; c) _____

In class:

Student 1: I think *Harry Potter* is mainly about the right & the evil because Harry always tries to do the right things and fights against the bad people.

Student 2: In my opinion, *Harry Potter* is about friendship & happiness because Harry thinks friendship is the most important thing and he is very happy to help his good friends when they are in trouble.

Student 3: As I notice, I believe *Harry Potter* is about love & hate because the movie shows Harry's deep love to Jenny and his deep hate to Ridel…

Teacher: What must we do if we want to be successful in the real world?

Students: If we want to be successful in the world, we must try our best to overcome difficulties/be strong/be sure of ourselves/have many true friends…

Teacher: Fabulous job. Remember these good ideas. Remember to smile, and a happy life you'll get, I think.

Step 4 Task Three

| Interview the audience | | |
| --- | --- | --- |
| Teacher's Activities | Students' Activities | Purposes |
| Offer students a situation to create dialogues. Pick out useful sentence patterns for students. Encourage and help students to speak. Help to select and reward the best performance. | a. Act as a reporter from Guangzhou TV Film Channel and audiences. b. Watch the performance, communicate, exhibit and appraise through comparison. | a. To practice some useful phrases and vocabulary. b. To encourage co-operation and creativity. c. To achieve a group or class product and a sense of achievement. d. To develop ability of appreciating art and literature. |

In class:

(*The teacher plays different effect shots of the film in the right corner of the screen and gives students a real situation to interview.*)

Situation: *Harry Potter* attracts so many people, both male and female, young and old. The child actor Daniel Radcliffe as Harry Potter also becomes popular. Suppose you are a reporter from *Guangzhou TV Film Channel*, you are making a programme about "Talking about *Harry Potter*", please interview some audiences to know how they like the movie.

You may ask such questions:

(1) Do you like *Harry Potter*? Do you like to watch magic tricks?

(2) What do you think of Daniel's performance in this movie?

(3) What impression does Harry leave you?

(4) How do you like the movie? What have you learned from the movie?

(5) Do you think that Harry's experience in Hogwarts is important to his life?

(6) Do you think we can learn about the real world by watching movies?

(*The students find joy and happiness by performance and watching. They choose the excellent reporter, the funniest audience and the best English speaker. The teacher gives them small presents as encouragement. The class atmosphere has reached high tide. The following is one of their interviews.*)

R = Reporter    A = Audience

R: Today in our programme "Talking about *Harry Potter*", we will interview a group of teenagers from No. 5 Middle School of Guangzhou. Welcome, boys and girls.

A: Thank you.

R: Do you like Harry Potter?

A: Yes.

R: Is Harry Potter handsome?

A: No, I don't think he is handsome but very cool.

R: How do you feel about Harry Potter? What kind of person is he?

A: I think Harry is a superman because he has magic power.

A: I think Harry is a kind-hearted person because he is always helpful to his friends.

A: In my opinion, Harry is sort of heroic. When he was fighting against the big snake, he displayed extraordinary courage...

R: What do you think of Daniel's performance in the movie?

A: Oh, I think it is a big success because he brings me into a magic world by his vivid action.

R: Do you think we can learn about the real world by seeing films?

A: Yes. I think so. You see, Harry's experiences with magic teach him about the real world. This is a good example.

R: Thank you for this interview. Bye.

A：Good-bye.

Step 5 Assessment & Summary

| Internet assessment | | |
|---|---|---|
| Teacher's Activities | Students' Activities | Purposes |
| Show the Internet assessment form. | Visit my website and finish the assessment form. | To focus students' attention on learning. To improve classroom instruction, support student learning and respond to student needs. |

Teacher's remarks：Well. In this lesson, I believe everyone has a delightful time and has gained pleasure and knowledge from *Harry Potter*. And I'm satisfied with you because the competitors have shown us not only positiveness but also creativity. All of you are polite, friendly and cooperative. I believe your violent desire and hardworking attitude will make you remarkable in your English study. Now homework for you.

Step 6 Homework

①Introduce a good film；②Make a movie poster；③Finish a questionnaire on entertainment.

## 九、教学反思

中学生很喜欢看电影，利用原版电影教英语文化无疑是一种良策。这不仅仅因为"兴趣是最好的老师"，更重要的是原版电影媒介能够使英语学习自然、生动、高效，使知识传播和文化吸收形象、深刻而快捷。*Harry Potter* 是中学生津津乐道的一部电影，不少学生虽然在课前已经看过这部电影，娱乐的效果是达到了，但是很少有学生对电影中的语言精华及文化内涵进行深入的思考。因此，我在设计这堂课的时候侧重点在于文化教学的层面，将电影内容和课程教学有机地整合在一起，主要利用了一些有效的教学原则，如整合原则、为交际服务原则、通过多样化手段导入文化内容原则、人性教育原则、比较教育原则、弘扬民族文化原则、人文关怀原则。我根据《新课标》的任务型教学理论总共设计了由五个由简到繁、由易到难、前后相连、层层深入、环环相扣的任务组成的任务链：首先在放映电影之前暂时不告诉学生电影名称，先让学生以小组为单位利用学过的情态动词制定在电影院观看影片的一些规则。这样做一方面吊起了学生的胃口，激励学生在真实的环境里得体地应用情态动词；另一方面，使学生学习在公共场合如何表现出良好的文明礼貌素养。然后由学生介绍 Harry Potter 的作者及主要演员，对该影片的文化背景知识进行必要的介绍，让学生开始进入英语文化的氛围。第三个任务是观看和欣赏原版英语电影的三个精彩片段：片段1，Harry Potter 的悲惨的童年生活；片段2，Hogwarts 学校与魔法；片段3，Harry Potter 与巨蛇及坏巫师的搏斗。在放映的现场，我采用了师生互动、边看边讲的方法对影片中的重点和难点进行精讲。比如，对生词、习惯用语进行解释，对生活习惯进行介绍，并且接受学生的提问等，力争让每一个学生听懂每一句话，引导学生对正义与邪恶、爱与恨、友谊与幸福、成功与失败等人生主题进行思考。第四个任务是交际活动，让学生扮演广州电视影视频道的记者去采访观众对 Harry Potter 这部影片的看法，让学生在真实的情景中运用所学到的知识和技能表达自己的观点，交流彼此的思想，学会从不同的角度去欣赏文学艺术。为了了解学生观看影片的收益，我在观看影片的过程中通过听力理解、问答、复述、讨论、访谈等形式对学生的学习效果进行了考查，而且在作业布置方面要求学生对同学们的业余娱乐活动进行调查，并且在网上完成一个文化教学评估表，另外还要求他们制作一张电影海报或者介绍一部自己喜欢的影片。这些作业会作为学习成果在班上展览、交流、评比，之后存入学生的档案袋。整个课堂气氛活跃，师生互动比较多，完成了教学设计中的内容和任务，达到了教学目标的要求。我觉得需要改进的地方是练习偏多，留给学生思考的时间不够。

## 十、教学点评

观看电影是一个语言输入的过程，但真正掌握一门外语还需要一个输出的过程。在本节课，张老师较好地将电影欣赏与单元教学内容有机整合，将语言教学与文化教学有机结合起来，合理设计和实施了语言的输入与输出过程。首先在影片的选择上，英文原版电影 Harry Potter 语言难度适当，发音清晰地道，内容能引起学生的兴趣，几乎涵盖了语言学习中的语音、语调、节奏、用词、思维、感情等几大要素，有语言的精华，也符合高一学生的年龄特点、学习兴趣和学习水平；其次在欣赏电影的过程中，张老师合理地处理了教与学的关系，把握了电影教学与文化教学的要领，通过介绍文化背景、引入剧本片段、问题讨论、问与答、提取故事梗概、听力理解、影片评论、现场采访等形式讲授英语视、听、说、读、写的技巧和电影文化知识，以及电影艺术审美的要领，从而帮助学生对看到的电影内容进行提炼和提升，使之内化为学生自身的能力，教师的主导作用也得到了充分发挥。教学设计体现了《新课标》的任务型教学理念：Making our rules for cinema—Meeting the writer & the child actors—Film appreciation—Interview the audience—Internet assessment 五个步骤环环相扣。通过以上任务链的完成，加上制作精美的课件，整个课堂自始至终都沉浸在跨文化交际的互动氛围之中，做到了视、听、说、读、写交融，语言与文化并重，受到了学生的普遍欢迎。不足之处是：课堂容量大，老师讲话语速急，学生听起来有些辛苦，希望改进。

# 第七章　广州市海珠区集团学校联动教研

## 课例七　沪教版八年级下册 Unit 6 Pets Grammar 语法课*

### 一、教学内容

This unit is based on the topic of pets and pet ownership. In the grammar section, we learn the formation and usage of manner adverbs and their comparative and superlative forms and usage. Adverbs generally modify verbs, adjectives, adverbs and are used as gerunds to indicate time, place, manner, degree or frequency. The grammar in this lesson is taught in the context of the unit's topic, and grammar is learned and used in situations.

### 二、学情分析

The students in Grade 8 are simple, inquisitive and eager to express themselves. Students have some experience with the topic of pet keeping, and most of them have a strong interest in cute pets for the course. In addition, in the first book of the eighth grade, students also learned the use of adjectives, the comparative and the superlative form and structure of adjectives, the comparative and the superlative of adverbs have a certain knowledge of adverbial metamorphosis, which can lay a certain foundation for students to transfer their learning. However, the students' self-confidence in learning English is not enough, and the teacher needs to encourage them to speak boldly.

---

\*　执教：广州市海珠区教育发展研究院张志梅；点评：广州市南武中学王迪雅，广州市南武中学附属学校卢兰芬。

## 三、教学目标

Students will be able to:

(1) study the formation and usage of adverbs;

(2) learn the comparative and superlative forms and usage of adverbs;

(3) learn to use the comparative and the superlative of adverbs correctly in context;

(4) learn the skills of taking care of pets and how to run a pet store, etc.

## 四、教学重点、难点

Focus: To learn the formation and usage of adverbs and their comparative and superlative forms.

Difficulty: To distinguish the use of easily confused adverbs such as hard, fast, late, well, etc.

## 五、教学过程评析

Activity 1: Lead in

Purpose: Lead in the topic and arouse students' interest about the topic.

Look at the pictures and talk about Ella and her pet dog.

(1) How does the pet dog love Ella? Faithfully.

(2) How did Ella play with her dog? Excitedly.

(3) How did the dog eat its tasty food? Happily.

(4) How did Ella take the pet dog to the pet shop? Sadly.

(5) What do the words "Faithfully, Excitedly, Happily, Sadly" have in common?

Discovery 1: Adverb = Adjective + ly.

Discovery 2: 以 y 结尾的形容词把 y 改为 i + ly, 如:

hungry—hungrily, easy—easily, heavy—heavily, 特例 shy—shyly

Activity 2: Grammar in form

Purpose: Draw students' attention to the form and functions of adverbs.

Play a game and find partners.

Discovery 3: 形副同形, 如 hard/fast/late/high/low/early/enough/long/straight

Discovery 4: 以 le 结尾的形容词需去 e + y, 如:

gentle—gently, comfortable—comfortably, possible—possibly

Discovery 5：以 ll 结尾的形容词需 +y，如 full—fully，dull—dully

Discovery 6：不规则：good—well，

Discovery 7：Adverbs modify adjectives/verbs/adverbs（functions）

Activity 3  Grammar in use

Purpose：Consolidate the use of adverbs in real context.

*Task* 1：Mr. Happy is giving advice on how to improve their service（服务）. Can you help finish it?（P88）

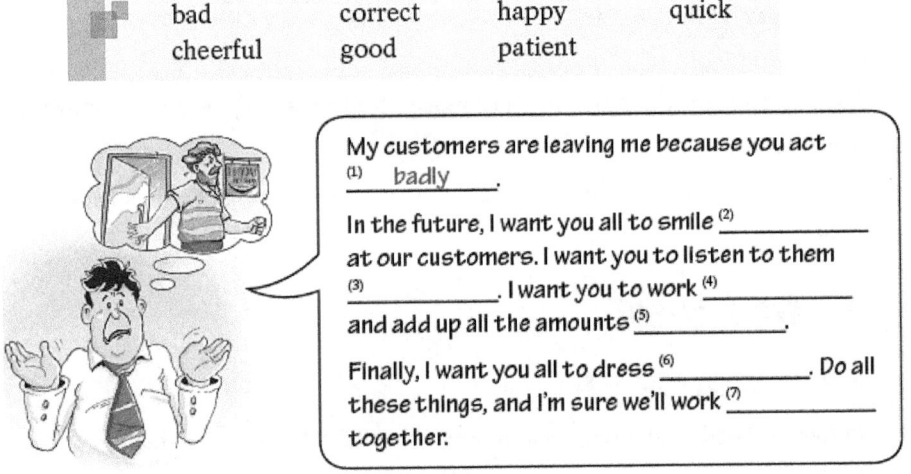

| bad | correct | happy | quick |
| cheerful | good | patient | |

My customers are leaving me because you act (1) __badly__.

In the future, I want you all to smile (2) _____ at our customers. I want you to listen to them (3) _____. I want you to work (4) _____ and add up all the amounts (5) _____.

Finally, I want you all to dress (6) _____. Do all these things, and I'm sure we'll work (7) _____ together.

In class：Students can use cheerfully, patiently, quickly, correctly, well, happily.

*Task* 2：After talking to the workers, there are many changes.

Before　　　　　After　　　　　Future

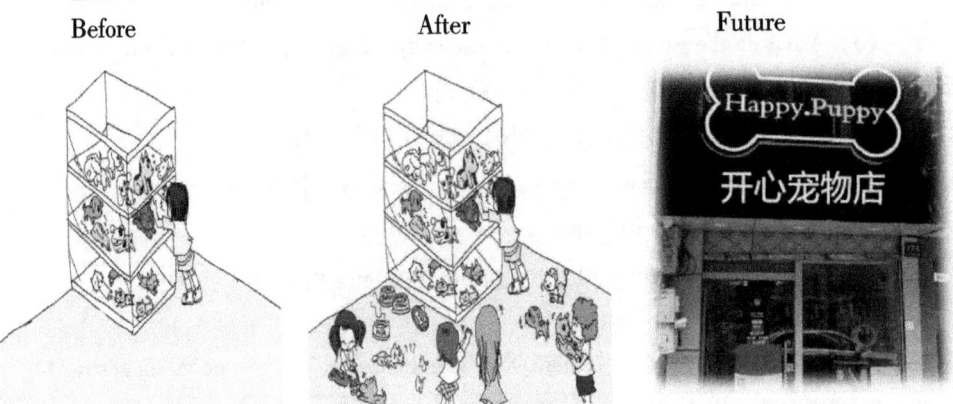

The workers offer help _____ (quick) than before. more quickly/the most quickly

They also work _____ (careful) than before. more carefully/the most carefully

Besides, they work _____ (fast) and _____ (hard) than before. faster/the fastest, harder/the hardest

What's more, the shop closes _____ (late) than before. later/the latest

Discovery 8：比较级标志词：than, much, even, a little

Discovery 9：最高级标志词：in + 范围, one of..., of all, among

In class：Learn about the comparatives and superlatives of adverbs.

*Task* 3：To become better, they should do better. Will you choose the comparative or superlative?

Purpose：Learn about the comparatives and superlatives of adverbs in real context.

First, the boss should think further/the furthest (far) for the pet shop.

Secondly, the workers must learn more/the most (much) about pet care (护理).

Besides, the workers should behave (表现) better/the best (good) than before.

Lastly, if some workers work much worse/the worst (bad) than others, they should be paid less/the least (little).

Discovery 10：The comparative & superlative forms of far, much, well, badly, and little are irregular.

far — farther/further — farthest/furthest

much — more — most

well — better — best

badly — worse — worst

little — less — least

*Task* 4：Emma interviewed 40 people to find out which pet centre is the most popular. Help her complete her report. (P89)

| Pet centre | Good animal doctors | Good helpers | Number of visits |
|---|---|---|---|
| TEP | | | |
| LOVE | | | |
| Ken's | | | |
| Heart | | | |

I interviewed 40 people who keep pets at home. They think the animal doctors at TEP check pets (1)_____ (carefully) and the helpers help look after pets (2)_____ (patiently) than those at LOVE and Ken's. However, among the four pet centres, people go to Heart (3)_____ (regularly). They think the animal doctors and helpers there did their jobs (4)_____ (well). They seldom go to Ken's because the animal doctors there usually work (5)_____ (slowly) than those in the other centres. Of all these four pet centres, Ken's helpers care (6)_____ (little) about pets.

In class: Students can use more carefully/patiently/slowly, but they are not sure of the most regularly/best/least. They need more practice.

Task 5 Share your advice

Purpose:

Mr. Happy is sharing his experience on how to keep pets with Ella. Can you help finish the advice?

Tips: feed—regular（规律的）

play with…— patient

treat— careful

do XX's job— good

make it live— comfortable

…

As a pet owner, you have to learn more about how to keep a pet.

First, you should feed your pet regularly.

Besides, you should play with it patiently.

Most importantly, you should treat it carefully when it is sick.

You also need to do your job as an owner the best.

Lastly, make it live comfortably.

If you follow the advice, I am sure you will have a good relationship with your pet.

## 六、教学点评

The English Curriculum Standards require that the form of language be organically combined with its meaning and communicative function, and that the rules of language be internalized in actual language use, so that students can accurately use the language for effective communication. Larsen-Freeman proposed a three-dimensional system of grammar: form, meaning and use. The design of this lesson also follows the three-dimensional teaching framework of form-meaning-use. Firstly, students are asked to fill in the adverbs that appear in the listening audio; Secondly, students are asked to find out and summarize the forms of adverbs; Then, students are asked to use adverbs in real-life situations through the unit's scenario of pet-raising and to explore the usage of adverbs modifying verbs and adverbs modifying adjectives. Finally, the task of making suggestions about pet ownership is used to consolidate students' knowledge of the grammar content of the lesson. This lesson also realizes the link between input, intake and output.

从上课效果来看，目标达成度高。导入部分的看图说话一下子把学生的积极性调动起来了，整个场面显得轻松、活泼、生动。Find partners 的游戏帮助学生快速归纳副词在意义、形式和用法上的特征；Grammar in use 的环节充分利用教材资源，依据任务型教学以及建构主义的理念，在 Before, After, Future 三个情境中形象生动地呈现副词的原级、比较级和最高级，加强学生对语法运用的训练的同时，注重提高学生用英语获取信息、处理信息和解决问题的能力。学生积极举手发言，提高了学生听、说、读、写多方面的能力，培养学生的学科素养，突出英语教学的育人功能。建议进一步深入挖掘关爱动物和对人与自然的思考方面的主题。

# 第八章 广州市"百千万人才培养工程"第二批"中学名教师"培养项目跟岗活动

## 课例八 How to Write a Survey 应用文写作课[*]

### 一、教学背景

活动对象：广州市基础教育系统新一轮"百千万人才培养工程"第二批"中学名教师"培养项目高中英语文2班全体成员和海珠区全体高三英语老师。

活动时间：2015年3月31日。

活动地点：广州市南武中学校本部（海珠区同福中路362号）。

### 二、教材分析

**广东省高考英语基础写作考查情况 1**

| 年份 | 2007 | 2008 | 2009 | 2010 |
|---|---|---|---|---|
| 题材 | 校园偶像调查 | 校园墙报通讯 | 采访报道 | 射击项目介绍 |
| 命题形式 | 中文表格 | 中文提纲 | 中文提纲 | 中文提纲 |
| 话题 | 谁是你的偶像 课标话题（简称课话）7 个人感情、21 热点 | 公共场所禁烟 课话 3 环境、13 健康、21 热点 | 中小学生近视问题 课话 13 健康、21 热点 | 体育时事热点 课话 15、21 热点 |
| 考查要素 | 调查时间、问题对象、差异、排序、理由 | 背景、时间、事件 | 时间、对象、主题、基本信息、原因、建议、提示 | 内容、时间、范围、目标、措施、相关数据-百分比 |

---

[*] 执教：广州市海珠区教育发展中心张志梅；点评：广州市"百千万人才培养工程"高中英语文2班老师：孙文经、刘敏莉、刘峰、高道兴、张楠、赵玉书、谢莉。本课例获广州市高三有效教学案例三等奖。

**广东省高考英语基础写作考查情况 2**

| 年份 | 2011 | 2012 | 2013 | 2014 |
|---|---|---|---|---|
| 题材 | 图书信息及报道 | 传奇人物介绍 | 移民火星的快讯 | 人物报道 |
| 命题形式 | 中文提纲 | 中文提纲 | 中文提纲 | 中文提纲 |
| 话题 | Battle Hymn of the Tiger Mother 教育方式<br>课话 2 家庭、21 热点 | Allan Stewart 80 多岁硕士<br>课话 2 周围人、21 热点 | 30 名移民火星志愿者<br>课话 9 计划愿望、21 热点 | Richard Avis 寻找 time twins<br>课话 2 周围人、6 兴趣、21 热点 |
| 考查要素 | 书名、作者、出版时间、内容、效应、相关报道 | 姓名、国籍、出生日期、世界纪录、学习态度、学位 | 志愿者条件、时间、地点、专家观点、志愿者观点 | 人物、出生日期、时间、目的、相关信息、计划 |

（1）基础写作题材贴近考生的学习和生活的热点问题。历年来高考作文题的题材都非常贴近考生的学习生活，如校园活动、校外见闻、交友、旅游以及与考生有关的话题讨论等。可以预料 2015 年高考写作题的题材还会在这些范围之内，并为所有考生熟悉。

（2）写作的体裁主要是应用文。具体说来是新闻体裁，命题形式多为看图表说明图表内容，介绍人物或者项目，或者根据表格信息写通讯报道、调查等应用文。

（3）必考信息点：时间、地点、对象、目的、原因、数据、结论……

（4）调查报告包含高考基础写作的必考信息点，需要将图表信息转换为文字信息，是一种非常实用的文体，但同时也是学生认为难度较高的一种体裁。需要有针对性地进行写作方法和策略的指导。

## 三、学情分析

The students I will teach are the ones of Senior Grade 3 from Nan Wu Senior High School. They are graduates and have already organized a lot about the basic writing. So the students are familiar with the requirements and characteristics of the basic writing tasks. So this is a writing revision and I try to have the students adopt their knowledge and skills to accomplish a new task, through which they will be able to avoid some common mistakes and Chinglish and develop their skills and strategies.

## 四、教学目标

Students are able to:

(1) grasp the writing characteristics of the survey;

(2) learn to combine and express the key points by using complex sentences and polish the survey in class;

(3) have both self and peer evaluation according to the standards: ①information completeness; ② the varieties and correctness of the sentence structures; ③coherence; ④audience awareness;

(4) Students will be able to concern about national and international issues;

(5) Develop student's sense of group cooperation as well as patriotism.

## 五、教学重点和难点

Important points:

(1) Help students grasp the writing characteristics of the survey.

(2) Enhance students' abilities to combine and express the key points by using complex sentences.

(3) Improve the writing strategies.

Difficult points:

Enhance students' abilities to combine and express the key points by using complex sentences.

Students have self-evaluation and peer evaluation effectively.

## 六、教学策略和方法

Teaching Methods: Communicative Teaching and Task-based Methods

Teaching Aids: Blackboard, Computer-based Multi-media

## 七、教学过程

| Teacher's Activities | Students' Activities | Purposes |
| --- | --- | --- |
| Warm up and lead in<br>• Introduce the learning objectives<br>• Lead in the topic with a small quiz | • Listen and recall what is socialist core values | • To motivate students to get interested in the class as well as to lead in the topic.<br>• To make students know the learning objectives. |
| Pre-writing activity: Brainstorming<br>• Do you love our motherland?<br>• What can we do for it? | • Brainstorm<br>• Listen, think, discuss and present | • To activate their stored information of the understanding of patriotism. |
| While-writing activity<br>• Introduce the task<br>• Have the students discuss and cooperate<br>• In groups of four, students analyze a sample recommendation letter in terms of the structure, effectiveness of the example, language and grammar. | • Analyze the task<br>• Use the writing strategies<br>• Learn by cooperation | • To make students be the center of the class, making them develop their self-study and cooperative ability. |
| Post writing activity<br>• Show the evaluation form | • Self-evaluate<br>• Peer evaluate | • Have both self and peer evaluation according to the standards: a. information completeness; b. the varieties and correctness of the sentence structures; c. coherence; d. audience awareness<br>• Better their writing as well as give students confidence and positive energy |
| • Homework | | |

## 附：广东高考基础写作的写作策略

### 广东高考基础写作的写作策略1——Analyze the task

| 文体 | 读者 | 人称 | 时态 | 语言特点 |
|---|---|---|---|---|
| 应用文、调查报告 | 其他人 | 第三人称 | 一般现在时为主 | 真实性、针对性、逻辑性 |

### 广东高考基础写作的写作策略2——Draft the Chinese outline with 5 sentences

| 内容要点 | 要点整合 | 5句话中文提纲 |
|---|---|---|
| 1. 有关"爱国"的调查时间、地点、对象；<br>2. 调查结果统计；<br>3. 你的观点和理由。 | 1. 有关"爱国"的调查时间、地点、对象、内容；<br>2. 某市民和某果农；<br>3. 某教授和某大学生；<br>4. 几位"90后"；<br>5. 我的观点和理由。 | 1. 2014年国庆节期间，央视（CCTV）在全国范围内对国民进行了一项有关"你热爱祖国吗？你用哪些实际行动表明你爱国？"的调查。<br>2. 某市民（认为）做好日常工作就是对祖国做贡献。（连词1—）（站在）某果农（的立场,）不卖烂梨（就是爱国）。<br>3. 某教授（的观点是）祖国的强大就是自己的光荣。（连词）某大学生（建议/坚持）把垃圾扔进垃圾箱，这也是爱国（的实际行动）。<br>4. 几位"90后"（觉得）好好享受7天长假最重要，不要太关注这么严肃的问题。<br>5. 作为一名教师，在我看来，很有必要在日常教学中培养青少年的爱国意识，因为爱国不仅是一种情感，更是每个公民的责任。 |

### 广东高考基础写作的写作策略3——Write the correct words/phrases/patterns

| 5句 | words/ phrases | Sentence patterns |
|---|---|---|
| No. 1 S | 1. 爱国 | 1. 对……人进行有关……的调查 do/make/conduct/carry out a survey among sb. on/about sth.（survey format） |
| No. 2 S | 2. 市民<br>3. 做好日常工作<br>4. 对祖国做贡献<br>5. 果农<br>6. 不卖烂梨 | 2. A 等于 B<br>A equals B<br>A is equal to B<br>A is synonymous with B<br>Paris has always been synonymous with elegance, luxury and style. 巴黎一直是优雅、奢华和时尚的代名词。<br>3. 做 A 事就是做 B 事。<br>Seeing is believing.<br>To see is to believe. |

续上表

| 5 句 | words/ phrases | Sentence patterns |
|---|---|---|
| No. 3 S | 7. 教授<br>8. 祖国的强大<br>9. 自己的光荣<br>10. 大学生<br>11. 垃圾<br>12. 垃圾箱 | 4. Sb holds the view that 引导同位语从句<br>5. Sb suggests/advises/requests that 引导宾语从句，从句中使用虚拟语气 |
| No. 4 S | 13. "90后"<br>14. 享受7天长假<br>15. 关注这么严肃的主题 | 6. 宁愿做A事而不愿意做B事<br>Prefer to doing A to doing B<br>Would rather do A than do B<br>Would do A rather than do B |
| No. 5 S | 16. 培养<br>17. 青少年<br>18. 爱国意识<br>19. 情感<br>20. 责任 | 7. 我认为做某事很有必要因为……<br>I maintain/suppose that doing sth is of great importance for the reason that…<br>8. 不但是A，更是B……<br>more A than B |

广东高考基础写作的写作策略4——Write the sentences beautifully

| 高级的语法结构 | 举例 |
|---|---|
| 词的活用 | be important = be of importance |
| 介词短语 | |
| 非谓语 | |
| 同位语 | |
| 定语从句 | |
| 状语从句 | |
| 宾语从句 | |
| 被动语态 | |
| 强调、倒装…… | |

**广东高考基础写作的写作策略 5——Reach coherence by transitional words**

| 表时间 | up to now, currently, recently |
|---|---|
| 表原因 | because of, on account of, as a result (of), owing to, due to, for the reason that… |
| 表递进 | What's more, besides, to make the matter worse, |
| 表转折 | however, otherwise, nevertheless, even if/though |
| 表条件 | so long as, on condition that, |

**广东高考基础写作的写作策略 6——Self and peer evaluation of the writing**

| 标准 | 指标 | 优点 | 改进 |
|---|---|---|---|
| 内容的完整性<br>(Completeness) | 1. 要点齐全 | | |
| 句子结构的正确性<br>(Correctness) | 2. 时态语态 | | |
| | 3. 人称准确 | | |
| | 4. 单词拼写 | | |
| 句子结构的复杂性<br>(Variety) | 5. 介词短语 | | |
| | 6. 非谓语 | | |
| | 7. 同位语 | | |
| | 8. 定语从句 | | |
| | 9. 状语从句 | | |
| | 10. 宾语从句 | | |
| 信息内容的连贯性<br>(Coherence) | 11. 篇章连贯 | | |
| 读者意识<br>(Audience Awareness) | 12. 语言得体 | | |

# 八、教学点评

## 观课有感

有幸听了一场高质量的基础写作课,心里甚是高兴,特写下感悟。

在张老师的优美、自然、流畅的全英语言的引导下,学生在轻松、愉快的氛围中完成了本节课的教学任务,整节课称得上是一场具有个人特色、创新写作、科学实惠、学生受用的课型。值得我们学习与借鉴，其优点：

### 1. 巧用支架理论，为写作搭建审题与语言要点支架

首先，张教师启发学生如何审题，如何就题目的要求展开思考，如何开拓自己写这种题材的作文的思路等。其次，根据写作内容帮助学生搭建语言要点支架。最后，引导学生不断说或写出与题目相关的潜伏于意识之中的各种信息。

### 2. 巧用支架理论，为写作搭建句子与结构支架

首先，张老师从开始上课起就引导学生展开写作思路，顺着学生的思路，或交谈或提问，帮助他们搭好文章结构支架。其次，张老师指导学生要注意句与句之间的衔接方法，鼓励学生调出大脑中存储的相关信息，按照框中所给的信息进行整合与取舍。

### 3. 巧用支架理论，为写作搭建语篇与情感支架

首先，张老师巧用英语句子渗透德育教育，于无声处胜有声，这是教育的最高境界。其次，搭好总体语篇支架（汉语版），鼓励学生大胆尝试填空，用表扬浸润学生心田，让课堂活跃起来。最后，整场课采用小组合作学习、分组记分、分组板演、教师点拨的方式进行，让课堂高潮迭起。

总之，整节课以"过程教学法"为依托，在写作中注重支架的搭建，注重学生写作兴趣的培养，化被动为主动，并且将写作的整个过程融为一体，简约高效，能有效提高学生的写作水平，提升其写作能力，是一种值得借鉴和推广的高中英语控制性写作训练法。

# 第九章　广州市"百千万人才培养工程"第二批"中学名教师"培养项目跟岗以及海珠区高二英语教研活动

**课例九**　Topic 10 Festivals，Holidays and Celebrations 课标话题写作课①

## 一、授课背景

本课是实践导师给"百千万人才培养工程"高中英语文 2 班全体成员以及海珠区全体高二英语老师展示的写作教学示范课，时间是 2017 年 5 月 11 日，地点是广州市第五中学。

## 二、教材分析

1. On the characteristics of the NMET Writing （2014—2016）

| | | 题目要求 | 命题分析 |
|---|---|---|---|
| 2016 | 卷Ⅰ | 假定你是李华，暑假想去一家外资公司兼职，已写好申请书和个人简历（resume）。给外教 Ms. Jenkins 写信，请她帮你修改所附材料的文字和格式（format）。 | 纵观近三年全国卷高考书面表达，可以发现有如下命题特点：<br>1. 体裁以书信类为主<br>近三年全国卷高考书面表达基本都为书信，属于应用文的范畴。其中 2016 年全国卷Ⅲ和 2015 年全国卷Ⅱ的电子邮件都属于书信类；2014 年全国卷Ⅱ的征文也可划归为书信类，只不过没有格式的限制。 |
| | 卷Ⅱ | 假定你是李华，你校摄影俱乐部（Photography Club）将举办国际中学生摄影展。请给你的英国朋友 Peter 写封信，请他提供作品。信的内容包括：①主题：环境保护；②展览时间；③投稿邮箱：intlphotoshow @ gmschool. com。 | |

---

① 执教：广州市海珠区教育发展中心张志梅；点评：广州市第九十七中学庄英如。

续上表

| | | 题目要求 | 命题分析 |
|---|---|---|---|
| 2016 | 卷Ⅲ | 假定你是李华，之前与留学生朋友 Bob 约好一起去书店，但因故不能赴约。请给他写封邮件，内容包括：①表示歉意；②说明原因；③另约时间。 | 2. 给出的信件格式提示逐年减少<br>近三年对信件格式的提示逐年减少。2014 年书信的开头和结尾都已给出；2015 年两套卷中一套给出了开头，另一套给出了结尾；2016 年三套卷对于开头和结尾没有任何提示。<br>3. 写作形式大都为提纲类作文，但开放性增大<br>近三年的全国卷书面表达主要为提纲类作文，而且开放性逐年增大，给出的文字提纲高度简洁、概括，给考生留有较大的发挥空间。<br>4. 所选题材均与考生的日常生活密切相关<br>近三年全国卷书面表达的题材都与考生的日常生活密切相关，涉及中学生的学习、生活及中学生所熟悉的社会话题等，有利于考生在考场上的发挥。这些话题都体现了英语语用性，具有"生活化"气息。 |
| 2015 | 卷Ⅰ | 假定你是李华，你校英文报"外国文化"栏目拟刊登介绍美国节日风俗和中学生生活的短文。请给美国朋友彼得写信约稿，要点如下：<br>①栏目介绍；②稿件内容；③稿件长度：约 400 词；④交稿日期：6 月 28 日前。 | |
| 2015 | 卷Ⅱ | 假定你是李华，计划和同学去敬老院（nursing home）陪老人们过重阳节（the Double Ninth Festival）。请给外教露西写封邮件，邀她一同前往，内容包括：①出发及返回时间；②活动：包饺子、表演节目等。 | |
| 2014 | 卷Ⅰ | 假定你是李华，计划暑假期间去英国学习英语，为期六周。下面的广告（见图 1）引起了你的注意，请给该校写封信，询问有关情况（箭头所指内容）。 | |
| 2014 | 卷Ⅱ | 一家英语报社向中学生征文，主题是"十年后的我"。请根据下列要点和你的畅想完成短文。<br>①家庭；②工作；③业余生活。 | |

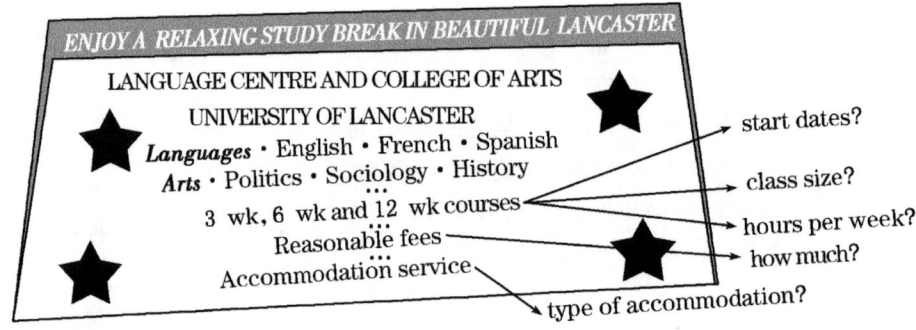

图 1

2. On the topic: Mother's Day

I choose Topic 10, Festivals, holidays and celebrations because it is one of the 24 topics and a topic closely related to our real life. What's more, the topic can interpreter my teaching belief. That is, Life should not only be lived, it should be celebrated! Bread is the main staff of people.

## 三、学情分析

The students I will teach are the ones of Senior Grade 2 from No. 5 Middle School. They have already contacted but organized inadequately about the national writing. So the students are not quite familiar with the requirements and characteristics of the national writing tasks. Some students even don't know how to write when they see such kind of writing tasks. In this writing lesson, I try to stimulate their background knowledge via speaking, then have the students adopt their knowledge and skills to accomplish a similar writing task with the help of thinking maps, through which they will be able to brainstorm ideas and better their writing skills and strategies.

## 四、教学目标

(1) Language abilities:

①read a Mother's Day poem correctly and emotionally;

②discuss in groups of three and recommend a nice restaurant in front of the class;

③write a heartwarming letter of invitation to their moms inside Mother's Day card.

（2）Learning abilities: take an active part in discussion, cooperation with teachers and classmates.

（3）Thinking qualities: peer evaluate the writing to improve the logical and critical thinking with the help of thinking maps.

（4）Cultural qualities:

①appreciate Chinese traditional culture and raise cross-culture awareness;

②dedicate their cards to their mums and show gratitude and love to them on Mother's Day.

## 五、教学重点和难点

Important points:

（1）Help students grasp the writing characteristics of the invitation letter.

（2）Encourage students to choose suitable vocabulary to show their love to moms.

（3）Enhance students' abilities to reason and evaluate with the help of thinking maps.

（4）Improve the writing strategies and efficiency.

Difficult points:

（1）Enhance students' abilities to reason and evaluate with the help of thinking maps.

（2）Students have self-evaluation and peer evaluation effectively.

## 六、教学过程

| Teacher's Activities | Students' Activities | Purposes |
| --- | --- | --- |
| Warm up and lead in Appreciate a Chinese Traditional poem<br>• Make a self-introduction and introduce the participants.<br>• Play the song and poem. | Pair Work<br>• Appreciate a traditional song<br>• Read the poem in pairs.<br>• Think: What is mother's love like in the poet's eye? | • To break the ice and motivate students to get interested in the class as well as to lead in the topic.<br>• To make students know the learning objectives. |

续上表

| Teacher's Activities | Students' Activities | Purposes |
|---|---|---|
| Pre-writing activity:<br>Speaking: *Let's vote for a nicer restaurant*<br>• How do you celebrate Mother's Day?<br>• Can you recommend a nice restaurant for my mom? | Group work<br>• Listen, think, discuss and present in groups of three.<br>• Brainstorm the ideas about how to recommend a nicer restaurant.<br>• Learn by cooperation. | • To activate their stored information and life experience of the understanding of what a nice restaurant is and make informed decisions. |
| While-writing activity<br>*Make a heartwarming Mother's Day card*<br>• Introduce the writing task.<br>• Have the students write on their own. | Personalized output<br>• Select the suitable vocabulary.<br>• Analyze the task by using the thinking map.<br>• Use the writing strategies. | • To make students be the center of the class, making them develop their self-study and creative ability.<br>• Complete a personalized invitation letter inside the Mother's Day card. |
| Post writing activity<br>Peer Evaluation<br>• Show the evaluation form. | Critical thinking<br>• Read the writing in class.<br>• Peer evaluate.<br>• Encourage each other. | Have peer evaluation according to the standards:<br>a. reasonable paragraphs<br>b. beautiful vocabulary<br>c. diverse sentences<br>d. natural coherence<br>e. tidy handwriting<br>• Better their writing as well as give students confidence and positive energy. |
| Summary<br>Show them a poem written by the teacher | Reflection<br>• Speak out the love to moms.<br>• Share the harvest and feeling. | • Have a sense of accomplishment.<br>• Deeper their understanding of Mother's Day. |
| Homework | Please dedicate your card to your mum and show your love to her on Mother's Day. | • Learn to express gratitude and love to mom.<br>• Build up closer relationship. |

## 七、教学点评

教学准备有两种思路：一种是顺向思考，另一种是逆向设计。在教学大纲时代，教师大都采用顺向设计，即基于教学内容安排学习活动。逆向设计是有了课程标准之后提出的新思路，教师首先将课程标准转换成学习目标，并据此设计与目标相匹配的评价，再来设计学习活动。本节写作课采用逆向思路进行设计，教师对近三年的全国卷作文题进行命题分析，发现全国卷的命题具有以下特点：①体裁以书信类为主；②给出的信件格式提示逐年减少；③写作形式大都为提纲类作文，但开放性增大。基于以上分析，本节课选取课程标准话题10——节日与庆祝作为教学目标，结合即将到来的母亲节设置说与写的情景，在分析和解决问题的过程中，训练学生的综合语言运用能力。本课例是基于以上思路的写作课型的成功探索。笔者认为本节说写结合课具有以下亮点。

### 1. 以主题为引领，创设真实情景

本节说写课以即将到来的母亲节和母爱为主题，先以一首诗歌《游子吟》作为引入，引起学生的共鸣。接着，教师设置 speaking 情景"教师远在老家年事已高的妈妈将来广州游玩，请学生帮忙推荐一家适合与妈妈在母亲节当天共进晚餐的餐厅"，并请学生在小组讨论，推选出一家美味的餐厅。然后在 writing 部分，要求学生写一封邀请信，邀请妈妈母亲节共进晚餐。最后以张老师自我创作的诗歌《母亲节》作为结束。这是一节充满爱的写作课，不仅在课堂上训练了学生的语言能力，更将语言教学延伸到课后，布置学生课后制作母亲节卡片，在母亲节当天献给自己的妈妈并与妈妈共进晚餐，深化了学生对母亲节的情感认知，以及在生活中敢于对亲人表达爱的情感态度。本节"以说带写"的写作课理清并抓住了主线，将主题引领作为整合的起点，体现了综合性、实践性和关联性的学习过程。

### 2. 教学活动设计科学合理

教学活动是教师与学生之间开展的一系列有组织、有计划的学习活动，它应具备引起注意、明释内容、调适形式和关注结果等逻辑元素。本节课由于是借班授课，教师在自我介绍时使用自己当年在五中任教的照片以及已毕业的学生的照片作为素材，消除了与学生之间的陌生感，拉近了与学生之间的距离。在选取学生上台展示推荐的餐厅时，由于是公开课，学生不好意思上台，教师自创了"President 习"的点名游戏，活跃课堂气氛，消除了学生的紧张感。在 speaking 和 writing 部分，两个活动都具有一定的开放性。教师布置任务后分别提供了两个 thinking map 搭建"脚手架"以帮助学生完成任务，将 speaking

和 writing 紧密结合，强化铺垫，激活学生写作的内容图式、形式图式和语言图式。课后作业是布置学生制作完成母亲节邀请母亲共进晚餐的邀请卡，将教学活动延伸至课外，进一步升华了本课的主题"母亲节与爱"，把语言教学与生活实践相结合，培养了学生热爱母亲、敢于表达爱的情感态度与价值观。

### 3. 评价适时、适度、具体、正面，激励功能充分发挥

有效的课堂评价应具有以下两点功能：首先，教师应当对学生的表现做出即时、中肯的评估，让他们知道自己的回答或表现有哪些可取之处，让他们在体验学习成功的快乐的同时，意识到自己存在的不足，并维护其自尊心。体验成功的欢乐和维护自尊心这两点都能激发学生参与课堂活动的积极性，这种积极状态是学生内心深处受到激励后形成的更强的表现欲。其次，教师的有效评价不仅预示着前一段交流的结束，评价中的部分话语还能将交流继续推向深入，引发师生、生生之间新一轮交流和更多的话语输出，形成更积极的语言输出和交流状态。

本节课的评价主要有教师的即时评价和写后写作评价两种。在学生回答问题或完成任务之后，教师能够结合具体情况，及时给出具体、中肯、真诚的评价。例如，在两位学生合作朗读完诗歌《游子吟》之后，教师先肯定两位朗读者的朗读，"Your reading is very beautiful. I really enjoy the poem."，之后用转折词 but 恰当指出朗读中一些发音错误，并带领全班同学齐声朗读。在学生推荐餐厅之后，教师根据学生的推荐理由，结合眼神和动作，给出"You are so considerate."的评价，这一评价具体、真诚，不仅对学生推荐时能够给予具体的推荐理由做出评价，还赞美了学生善解人意的优秀品质。学生推选出美味的餐厅之后，教师给予推荐者小礼物作为奖励，并鼓励学生"If you open your month, you can always have presents."。教师对学生的反馈不仅有口头的，还有物质的，更有激励性的语言鼓励学生在接下来的任务中主动参与活动。在写作反馈中，教师设计了具体的评价量表供学生进行同伴互评。该评价量表是本写作课的一大亮点。该量表避免关注学生的语言错误，而是根据本节写作课的教学目标设计量表，从篇章结构、词汇运用、衔接手段、书写等角度在闪光点和增分点两方面关注学生的正面表现，给予学生积极的反馈。

由于上课环境的限制，学生按照会议室座位就坐，在完成学习任务的过程中难以有效合作沟通，教师不便于在学生中间走动以调动学生的积极性，因而本节课任务的推进比较慢。建议教师调整上课的节奏，把握上课时间，留给学生更多的时间进行写作与评价。另外，为了使说写结合更加紧密，建议在写作任务的设置上设计与 speaking 部分相关的写作要点，如"邀请妈妈到该餐厅用餐的理由"等，有利于学生在写作中有更好的发挥。

# 第十章 广州市第四批初中英语骨干教师第六组跟岗活动

## 课例十 上教社 Going on Safari 整本书阅读示范课*

### 一、授课背景

听课对象:广州市第四批初中英语骨干老师第六组以及番禺区部分初中英语老师。

时间:2019年9月20日。

授课对象:广州市化龙中学初三6班(年级普通班)。经过两年多的学习,学生对初中英语词汇和语法有一定的了解,具备了一定的听、说、读、写能力。该班学生思维活跃,乐于参与思考和互动,但是词汇量明显不足,阅读能力有待进一步提高。

教学内容:上海外语教育出版社出版的 Going on Safari《畅游野生动物园》,属于课标24个话题中的 Topic 20 Nature, Animals and Plants。该书讲述了主人公 May 畅游非洲野生动物园的经历,包括四个主要部分:Getting Ready to Go(准备出发);Arriving in Africa(到达非洲);Seeing the Animals(观看动物);A Narrow Escape(死里逃生)。本课围绕 May 的经历,以读为切入口,围绕故事情节的发展,在小组分享、合作中把阅读与听、读、写等语言技能有机结合起来。

教学准备:Give the students a vocabulary list of the whole book in advance, providing the phonetics and the specific pages and lines. To facilitate the students to sweep the vocabulary obstacles and understand the contents of the book.

---

\* 执教:广州市海珠区教育发展研究院张志梅;点评:2019年广州市初中英语骨干教师第四批第六组老师易翠红、郭淑爱、周可芬、赖长春、陈婉冰、梅晓燕、雷晓莲、赵金龙。此课例在上海外语教育出版社举办的2019年《新课标》背景下中学英语"全景阅读"教学论坛(广东站)上进行了交流,时间为2019年12月16日。

## 二、学习目标

Students will be able to:

(1) listen and pay attention to the pronunciation, the stress, the pause, the intonation of the book;

(2) try to read the song and the book correctly and emotionally by using imitation skills;

(3) think for themselves and ask classmates questions according to what they read;

(4) work in groups and share what they think of the book in front of the class;

(5) take an active part in discussion, cooperation with teachers and classmates;

(6) evaluate the song and peer evaluate the presentation to improve the logical and critical thinking with the help of thinking maps;

(7) raise the awareness of protecting wild animals.

## 三、教学评析

### 1. Warming up

由于是借班授课,而且学生刚好结束课间跑操,使用了当时歌单上最新最火的歌曲《说好不哭》(*Won't Cry*)作为引入,让学生放松,进入状态的同时思考和学习,从词、曲、歌手、乐队、视频、主题等方面欣赏英语歌曲,学习使用有用的句型表达情感。另外温馨提示学生,能够站出来讲英语的人都可以获得小礼物,鼓励他们积极参与。很高兴发现音乐很快消除了师生之间的陌生感。

让学生谈论长隆野生动物园的照片,激活他们的背景知识,自然过渡到走进非洲的野生动物园。

### 2. 读前 Pre-reading

First, Read for prediction. 让学生看书的封面和书名,预测整本书的内容。

Second, Read for main idea. 让学生阅读书的目录,预测整本书的大意。

Third, Read for what you want to know. 让学生使用正确的语音语调读前置问题,带着自己感兴趣的问题去读。

Read the pre-reading questions (P2) with correct tones.

G: general questions 一般疑问句↗　　S: special questions 特殊疑问句↘

A: alternative questions 选择疑问句↗↘　　T: tag questions 反意疑问句↘↗

(1) Where can you go on safari [səˈfɑːri]? ↘ (S)

(2) Are there tigers in Africa? ↗ (G)

(3) What are the Big Five? ↘ (S)

(4) What is the only thing you can shoot on safari [səˈfɑːri]? ↘ (S)

(5) Why are there white markings (斑纹) around some antelope's [ˌæntɪləʊps] tails? ↘ (S)

(6) Are hippos [ˌhɪpəʊs] (河马) as dangerous as lions? ↗ (G)

(7) How fast can a cheetah [ˌtʃiːtə] (猎豹) run? ↘ (S)

(8) Which are more dangerous, hippos ↗ or lions? ↘ (A)

(9) Where can you go on safari, in Asia ↗ or in Africa? ↘ (A)

(10) There are tigers in Africa, ↘aren't there? ↗ (T)

3. 读中 While-reading

Listen to Part 1 (*Getting Ready to Go* 准备出发) carefully and tick the things may needs to pack.

Fourth, Read Part 2 (*Arriving in Africa* 到达非洲) in a group of 4 with imitation skills and ask the listeners questions designed by the teacher. Other students listen and record the performance of the group according to the evaluation form.

四人小组使用模仿技巧在讲台上朗读第2部分，然后向其他同学询问老师设计的问题；其他同学听的同时根据评价表记录小组的表现。

(1) Is James a game ranger?

(2) Why was the poacher going to kill an elephant?

(3) How often does a wild lion usually eat?

(4) Is Mosses James' tracker? Why?

2 groups had presentations in front of the class.

Fifth, Read Part 3 (*Seeing the Animals* 观看动物) in a group of 5 and then prepare your own questions to ask your classmates.

五人小组阅读第3部分（*Seeing the Animals* 观看动物），然后准备自己提问同学。其他同学听的同时根据评价表记录小组的表现。

2 groups had presentations in front of the class.

(1) Are there pandas in Africa?

(2) What are the Big Five?

(3) Why do antelopes have white markings?

(4) What will happen if people don't protect rhinos?

(5) How high can Buffalos grow up to?

(6) What are giraffes famous for?

(7) Which animal run faster, a cheetah or a wildebeest?

(8) Who feeds the animals in a safari?

(9) How long does a baby elephant spend inside its mother?

(10) What is the relationship between humans and animals?

4. Post-reading

Peer evaluation: Let's vote for the best readers.

They can read the pages correctly.

They can read the pages fluently.

They can read the pages emotionally.

Self-evaluation: Recall what you have learned and share it in class with the help of the thinking map below.

*Thinking Map*: Share with my learning

| Content（内容） | Opinions（看法） | Reasons（理由） | Feelings（感悟） | Others |
|---|---|---|---|---|
| Won't Cry | The song is worth listening to. = The song is worthy to be listened to. = The song is worthy of being listened to. The song is worthwhile listening to. = The song is worthwhile to listen to. | Because/As/Since/ For the reason that I enjoy/am fond of/ am crazy about/ fall in love with the… lyric [ˌlirik] 歌词/ melody [ˈmelədi] (曲调)/singer/movie/story… | Songs are like sunshine/dew/…They can help us a lot. Relax oneself/ experience different cultures/ encourage … | |
| Going on Safari | be worth doing = be worthy to be done = be worthy of being done = be worthwhile doing = be worthwhile to do | The reasons are as follows. The reason why I love it is that… There are several reasons. | Books are like friends./…They can help us know the world better.… | |

5. 作业 Assignment：

Sixth, read Part 4 (*A Narrow Escape* 死里逃生) and finish writing the summary of May's trip on Page 44.

## 四、教学反思

本节课教学目标达成度比较高，反思学生的表现，结合听课老师的反馈，优点如下。

（1）为学生准备了整本书的词汇表，为学生阅读搭建了词汇的"脚手架"，大大提高了学生说的准确性和流畅性。

（2）教学目标：体现核心素养在课堂教学中的具体操作实施，带领学生走进野生动物的世界，培养保护动物的自然观，也培养学生模仿朗读、获取信息、询问信息的微技能，把中考听说考试的备考与发展学生的核心素养有机结合起来。

（3）教学活动：体现了以学生为主体的课堂教学观，充分调动了学生学习的积极主动性，进行了激发好奇心和求知欲的思维训练，而且尝试让思维可见、可听。从学生的表现来看，他们积极举手发言，提出了一些有思维火花的问题，教师也收获了孩子们天真烂漫的笑容。

（4）教学评价：适时适度，激励学生，培养了学生的自信心和成就感。本节课中教师自始至终对学生循循善诱，用心聆听，并且根据学生的语言输出及时中肯地进行评价。同时也充分考虑了参与听课的20多位老师的需要，让老师们参与投票，观察学生表现，现场答疑，评课等，发挥老师们教研活动的主人翁精神，调动了他们工作的主动性和创造性。

本课不足之处在于：教师对学生的了解不够，导致设计的内容偏多，偏难，加之受教室环境的限制，学生难以进行高效的小组合作沟通，导致课堂节奏掌握得不太好，从学生的口头语言和习作中看出语言输入的质量有待提高。此外，课堂上如何做到既给学生鼓励，又能够及时纠正学生错误仍然需要改进。

## 五、教学点评

2019年9月20日，市级骨干教师培训之实践导师跟岗进入第五天，我们第6组一行8人，早早来到了绿树葱葱、环境优雅、负离子极高的化龙中学。今天我们终于领略到了实践导师张老师的整本书阅读现场示范！张老师的教学设计融育人目标于教学内容与教学过程之中，教学目标体现英语学科核心素养，课堂紧紧地抓住了上课学生和听课老师们的心，特别是学生认真听讲、积极发言和热烈讨论，让我们觉得这真的不只是一节英语课，而是名师典范与育人楷模的彰显。课后，我们集中到会议室进行评课。导师张志梅老师就初中阅读教学提出了独到的看法，也为化龙中学、石楼中学全体英语教师怎样针对农村地区提高学生英语阅读能力阐述了她的见解，并提出了宝贵建议，同时也对赵老师的课用全英进行了精准的评价。整个过程，我们积极深入研讨，受益匪浅。张老师赞扬赵老师上课有张力，有耐心，对教学充满了激情；课前做好备课的充分准备，教学重点和难点突出，任务一环紧扣一环，学生参与度高。张老师一向强调：Thinking is learning。她希望我们在以后日常的教学中要关注每个学生的学，注意训练学生的思考能力，鼓励学生开口大胆说。尤其是要对学生进行思维训练和创新能力的培养，同时在设计教学环节中彰显合作精神，让学生在合作中发现问题，从合作中获得成功感。

### 附："基于核心素养的初中英语整本书阅读教学课例研究"专题发言

Good morning! Ladies and gentlemen!

I am very grateful and more than happy to have this opportunity to share some of my teaching ideas and experiences today.

My topic is "A Case Study on English Reading Teaching of the Whole Book in Junior High School Based on Core Literacy". The main contents include the related background, a brief introduction of my lesson, teaching procedures and analysis; teaching reflection and perspective.

As we all know, reading is a lifetime spiritual activity. Reading ability is one of the most important abilities of the students. Guangzhou and the whole GD-HK-Macao Greater Bay Area are promoting the intelligent growth reading among primary and middle school students. In this context, It is our responsibility and mission to promote this meaningful project. Our Haizhu District has started to read the whole book in the classroom.

Some research results show that teaching whole books, can effectively stimulate students' interest in reading and improve students' language ability, thinking ability and aesthetic ability. As a matter of fact, the significance of reading the whole book in English learning is more and more recognized and valued.

Two recent educational studies in the United States provide theoretical support for the promotion of the reading of the whole book. According to a study on grit in the Chicago public schools among thousands of high school juniors, it turns out that grittier kids were significantly more likely to graduate.

One characteristic emerged as a significant predictor of success. It wasn't social intelligence, it wasn't good looks, physical health, and it wasn't IQ. It was grit. Grit is passion and perseverance for very long-term goals. Grit is having stamina. Grit is sticking with your future. Day in, day out, not just for the week, not just for the month, just for years. And working really hard to make that future a reality.

Another study is an idea developed at Stanford University by Carol Dweck, and it is the belief that the ability to learn is not fixed. But that it can change with your effort. Dr. Dweck has shown that once kids fall in love with reading, they are much more likely to persevere when they fail. Because they don't believe that failure is a permanent condition. So growth mindset is a great idea for building grit. Which is not only beneficial to children's English learning, but also beneficial to all of their lives.

It is clear that, compared with the daily textbook reading, reading a whole book will need more patience and perseverance, so it will also help to train the students' growth mindset. But how to integrate the whole book into the daily teaching is a very tough task. How to combine the core literacy and the reading teaching with the greatest perplexity of the teachers? After the co-discussion of the teachers in our central group, we decided to choose the case study as the starting point and the focus point.

Miss Luo Xuemei, from the affiliated High School of South China Normal University, lectured a demonstration class on Jack London's novel *The Call of the Wild* in Class 2, Grade 1 of Nanwu High School; Mr. Sun Jian, from Shanghai International Studies University worked as an expert in the activity. Besides, we have invited teachers from distinguished high school English workshops of Guangzhou; teachers from brother and sister schools in Guangzhou. Like the affiliated High School of South China Normal University, Guangzhou Foreign Language School and more as well as all the English teachers of Senior One in our district.

The teachers think highly of Miss Luo's class. This is also a milestone for us to study the teaching of reading throughout the whole book. I particularly appreciate Miss Luo for her outstanding guidance in using the mind map as a learning tool to enable students to move from shallow to deep learning through multi-dimensional tasks.

Since then, we have gradually carried out the reading teaching of the whole book in the whole district. It is also more and more popular with teachers and students.

In order to further promote the reading teaching of the whole book in the junior high school, I had an open class in Hua Long Junior High School on September 20th, 2019, teaching the book named *Going on Safari*, published by the Shanghai Foreign Language Education Press. I'd like to share this lesson from the procedures including the preparation, lead-in, pre-reading, while-reading, post-reading, evaluation, and teaching reflection with a view to guide the students' to read happily, walk into the world of wild animals and cultivating students' view of protecting animals and nature, especially develop their micro-skills of imitating the reading, getting information and asking information, and hopefully combine the preparation of the listening and speaking test of Guangzhou and the development of the students' core literacy.

# 第四篇　成果推广

　　本篇介绍笔者开展联动教研行动研究有关的成果，包括课题研究过程中提炼的论文、案例研究、语言与文化的融合教学、双语教学、最新中考试题评析、区域学业水平监测质量分析和媒体报道等。这些成果是通过对常规教研工作深入研究和在实践中不断摸索、总结提炼的，包含了对于特定问题的见解、解决方案和教学思想。另外也精选了笔者在课题前积累的论文、课例、实验报告、考察报告、教学模式研究等，它们是课题研究宝贵的参考和支持。正是前前后后的积累让我们的联动教研更富有深度和内涵，也为我们提供了更多解决问题和创新的可能性。通过对这些成果的审视和思考，我们能够从中发现教育工作的真谛和意义，以及我们在其中扮演的角色和使命，激励我们在今后的研究过程中不仅要关注提炼课题成果，还要注重学会反思和学会生活，成为具备丰富经验和智慧的教育者，为学生们提供更优质的服务，推动教育事业的可持续发展。也希望通过分享我们在教研当中的创新思维和实践经验，为同行提供参考和启发。

# 第一章　育人蓝图引领的初中英语单元整体教学*
## ——以牛津沪教版八年级下册 Unit 1 Helping Those in Need 单元复习课为例

### 一、引言

今年是全面贯彻落实党的二十大精神的开局之年，是"十四五规划"承上启下关键之年。为全面贯彻落实党的二十大精神，促进教育高质量发展，广东省广州市海珠区教育发展研究院与区内外学校共建共享"深教研"平台，组织"聚焦新课标"系列教学展示活动。活动以广州市五中东晓学校为样本学校，由驻点调研、教研员的课例展示和市区联动教研等部分组成。本文基于笔者在广州市的课例展示，探讨初中英语单元整体教学的联动教研区域实践。

《义务教育英语课程标准（2022年版）》提出：英语课程应加强单元教学的整体性，推动实施单元整体教学。教师要强化素养立意，围绕单元主题，充分挖掘育人价值，确立单元育人目标和教学主线；深入解读和分析单元内各语篇及相关教学资源，并结合学生的认知逻辑和生活经验，对单元内容进行必要的整合或重组，建立单元内各语篇内容之间及语篇育人功能之间的联系，形成具有整合性、关联性、发展性的单元育人蓝图。《新课标》倡导教师在教学中遵循学习活动观。教师要有意识地为学生创设主动参与和探究主题意义的情境和空间，使学生获得积极的学习体验，成为意义探究的主体和积极主动的知识建构者。《新课标》提出教学评价应贯穿英语课程教与学的全过程。[1]单元评价

---

\* 本文原发表于《21世纪英语教育》2023年第343期。本文为广东省教育研究院2022年中小学英语教育专项研究课题"聚焦单元整体教学的中学英语联动教研行动研究"（课题编号：GDJY-2022-A-yyb33）的阶段性研究成果，并获2023年广东省中小学外语教育论文评选一等奖。

① 中华人民共和国教育部：《义务教育英语课程标准（2022年版）》，北京师范大学出版社2022年版，第47-48页。

② 中华人民共和国教育部：《义务教育英语课程标准（2022年版）》，北京师范大学出版社2022年版，第50页。

应根据单元教学目标，围绕核心素养综合表现进行设计，通过多元主体参与的方式，采用多种手段和形式组织实施。②

总之，《新课标》对实施单元整体教学有明确的描述。强调要依据单元育人蓝图实施教学，使学生逐步建构起对单元主题的完整认知，促进正确态度和价值观的形成。①

## 二、构建单元育人蓝图

牛津沪教版八年级下册 Unit 1 Helping Those in Need 单元主题属于《新课标》"人与社会"范畴下的"社会服务与人际沟通"主题群，子主题内容为"志愿服务与公共服务"。② 本单元各语篇主要以"帮助有需要的人"为话题，以志愿服务为主线，三个小观念围绕着大观念，大观念指挥着三个小观念。具体结构如图1所示。

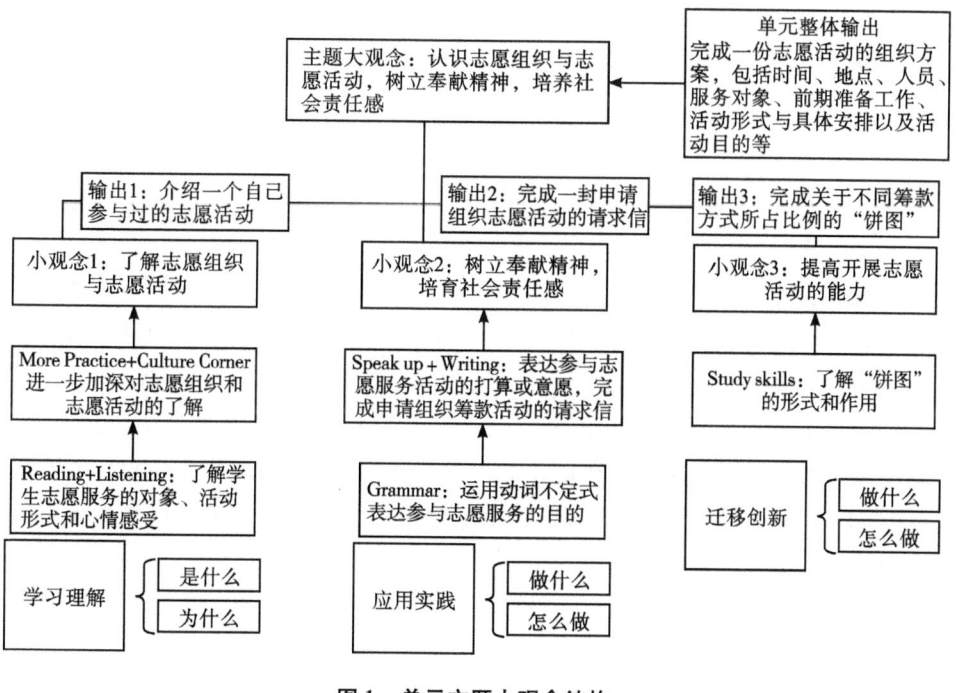

图1 单元主题大观念结构

---

① 中华人民共和国教育部：《义务教育英语课程标准（2022年版）》，北京师范大学出版社2022年版，第53页。

② 中华人民共和国教育部：《义务教育英语课程标准（2022年版）》，北京师范大学出版社2022年版，第58页。

如图1所示，三条教学主线分别为学习理解、应用实践、迁移创新。单元整体输出为完成一份志愿活动的组织方案，助力实现以下单元育人蓝图：①了解志愿服务的目的、形式、内容和意义；听取筹款活动的电台采访录音；掌握动词不定式做状语和宾语的用法；谈论自己打算参加的志愿服务活动。②了解不同的志愿组织；理解志愿服务的重要性；建立良好的道德风尚，培养奉献精神和社会责任感。③从文本中提取关键信息，利用思维导图构建写作框架并完成筹款活动申请书，有逻辑、有创意地表达思想。④在学习活动中积极与他人合作，共同完成志愿工作计划和互相评价，尝试用不同策略解决学习问题。

## 三、单元整体复习课教学设计

### （一）学情分析

广州市第五中学东晓学校初二1班共39人，该班参加2023年3月海珠区学业质量监测，数据显示该班学生的各项技能水平低于区平均水平，写作能力是短板。笔者通过驻点调研发现，主要原因是疫情期间线上教学时间长，学生学习松散，有的甚至出现了严重的心理问题。大部分学生对熟悉的词汇和语法不会灵活运用，能力较好的学生上课积极，但注意力不集中，学困生则迫切需要建立自信心。

基于学情的改进策略：①针对词汇问题，引导学生在生活化的情景和多模态语篇中理解和掌握核心词汇的意义、词性和功能；②针对语法问题，帮助学生意识到语法知识是"形式－意义－运用"的统一体，目的是在语境中运用和表达意义；③针对写作能力弱，注意力不集中的问题，鼓励学生以参与听、说、读、看活动为主，写的活动安排在课后作业中；④针对学困生自信心不足的问题，搭好"脚手架"，鼓励其在小组合作中尝试完成难度低的任务，带给他们快乐、勇气和自信心。

### （二）教学内容设计

本课属于单元整体复习，也是本单元的最后一课。单元的整体输出为完成一份志愿活动的组织方案。为了让学生顺利完成任务，采用产出导向法设计。

What：使用主题链的形式选取对单元主题意义有建构的多模态语篇，包括：①听歌曲 Count on Me，学生通过介绍这首歌，复习巩固本单元话题词汇的意义、词性和功能；②关于 C21 Volunteers 的视频，背景音乐还是 Count on Me，但是内容为 C21 International School 的志愿者帮助儿童的情景，视频复现单元核心词汇，同时帮助学生理解志愿服务的目的、形式、内容和意义等，也拓宽其国际视野；③Jiang Xu's Plan 是广州市第六中学姜同学写的志愿工作计划的录音，把学生从国外拉进现实生活，引导学生听读并且完成"鱼骨图"，包括服务对象、目的、时间、地点、计划和预期结果等，同时让学生评价 Jiang Xu's Plan，对好计划的标准心中有数；④Show Time，要求学生在四个真实的情景中选择一个，包括南华西敬老院、和谐动物收容所、东晓校园、彩虹社区，小组合作完成志愿工作计划，小组展示，评出最佳组；⑤Poem Time，集体朗读一首关于关怀世界的诗歌。

How：以英语教学活动观为依据，师生共建一段学习旅程：从"帮助朋友"，到"帮助儿童、老人、动物、社区、世界"，结尾留白。

Why：在努力为学生减负的基础上，让他们学得更开心有效，增强成就感和自信心。

## （三）课时教学目标

本课将达成单元育人蓝图目标 4，学生将能够：①Review the words and expressions of Unit 1. ②Understand the meaning of the voluntary work. ③Learn to make plans to help those in need and share them in groups. ④Peer assess the learning.

## 四、依据育人蓝图实施教学

2023 年 5 月 4 日，笔者在广州市初中英语单元整体教学市区联动教研活动中进行课例展示，授课对象为广州市五中东晓学校初二 1 班。在教学过程中依据育人蓝图，通过学习理解、应用实践和迁移创新等活动，引导学生整合性地学习语言知识和文化知识，进而运用所学知识、技能和策略，围绕主题表达个人观点和态度，解决真实问题，达到在教学中培养学生核心素养的目的。[1]

Activity 1 Song Time 感知注意

设计意图：To warm up and review the words and expressions of Unit 1.

教学评析：教师通过感知与注意活动创设主题情境，激活学生已有的知识经验。[2] 学生听歌曲 *Count On Me*，视频含有中英文字幕，歌曲朗朗上口，重复

---

[1] 中华人民共和国教育部：《义务教育英语课程标准（2022 年版）》，北京师范大学出版社 2022 年版，第 48 页。

[2] 中华人民共和国教育部：《义务教育英语课程标准（2022 年版）》，北京师范大学出版社 2022 年版，第 14 页。

率高，有效帮助学生理解"help friends in need"的含义。在轻松友好的氛围中，老师走近学生采访："Do you like Connie, the singer? How do you feel after listening to her song?"学生对同龄歌手 Connie 及其歌曲都非常喜爱，也对新老师热情起来。老师趁热打铁，设置了以语篇的形式介绍歌曲的填词任务，告诉学生可以使用教材单元词汇表，学生积极举手发言，达成了本课目标①。歌曲拉近了师生距离，也扫除了通往育人蓝图的词汇障碍。

Activity 2 Video Time 学习理解

设计意图：To help students to think the meaning of voluntary work.

教学评析：教师引导学生通过学习理解类活动，建立信息间的关联，形成新的知识结构，感知并理解语言所表达的意义。① 引入 C21 国际学校 *Help Kids in Need* 的视频，背景音乐还是 *Count on Me*。学生观看视频后互相采访："What are the teenagers doing? How do the children feel? Why are volunteers so happy?"关于第 3 个问题，学生的回答是"Because helping kids is helpful/happy."。学生有创意，了解了志愿组织、活动及意义，达成了本课目标②，也助推育人蓝图中小观念 1 的形成。

Activity 3 Reading Time 应用实践

设计意图：To analyze a voluntary work plan and encourage students to give likes.

教学评析：在学习理解类活动的基础上，引导学生基于所形成的结构化知识开展描述、阐释、分析、应用等多种有意义的语言实践活动，内化语言知识和文化知识，加深对文化意涵的理解，巩固结构化知识，促进知识向能力的转化。② 教师引导："C21 volunteers are very kind and friendly. In Haizhu District, there are also many kind-hearted volunteers. Now a boy from No. 6 Middle school wants to share his plan."学生从国外回到课堂，读 Jiang Xu's Plan，梳理结构化知识，用思维导图描述"to help the elderly who suffer from illness and pain, plan to clean the room, decide to put up some beautiful pictures, offer to wash the clothes, would love to sing and dance, wish to make the elderly happy"等要点，阐释动词不定式表达目的和计划，运用评价表为 Jiang Xu's Plan 点赞。进一步

---

① 中华人民共和国教育部：《义务教育英语课程标准（2022 年版）》，北京师范大学出版社 2022 年版，第 49 页。

② 中华人民共和国教育部：《义务教育英语课程标准（2022 年版）》，北京师范大学出版社 2022 年版，第 50 页。

理解志愿服务做什么，怎么做，指向本课目标③，也激励学生向优秀的同龄人学习，树立奉献精神，培养社会责任感，助推育人蓝图中小观念 2 的形成。

Activity 4 Show Time 迁移创新

设计意图：To help students reflect and improve their learning.

教学评析：坚持学创结合，引导学生在迁移创新类活动中联系个人实际，运用所学解决现实生活中的问题，形成正确的态度和价值判断。[①] 教师引导："Dongxiao volunteers have been working very hard all the time. It's time for you to continue this good job. You can choose a place, then discuss in groups and share your plan in class." 教师对东晓中学志愿者的表扬给了学生鼓舞，学生从 Nanhuaxi Nursing Home, Hexie Animal Shelter, Dongxiao School, Rainbow Community 中选择和适度发挥，有 1 组选了帮助社区贫困孩子，有 2 个组都选了帮助动物。例如第 1 组：

Greetings：Hello, everyone! My name is...

Student A：In order to help animals, we are going to Hexie Animal Shelter this Saturday.

Student B：First, we plan to help animals have a bath.

Student C：Next, we decide to play with animals.

Student D：Finally, we would love to find new homes for them.

Together：We wish to bring joy, peace and hope to the homeless animals. Welcome to join us! That's all. Thank you!

可见学生运用了单元核心词汇，内化了 in order to do, plan/decide/would love to do, wish to do 等结构化知识，整体输出了志愿活动的组织方案，包括目的、时间、地点、人员、服务对象、活动形式与具体安排等，并选出了最佳志愿活动计划，体现了能力向素养的转化。达成本课目标（③④），推进了单元育人蓝图的实现。

Activity 5 Poem Time 呼应主题

Helping those in need

Robot：Help those in need, lend a hand,

Make them smile, help them stand.

Students：With love and care in our heart,

---

① 中华人民共和国教育部：《义务教育英语课程标准（2022 年版）》，北京师范大学出版社 2022 年版，第 3 页。

Let us do our part, each day to start!

**教学评析**：教师扮演机器人邀请学生朗读诗歌，大大激发了学生的兴趣，达到了情感价值观的升华。

Activity 6 Summary Time

**教学评析**：学生利用流程图回顾学习旅程：Helping friends—kids—elderly—animals—environment—community—nature—world，结尾留白，老师点明这是一段关于爱与成长的旅程，也是新的育人蓝图的起点，延伸了单元主题大观念。

Activity 7 Homework

**Must-do**（必做）：选择你喜欢的志愿工作，并写一个计划。

**Optional**（选做）：写"一节有趣的英语课"的日记。

**教学评析**：从作业反馈看，全班有32人完成了必做题，说明对写作增加了信心。更可喜的是有28人写了日记，如吴同学写道："我很高兴在英语课上采访了同学。这不仅巩固了第一单元的知识，加深了印象，还学会了如何介绍志愿工作，对我的英语学习很有帮助。我对老师的印象十分深刻，她上课风趣幽默，把生涩难懂的知识变得简单易懂，让人情不自禁地沉浸在知识的海洋里。下课后，我们都还意犹未尽，期待以后还能有机会上老师的课！"学生内化了单元知识，获得了积极的情感态度，这是单元育人蓝图的出发点和落脚点。

## 五、结语

在初中英语单元整体教学中，育人蓝图就像亲切的向导，指引教师依据课标，以主题意义的探究和生成为主线，整合课内外资源，基于学情整体规划教学内容，合理设计教学目标。在教学中遵循学习活动观的路径，关联设计递进活动，适时搭建脚手架，使活动的推进贴近学生，服务于单元产出，学生在探究真实而有意义的学习旅程中，润物细无声般地获得核心素养的提升。在联动教研活动中，专家、教研员和一线老师共同探讨初中英语单元整体教学，有助于深入理解单元育人价值，优化课程结构，丰富课程内容，完善评估体系，打造精品案例[①]，促进教师发展。育人蓝图引领的单元整体教学是提升教学质量的抓手，也是老师们的困惑所在。"聚焦新课标，共享深教研"的课例展示则

---

① 梅德明、王雪梅、李硕：《落实课标，素养导向，擘画高中英语课程建设蓝图》，载《中小学英语教学与研究》2023第3期，第2、第6页。

构建了实践导向的学习和研究共同体[①]，提高了学生的参与度，着力引导教师准确、深刻领会课程理念、目标和要求，并转化为切实有效的教学实践，对《新课标》落地、提高区域教学质量有深远的意义。《新课标》背景下，我们需要深入研究"单元复习课"如何体现主题意义与语言形式的深度融合，如何引导学生深度学习，以及更科学有效地评价教学效果，达到语言学习和育人蓝图统一的目的。

---

[①] 中华人民共和国教育部：《义务教育英语课程标准（2022年版）》，北京师范大学出版社2022年版，第75页。

# 第二章　基于单元整体教学的初中英语作业设计研究*

## 一、引言

《义务教育英语课程标准（2022年版）》明确指出：加强单元教学的整体性，推动实施单元整体教学。①作业的设计既要有利于学生巩固语言知识和技能，又要有利于促进学生有效运用策略，增强学习动机。教师应根据不同学段学生的认知特点和学习需求，基于单元教学目标，兼顾个体差异，整体设计单元作业和课时作业，把握好作业的内容、难度和数量，使学生形成积极的情感体验，提升自我效能感。教师应创设真实的学习情境，建立课堂所学和学生生活的关联，设计复习巩固类、拓展延伸类和综合实践类等多种类型的作业。②

然而，因为应试的压力大，初中英语教学中存在作业考试化的倾向。学生的学习时间过长、学习负担过重等问题依然严重。作业形式过于简单，而且其中的大部分都是将重点放在了对课堂上所学知识与技能的机械性重复练习上，存在很大的随意性，缺少系统性和科学性。学生很少有机会进行合作性探究，也难以进行开放性思考和多元化问题解决。教师对学生作业的评价通常只关注是否符合标准答案，这不仅削弱了学生对语言学习的兴趣，也阻碍了高阶思维能力的发展。

基于《新课标》对"单元整体教学"的要求，需要教师对"单元作业设计"进行全面的思考，并探讨提高初中英语作业有效性的方法策略，达到既符合课标要求又促进学生身心健康发展的效果。

---

\*　本文即将发表于《基础教育论坛》2024年第1期（总459期）。
①　中华人民共和国教育部：《义务教育英语课程标准（2022年版）》，北京师范大学出版社2022年版，第47页。
②　中华人民共和国教育部：《义务教育英语课程标准（2022年版）》，北京师范大学出版社2022年版，第57页。

## 二、基于单元整体教学目标确定作业目标

在日常教学中，每个单元都有相应的教学目标，而作业应该是助推单元目标实现的有效手段。因此在设定单元内分课时作业目标之前，为了确保作业的可信度和效度并最终达到单元教学目标，教师应该综合考虑单元整体教学目标、分课时教学目标以及作业目标，使它们相辅相成。

比如牛津沪教版八年级下册 Unit 1 Helping Those in Need 单元主题属于《新课标》"人与社会"范畴下的"社会服务与人际沟通"主题群，子主题内容为"志愿服务与公共服务"。该单元各个语篇主要以"帮助有困难的人"为话题，以志愿服务为主线，教师对单元内容进行了必要的整合和重组，并制定了单元教学目标、分课时教学目标和分课时作业目标（详见表1至表3），以充分发挥作业巩固内化课堂教学内容的作用，实现课内学习与课后学习的互补。

**表1 牛津沪教版八年级下册 Unit 1 Helping Those in Need 单元整体教学目标**

| |
|---|
| 1. 了解志愿服务的目的、主要形式、内容和意义；听取有关筹款活动的电台采访录音，巩固提取和记录关键信息的倾听技巧；掌握动词不定式做状语和宾语的用法，通过小组活动，谈论自己打算参加的志愿服务活动。 |
| 2. 了解不同的志愿组织，理解志愿服务的重要性；建立良好的道德风尚，培养奉献精神和社会责任感。 |
| 3. 从文本中提取关键信息和要点；利用"蛛网图"构建写作框架并完成一封给校长的筹款活动申请书；有逻辑、有创意地表达自己的想法。 |
| 4. 在学习活动中积极与他人合作，共同完成自己的志愿工作计划和评价同学的计划；并且尝试用不同的策略来解决语言学习中的问题。 |

**表2 牛津沪教版八年级下册 Unit 1 Helping Those in Need 分课时教学目标**

| | |
|---|---|
| 课时1教学目标 | Getting Ready：听取有关筹款活动的电台采访录音，讨论"帮助有困难的人"的话题。 |
| 课时2教学目标 | Voluntary Work：阅读并了解学生志愿服务的对象、活动形式和心情感受等。 |
| 课时3教学目标 | More Practice：进一步加深对志愿组织和志愿活动的了解。 |
| 课时4教学目标 | Culture Corner：了解联合国儿童基金会，关注慈善机构。 |

续上表

| 课时 5 教学目标 | Grammar & Speaking：掌握动词不定式作宾语、宾补和目的状语的用法。 |
|---|---|
| 课时 6 教学目标 | Writing & Study Skills：使用"蛛网图"和"饼图"构思写作框架，完成向校长申请组织筹款活动的信件。 |
| 课时 7 教学目标 | Revision & Assessment：完成志愿活动的组织方案，并且进行自我评价和相互评价。 |

表3　牛津沪教版八年级下册 Unit 1 Helping Those in Need 分课时作业目标

| 课时 1 作业目标 | 学生通过介绍歌曲 Count on Me，复习巩固本单元话题词汇的意义、词性和功能。 |
|---|---|
| 课时 2 作业目标 | 梳理阅读语篇的"鱼骨图"，包括组织者、受惠者、目的、时间、地点、形式和预期结果等，对好计划的标准心中有数。 |
| 课时 3 作业目标 | 观看和评价 C21 International School 的志愿者帮助儿童的视频，帮助理解志愿服务的目的、形式、内容和意义等，拓宽学生国际视野。 |
| 课时 4 作业目标 | 阅读同龄人写的志愿工作计划，把学生拉进现实生活。 |
| 课时 5 作业目标 | 运用课堂语法口头表达参与志愿活动的意愿。为课时 6 做准备。 |
| 课时 6 作业目标 | 选择真实的情景，包括敬老院、动物收容所、校园、社区，小组讨论感兴趣的志愿活动。 |
| 课时 7 作业目标 | Robot poem，一首由机器人写的关怀世界的诗歌，引导学生思考要帮助的 those 不仅仅是人，还可以是全世界，深化主题意义。 |

由此可见，单元内分课时作业目标与分课时教学目标以及单元教学目标高度关联。通过作业，学生可以更深入地理解课堂所学内容，拓宽学习资源，调整学习策略，并培养良好的学习习惯。在对课堂上所学的知识与技能进行强化的过程中，作业还有助于提高学生的学习责任心和积极性、学习兴趣和信心、元认知能力、问题解决能力和创新实践能力，更好地激发他们的学习动机。

## 三、以目标为导向，遵循作业设计的原则

### （一）趣味性原则

在设计作业时，教师不仅要考虑教学需要，还要充分关注学生对新鲜事物的好奇心，努力提高作业的趣味性。首先，通过选择有趣的话题和内容来吸引学生的注意力，例如使用有趣的故事、音乐、影视片段或游戏等元素。其次，使用多种媒体技术，如视频、音频、网站或应用程序，使学习过程更加生动有趣。此外，还可以设计一些创意性的任务，如设计海报、编短剧等，让学生能够发挥想象力和创造力，增添他们参与英语学习的乐趣。

### （二）实践性原则

学生的英语语言能力只有通过大量的语言实践才能得到培养和提高。有些扩展型的课外作业，如调查、采访报告等，需要学生实践完成。因此，在设计此类作业时，需要以教材为依托，结合学生的生活实际，鼓励学生积极主动地参与实践活动，让学生通过作业的完成深入理解和运用所学知识，增强其实践能力。此外，让学生在完成作业的过程中逐渐形成自己的学习风格，发展学生的自主学习能力以及创造性地解决问题的能力。

### （三）多样性原则

作业的设计是在对学生依据课标应达到的学习能力和所预期的教学效果进行全面考虑的基础上进行的，它并不是一个随意的过程。所以，老师应该针对水平存在差异、兴趣多样化、要求不一样的学生，在作业的设置上采取多样化的形式、多元化的评价方式，让他们能够在符合自己的水平、兴趣、未来发展需要的情况下，进行与之相适应的学习活动，从而达到因材施教的目的，达到"减负"和"增效"的效果。

## 四、基于单元整体教学的作业实施与评价

### （一）根据主题大观念布置整合性的作业

在单元的整体教学中，活动的设置应当以对主题意义的探索为基础，因而作业的设置应注重多个输出活动的相关与扩展，并将所学的语言知识、文化知

识、语言技能和学习策略结合起来,从而使得作业能够更好地为本单元的整体教学目的服务。

比如以牛津沪教版八年级下册 Unit 3 Traditional Skills 为例,单元主题属于《新课标》"人与自我"范畴下的"生活与学习"主题群。该单元各语篇以"传统技艺"为话题,以各种中国传统技艺的历史和特点为主线,但各个课型关联度较弱,对于学生在校园活动中的主创性拓展不够,需要在作业中加强与子主题内容"丰富、充实、积极向上的生活"的联系,培养学生"勤于动手,乐于实践,敢于创新"的精神。因此,教师可以根据单元主题大小观念进行整合性的作业设计,让学生选择生活中熟悉的手工艺人,完成一份宣传海报。在海报中,既要有对已学内容的综合输出,又要有"保护中华优秀传统工艺"的建议,最终形成单元主题大观念"劳动实践,劳动品质与工匠精神"①。

(二) 创设真实情境激发学生完成作业的内在动机

创设真实情境是指将学生置于具有现实感和真实性的情境中,让他们感受到所学知识的实际性和重要性,激发学生完成作业的内在动机。在设计作业时,可以选取与学生生活相关的话题,让学生能够将所学知识与自己的生活联系起来。例如,前面表3中,牛津沪教版八年级下册 Unit 1 Helping Those in Need 课时6的作业设计,教师设置了以下真实的情景:敬老院、动物收容所、学校志愿者、社区捐书筹款,给学生选择的机会和适度发挥的空间,激发了学生的学习兴趣。学生能够运用单元词汇和语法知识,小组分享志愿服务计划并且评价优秀小组计划,在真实的场景中运用所学知识,促进语言知识的内化和迁移,获得真实的情感体验,激发了他们参加志愿活动的动机。这是最重要的育人目标,也是单元整体教学的出发点和落脚点。

(三) 基于单元整体教学实施作业评价

《新课标》提出教学评价应贯穿英语课程教与学的全过程,包括课堂评价、作业评价、单元评价和期末评价等。教学评价应充分发挥学生的主体作用。教学过程中,教师应引导学生成为各类评价活动的设计者、参与者和合作者,帮助他们学会开展自我评价和相互评价,主动反思和评价自我表现,促进

---

① 中华人民共和国教育部:《义务教育英语课程标准(2022年版)》,北京师范大学出版社2022年版,第16页。

自我监督性学习,并在相互评价中取长补短,总结经验,规划学习。[①]

首先,单元作业评价的全程化实施可以帮助学生更好地了解自己的学习成果,促进其在学习过程中进行反思并获得提高。因此针对不同类型的作业,老师也需要设计相应的评价标准。例如,针对牛津沪教版八年级下册 Unit 1 Helping Those in Need 单元作业评价可以按照表 4 进行学生自评、互评和教师评价。

表4　牛津沪教版八年级下册 Unit 1 Helping Those in Need 单元作业评价表

| 序号 | 标准 | 自评 | 互评 | 师评 |
| --- | --- | --- | --- | --- |
| 1 | 自信地介绍自己 | | | |
| 2 | 使用"(in order) to do"不定式表示目的 | | | |
| 3 | Know whom/when/where to help<br>知道何时何地帮助谁 | | | |
| 4 | 使用"plan/decide/offer/would love to…"不定式做宾语 | | | |
| 5 | 使用"wish to do"表达预期效果 | | | |
| Level | Excellent; Good; So-so. | | | |

其次,个性化的评价反馈可以帮助学生更全面地了解自己在英语学习中的实际情况,以便他们能够有针对性地进行改进。老师可以根据学生的能力水平、学习风格和学习兴趣等因素来分类评价。在给学生提建议前,老师可以先鼓励学生提出自己的看法,并一起探讨如何更好地改进,目的是帮助每一个学生进步。

## 五、结语

在"教—学—评"一体化的单元整体教学视野下,老师要对作业这一教育中的关键环节的作用和价值展开深入探讨。为了更好地减轻学业负担并提高效率,教师需要进一步细化作业设计和评价,并充分利用信息技术手段增加作业反馈渠道。通过真实有趣的作业和丰富的实践活动,学生巩固和运用了语言知识,体验了英语作业的乐趣。此外,全程化、多元化、个性化的评价为学生的学和教师的教提供了及时、准确的信息反馈。这样的作业设计和评价方式将充分体现其激励作用,培养学生核心素养,实现英语学科的育人目标。

---

① 中华人民共和国教育部:《义务教育英语课程标准(2022 年版)》,北京师范大学出版社 2022 年版,第 53 页。

# 第三章 "双新"背景下高中英语视频教学中培养学生文化意识的研究*
## ——以人教版选择性必修三 Unit 1 Art Video Time《清明上河图》为例

## 引言

党的二十大报告中提出要完善人才战略布局，推进文化自信，推动中华文化更好地走向世界。文化是人存在的根和魂。文化意识帮助学生成长为有文化修养和社会责任感的人。文化修养是个体自主发展和参与社会的必要基础。自主发展和社会参与，则是促使个体适应社会和实现个人价值的重要前提与根本保证。文化意识突出强调个人修养、涵养、内在精神，追求真善美的统一，直接涉及培养什么人、怎样培养人、为谁培养人的问题，意义重大。①

《普通高中英语课程标准（2017年版2020年修订）》指出文化意识体现了英语学科核心素养的育人价值导向，将立德树人这一根本任务落到实处。《高中课标》明确地把学生"文化意识"的培养列入到英语教学之中。

《义务教育英语课程标准（2022年版）》（以下简称"《义教课标》"）指出，"文化意识是指对中外文化的理解和对优秀文化的鉴赏，是学生在新时代表现出的跨文化认知、态度和行为选择。文化意识的培育有助于学生增强家国情怀和人类命运共同体意识，涵养品格，提升文明素养和社会责任感"。《新课标》在"课程性质"中指出，"英语课程体现工具性和人文性的统一"，教师应通过英语课程帮助学生"比较文化异同，汲取文化精华，逐步形成跨文

---

\* 本文原发表于《课堂内外·高中教研》2023年第9期，收录于本书时略有改动。本文为广东省教育研究院2022年中小学英语教育专项研究课题"聚焦单元整体教学的中学英语联动教研行动研究"（课题编号：GDJY－2022－A－yyb33）的阶段性研究成果。

① 梅德明：《基于学科核心素养发展的英语课程改革》，载上海市英语教育教学研究基地公众号，2019－11－18.

化沟通与交流的意识和能力，涵养家国情怀，坚定文化自信，形成正确的世界观、人生观和价值观"。

无论是《高中课标》还是《新课标》中，语言技能除了包括听、说、读、写，还增加了"看"。之所以增加"看"这一语言技能，主要是因为信息技术时代人们获取信息的方式发生了变化，特别是观看视频成为当代人们获取信息的主要途径之一，它既是信息输入的方式，也是信息表达的方式。人们通过"看"来接收信息、理解信息和运用信息，同时也通过视觉表达（visual representation），即创建视频、图片、图表、标识等来表达信息。

人教版新教材非常重视"看"技能的培养。首先，教材中增加了大量图片、图表，尤其是真实照片。每个单元的首页是一幅主题图，画面美观、内涵丰富，能够激发学生对单元话题的联想与期待。其次，每个单元都有 Video Time 板块，通过视频材料拓展单元话题内容，扩大学生的文化视野。Video Time 对于单元主题意义的探究起着不可或缺的作用，同时与单元其他语篇构成关联，共同指向单元主题观念的构成。基于此，本文以人教版选择性必修三 Unit 1 Art Video Time《清明上河图》教学为例，探讨文化意识的培养，以增强学生对中华优秀传统文化的认同感和民族自豪感。

## 一、单元整体设计与视频教学有机结合的概述

### （一）单元整体教学设计

实施视频教学，教学设计是最关键的一步。虽然教学设计对教师来说并不陌生，但由于目前专门针对英语视频文化课程的设计尚处于起步阶段，许多英语教师尽管已经认识到视频教学的重要意义，但在实践中却缺乏准确定位且未能深入实施。在新教材中，视频和单元整体教学是密切相关、相辅相成的，教师需要把握视频内容与单元各个语篇的内在逻辑及其对单元主题意义建构的作用，做好单元整体教学设计，才能使视频教学与单元整体教学有机结合，达到最佳的教学效果。

### （二）教学设计案例

本单元是人教版选择性必修三 Unit 1 Art，单元的主题是"Human and Society"，涉及"历史、社会与文化"。单元内容分析和整体设计分别见表 1 和图 1。

表1 《清明上河图》单元内容分析

| 语篇板块 | 语篇类型 | 语篇内容 | 主题意义 |
| --- | --- | --- | --- |
| Reading and Thinking | 知识性小品文 | 介绍西方绘画艺术发展的重要历史时期的艺术风格、特点、杰出代表及其作品。 | 了解西方艺术绘画史,探讨其发展变化的历程。 |
| Learning about Language (Build up your vocabulary) | 说明文 | 介绍印象派的艺术特点以及著名的印象派画家莫奈的创作主题。 | 了解印象派的艺术特点及代表人物,体会艺术魅力。 |
| Using Language (Talk about works of art) | 主题演讲 | 介绍我国水墨动画片的代表作品及其创作背景、内容、艺术特色及中国水墨动画片的未来。 | 了解我国动画史,激发对中国传统绘画艺术的兴趣,增强文化自信。 |
| Using Language (Write an art exhibition announcement) | 应用文 | 介绍中国古代艺术藏品展览信息,包括展览的主题、亮点、目的和意义,以及有关展览的实用信息。 | 感受艺术在跨文化交流中的独特价值,激发参与艺术交流活动的热情。 |
| Project | 脱口秀 | 介绍艺术家生平及成长经历。 | 了解和探究中外艺术家,增长见识,提升艺术修养。 |
| Video Time | 说明文(视频) | 介绍中国传世名画《清明上河图》,包括画作的基本信息、内容及历史和艺术价值。 | 体验中华传统文化艺术作品的魅力,理解其艺术、历史价值,比较中西方文化异同,提高审美情趣、跨文化交流的意识以及加强文化遗产保护意识。 |

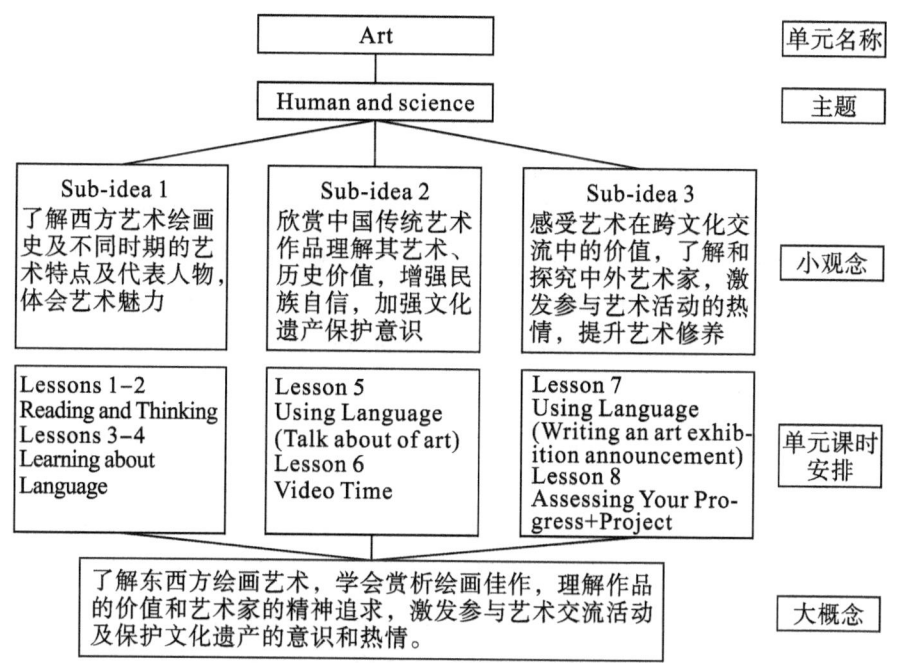

图1 单元整体设计

本课视频介绍《清明上河图》,属于单元第6课时。学生在前面已经学习了西方艺术绘画史、印象派的艺术特点及代表人物,探讨了西方艺术发展变化的历程并体会了西方艺术的魅力。《清明上河图》作为中国传统艺术代表和珍贵文化遗产,其视频教学重点是营造文化交流的语境,挖掘英语讲解语篇的文化内涵,帮助学生更好地了解中国传统文化,增强文化自信心。另外,通过比较西方绘画艺术,使学生深入了解中西方艺术文化的异同,感受到不同文化背景下的艺术美,培养良好的审美情趣,加强文化遗产保护意识和跨文化交流的意识,从而达到丰富单元主题意义,助力单元大观念形成的目的。

## 二、基于视频语篇分析,挖掘文化内涵,确定文化教学探究的维度

视频作为一种多模态语篇,能够再现现实生活经验,加强与观看者的互动,建构语篇整体意义。通过语篇分析,我们对作品不仅可以"知其然"(knowing what),而且可以"知其所以然"(knowing how)。对于视频语篇也必须分析它具有什么样的文体特征、内容结构和语言特点,学生基于语篇分析进行深度思考和理解,才能充分输入,为输出做准备。

## 《清明上河图》视频语篇分析

No doubt, one of the most admired Chinese paintings of all time is the *Qingming Shang He Tu* or *Along the River During the Qingming Festival*. The painting is on a silk scroll that is 24.8 cm wide and 528.7 cm long, bearing Emperor Huizong's name. It was painted by Zhang Zeduan, who was a court painter during the Northern Song Dynasty. This amazingly detailed painting quickly became a national treasure. Over the centuries that followed, hundreds of copies of it were made, many of which became national treasures themselves. Although the original painting was lost for some time, it is now proudly placed in the Palace Museum in Beijing. The painting is exhibited for only brief periods every few years. However, using computer animation, the painting has been remade into an animated digital version for all to enjoy. It contains moving characters and objects, showing life along the Bian River during the Qingming Festival, a time when Chinese people visit their ancestors' graves.

Flowing from right to left, the painting begins by showing the countryside outside Bianjing City, the capital of China at that time. There are a few houses and a few people traveling back to Bianjing. The scene soon becomes more crowded. The road beside the river becomes packed with restaurants, and the river becomes full of boats. Then we see the Rainbow Bridge arching over the river. On both sides of the bridge are people selling food and drink, while travelers pass by. Soon, the city begins to emerge. We see temples, inns, and large houses. The roads are now filled with people travelling on foot, and in carts and sedan chairs. Then we come to the first city gate. Through the gate is passing a line of camels carrying goods. In the city, there are butcher shops, doctor's clinics, hotels, inns, houses, and fabric shops. The streets are still crowded with people, but most of them are relaxing and taking it easy.

The painting ends here, but the scroll does not. About half of the scroll has the seals of its previous owners, along with poems praising the painting's beauty. There is also a note which gives a short biography of Zhang Zeduan. These seals and poems, along with the note, are the reasons why many experts claim this to be the original painting. The *Qingming Shang He Tu* is not only a true work of art, but it also gives us a rare insight into daily life in ancient China. So often, history only contains the stories of emperors, generals, and important events. This painting's great appeal is that it provides us with a look into ordinary people's lives in the Song Dynasty.

## （一）挖掘文化内涵

《清明上河图》视频语篇属于说明文，语言为陈述句，结构清晰，分三部分展开。第一部分介绍了这幅画作的概况，包括画家的身份、画作的尺寸大小、主题内容等信息；第二部分依照从右到左的观赏顺序展示了这幅画作的内容细节；第三部分总结了这幅画作独特的历史、文化和艺术价值。

视频材料中出现了较多学生不熟悉的语言。在第一部分介绍画作概况时，出现 silk scroll，需要引导学生注意卷轴式画作的欣赏顺序，为接下来了解画作内容做准备；在介绍画作近况时，视频提到了 computer animation，这为后续讨论如何传播中华艺术做了一些铺垫。第二部分介绍画作内容细节时，出现了与画作时代背景匹配的建筑与活动，如 inns、carts、sedan chairs、a line of camels、butcher shops，内容信息量较大，语言与画面均传达出北宋都城汴京当时的城市面貌和人民生活状况。在对这一部分内容的处理中，要辅以细节图片的展示，让学生更深刻地感受作品魅力与作品的历史价值，加强学生的文化遗产保护意识。第三部分总结画作的艺术价值，其中的评价"This painting's great appeal is that it provides us with a look into ordinary people's lives in the Song Dynasty."很好地概括了其历史价值。但学生欣赏《清明上河图》时看到的多是社会繁荣的景象，故在此引入第二则听力材料，介绍画作中也描绘了当时的社会问题，引导学生辩证思考，加深学生对其艺术价值、历史价值的认识。[①]

## （二）确定文化教学探究的维度

材料中的语言词汇丰富，包括大量描述建筑和社会风貌的词汇与重点语块，如 visit their ancestor's graves、be packed with、arch over、doctor's clinic、lose control of、in decline 等。语言风格相对正式，复合句式较多，在理解过程中需要展示部分语篇。

《清明上河图》不仅是中国文化的瑰宝，也有助于促进中西方文化间的相互理解、交流和合作。要求学生在"看"的过程中有选择地记录所需信息，理解所"看"语料中非文字资源传达的意义，更加深刻地感受艺术作品的魅力，理解其非凡的历史价值和艺术价值，激发他们对艺术的好奇心，同时也有助于加强学生的文化自信和文化遗产保护意识。总之，语篇非常适用于凸显文化意识培养的视听说教学。

---

① 参见广州市第41中学沈丽芬参加广州市海珠区第六届"明珠杯"高中英语教学比赛课例。

## 三、准确把握课标中"看"的要求，结合学情确定文化意识的培养目标

### （一）把握课标要求

《高中课标》自新中国成立以来在语言技能中首次增加了"看"的技能，指出语言技能中的看通常指利用多模态语篇中的图形、表格、动画符号以及视频等理解意义的技能。[①] 理解多模态语篇除了需要使用传统的文本阅读技能之外，还需要观察图表中的信息、理解符号和动画的意义。鉴于这种技能在新媒体时代日趋重要，《高中课标》有明确的教学建议，指出文化知识的教学应以促进学生文化意识的形成和发展为目标。文化学习不仅需要知识的积累，还需要深入理解其精神内涵，并将优秀文化进一步内化为个人的意识和品行。这是一个内化于心、外化于行的过程，涉及几个步骤的演进和融合：感知中外文化知识—分析与比较，认同优秀文化—赏析与汲取，加深文化理解—认知与内化，形成文明素养—行为与表征。[②]

### （二）增强文化意识

学生通过义务教育课程的学习，对中外文化知识已经有了诸多积累，进入高中后将进一步扩大中外文化知识的学习范围，丰富学习的内容，学会用英文讲述好中国故事。教师在中外文化知识的教学中，应通过创设有意义的语境、恰当利用信息技术、基于语篇所承载的文化知识，引导学生挖掘其意义与内涵，帮助学生在语言练习和运用的各种活动中学习和内化语言知识和文化知识，通过感知、比较、分析和鉴赏，加深对文化异同的理解，提高对文化差异的敏感度和跨文化交际能力，帮助学生坚定文化自信，增强国家意识。

本节课的授课对象为高二年级学生，经过一年半的高中学习，学生对"人与社会"的主题较为熟悉。在学习此课前，学生已完成本单元的学习，掌握了一定的绘画艺术相关知识及其表达方式，但对《清明上河图》的认识只停留在零散的信息点上，如画者的身份或描绘的时代等，而对于此作品的具体

---

① 中华人民共和国教育部：《普通高中英语课程标准（2017年版2020年修订）》，人民教育出版社2020年版。
② 梅德明、王蔷：《新时代义务教育课程新发展——义务教育英语课程标准（2022年版）解读》，载《基础教育课程》2022年第10期，第19-25页。

内容、特点以及它在艺术和历史方面的价值并无深层的探讨，也很少尝试运用已有语言及知识流畅地描述绘画作品。

《清明上河图》长达 5 米，其中刻画了 800 个人物形象，细致地描绘了宋朝汴京城的场景。学生要在课堂有限的时间里，了解并理解其大致内容，需要老师充分调动学生的求知欲，通过活动的有效设置让学生主动、积极地观察画作内容。同时学生要欣赏此画，分析它的特点，并归纳其艺术和历史价值，教师必须提供足够的铺垫及语言"脚手架"，帮助学生理清逻辑，扫清表达障碍。

（三）学习目标

| | |
|---|---|
| 单元教学目标 | 经过本单元的学习，学生能够：<br>（1）了解西方绘画艺术的历史及不同时期的代表人物和代表作，把握不同历史时期西方绘画作品的特色及其变化的因素，能够自觉运用话语标记，简短地介绍艺术作品。<br>（2）了解中国绘画艺术及相关代表作品，感受中华艺术的魅力，对其在历史研究及文化传承方面的重要性发表自己的看法，增强文化自信，促进学生文化意识的形成和发展。<br>（3）了解艺术展览推介文的内容要素和语言特点，学会快速而准确地获取关键信息并能够写一则艺术展览公告，提高传播中华艺术的意识和能力。 |
| 课时教学目标 | 经过本节课的学习，学生能够完成单元教学目标（2）：<br>（1）了解视频中《清明上河图》展示的大致内容，识记描述建筑和社会风貌的词汇（如 temple、inn、city gate、fabric shops）和短语结构（be packed with、arch over、lose control of、in decline、give an insight into）的用法，将其运用于画作介绍中。<br>（2）运用本课相关语言描述《清明上河图》及其艺术价值和历史价值，增强对中华优秀传统文化的自豪感，坚定文化自信。<br>（3）结合自己对现代广州的理解，尝试创造属于自己的艺术作品——广州版《清明上河图》中的一个场景，并运用本节课学习的语言简单描述自己的作品，提高跨文化交流的意识，加强文化遗产保护意识。 |

## 四、营造文化交流的语境，提高跨文化交流的意识和能力

文化意识的不同发展水平之间存在递进关系，通过不同含义的词语表现出来，如：

一级：了解中外优秀文化，形成正确的价值观，感知所学内容的语言美和意蕴美。

二级：感悟中外优秀文化的精神内涵，树立正确的价值观，理解和欣赏所学内容的语言美和意蕴美。

三级：分析、鉴别文化现象所反映的价值取向，自觉坚定文化自信，吸取优秀文化，具有正确的价值观、健康的审美情趣和道德情感。

就中外优秀文化而言，了解、感悟其精神内涵，吸取优秀文化表现为三个不同的层次。同样，对所学内容的语言美和意蕴美，从感知到理解和欣赏，再到培养审美情趣，也是一个逐步提升和深化的过程。文化意识包括综合运用特定学习方式下所孕育出来的世界观、人生观和价值观等内在动力系统，三级的综合品质自然落到了具有正确的价值观、健康的审美情趣和道德情感，体现了水平质性差异描述的系统性。

在《清明上河图》视频教学中，教师可以运用情景教学法，充分利用信息技术营造文化交流互动的语境，让学生们在真实的情境中开展多层次的语言互动实践。新教材中《清明上河图》视频巧妙地融合了现代科技手段，如3D建模、虚拟现实等，高度还原出该画作中的场景和人物，以及色彩、线条等细节。还专门为该画作创作配乐，并根据画面的变化和情感变化调整配乐，使观众更加沉浸在画面氛围中，有身临其境的感觉，更容易理解和欣赏这幅传世名画的艺术魅力。下面是本课的教学活动和任务链设计。

| 语步 | 教学活动 | 设计意图 | 互动模式 & 时间 |
| --- | --- | --- | --- |
| | | Pre-listening | |
| Activity 1：Lead-in 了解和感知语言美和意蕴美 | T presents a short film to ask Ss to guess which painting does it show. | 利用《清明上河图》的全景视频创设情景，激活学生的背景知识以及激发学生对该画作的兴趣。 | CW 2′ |
| | T shows the recruitment advertisement of the museum and asks Ss to share their knowledge on *Qingming Shang He Tu*. | 创设真实情境，让学生担任 part-time guides in the Palace Museum。先了解学生对《清明上河图》的认识情况，然后串联本课核心任务链。 | CW 2′ |

续上表

| 语步 | 教学活动 | 设计意图 | 互动模式 & 时间 |
| --- | --- | --- | --- |
| While-listening ||||
| Activity 2：Watch, listen, and summarize 理解和欣赏语言美和意蕴美 | T guides Ss to first predict whether the statements are true or false, then check the answers after watching the video and summarize the basic information of *Qingming Shang He Tu*. | 一方面通过正误判断训练学生听取信息的能力，让学生在观看视频过程中把握视频大意，另一方面通过思维导图的展示让学生了解需要掌握的听力框架，为接下来的口头描述活动做铺垫。 | IW 6′ |
| Activity 3：Watch, take notes and share 欣赏和比较审美情趣 | Ss watch the video again and fill in the blanks to work out what was shown in the painting. T draws Ss' attention to the key words describing buildings and activities. | 再次观看视频第二部分，获取画作展示的内容信息，学生填空，教师通过图片展示引导学生有效关注描述画作中建筑和社会活动的关键词，为接下来的介绍做铺垫。 | IW 5′ |
| | Ss introduce part of the painting compared with the western paintings in class. | 学生根据所学的语言描述《清明上河图》的部分内容，聚焦欣赏建筑的多样性和社会活动的丰富性，比较它和西方绘画艺术的异同，在组内分享讨论，并在全班展示分享。 | IW & GW 8′ |
| Activity 4：Listen, notice and take notes 鉴赏和评价价值取向 | Ss summarize the importance of *Qingming Shang He Tu* based on what was learned, and critically view the life shown on the painting through the second listening material. | 学生根据前一部分视频中的内容总结归纳《清明上河图》的艺术价值，并通过第二段听力材料，批判性地看待当时的社会生活经济状况，对艺术作品或文化保持敏锐的感知和开放的心态，领悟其独特的历史价值，坚定文化自信。 | IW & CW 6′ |

续上表

| 语步 | 教学活动 | 设计意图 | 互动模式 & 时间 |
|---|---|---|---|
| Post-listening ||||
| Activity 5：<br>Speak and share<br>应用和实践<br>道德情感 | Ss think of some methods to protect and promote *Qingming Shang He Tu* and share their opinion to the whole class. | 学生利用所学思考如何保护和推广《清明上河图》，在组内讨论并在全班口头分享，感受历史与文化的厚重，以此增强学生对中华优秀传统文化的认同感和民族自豪感，提高保护文化遗产的意识。 | IW & GW<br>3′ |
| Activity 6：<br>Speak and share<br>迁移和创新<br>文化意识 | 学生以小组为单位，为广州版《清明上河图》设计一副描绘现代广州的画卷，并用语言描述出来。 | 为学生设计小组成员活动人物，让每位同学都参与其中，内化并尝试运用本课所学描写绘画作品内容的句子，推动迁移创新；让学生身体力行，能在生活中拓展和升华美，加入到保护和传承传统文化艺术的行列中来。 | IW & GW<br>8′ |

续上表

| 语步 | 教学活动 | 设计意图 | 互动模式 & 时间 |
|---|---|---|---|
| Homework<br>迁移和创新<br>跨文化交流 | Must-do：<br>Make an oral speech to introduce *Qingming Shang He Tu* based on the mind map. 学生根据课堂的思维导图准备一个口头演讲介绍《清明上河图》，包括《清明上河图》的基本信息、画作展示的内容、画作的艺术价值和历史价值以及保护、推广《清明上河图》的措施等。<br>Optional：<br>应用文写作：假如你有机会当一天故宫博物院的志愿解说员，专门向外国人介绍北宋张择端的《清明上河图》。请你写一篇英语解说介绍，内容包括以下要点：<br>1. 画的概要；<br>2. 画中的细节亮点；<br>3. 画的历史和艺术价值。 | 《清明上河图》是中国传统文化中的经典之作，它不仅在中国具有重要的历史、文化和艺术价值，也成了中外交流中的重要桥梁。在国际交流中引入这样一个充满历史和文化内涵的中国传统文化符号，我们可以更好地学习和吸收其他文化背景下的经验和智慧，丰富自己的视野和思想，同时也能推动中华文化更好地走向世界，为推动人类文明的发展贡献一份力量。 | IW<br>20′ |

注：IW = Individual Work　　GW = Group Work　　CW = Class Work

通过以上对《清明上河图》多层次的语言实践活动，学生从感知理解到欣赏比较，再到培养审美情趣等都得到了提升和深化。首先观看《清明上河图》的全景视频，初步感知其中的语言美和意蕴美。例如观察到江上鱼跃水中，可以感受到诗意的美；看到市井百态的生活场景，则能感受到现实主义的意境。在感知的基础上，让学生带着担任 part-time guides in the Palace Museum 的任务，理解人物、建筑、动物等元素与社会背景、文化内涵的联系，以及艺术家表现技巧的运用，更好地领会其中的语言美和意蕴美，比较其与西方绘画艺术的异同。在理解的基础上，对《清明上河图》进行评价和欣赏，从心理和情感上产生共鸣。例如，欣赏画面色彩的协调、结构的完整性、细节描绘的精致等方面，以及对艺术家的创意和高超技艺产生赞赏和敬意等。在欣赏的基础上，形成对《清明上河图》的个性化、深入的理解和欣赏，建立起自己独特的审美情趣、价值取向和道德情感，提高跨文化交流的能力①。

## 五、基于学生参与教学活动的行为表现进行文化意识的多元评价，促进核心素养的形成

《高中课标》指出：普通高中英语课程应建立以学生为主体，促进学生全面、健康而有个性地发展的课程评价体系。评价应聚焦并促进学生英语学科核心素养的形成及发展，采用形成性评价与终结性评价相结合的多元评价方式，重视评价的促学作用，关注学生在英语学习过程中所表现出的情感、态度和价值观等要素，引导学生学会监控和调整自己的英语学习目标、学习方式和学习进程。②

基于文化意识培养的视频教学评价应该以学生文化意识的养成以及跨文化交际能力的发展为评价对象而做出价值判断。文化意识与跨文化交际能力不是实际反应本身，而是在特殊情景下以特定方式反应的内部准备状态或者内在倾向性，它所需要的是一种对行为表现的衡量方式，体现学生掌握英语文化知识并且能够得体运用这些知识的能力。这类评价通常只是由一些可观察的指标间接地推断和度量。因此，本视频教学中关于文化意识的评价应该基于学生参与教学活动的行为表现、态度、兴趣、审美情趣、道德情感、价值观等项目，参照新课标中关于文化意识的具体描述，设计出有针对性的多元评价指标进行。

### （一）诊断性评价

如在学习视频之前，通过问答或者测试先了解学生对《清明上河图》的知晓情况，以便设计有针对性的教学活动。

### （二）形成性评价

对学习过程进行全程性评价，本课结束后，可以让学生根据评价表尝试自我评价和相互评价。这种评价方式鼓励学生积极参与课堂活动，帮助他们自主发掘学习兴趣和潜能，达到"以评促学"的教学目标。

---

① 参见广州市南武中学陈家宜参加广州市海珠区第六届"明珠杯"高中英语教学比赛课例。
② 中华人民共和国教育部：《普通高中英语课程标准（2017年版2020年修订）》，人民教育出版社2020年版，第80－92页。

**Assessment**

| In this lesson, I have… | Self-Assessment | Peer-Assessment |
|---|---|---|
| mastered the new expressions in the video. | | |
| made a clear introduction of *Qingming Shang He Tu*. | | |
| understood the value of *Qingming Shang He Tu*. | | |
| come up with some methods to promote *Qingming Shang He Tu*. | | |
| shared my introduction and opinion with confidence in my group. | | |

☆ stands for "Not so good", ☆☆ stands for "Good", ☆☆☆ stands for "Excellent".

## （三）项目式评价

通过项目式教学活动，如 Activity 6：学生结合自己对现代广州的理解，尝试创造属于自己的艺术作品——广州版《清明上河图》。① 这个项目可以评价学生是否具有艺术表达和创意表现的兴趣和意识，能在生活中拓展和升华美等。

Create a scene of modern Guangzhou for "Nanguo Shangdu" & Assessment

| Character | Task | Useful expressions | Items | Score |
|---|---|---|---|---|
| Student 1 | Name of your scene | 1. The name of our scene is… <br> 2. With this name, we intend to… | 1. Voice, loud and clear? <br> 2 points | |
| Student 2 | Design of the background | 1. Flowing from…to… <br> 2. The painting begins by…then we see… | 2. Description, clear? <br> 2 points | |
| Student 3 | Design of the activity | 1. We see sb doing sth <br> 2. People are doing sth in some place | 3. Creation, cool? <br> 2 points | |
| Student 4 | Purpose | 1. The reason why I choose this activity is that… <br> 2. The activity can reflect … | 4. Introduction, attractive? <br> 2 points | |

---

① 参见中山大学附属中学李旸参加广州市海珠区第六届"明珠杯"高中英语教学比赛课例。

### (四) 终结性评价

终结性评价是对学生学习成果的总结和评估，适合针对学生对《清明上河图》的理解和应用能力进行评价。如作业可以设计为根据思维导图准备一个口头演讲介绍《清明上河图》，以及当一天故宫博物院的志愿解说员，专门向外国人介绍北宋张择端的《清明上河图》等。可以利用学生的口语表现和应用文写作完成的情况来评价其是否能结合自己的文化背景和对画作的理解与其他文化背景的人进行跨文化交流，包括分享观点、比较不同文化等。

总之，积极有效的评价应贯穿英语文化教学的全过程，应是形成性评价与终结性评价的有机结合。教师在教学过程中，应特别重视根据教学的需要创造性地发展和使用不同的评价工具，调整形成性评价和终结性评价在学生学业成绩中的比例，真正发挥评价促学促教的作用。

## 六、思考

在"双新"背景下，高中英语视频教学的发展已经成为一种趋势。随着信息技术的快速发展，视频资源的获取和使用也变得越来越便捷。如何在这一背景下，培养学生的文化意识，提高他们的跨文化交际能力，是需要我们不断探讨的问题。

首先，我们应该注重选择优质的视频资源。只有选择符合学生年龄和水平的视频资源，才能真正激发学生的学习兴趣，拓展他们的文化视野。

其次，我们应该通过多种方式，全面提升学生的文化意识。除了视频教学外，还应该进行实地考察、讨论交流、综合实践等多种形式的教学活动，使学生在不同的场景中，更加深入地理解和感受不同文化之间的联系和差异。

最重要的是，教师要充分发挥学生的主体作用，鼓励他们积极参与跨文化交流。我们要清楚地认识到不同民族由于地理、自然环境等种种因素的影响，其生活方式也不尽相同，因而文化带有民族性；文化是多元的而不是一元的；文化是变化的而不是静止的。为此，教师要努力营造文化交流的语境，培养学生的文化意识，使文化教学与语言技能的培养同步进行，从而为学生的发展搭建国际性平台，提高学生的全球意识和跨文化的交往能力，培养文化自信，推动中华文化更好地走向世界。

## 第四章　读后续写的文化转向与运用"TEAMS"框架提升学生文化意识初探*
——以2023年新高考英语全国Ⅰ卷为例

### 一、新课标理念下高考读后续写中文化意识的测评

《普通高中英语课程标准（2017年版2020年修订）》考试命题建议指出，写作的主要考试形式为：故事续写、看图写报告、命题作文和概要写作。①读后续写作为排在首位的考试形式，是新高考采用的创新型写作形式。该形式将阅读与写作相结合，既考查阅读理解能力，也考查创造性写作能力，关注语言的输入与输出效果，着眼于提升学生的英语学科核心素养。《高中课标》指出：文化意识指对中外文化的理解和对优秀文化的认同，是学生在全球化背景下表现出的跨文化认知、态度和行为取向。文化意识体现英语学科核心素养的价值取向。文化意识的培育有助于学生增强国家认同和家国情怀，坚定文化自信，树立人类命运共同体意识，学会做人做事，成长为有文明素养和社会责任感的人。②《义务教育英语课程标准（2022年版）》提出培育文化意识，能够了解不同国家的优秀文明成果，比较中外文化的异同，发展跨文化沟通与交流的能力，形成健康向上的审美情趣和正确的价值观，加深对中华文化的理解和认同，树立国际视野，坚定文化自信。③鉴于两个新课标都明确地把学生"文化意识"的培养列入到英语教学目标之中，新高考读后续写中不断体现文化

---

\* 本文原发表于《广东教育》2023年第9期。本文为广东省教育研究院2022年中小学英语教育专项研究课题"聚焦单元整体教学的中学英语联动教研行动研究"（课题编号：GDJY-2022-A-yyb33）的阶段性研究成果。

① 中华人民共和国教育部：《普通高中英语课程标准》，人民教育出版社2020年版，第16、第59页。

② 中华人民共和国教育部：《义务教育英语课程标准》，北京师范大学出版社2022年版，第4页。

③ 李昂、孙佳星：《巧用原卷分析法助力读后续写情节设计》，载《广东教育·高中》2023年第6期。

意识的考查维度，这一点在 2023 年新高考英语全国卷的读后续写试题中尤为突出。本文以 2023 年新高考英语全国 I 卷读后续写真题为例，尝试利用 TEAMS 框架指导学生有效梳理原文、合理构思情节、恰当使用描写手段丰富续文的文学色彩，提高学生文化意识和写作能力。

## 二、2023 年新高考英语全国 I 卷读后续写试题的文化转向

阅读下面材料，根据其内容和所给段落开头语续写两段，使之构成一篇完整的短文。

When I was in middle school, my social studies teacher asked me to enter a writing contest. I said no without thinking, I did not love writing. My family came from Brazil, so English was only my second language. Writing was so difficult and painful for me that my teacher had allowed me to present my paper on the sinking of the Titanic by acting out a play, where I played all the parts. No one laughed harder than he did.

So, why did he suddenly force me to do something at which I was sure to fail? His reply: "Because I love your stories. If you're willing to apply yourself, I think you have a good shot at this." Encouraged by his words, I agreed to give it a try.

I chose Paul Revere's horse as my subject. Paul Revere was a silversmith（银匠）in Boston who rode a horse at night on April 18, 1775 to Lexington to warn people that British soldiers were coming. My story would come straight from the horse's mouth, not a brilliant idea, but funny; and unlikely to be anyone else's choice.

What did the horse think, as he sped through the night? Did he get tired? Have doubts? Did he want to quit? I sympathized immediately. I got tired. I had doubts. I wanted to quit. But, like Revere's horse, I kept going. I worked hard. I checked my spelling. I asked my older sister to correct my grammar. I checked out a half dozen books on Paul Revere from the library. I even read a few of them.

When I handed in the essay to my teacher, he read it, laughed out loud, and said, "Great. Now, write it again." I wrote it again, and again and again. When I finally finished it, the thought of winning had given way to the enjoyment of writing. If I didn't win, I wouldn't care.

Para 1: *A few weeks later, when I almost forgot the contest, the news came.*

Para 2: *I went to the teacher's office after the award presentation.*

本篇读后续写原文讲述一名英语为第二语言的中学生在老师的鼓励下参加

写作比赛并通过努力取得成功的励志故事。跟以往读后续写的试题比较，文化元素是本次试题中最突出的特点（见表1）。

表1  2023年新高考英语全国 I 卷读后续写文化特色解读

| 文化符号 | 巴西家庭、英语作为第二语言、学校写作比赛、泰坦尼克号、保罗·里维尔骑马警示、文化人物 Paul Revere、美国独立战争历史背景 |
| --- | --- |
| 文化背景 | Paul Revere（保罗·里维尔）是美国马萨诸塞州波士顿的一位银匠、实业家，也是美国独立战争时期的一名爱国者。保罗·里维尔是位杰出的军人，他协助组建了一个针对英军的情报与警报系统。他最著名的事迹是在列克星敦和康科德战役前夜警告民兵英军即将来袭。美国诗人亨利·沃兹沃思·朗费罗于1861年发表诗作《保罗·里维尔骑马来》，对此事件进行了戏剧化的诠释，战役结束后，里维尔重拾他的银匠与铸造生意，并在1800年成为美国第一位成功制作铜片作为军舰防护板的人。 |
| 文学色彩 | 通过讲述保罗·里维尔的马的故事，"我"给人留下深刻的印象，也体现了语言和文化交流的重要性。采用"从马嘴里说出来"的可信方式，增强了故事的趣味性和幽默感，使整篇文章更加生动有趣，也可以看出"我"的文学写作技巧。 |
| 文化价值 | 含有鲜明的人文关怀，关注人的价值、人的发展，以及人与自我、人与社会的关系。"青少年"是对个人体验情境的限定，它与考生自己的生活经历和体验，以及与成长的主题紧密相连，使考生能够充分展示个性化的思考，表达出他们真实的思想和感情。文章表达了一种积极、开放的学习态度。尽管英语不是"我"的母语，但"我"并没有因此放弃学习，反而在老师和家人的帮助下，选择跨文化视角，扩大阅读量并反复修改，逐渐掌握了英语写作技巧，最终赢得比赛。这种学习态度，可以鼓励同样是英语作为二语的中学生读者拓宽视野、勇于运用跨文化知识创造性地解决问题，提高跨文化交流和理解的能力。而跨文化交流能力恰恰是全球化时代人们必备的综合能力，它不仅帮助人们更好地融入不同文化环境，同时也有助于树立人类命运共同体意识，促进不同文化之间的相互理解和尊重。 |

从表1可以看出，本次试题体现了明显的文化转向，丰富的文化元素激发学生在阅读过程中进行思考，鼓励多元思辨和发散思维，灵活开放的写作情境引导学生在语言学习过程中注重辨析语言和文化中的具体现象，梳理和概括信息，从跨文化的视角评判事物和不同观念，个性化地、创造性地表达自己的观点和想法。在加强语言表达能力考查的同时，加强对文化意识的考查，也增加了续写的难度。

## 三、"TEAMS" 框架在读后续写中的运用

新高考实施以来，在多数地区，读后续写成为得分率最低的题型。失分项主要集中在内容（情节单薄、不符合主题）、语言（词汇和语法使用的准确性低、丰富性不足）和语篇（衔接不紧凑、逻辑不连贯）等方面。要想突破读后续写的难点，首要任务是构建好读后续写框架，写作时才能思路清晰。下面以2023年新高考英语全国Ⅰ卷读后续写真题为例，尝试运用操作性强的 TEAMS 框架[①]写出与原文衔接合理、语意连贯、逻辑相符又体现文化意识的续文。

T 指 Transitional sentence（衔接句）或 Theme（主题句）；

E 指 Emotion /Environment（心理描写/环境描写）；

A 指 Action［动作（链）］和 Appearance（外貌神态描写）；

M 指 Monologue/Conversation（独白/对话）；

S 指 Style（语言风格）[②]。

其中，Action 是助推情节所必要的，Emotion、Environment、Appearance、Monologue、Conversation、Style 的写作顺序和次数可根据故事情节的需要适当调整。

### Step 1 梳理原文，探究 Theme

| | |
|---|---|
| Who | "我": a middle school student, writing was difficult and painful…<br>社会学老师: my social studies teacher, encouraged me…<br>Paul Revere 的马不容忽视：是作者写作的灵感来源，通过马的视角来展开想象和描绘，马也代表作者内心的挣扎，启发学生运用跨文化知识创造性地解决问题。 |
| When | when I was in middle school |
| Where | in middle school |
| What | 学生一开始拒绝参加写作比赛，老师鼓励并提供指导，学生最终交稿。<br>特别要找出矛盾冲突（conflict），它是故事情节的驱动力，可以在原文中直接标记相关词句。原文第二段首句 "So, why did he suddenly force me to do something at which I was sure to fail?" 体现了冲突，即作者对写作没有信心，但老师却迫使他参加写作比赛。"我"参不参加写作比赛？ |

---

① 邱彩花等：《用 TEAM 框架突破高考英语读后续写》，西北工业大学出版社2022年版，第7页。

② 孙依依等：《高中英语读后续写全攻略》，上海外语教育出版社2023年版，第3页。

续上表

| Why | 英语是第二语言，学得很痛苦，缺乏自信。 |
|---|---|
| How | 学生内心的挣扎是故事中的主要冲突，老师的鼓励、支持是化解冲突的关键。 |
| Theme | 定义：主题（theme）是某种观念、某种意义、某种对人物或事件的诠释，是体现在整个作品中对生活的深刻而又融贯统一的观点。<br>作用：①传达作者观念；②引领续写方向；③使文章基调统一。<br>方法：（1）直接在原文中找到体现主题的句子，它通常完整地出现在首段、中间段或末段。原文第4段中"I got tired. I had doubts. I wanted to quit. But, like Revere's fabled horse, I kept going."这句话体现了主题，即在面临挑战和困难时要坚持不懈，才能取得成功。<br>（2）需要通过各种线索概括出主题，线索可以为贯穿全文的人、事、物、情感等，如题目、关键词、一些反复出现的信息等。 |
| Tip 1 | 建议运用原卷分析法梳理原文，也就是直接在试卷卷面及草稿纸上开展可视化的分析，如圈出主要人物，标出人物之间的关系、性格、情感、环境等关键词句。（李昂、孙佳星，2023） |

**Step 2　合理构思，搭建"TEAMS"**

Para 1 When I almost forgot the contest, the news came.
在我快忘记这个比赛的时候，有消息了。
Tip 2：6A（Actions）或"6所"（所见、所听、所说、所做、所想、所感）助推情节，用 Q-A（问答）模式列提纲

（T1 衔接句1）开头语交代有消息了，接下来可以从消息内容的角度展开提问，答案就是构思的情节。

| Q1：What is the news? What did you hear/see? | A1 + Environment |
|---|---|
| Q2：How did you feel at the news? | A2 + Emotion |
| Q3：What did you say at the award ceremony? | A3 + Monologue |
| Q4：How did the audience react? | A5 |
| Q5：Why did you go to the teacher's office? | A6 + Emotion |

（T2 衔接句2）根据第二段段首句反向推理，"我"迫不及待地去老师办公室分享好消息。

续上表

| Para 2 I went to the teacher's office after the award presentation. 颁完奖后我去了老师办公室。 ||
|---|---|
| (T3 衔接句3）承上（衔接首句的内容），段首句涉及的人物有 I，事物是 the office。根据句意，衔接句从 office 的角度展开更为合适，从颁奖典礼转场到办公室，转场是情节时空切换的重要标记，有助于增加画面感。 ||
| Q1：What did I see/do/hear in the office? | A1 + Appearance |
| Q2：What did the teacher/others say/do? | A2 + M（Conversation） |
| Q3：How did I feel? | A3 + Emotion |
| Q4：What was the ending? | A4 |
| Q5：What did I learn from this experience? | T4（Theme）点明呼应升华主题 |

**Step 3　运用"TEAMS"，增添文采**

| | |
|---|---|
| Theme<br>点明主题<br>呼应主题<br>升华主题 | （1）自然式结尾：从开头能直接推测结尾，总结全篇，点明主题。<br>As I walked home, I knew English writing was not my pain any more.<br>（2）首尾呼应式结尾：直接复现原文关键词，或把原文关键词以词性或词形变化的方式进行重复，或改写关键句进行重复，呼应主题。<br>As I walked home, the thought of winning had given way to the motivation of writing.（把原文中的 enjoyment 改为 motivation。）<br>（3）寓情于景式结尾：即以景代情，呼应主题。<br>As I walked home, I felt as if the gentle breeze was whispering, "Anything is possible if you keep trying."<br>（4）议论+反思式结尾：议论形式+心理活动，升华主题。<br>Looking back at the writing contest, I realized that his guidance had been invaluable in shaping my outlook towards life.<br>（5）留白式结尾：通过描写画面（动作、变化等）升华主题，给读者留下遐想的空间。<br>Like Paul Revere horse, I will keep going and going. |
| Environment<br>描述背景<br>创设氛围<br>推动情节<br>烘托情绪 | 自然环境描写：昼夜更迭、草木鸟兽、细节环境等。<br>With bright sunshine flooding the room 阳光洒满房间<br>The blue sky is dotted with many floating clouds. 蓝蓝的天上白云飘<br>社会环境描写：时代背景、人物生活环境等。<br>The technology of the 21$^{st}$ century have changed the way we live. |

续上表

| | | |
|---|---|---|
| Emotion<br>展现人物内心世界，<br>揭示人物性格特征 | 表示喜怒哀乐的名词、形容词、副词<br>介词短语（to one's surprise、in relief、in panic…）<br>so…that…等表达人物的情感。<br>借景抒情：A brilliant, deep blue sky arched high over the moorland. | |
| Appearance<br>烘托情感<br>刻画心理 | 眼睛 with tears streaming down one's face<br>嘴巴 blow a fuse（七窍生烟）<br>眉毛 arched eyebrows（弯起的眉毛，表示疑问或好奇）<br>面部表情 one's face splits into a wide smile | |
| Actions<br>推动情节发展<br>刻画人物性格<br>反映人物情感<br>调节叙事节奏 | 可以使用以下句式构成动作链：<br>（1）When A did sth., B did sth.<br>When I got up in the middle of the movie, Emmett whispered…<br>（2）A was doing sth. as B did sth.<br>Everybody was complaining as I inched out.<br>（3）v-ing, sb. do/did sth., v-ing<br>After scratching up a wet towel, Josh rushed downstairs with his daughter, covering her nose from the choking smoke.<br>（4）v-ed（情绪类形容词），主句，v-ing<br>Exhausted and drained, she sat by the footpath, resting her aching feet.<br>（5）（身体部位）+v-ing/ved, sb. do/did sth, 或（with+情绪类名词）sb. do/did sth.<br>Hands trembling with excitement, Lucy opened the box merrily. | |
| Monologue<br>呼应前文内容<br>推动情节发展<br>刻画人物性格<br>表达人物情绪<br>改变文字节奏 | 直接说：<br>（1）对话标签（sb. said 或 said sb.）后接 doing/done 作伴随状语或独立主格作状语用来增加动作描写。如：<br>"I'll get you a special gift," she said, heading for the sitting room.<br>（2）对话标签（sb. said 或 said sb.）后接并列谓语或者并列句，用来增加动作描写，让情节发展更加流畅。如：<br>"Drive safely," the old man said, and waved goodbye to us.<br>间接说：<br>（3）无显性的对话标签（sb. said 或 said sb.），引号内用句号，后接完整的句子，承接引号内句子的语义。如：<br>"I'm really disappointed with all of you." He turned around, slammed the door and rushed out. | |

续上表

| | |
|---|---|
| Style<br>语言沿袭<br>保持原文风格 | 在读后续写中，丰富的描写手法非常重要，但作为一个完整的故事，还需注意续写与原文语言风格保持统一，即语言沿袭，可从"三个一致"的角度保持原文风格。<br>A. 用词特点一致<br>（1）日常词汇（"小"词）：<br>social studies, writing contest, essay, subject, spelling, grammar…<br>（2）专业词汇（"大"词）：<br>Titanic, Paul Revere's horse, straight from the horse's mouth, Lexington…<br>B. 描写角度一致<br>（3）Emotion/Environment: did not love writing, difficult, painful, tired, doubts, wanted to quit, sympathized, encouraged, enjoyment…<br>（4）Actions: acted out a play, checked out books, handed in the essay, laughed…<br>（5）Monologue: "Because I love your stories. If you're willing to apply yourself, I think you have a good shot at this." "Great. Now, write it again."<br>C. 修辞手法一致<br>（6）拟人（personification）: What did the horse think, as he sped through the night? Did he get tired? Have doubts? Did he want to quit?<br>（7）明喻（simile）: But, like Revere's horse, I kept going.<br>My story would come (as if it were) straight from the horse's mouth.<br>用"straight from the horse's mouth"这个习语来说明故事的来源可靠，就好像从马嘴里直接听到它说出来一样。<br>（8）暗喻（metaphor）：多用 be 动词来联系。<br>She was a shining star on the stage.<br>（9）反问（rhetorical question）: Did he get tired? Have doubts? …<br>（10）排比（parallelism）: I worked hard. I checked my spelling. I asked my older sister to correct my grammar…<br>（11）重复（repetition）: I wrote it again, and again and again.<br>（12）无灵句（inanimate）：无灵主语（时间、地点、情感、自然现象、身体部位、抽象概念）+ 有灵动词的组合，如：<br>When I finally finished it, the thought of winning had given way to the enjoyment of writing. （抽象概念 the thought + 有灵动词 had given way to） |

**续上表**

| | |
|---|---|
| Style<br>语言沿袭<br>保持原文风格 | （13）夸张（hyperbole）：使用动词；使用形容词或者副词；使用数量词；使用介词短语。<br>I have been waiting for ages! He's incredibly tall.<br>（14）引用（quotation）：引用名人名言，提高文章的可信度和说服力。<br>"I have a dream," as Martin Luther King declared in his iconic speech.<br>（15）对照（contrast）：对比事物的相似和不同点来强调差异、衬托形象、突出情感，增强表现力。<br>The city was noisy, but the country was quiet.<br>（16）虚拟语气：If I didn't win, I wouldn't care. |

## 四、评价"TEAMS"，提升文化意识

评价反馈是读后续写的关键环节，能够深化学生的主题意义体验。在学生写作前，教师需要提供和解释"TEAMS"读后续写评价表（见表2）。这既能让学生有清晰明确的续写目标，把握写作要点，又能让学生从读者视角审视内化主题意义，推进真实、丰富而强烈的主题意义体验。在学生完成续写后，可以先让学生进行自评，反思个人写作的优缺点，并修改不足之处。然后，引导学生开展互评，以使学生在思维碰撞中发掘同伴作品的闪光点，取长补短，反思个人学习，升华对主题意义的理解，共同提高写作能力和文化意识。下面运用表2对下列续文进行评价（斜体部分为给定的提示语）。

One possible version 1：

*A few weeks later, when I almost forgot the contest, the news came.* The list of winners was posted on the notice board at school. Seeing my name on it, I couldn't believe my eyes. Then I was told to attend the award presentation, and I couldn't help but feel nervous about presenting my essay. But when I heard my name being announced, like Revere's horse, I plucked up my courage and strode onto the stage. The audience burst out laughing as they enjoyed the story straight from the horse's mouth. With all the self-doubt vanishing, I was eager to share the trophy with my teacher.

*I went to the teacher's office after the award presentation.* Through the half-closed office door, I saw my teacher buried in grading papers. I tiptoed over to him. "Congratulations!" No sooner had I approached him than my teacher gave me a big bear hug. "Thank you, teacher, without your encouragement, I couldn't have won the prize!" I shed tears of joy. "If you're willing to apply yourself, I believe you will always have a good shot." My teacher smiled. As I walked home, I felt as if the gentle breeze was whispering, "Anything is possible if you keep trying."

表2 "TEAMS"读后续写评价表

| Aspects | Detail | Self-evaluation | Peer evaluation |
| --- | --- | --- | --- |
| Theme 主题 | As I walked home, I felt as if the gentle breeze was whispering, "Anything is possible if you keep trying." | 优点：情景交融，感受到主人公内心的愉悦和希望。<br>提升点：可以使用议论+反思式结尾或者留白式结尾进一步升华主题。 | 共商改进：<br>Looking back, the most important lesson I have learnt is that we should try and overcome new challenges in life. |
| Environment 环境描写 | The list of winners was posted on the notice board at school. | 优点：简洁的环境描写，让读者知道奖项公示的地点和方式。<br>提升点：可使用形容词和形象比喻来使描写更具吸引力。 | 共商改进：<br>on the prominent notice board, "prominent" 非常显眼的位置，引人注目。 |
| Emotion 情感描写 | Seeing my name on it, I couldn't believe my eyes. I couldn't help but feel nervous about presenting my essay. | 优点：具体的视觉形象描绘表达"我"的惊喜和兴奋之情，否定词"couldn't help but"既表现出紧张心情又表达对演讲的重视。<br>提升点：可使用手心冒汗或者心跳加速等具体生动的描述。 | 共商改进：<br>With my heart racing, I couldn't help but feel nervous about presenting my essay. |
| Appearance 外貌神态 | I saw my teacher buried in grading papers. | 优点："buried in" 这个形象描写和 "grading papers" 使老师辛勤工作的神态跃然纸上。<br>提升点：可添加表现老师情绪的描写，体现老师敬业乐业。 | 共商改进：<br>I saw my teacher buried in grading papers, his face beaming with accomplishment. 脸上洋溢着成就感 |

续上表

| Aspects | Detail | Self-evaluation | Peer evaluation |
|---|---|---|---|
| Actions 动作描写 | The audience burst out laughing as they enjoyed the story straight from the horse's mouth. | 优点:"burst out laughing"生动展现观众的情感反应。同时,"straight from the horse's mouth"习语增加与原文融洽度。<br>提升点:可添加细节,让读者身临其境。 | 共商改进:<br>The audience <u>leaned forward</u>, bursting out laughing as they enjoyed the story straight from the horse's mouth. |
| Monologue 独白/对话 | "Congratulations!" "Thank you, teacher, without your encouragement, I couldn't have won the prize!" I shed tears of joy. | 优点:表达了老师的祝贺,"我"对老师的感激和获奖的喜悦。<br>提升点:增加对话标签(sb. said 或 said sb.),让情节发展更加流畅。修改 shed tears of joy,更符合"I"。 | 共商改进:<br>"Thank you, teacher", I said. "Without your encouragement, I couldn't have won the prize!" I felt very emotional. |
| Style 风格 | 用词特点一致:<br>present my essay, Revere's horse,<br>描写角度一致:<br>"If you're willing to apply yourself, I believe you will always have a good shot." My teacher smiled.<br>修辞手法一致:<br>明喻(simile) Like Revere's horse, I plucked up my courage and strode onto the stage. | 优点:将 Revere's horse 这个文化历史元素转化为生动的故事情节,提高了历史认知能力和文化意识;对原文中老师最具有启发的语句进行改写及明喻的使用都增加了与原文的融洽度。<br>提升点:在描写角度和修辞手法方面可以增强一致性。 | 共商改进:<br><u>I had doubts. I wanted to quit.</u> But like Revere's horse, I plucked up my courage and strode onto the stage.<br>使用对照,突出"我"内心的情感变化,吸引读者注意力。 |

续上表

| Aspects | Detail | Self-evaluation | Peer evaluation |
| --- | --- | --- | --- |
| Overall 总体 | "TEAMS" 总体评价：<br>T：探究了跨文化背景下"我"面临挑战时坚持不懈、勇于创新，最终取得成功的主题意义。<br>E：通过介绍学校布告栏、颁奖现场和老师的办公室等地方，营造了具体的时空背景；通过主人公的内心变化和老师之间的互动，表达出惊喜、紧张、勇气、自信、感激等复杂情感。<br>A：登上领奖台、和老师拥抱等动作描写，使故事更加具体生动；老师在办公室批改作业的神态体现了老师敬业乐业的精神。<br>M：师生对话表达了老师对"我"的祝贺，"我"对老师的感激。<br>S：将 Revere's horse 这个文化历史元素转化为生动的故事情节，提高了历史认知能力和文化意识；对原文中老师最具激励的语句进行改写增加了与原文的融洽度，充满人文关怀；采用了比喻、拟人、引用习语等修辞手法，丰富了续文的文学色彩。<br>提升点：可以增加更多关于参赛经历和故事细节的生动描写，另外还可以进一步提炼和升华主题意义。 | | |

## 五、结语

2023年全国新课标Ⅰ卷的读后续写试题体现了明显的文化转向，在加强语言表达能力考查的同时，加强了对文化意识的考查，引导学生通过跨文化视角，运用跨文化知识创造性地解决问题，也增加了续写的难度。读后续写的文化转向促使教师重新审视教学内容、步骤和方法。运用"TEAMS"框架，可以指导学生在理解语篇内容和文化意蕴的基础上，紧扣主题意义进行合情合理的续写，并且通过自评和互评提升文学色彩和写作效果，这一过程有助于学生融合语言知识和文化知识，提高创造性地表达观点、意图和情感的高阶思维能力和文化素养，也有助于践行学思结合、学用结合、用创为本的英语学习活动观，深化学生对主题意义的理解，落实"教—学—评"一体化，实现深度学习和核心素养发展的目的。今后要进一步探索运用"TEAMS"评价和高考读后续写评分标准的协同，使两者相得益彰，共同提高学生的文化意识和写作能力。

# 第五章 基于学业水平监测的读后续写分析与"TEAMS"讲评研究*
## ——以 2023 年 6 月广州市高二英语八区联考读后续写试题为例

《普通高中英语课程标准（2017 年版 2020 年修订）》指出：高中英语学业质量水平既是指导教师开展日常教学的依据，也是阶段性评价、学业水平考试和高考命题的重要依据。高中英语学业质量水平中，水平一主要用于检测必修课程的学习结果，是高中学生在英语学科应达到的合格要求，也是高中英语学业水平考试命题的主要依据；水平二主要用于检测选择性必修课程的学习结果，也是英语高考命题的主要依据。[①]依据《高中课标》要求，2023 年 6 月广州市高二英语八区联考属于水平二测试，考试范围为选择性必修一（第 2、第 3、第 4、第 5 单元）、选择性必修二（第 1、第 2、第 3、第 4 单元）。按照《高中课标》水平二对写作的要求（能概述所读语篇的主要内容或续写语篇），在试题中包含了读后续写的考查。笔者对本次质量监测学生的读后续写答题情况进行分析，探讨运用 TEAMS 框架有针对性地讲评指导策略。

## 一、试题分析与师生作文

读后续写（满分 25 分）

阅读下面材料，根据其内容和所给段落开头语续写两段，使之构成一篇完整的短文。

Many years ago, a little boy named Antonio lived in Italy with his grandfather, who was a stone cutter. He liked to go with his grandfather to the stone yard. While

---

\* 本文原发表于《教学考试·高考英语》2023 年第 6 期。本文为广东省教育研究院 2022 年中小学英语教育专项研究课题"聚焦单元整体教学的中学英语联动教研行动研究"（课题编号：GDJY – 2022 – A – yyb33）的阶段性研究成果。

[①] 中华人民共和国教育部：《普通高中英语课程标准》，人民教育出版社 2020 年版，第 51、第 83 页。

his grandfather was busy cutting the stone blocks, Antonio would play among the chips. Sometimes he would make a small statue out of soft clay; sometimes, he would try to cut a statue from a piece of rock. Antonio showed so much skill that his grandfather was delighted. "The boy will be a sculptor someday."

There lived in the same town a rich man called Count. Sometimes Count would have a grand dinner, and his rich friends from other towns would come to visit him. Then Antonio's grandfather would go up to Count's house to help with the work in the kitchen, for he was a fine cook as well as a good stone cutter.

One day, Antonio went with his grandfather to Count's great house. Some people from the city were coming, and there was to be a grand feast. The boy could not cook and was not old enough to wait on the table. But he could wash the pans and kettles, and as he was smart and quick, he could help in many other ways.

All went well until it was time to spread the table for dinner. Suddenly, there was a crash in the dining room, and a man rushed into the kitchen with some pieces of marble（大理石）in his hands. He was pale and shaking with fright.

"What shall I do? What shall I do?" he cried. "I have broken the statue that was to stand at the centre of the table. I cannot make the table look pretty without the statue. What will Count say?" And now all the other servants were in trouble. Count would be very angry.

Para 1: *Then little Antonio went up to the man who had caused the trouble.*

Para 2: *When the guests came in for dinner, the first thing they saw was the yellow lion cut out of butter.*

原文属于《高中课标》"人与自我"及"人与社会"的主题语境。故事以人物为线索展开，小男孩 Antonio 是雕刻匠人的孙子，有雕刻的天赋且从小耳濡目染，练就了很好的雕刻技能。一次爷孙两人在富人 Count 家做临时帮工时，仆人不小心打碎了一个很重要的装饰餐桌的雕塑品，眼看宴席即将开始，仆人非常惊慌无助。此时，Antonio 挺身而出，用牛油雕刻了一头狮子替换打碎的雕塑品，帮助仆人渡过难关。

老师范文:

Then little Antonio went up to the man who had caused the trouble. "If you had another statue, could you arrange the table?" he asked. "Certainly," said the man. On the kitchen table, there lay a large square lump of butter. With a kitchen knife in his hand, Antonio began to cut and carve this butter. With each stroke under his skilled hands, he gently sliced into the butter, creating precise lines and shapes. Finally, a crouching lion stood proudly before him. All the servants crowded around to see it. "How beautiful!" they cried.

When the guests came in for dinner, the first thing they saw was the yellow lion cut out of butter. "What a stunning statue!" they exclaimed. Curious, Count asked the head servant where he had found such an amazing statue. "It was carved by a little boy just an hour ago," the servant said with trepidation. Instead of getting angry, Count said happily, "The new statue is better than the old one. Now let me meet the great sculptor!" His grandfather smiled, "The boy will be an excellent sculptor someday."

学生习作:

Then little Antonio went up to the man who had caused the trouble, " I have an idea." Antonio said to the man. "You? But you are just a little boy." The man didn't trust little Antonio. Antonio just found a block of butter and started to cut it without saying a word. His grandfather just smiled and looked at his grandson. He knew Antonio could make it. After a while, the butter turned into a yellow lion. The other servants couldn't believe it was made by a little boy. The man who caused the trouble laughed and shook hands with little Antonio with gratitude. Then, they put the yellow lion at the centre of the table.

When the guests came in for dinner, the first thing they saw was the yellow lion cut out of butter. They were all surprised by the special statue. When Count came in, he also noticed the lion. He picked up and asked, "Who cut this amazing statue with butter?" All the servants looked at little Antonio, "It's me, I cut the statue." Count was surprised by this little boy. He also said to Antonio's grandfather, "You have a grandson as good as you." His grandfather laughed happily and Antonio laughed, too.

## 二、问题诊断与改进策略

本次读后续写的评分标准与全国卷评分标准保持一致，包括：与所给短文及段落开头语的衔接程度；内容的丰富性及与所给内容的逻辑衔接程度；语法结构和词汇的丰富性和准确性；上下文行文的连贯性。阅卷数据显示：全区考生3144人，全体平均分14.4分，得分率为57.6%，最高分为24分，有44人0分，零分率占1.4%，标准差4.2，难度系数为0.58。从平均分和难度系数看，全卷难度系数为0.65，而读后续写难度系数为0.58，是所有能力板块中通过率最低的，说明读后续写是学生最需要提高的题型。存在的主要问题如下：

（一）语篇（衔接不紧凑、逻辑不连贯）

（1）续写未能与给出的首句连接，如第一段首句讲"Antonio went up to the man who had caused the trouble"，但部分考生紧接着的续写却是Antonio与Count进行对话互动。

（2）对第二段首句关键词butter单词意思不理解，导致第一段情节与第二段不一致，具体表现为在第一段中，出现Antonio使用marble进行雕刻而不是使用butter，又或mix the marble with butter等。

（二）内容（情节单薄、不符合主题）

（1）部分考生缺乏生活常识，逻辑不严谨，没注意当时时间紧，Antonio年纪小，力气弱，而石头坚硬，不可能在短时间内使用石头完成雕刻，更不可能用石头雕出多个作品，因而出现了如"Antonio came with some small statues made up of the marble."的错误。

（2）缺乏文化背景知识，角色言行失当，如写到Antonio坐在宴席上回答Count的问题。

（三）语言（词汇和语法使用的准确性低、丰富性不足）：

（1）拼写错误，如comforted写成comfored, create写成creat, breaking写成broking, delightedly写成delightly, afraid写成afriad, perfect写成prefect, nodded写成nudded/noded, praising写成prising, voice写成voise, solve写成slove, calm写成clam, solved写成soluted, 等。

（2）不规则动词错误，如hided (hide), hitted (hit), standed (stand), cutted (cut), though/through/throught (think), shaked (shake), broked (break), heared (hear)、replyed (reply)，以及将 broken 和 known 当成过去式等。

（3）各种语法错误，如主谓一致错误、时态错误、双谓语等。

针对以上问题，采用以下改进策略：针对语法词汇的准确性问题，要求老师指出错误所在，学生先自改，后与同伴互改，做到拼写和语法正确；写作时间安排也是影响本次考生写作产出的一个重要因素，很多学生都反映时间不够，所以，在写作时间分配上也要对学生加强指导；针对语篇衔接和内容丰富性问题，建议尝试运用 TEAMS 框架进行讲评。

## 三、"TEAMS"框架在读后续写讲评课中的运用

下文以联考读后续写试题为例，运用"TEAMS"框架[①]，让学生修改出与原文衔接合理、语意连贯、逻辑相符又有文采的续文。

T 指 Theme（主题）或 Transitional sentence（衔接句）；

E 指 Emotion /Environment（心理描写/环境描写）；

A 指 Action［动作（链）］和 Appearance（外貌神态描写）；

M 指 Monologue/Dialogue（独白/对话）；

S 指 Style（语言风格）[②]。

其中，Action 是助推情节所必要的，Emotion、Environment、Appearance、Monologue、Dialogue、Style 的写作顺序和次数可根据故事情节需要适当调整。

Step 1　读懂原文"TEAMS"

| | |
|---|---|
| Theme | 原文第 1 段最后一句"Antonio showed so much skill that his grandfather was delighted. 'The boy will be a sculptor someday.'"以及第 3 段最后一句"…and as he was smart and quick, he could help in many other ways."体现了主题意义，即 Antonio 表现出出色的雕刻技能，他聪明，反应快，是个多面帮手，日后会成为雕刻大师。 |
| Environment | 自然环境描写：昼夜更迭、草木鸟兽、细节环境等。如：<br>He liked to go with his grandfather to the stone yard.<br>社会环境描写：时代背景、人物生活环境等。如：<br>Many years ago, a little boy named Antonio lived in Italy with his grandfather, who was a stone cutter. |

---

[①] 邱彩花等：《用 TEAM 框架突破高考英语读后续写》，西北工业大学出版社 2022 年版，第 7 页。

[②] 孙依依等：《高中英语读后续写全攻略》，上海外语教育出版社 2023 年版，第 3 页。

续上表

| | |
|---|---|
| Emotion | 表示喜怒哀乐的名词、形容词、副词：如：<br>Count would be very angry.<br>介词短语（to one's surprise、in relief、in panic、with joy…），如：<br>He was pale and shaking with fright.<br>So…that…/感叹句等表达人物的情感。如：<br>Antonio showed so much skill that his grandfather was delighted. |
| Appearance | 面部表情、眼睛、嘴巴、眉毛等。如：<br>He was pale and shaking with fright. |
| Actions | 使用以下句式构成动作链：<br>When/While A did/was/were doing sth., B did/would do sth.<br>While his grandfather was busy cutting the stone blocks, Antonio would play among the chips.<br>（2）sb. do/did sth. + with 结构做伴随状语<br>Suddenly, there was a crash in the dining room, and a man rushed into the kitchen with some pieces of marble in his hands. |
| Monologue (Dialogue) | Monologue，如：<br>"The boy will be a sculptor someday."<br>Dialogue：对话内容 + 对话标签（sb. said/cried/asked…）+ 对话内容/并列谓语/并列句，用来增加动作描写，让情节发展更加流畅。如：<br>"What shall I do? What shall I do?" he cried. "I have broken the statue that was to stand at the centre of the table…" |
| Style | 读后续写需注意与原文风格保持统一，可从"四个一致"的角度保持语言沿袭。<br>A. 用词特点一致<br>（1）日常词汇（"小"词）：<br>little boy, grandfather, rich man, friends, cook, guests, yard, kitchen, house, clay, pans, kettles, table, dining room, dinner, trouble, butter…<br>（2）专业词汇（"大"词）：<br>stone cutter, sculptor, servants, feast, statue, marble…<br>B. 描写角度一致<br>（3）Emotion/Environment/Actions/Monologue（Dialogue）…（如上所述） |

续上表

| | |
|---|---|
| Style | C. 修辞手法一致<br>（4）排比（parallelism）：<br>Sometimes he would make a small statue out of soft clay; sometimes, he would try to cut a statue from a piece of rock.<br>（5）重复（repetition）：<br>"What shall I do? What shall I do?" he cried.<br>D. 句式特点一致<br>（6）存在句：<br>There lived in the same town a rich man called Count.<br>（7）原因状语从句：<br>…and as he was smart and quick, he could help in many other ways.<br>（8）until 引导的时间状语从句：<br>All went well until it was time to spread the table for dinner. |

## Step 2　学习范文"TEAMS"

| | |
|---|---|
| Transitional sentences<br>（T1/2/3 衔接句）<br>T4（Theme） | T1：第一段开头语交代小安东尼奥走向制造麻烦的男人，接下来可从 little Antonio 的角度展开提问，用 6A（Actions）或 6 所（所见、所听、所说、所做、所想、所感）助推情节。答案就是 T1。<br>Q1：What did he say?<br>T1："If you had another statue, could you arrange the table?" he asked.<br>可见 T1 衔接合理。<br>T2：根据第二段段首句 When the guests came in for dinner, the first thing they saw was the yellow lion cut out of butter. 反推，黄狮子雕刻完毕并摆设好了。Then, they put the yellow lion at the centre of the table. 衔接紧密。<br>T3：第二段段首句涉及的人有 the guests，事物是 the yellow lion，"What a stunning statue!" they exclaimed. 传达了客人们对于狮子的惊叹，也使叙述连贯。<br>T4 首尾呼应式结尾：直接复现原文关键词，或把原文关键词以词性或词形变化的方式进行重复，或改写关键句进行重复，呼应并升华主题。His grandfather smiled, "The boy will be an excellent sculptor someday." |
| Environment | 自然环境：On the kitchen table, there was a large square lump of butter. |

续上表

| | |
|---|---|
| Emotion | 表示喜怒哀乐的形容词、副词<br>Curious, Count asked the head servant…<br>Instead of getting angry, Count said happily.<br>介词短语：<br>the servant said with trepidation<br>感叹句："How beautiful!" they cried. "What a stunning statue!" |
| Actions | sb. do/did sth. +with 结构做伴随状语<br>With a kitchen knife in his hand, Antonio began to cut and carve this butter.<br>sb. do/did sth., v-ing<br>He gently sliced into the butter, creating precise lines and shapes. |
| Monologue<br>(Dialogue) | Monologue, 如：<br>His grandfather smiled, "The boy will be an excellent sculptor someday."<br>Dialogue, 如：<br>"If you had another statue, could you arrange the table?" he asked. |
| Style | A. 用词特点一致<br>（1）日常词汇（"小"词）：<br>little boy, grandfather, grandson, man, kitchen, knife, table, dining room, trouble, butter…<br>（2）专业词汇（"大"词）：<br>sculptor, servants, carve, statue…<br>B. 描写角度一致<br>（3）Emotion/Environment/Actions/Monologue（dialogue）…（如上所述）<br>C. 修辞手法一致<br>（4）排比（parallelism）：<br>With a kitchen knife in his hand, Antonio began to cut and carve this butter.<br>With each stroke under his skilled hands, he gently sliced into the butter…<br>（5）拟人（personification）：<br>A crouching lion stood proudly before him.<br>D. 句式特点一致<br>（6）存在句：<br>On the kitchen table, there lay a large square lump of butter. |

## Step 3 评价"TEAMS",提升习作

| Aspects | Detail | Self-evaluation | Peer evaluation |
|---|---|---|---|
| T1/2/3 衔接句 T4（Theme） | T1: "I have an idea." Antonio said to the man. T2: Then, they put the yellow lion at the centre of the table. T3: They were all surprised by the special statue. T4: His grandfather laughed happily and Antonio laughed, too. | 优点：T1、T2、T3衔接合理，T4欢乐的结尾充满正能量。提升点：T4可使用议论+反思式结尾升华主题。 | 共商改进：Not until then did Antonio realize the magic of helping others. |
| Environment | Then, they put the yellow lion at the centre of the table. | 优点：简要说明了黄色的狮子放在桌子中央。提升点：可增加关于环境的细节，使读者身临其境。 | 共商改进：句后添加 with golden rays of sunlight streaming in through the nearby window |
| Emotion | The man who caused the trouble laughed and shook hands with little Antonio with gratitude. | 优点：男子的行为和笑声传达了他的快乐和感激。提升点：laughed 不太符合语境。 | 共商改进：The man who caused the trouble smiled. |
| Appearance | 无。 | 提升点：可添加外貌神态描写，例如眼神中流露出的喜悦等。 | 共商改进：His eyes sparkled with genuine joy, reflecting his gratitude towards little Antonio. |

续上表

| Aspects | Detail | Self-evaluation | Peer evaluation |
|---|---|---|---|
| Actions | Antonio found a butter and started to cut it without saying a word. After a while, the butter turned into a yellow lion. | 优点：描述了发现黄油、切割并制成黄狮的过程。提升点：增加雕刻黄油的细节，使描写更生动。 | 共商改进：句间插入：His eyes fixed on the cutting line as his hands moved with precision. |
| Monologue/Dialogue | Antonio said to the man, "I have an idea." The man responded, "You? But you are just a little boy." "Who cut this amazing statue with butter?" "It's me, I cut the statue." He also said to Antonio's grandfather, "You have a grandson as good as you." | 优点：男人的质疑凸显了安东尼奥的才能。提升点：第一个对话标签 responded 不准确。He（Count）向安东尼奥的祖父称赞的话不符合人物身份。 | 共商改进："responded" 改为 "replied"；学范文修改 Count 的话：Count said, "The new statue is better. Now let me meet the great sculptor!" |
| Style | 用词特点一致：grandfather, grandson, servants, butter, dinner, statue, sculptor | 优点：grandfather, grandson, servants, butter, dinner, statue, sculptor 使语言沿袭。提升点：在描写角度和修辞手法可有更多一致性。 | 共商改进：情感描写角度一致：Instead of getting angry, Count said happily… |

续上表

| Aspects | Detail | Self-evaluation | Peer evaluation |
| --- | --- | --- | --- |
| Overall Improvement | Then little Antonio went up to the man who had caused the trouble, " I have an idea." Antonio said to the man. "You? But you are just a little boy." The man didn't trust little Antonio. Antonio just found a block of butter and started cutting it. His eyes fixed on the cutting line as his hands moved with precision. After an hour, the butter turned into a yellow lion. The other servants couldn't believe their eyes. The man who caused the trouble smiled. His eyes sparkled with genuine joy, reflecting his gratitude towards little Antonio. Then, they put the yellow lion in the centre of the table with golden sunlight streaming in through the nearby window.<br>When the guests came in for dinner, the first thing they saw was the yellow lion cut out of butter. They were all surprised by the special statue. When Count came in, he also noticed the lion. He picked up and asked, "Who cut this amazing statue with butter?" All the servants looked at little Antonio, "It's me, I cut the statue." Instead of getting angry, Count said happily, "The new statue is better than the old one. Now let me meet the great sculptor!" Everyone applauded. Not until then did Antonio realize the magic of helping others. | | |

## 四、结语

《高中课标》提出要突出学生在评价中的主体地位，关注学生的全面发展和进步。[①] 作为评价过程的主要参与者，学生应在教师的指导下，学习使用适当的评价方法和可行的评价工具，积极参与评价，发现和分析学习中的具体问题。应提倡学生开展自评和互评，加强学生之间、师生之间评价信息的互动交流，促进自我监督式的学习，并在相互评价中不断反思，取长补短，总结经验，调控学习，把教学评价变成主体参与、自我反思、相互激励、共同发展的过程和手段[②]。评价反馈是读后续写的关键环节，运用"TEAMS"框架，可以

---

①② 中华人民共和国教育部：《普通高中英语课程标准》，人民教育出版社2020年版，第51、第83页。

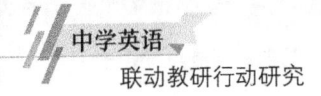

指导学生在读懂语篇的基础上，紧扣主题意义合理续写，通过自评和互评提升写作效果。这一过程有助于学生融合语言知识和文化知识，提高创造性地表达思想和情感的高阶思维能力，实现深度学习和发展核心素养的目的。

# 第六章 基于核心素养和学生说题的高中英语写作教学课例研究*

**摘 要**：分析目前高中英语教学中提高学生应试能力与培养学生核心素养之间的矛盾，以一堂高中英语写作教学课为例，从导入、写前、写中、写后、反思等教学环节阐述如何引导学生说题，提高学生的语言能力，发展学生的核心素养，真正落实以学生为主体的课堂教学。

**关键词**：写作教学　学生说题　主体地位　课例反思　核心素养

## 一、引言

当前，各地掀起了以构建学生核心素养为导向的教育教学改革浪潮。在我国，如何基于核心素养促进课程改革也成为研究的热点。但不可否认，在应试教育的学校文化背景下，大部分学校的英语课程针对核心素养的培养具有较大的随意性和盲目性。很多一线老师对如何落实英语学科核心素养目标不理解，在具体的实施过程中存在不少迷惘和偏差。笔者在学校的调研中常常看到，通过大量的习题、试卷讲评课，学生得到了答案，却不知道答案因何而来，面对新考题仍然茫然无措，升学成绩不理想，核心素养的培养更是被束之高阁，这些做法违背了新课改的宗旨和理念。本文针对区域调研中存在的问题，以试卷讲评课为切入点，在高二英语写作课堂中使用了让学生说题，教师更多走下讲台倾听，适时启发、引导、评价等教学策略，和一线老师面对面交流基于核心素养的教学目标设计与实施，共同探讨如何解决在日常英语课堂教学中不断提高应试能力与核心素养之间的矛盾。

---

\* 本文原发表于《英语教师》2017年第17期。本文为广东省十三五教育科学规划课题"新课程理念下学生说题教学的策略研究"（课题批准号：2016YQJK009）的成果之一。

## 二、课例介绍与分析

### （一）教学对象与内容分析

本课例为高二英语写作课，由广州市海珠区教育发展中心中学英语教研员张志梅执教，听课对象是广州市海珠区高二级和初一级全体英语教师，以及作者所带的广州市基础教育系统"百千万人才培养工程"第二批"中学名教师"高中英语第一工作室全体人员。课例时长为45分钟。授课的对象是广州市第五中学高二12班。该班是文科普通班，学生们还在进行模块学习，对全国卷的书面表达题型不熟悉，而所在的区即将按照全国高考的题型进行期末联考，老师们期待平时总在台上评价老师的教研员上一堂公开课，特别是高二的老师们很希望这次公开课的写作任务设计能够体现全国高考的理念和特点，为期末考试复习做准备。

作者通过分析2014—2016年这三年全国卷高考书面表达，发现命题有如下特点：①体裁以书信类为主，属于应用文的范畴。②给出的信件格式提示逐年减少。2014年书信的开头和结尾都已给出；2015年两套卷中一套给出了开头，另一套给出了结尾；2016年三套卷对于开头和结尾均没有任何提示。③写作形式大都为提纲类作文，但开放性增大，给出的文字提纲高度简洁、概括，给考生留有较大的发挥空间。④所选题材均与考生的日常生活密切相关，有利于考生在考场上的发挥。

又因为上课时间是2017年5月11日，恰逢母亲节前夕，所以选择了课标中24个话题中的Topic 10 Festivals, Holidays and Celebrations。而且非常凑巧，笔者80岁高龄的母亲临时决定近期将远道而来广州看望子女，陪伴母亲尝尝广州美食、逛逛街自然是表孝心的方式。笔者希望借此机会和师生一起认真研究，为母亲准备一个特别温馨的节日，也期待传达一种积极的生活态度和教育理念：生活不应该只是活着，应该庆祝！Life should not only be lived but it should be celebrated!

基于以上分析，设计了以下的写作任务：

Writing：你是_____，5月14号星期天是母亲节，你打算邀请妈妈一起共进晚餐，请你用英语给妈妈发一封电子邮件，告诉她关于母亲节你的计划，包括以下内容：

①写信目的；②晚餐的时间、地点、庆祝活动等信息；③你的祝愿。

写作任务为邀请信，学生根据提纲写作，开放性比较大，同时这是学生非常熟悉的话题，体现了英语语用性，富有生活气息，能够体现全国高考的特点。

### （二）学习目标

（1）语言能力：

Students will be able to:

- read a Mother's Day poem correctly and emotionally;
- discuss in groups of three and recommend a nice restaurant in front of the class;
- write a heartwarming letter of invitation to your mom inside Mother's Day card.

（2）学习能力：

Students will be able to: take an active part in discussion, cooperation with teachers and classmates.

（3）思维品质：

Students will be able to: peer evaluate the writing to improve the logical and critical thinking with the help of thinking maps.

（4）文化品质：

Students will be able to:

- appreciate Chinese traditional culture and raise cross-culture awareness;
- dedicate your card to your mum and show your love to her on Mother's Day.

## 三、教学过程设计与分析

本节写作课以即将到来的母亲节和母爱为主线，学生说写结合向听课老师展示语言输出的过程。下面重点阐述导入、写前、写中和写后四个环节的中学生如何说题，教师如何根据学生的说题语言及时调整教学行为，实现上述的教学目标。

### （一）热身导入

**1. 教师自我介绍**

由于是借班授课，教师在自我介绍时采用自己当年在五中任教的照片以及已毕业的学生的照片作为自我介绍素材，消除了与学生之间的陌生感，拉近了与学生之间的距离。

### 2. 学生欣赏英文版《游子吟》

Warm up: What is mother's love like?

A TRAVELLER'S SONG By Men Jiao
The thread in the hands of a found-hearted mother
Makes clothes for the body of her wayward boy;
Carefully she sews and thoroughly she mends,
Dreading the delays that will keep him late from home.
But how much love can the inch-long grass
Pay for three spring months of the sun light?

以一首孟郊的《游子吟》英文版童谣引入，学生听到可爱的童声，看到图文并茂的情境，马上产生共鸣。紧接着，教师提问"Do you like the song? Who's the writer of the poem?"让学生欣赏中华古典文学之美，然后通过思考"在诗人的眼里母爱是三春晖，在你的心里母爱又是什么？"这样的问题，帮助学生学会理解通俗易懂的表达母爱的词汇：慈母（fond-hearted mother）、游子（wayward boy）、寸草（inch-long grass）、春晖（spring sunlight），体会中国文化的博大精深。

### 3. 学生破冰游戏——选出"最美DJ"

教师邀请本班"最美DJ"为大家配乐朗读这首诗歌，但是学生当着200多位英语老师的面不敢举手。为了消除学生的紧张感，老师自创了一个游戏"Headmaster Qiu Laoda"（裘老大——师生对裘校长的亲切称呼），学生依次说Headmaster-Qiu-Lao-Da，说到Da的学生必须拍一下头，如果忘记拍头，就要成为DJ。结果学生很喜欢这个游戏，课堂气氛活跃起来。很快，两个女生被选中，她们走到师生面前表演，朗读任务在欢声笑语中完成。本环节运用音乐和图片让学生获得心灵的感动，为引入写作的话题做好了铺垫。

（二）写前活动

1. **教师设置个性化的 speaking 情景**

在学生获得内心情感共鸣的基础上，教师设置了如下 speaking 情景："教师远在老家年事已高的妈妈将来广州游玩，请学生帮忙推荐一家适合与妈妈在母亲节当天共进晚餐的餐厅"，学生小组讨论推选出一家美味的餐厅。目的是激活学生的背景知识，鼓励学生进行个性化的表达，通过合作增强学生学习的自信心和动力。师生对话如下：

T：As you mentioned, mother's love is like sunlight/honey brewed by bees./spring breeze/…

To me, mother's love is like a running river. All the yummy food is running to me from Hunan.

Look, this is my fond-hearted mum。

Ss：Hahaha…

T：My mum called me this morning and she is coming to Guangzhou to spend Mother's day. Please discuss in groups and recommend a nice restaurant for me, OK?

Ss：OK.

2. **制作 Thinking map**

老师引导学生 Brainstorm 完成 thinking map 1，明确推荐餐厅的思路和方向

*Thinking Map 1：Let's vote for a nicer restaurant*

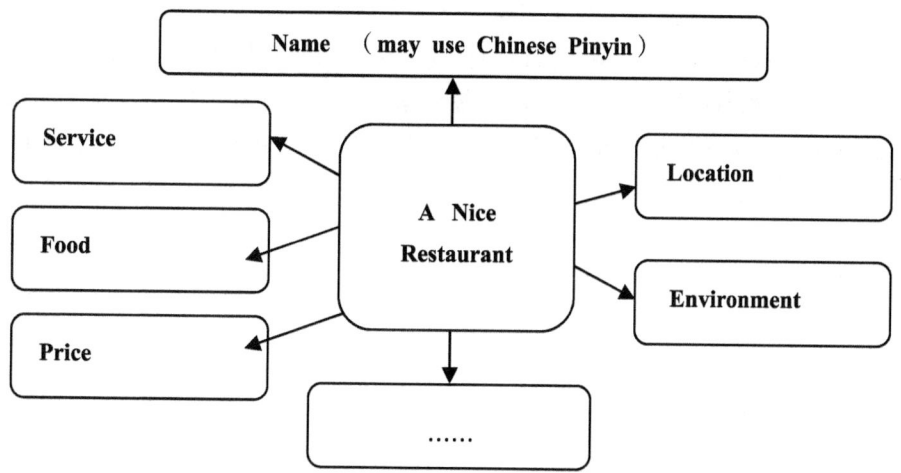

### 3. 学生小组讨论，推荐餐厅

学生经过小组讨论之后积极举手发言，老师选择两个小组展示，采用一人介绍，一人在黑板上记录有关餐厅的位置、环境、食物、服务、价格等关键信息的方式。教师要求全班同学认真听和记笔记，教师也仔细倾听，适时介入、启发、引导和评价。两个小组发言如下：

Group 1：(Two Boys) We recommend the White Swan Hotel. It is located in Shamian. It is near the Pearl River. It is amazing to have dinner in a river-view room. There are a lot of historical buildings near the hotel. Rainbow's mum can try prawn shrimps, turnip cakes and many local food. The waiters and waitresses are very refined and courteous, but the price is very high.

Group 2：(Two girls) We recommend Feng Chu Restaurant at Xiadu Road. It is near No.6 Middle School of Guangzhou. The food is tasty and the waiters and waitresses have good manners. After dinner, Rainbow can show her mum around the school campus and then do some shopping. I think it's better to buy a present for Rainbow's mum.

### 4. 全体师生评选出最好的餐厅

两组学生推荐完毕之后，全体师生通过举手表决的方式评选出更好的餐厅。结果，现场250多名师生共同选出the White Swan Hotel。大家鼓掌祝贺，胜出的组还获得了巧克力奖品。现场气氛热烈。

## （三）写中活动

### 1. 教师提供别具一格的作文题——制作母亲节卡片

教师为每一个学生准备一张封面精美、里面为母亲节邀请信的卡片，要求学生用英语邀请妈妈在母亲节共进晚餐，参加温馨的活动。这是之前speaking活动的拓展。为了帮助学生构思，老师提供了第二个thinking map，为学生独立写作做准备。

*Thinking Map 2：Outline a heartwarming letter of invitation to your mum*

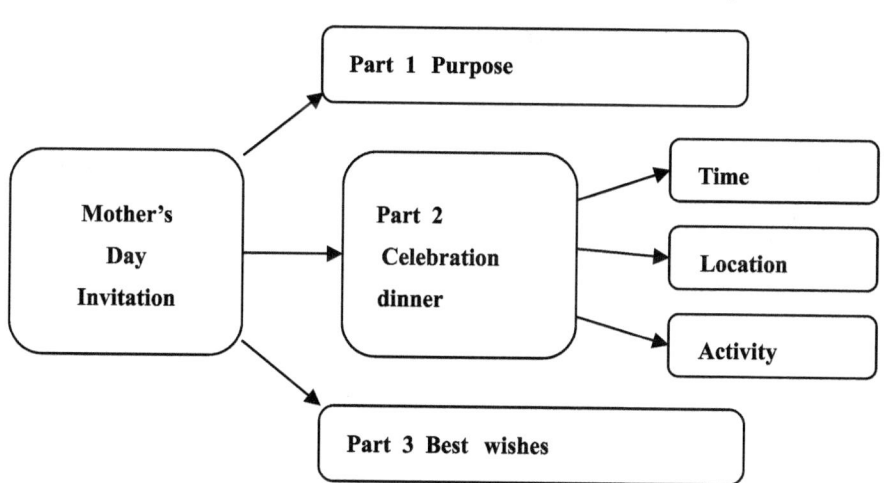

### 2. 学生自主学习，独立完成母亲节邀请信

学生凭借思维导图分析邀请信的格式和要求，梳理段落之间的逻辑关系，选择个性化的语言完成邀请信。如果有疑问，可以举手提问，现场多位老师为学生提供了及时的帮助。这个环节旨在培养学生独立思考和自主学习的能力。根据课堂观察，51位同学全部动笔进行了写作，说明题目的设计让学生有感而发。有32人在15分钟内完成了完整的邀请信，完成率62.7%，语言输出的量还是比较好的。

邀请现场听课老师和学生一起写作，体会做学生的感受。

老师们课后反映他们大概也需要15分钟完成任务。

### （四）写后活动

### 1. 教师指明评价方向

Peer-Evaluation Form

| 项目 Items | 闪光点举例（Shining Points） | 增分点提升（Potentialities） |
| --- | --- | --- |
| 1. 段落是否合理<br>（Reasonable Paragraphs） | | |
| 2. 词汇是否优美<br>（Beautiful Vocabulary） | | |

续上表

| 项目 Items | 闪光点举例（Shining Points） | 增分点提升（Potentialities） |
|---|---|---|
| 3．句式是否丰富<br>（Diverse Sentences） | | |
| 4．衔接是否自然<br>（Natural Coherence） | | |
| 5．书写是否工整<br>（Tidy Handwriting） | | |
| 激励语<br> | | Evaluator： |

## 2．学生充当小老师，主评习作

学生现场朗读习作，在投影仪上展示，邀请自己喜欢的同学充当小老师，互评提高。因为时间关系，课堂上点评了两位学生作品，展示如下。

| 学生作品 | 学生主评 | 教师补充 |
|---|---|---|
| 作品1 | Boy：I think Deng Xicong can use some beautiful vocabulary, such as approaching, high-end, and I like White Swan Restaurant, too. But the word "teached" is wrong, you should say "taught". | T：I can't agree with the little teacher more. I find more shining points about Xicong. It's amazing for him to use three attributive clauses, and more importantly, he must be a successful learner because he can use what we learn today. |

续上表

| 学生作品 | 学生主评 | 教师补充 |
|---|---|---|
| 作品2 | Girl: First, I like He Yuqin's beautiful handwriting. Second, she has three reasonable paragraphs, especially I think the last paragraph is good, because I hope my mom will be young forever. Third, I think doing housework is a great way to show love. That's all, thank you. | T: Fantastic comments! Just like Yuqin quotes, action speakers louder than words. With true love, start from small to pay back mom. Thank you. |

### 3. 全班集体朗读母亲节小诗，总结激励

Mother's Day—By Rainbow

Girls: The second Sunday of May

　　　Is a day to express love

　　　From the beginning of mumbling language

　　　We issued the world's first common voice: MaMa

Boys: You are the person to bring us to this world

　　　Because of you, we have love

　　　As this festival is approaching

　　　We dedicate the most beautiful gift to you

Together: I love you, dear mom

　　　Happy Mother's Day to all moms in the world!

### （五）家庭作业

Please dedicate your card to your mum and show your love to her on Mother's Day.

## 四、教学反思

本节课基本上实现了教学目标,反思学生的表现,结合听课老师的反馈[①],做得比较好的地方有以下几点。

### (一) 教学准备:为老师们展示了逆向思路的教学设计

教学准备有两种思路:一种是顺向思考,另一种是逆向设计。在教学大纲时代,教师大都采用顺向设计,即基于教学内容安排学习活动。逆向设计是有了课程标准之后再提出的新思路,教师首先将课程标准转换成学习目标,并据此设计与目标相匹配的评价,然后设计学习活动。本节写作课先对近三年的全国卷作文题进行命题分析,选取课程标准话题10——节日与庆祝作为教学目标,结合即将到来的母亲节设置说与写的情景,在分析和解决问题的过程中,训练学生的综合语言运用能力,是逆向型写作课型的大胆尝试。老师们普遍反映对这种不依靠教材和教参的课感兴趣,还认为其把中国文化和外国节日融合起来进行教学很有创意和推广价值。

### (二) 教学目标:体现核心素养在课堂教学中的具体操作实施

本课以主题为引领,抓住了主线,并且创设了真实的情景,把培养核心素养的目标具体化为学生环环相扣的实践活动,体现了综合性、实践性和关联性的学习过程,也使学生的语言能力、学习能力、思维品质、文化品质得到了发展。同时本课也架起中西文化的桥梁,这也是新课程改革倡导的中国情怀,国际视野。

### (三) 教学活动:把语言教学与生活实践相结合

教学活动是教师与学生之间开展的一系列有组织、有计划的学习活动,它应具备引起注意、明释内容、调适形式和关注结果等逻辑元素。他们是将课堂行为引向有效性的最关键途径。本课把 speaking 和 writing 紧密结合,强化铺垫,激活学生写作的内容图式、形式图式和语言图式。课后布置学生完成并赠送母亲节卡,邀请母亲共进晚餐,将教学活动延伸至课外,进一步升华了本课的主题"母亲节与爱",把语言教学与生活实践相结合,培养了学生热爱母亲、敢于表达爱的情感态度与价值观,也传递了生活的真谛:Life should not only be lived, but it should be celebrated!

---

[①] 评课反馈:广州市第九十七中学庄英如。

## （四）教学评价：适时适度，激励学生

有效的课堂评价应具有以下两点功能：首先，教师应当对学生的表现做出即时、中肯的评估，让他们知道自己的回答或表现有哪些可取之处，让他们在体验学习成功的快乐的同时，意识到自己存在的不足，并维护其自尊心。体验成功的欢乐和维护自尊心这两点都能激发学生参与课堂活动的积极性，这种积极状态是学生内心深处受到激励后形成的更强的表现欲。其次，教师的有效评价不仅预示着前一段交流的结束，评价中的部分话语还能将交流继续推向深入，引发师生、生生之间新一轮交流和更多的话语输出，形成更积极的语言输出和交流状态。[①] 本节课中教师自始至终对学生循循善诱，用心聆听，并且根据学生的语言输出及时中肯地进行评价，得到听课老师一致好评。

## （五）师生角色：学生说题，主体地位得到尊重

英国语言教学大师 Michcal West 曾经说过："外语是学会的，不是教会的。"这句至理名言足以说明学生在学习外语中的主体地位的重要性。本节课教师心中有学生，在每一个教学活动中让学生说了算。先邀请学生朗读英文版《游子吟》作为引入；接着在教师设置的 speaking 情景下，学生 Brainstorm，小组讨论推选出一家美味的餐厅；然后，完成写作后在全班分享和点评；最后以学生集体朗读教师创作的诗歌《母亲节》作为结束，布置学生课后装饰好母亲节卡片，在母亲节当天献给自己的妈妈并与妈妈共进晚餐，深化学生对母亲节的情感认知，以及在生活中敢于对亲人表达爱的情感态度。整节课都体现了学生是言语活动的主体，充分调动了学生学习的积极主动性，特别是教学评价中学生发出了更多的声音。同时也充分考虑了参与听课的 200 多位老师的需要，让老师们参与投票，和学生一起写作，观察学生表现，现场答疑，批改习作、评课等，发挥老师们教研活动的主人翁精神，调动了他们工作的主动性和创造性。

本节课不足之处在于，教师对学生的了解不够，导致设计的内容偏多、偏难，加之受会议室环境的限制，学生难以进行高效的小组合作沟通，教师对课堂的节奏掌握得不太好，从学生的口头语言和习作中看出语言输入的质量有待提高。此外，课堂上如何做到既给学生鼓励，又能够及时纠正学生错误仍然值

---

[①] 黄宏震：《英语课堂中学生积极参与状态举例及原因分析》，载《中小学外语教学（中学篇）》2015 年第 3 期，第 55-59 页。

得思考。有老师建议减少任务,给学生更多的时间进行写作与评价;或降低难度,如改为"邀请妈妈到该餐厅用餐的理由"等,以有利于学生在写作中有更好的发挥。

## 五、结束语

变革的时代也是令人迷惘的时代,在教育世界中倡导基于核心素养的课程发展具有划时代的意义。[①] 作为教研员,以课例研究的方式和一线老师直面时代的挑战,不断探索,相信能够集思广益,不仅提升个人专业能力,更为区域的教研和课改提供新视野,形成提升教育质量的合力。

---

① 钟启泉:《基于核心素养的课程发展:挑战与课题》,载《全球教育展望》2016年第1期,第3-25页。

# 第七章 "主题—探究—评价"活动课教学模式*

## 第一节 建模的背景和意义

### 一、进行创新性教学，培养创新人才是时代的需要，是英语教学理论与实践变革的必然趋势

21世纪英语教学已经越来越明显地表现出如下的发展和变化。

（1）英语文化素养越来越成为每一个公民以至于整个民族文化素养的重要内容和标志，因此英语教学要面向大众，面向每一个学生。

（2）英语教学的目标不应仅局限于单纯强调知识和技能，发展学生的认知能力，而应更关注学习的过程和方法策略，关注学生在情感、态度、价值观等方面的发展，特别是学生的个性和创造力的发展。

（3）英语教学模式已经从传统的过分重视语法和词汇知识的传授、重复机械练习的注入式模式逐渐转变为以激励学生为特征，以学生为主体的启发式模式。学生的自主学习、独立创新、个性发展受到更多的重视。

（4）英语基础课程内容越来越关注学生的经验，反映社会科技的最新发展，满足学生多样化发展的需要，发挥评价在促进学生潜能、个性、创造性等方面的提升作用，使每个学生具有自信心和持续发展的能力。

（5）英语教学不再是教师单纯地为学生付出，而是学生创造性生活的一部分。英语教学的过程是师生双方实现自己生命价值和自身发展的舞台。

（6）多媒体信息技术和互联网络为各个层次的英语教学提供了越来越丰富的资源。学生可以根据自己的需要选择学习内容和学习方式并及时得到反馈信息，学生之间可以相互帮助和分享学习资源，这为个性化学习和创新学习创

---

\* 本文原发于查有梁总主编《中学英语教学建模》（广西教育出版社2003年版）。本文被广州市教育局评为"广州市中小学、中等职业学校第三阶段教学设计与实施活动——发展性教学评价研究"的优秀成果二等奖（获奖时间：2005年12月）。

造了条件。这样，英语教学不是"授人以鱼"，而是要"授人以渔"。

我国的英语教学历来有重视基础知识、基本技能、基本方法，重视教师的主导作用的优良传统。学生对英语知识（特别是对语法和词汇）的掌握有较明显的优势，不少学生在国内外的各种考试中取得高分便是一个很好的明证。但我国学生实践能力弱，一到实际交际，往往听不懂也说不出。不少学习了近10年英语的高中毕业生不敢同英语国家的人士交谈，看不懂英语报刊杂志上的广告，更听不懂日常的英语广播、看不懂电视电影，学生综合英语运用能力和创造力贫乏，探索研究意识不足，个性发展不够，而这些正是21世纪有竞争力人才的关键素质所在。因此，英语教学的当务之急是更新教和学的方式，开拓教与学的渠道，使学生尽可能多地参与有交际意义的语言实践活动，亲身感受和直接体验语言学习和语言运用。为此，教师应为学生创设激发创新的机会和环境。

## 二、构建行之有效的英语活动课教学模式，是培养学生创新精神和实践能力的重要途径

英语教学的实践证明，单一的"学科课程"很难打破"应试教育"的桎梏，不适应素质教育的要求。因此，《全日制义务教育普通高级中学英语课程标准（试验稿）》（以下简称《标准》）指出："英语课程要面向全体学生，注重素质教育。课程特别强调要关注每个学生的情感，激发他们学习英语的兴趣，帮助他们建立学习的成就感和自信心，使他们在学习过程中发展综合语言运用能力，提高人文素养，增强实践能力，培养创新精神。"[①] 开设英语活动课程是英语教学深化改革的产物，是实现上述课程理念的具体实践，是学生接受素质教育的重要途径，特别是培养创新精神和实践能力的有效措施。这些重要的育人功能是由英语活动课的本质特点所决定的。

### 1. 英语活动课的含义和特点

有关英语活动课程，《标准》中有如下的说明："要根据学生的年龄特点和兴趣爱好，积极开展各种课外活动有助于学生增长知识、开阔视野、发展智力和个性、展现才能。教师应有计划地组织内容丰富、形式多样的英语课外活动，如朗诵、唱歌、讲故事、演讲、表演、英语角、英语墙报、主题班会和展

---

① 中华人民共和国教育部：《全日制义务教育普通高级中学英语课程标准》，北京师范大学出版社2001年版，第32页。

览等。教师要善于诱导，保护学生的好奇心，培养他们的自主性和创新意识。"① 从中可以看出，英语课外活动是指在学科课程以外，由学校有目的、有计划、有组织地通过多种活动项目和活动方式，综合运用英语知识和技能，开展以学生为主体，以实践性、趣味性、自主性、创造性、综合性等为主要特征的多种活动内容的新型活动课程。它和英语的学科课程、潜在课程共同构成现代英语课程体系的有机组成部分，是完成同一育人目标的不同途径。

### 2. 英语活动课教学的现状在很大程度上压抑了学生创新能力的发展

我国现行的基础教育仍然是以分科主义课程为基础的教育，在"应试教育"的学校文化背景下，大部分学校的英语活动课程远远落后于改革开放和经济发展的形势。管理不科学，认识不充分，评估考核不健全，开展活动的条件不完善，使得许多活动无法真正展开，其内容和形式没有形成系统化，具有较大的随意性和盲目性。尽管英语界的有识之士已经意识到改革活动课教学的重要性和紧迫性，积极地做出了一些有益的探索，但在具体的实施过程中仍然产生了一些迷惘和偏差。一是将活动简单化、学科化，认为只要学生动口动手了，就是在做活动，让学生一遍遍地做着与学科课堂大同小异的练习题、诊断题、竞赛题、模拟题……习题和试卷像一堵无法逾越的高墙，隔绝了学生的英语学习与感悟生活的联系。二是片面追求教学组织形式的活动化效果，满足于唱唱跳跳，课堂看上去热热闹闹、生动活泼，但过于天真的游戏和刻板的角色扮演，使活动缺乏现实感和真实性，达不到应有的质量和深度，教师创造性的劳动在这里打了折扣。三是功利主义与精英主义取向。一些贵族学校和所谓的重点高中为了追求宣传效应，急于推出成果，有意无意地推出高难度的"研究性学习"活动，在选题上往往脱离学生的现实生活，在组织上竟相聘请专家、外教担任指导顾问，不顾"课程成本"，却把绝大多数学生置于陪读地位。其结果是造成了大批英语学习的"失败者""自卑者"。根据最近对广州市来自 ABC 三类中学共 600 名中学生进行英语课外活动学习的问卷调查，结果显示 33% 的学生对学校的英语课外活动"兴趣不大"或"毫无兴趣"，69% 的学生认为学校无丰富多彩的英语课外活动，71% 的学生认为英语课外活动课"收获不明显"，可见学生的积极性还没有调动起来，英语活动课的巨大潜力还远远没有开发出来。

正因为目前对英语活动课型无论从理解和领会上，还是从内容和要求上，

---

① 中华人民共和国教育部：《全日制义务教育普通高级中学英语课程标准》，北京师范大学出版社 2001 年版，第 33 页。

甚至形成模式的操作和运用方面尚处于一个起步和探索阶段。因此，针对教学中存在的问题，建立起能充分调动师生双方的积极性和创造性，有效培养学生综合英语运用能力和创新能力的教学模式，不仅有助于提高英语活动课的教学质量，而且可以为从事英语活动课教学工作的一线教师提供一些可供借鉴的、有价值的启示和帮助。

## 第二节 对"主题—探究—评价"英语活动课教学模式的基本认识

### 一、"主题—探究—评价"英语活动课教学模式的概念

"主题—探究—评价"英语活动课教学模式指的是以创新教育思想和素质教育理论为指导，坚持以活动促进学生的综合英语运用能力和创新能力的发展为目标，引导激励学生自主参与有意义的主题活动，然后围绕主题以多种多样的方式与逻辑展开探究，学习如何分析和处理有关信息，综合概括主题的特征和本质，最后表达、交流并共享学习成果。以此为基本程序的英语活动课教学模式，在具体的教学过程中包括学生的学和教师的教。无论是对于教师还是学生，英语活动课都是一个学习英语和运用英语的过程，强调学生的主动探索和亲身体验。而教师既是活动的组织者、情感的支持者，又是活动的参与者、示范者、咨询者和促进者。在不同的活动阶段，教师的作用也相应发生变化：在确定主题阶段，主要是情境创设者、活动组织者和信息导航者；在实践探究阶段，主要转向学习辅导者、支持者和意志激励者；在成果交流阶段，教师则是总结概括者、促进迁移者以及创新能力的开发者。在具体的实施中，各阶段相互推进、相互融合，并没有明显的界线，如表1所示。

表1 "主题—探究—评价"英语活动课教学模式

| 活动程序 | 教师活动 | 学生活动 |
| --- | --- | --- |
| 确立探究主题 | 创设问题情境<br>激发学习兴趣<br>组织小组讨论<br>帮助形成主题 | 体验问题情境<br>浏览相关资料<br>小组交流讨论<br>选择活动主题 |

续上表

| 活动程序 | 教师活动 | 学生活动 |
| --- | --- | --- |
| 实践探究主题 | 跟踪活动进展<br>协同小组活动<br>提供指导建议<br>给予感情支持 | 自主参与活动<br>思考实践探究<br>咨询疑难问题<br>培养创新思维 |
| 成果表达交流 | 组织成果展示<br>引导小组互评<br>提供反馈信息<br>帮助形成观点<br>促进成果推广 | 成果便捷发布<br>充分交流沟通<br>推广学习成果<br>完成知识迁移<br>发展创新能力 |

## 二、理论依据

### 1. 创新教育理论指导

创新教育理论认为：创新是作为活动主体的人所从事的产生新思想和新事物的活动，其根本特征是变革、进步和超越。从个体意义上来考察，创新就是指个人以一种探究的态度产生个体水平上的新的经验。美国心理学家马斯洛就曾把创造性分为"有特别才能的创造性"和"自我实现的创造性"两种：前者是指科学家、艺术家、天才人物的创造性；后者人皆有之，但其创新活动不一定得到社会的承认，而只是个体自己才感受到的"前所未有"的新经验。中小学生的创新，主要是指后一种意义上的创新。美国心理学家奥托说："我们所有的人，都有惊人的创造力。"因此，教师要树立"人人是创造主人的意识"。

创新教育贵在创新，就是根据创新原理，以培养学习者具有一定的创新意识、创新思维、创新能力以及创新个性为主要目标的教育理论和方法，重在学生牢固、系统地掌握学科知识的同时发展学习者的创新能力。

创新总是与活动相伴的。创新在活动中产生，在活动中生成。没有了活动，也就没有了创新；没有了活动，创新教育就没有了中介，失去了灵魂。活动必须贯穿于创新教育的全过程。要千方百计地调动学生的积极性，让他们活起来，动起来，把创新的潜力开发起来。

可见，创新教育是为培养学生创新意识、学习探索创新方法、锻炼学生创新能力而开展的教育活动，它可以帮助学生克服因循守旧的思想意识和行为习惯，敢于怀疑和打破前人的旧思想、旧观念，敢于标新立异，尝试新的东西，掌握创新的途径和方法，使教育活动不停留在传授知识阶段，还使学生创造性地分析问题和解决问题，关注的是人作为活动主体最本质、最深层、最能动的素质，使素质教育有了一个更高的目标定位，为素质教育提供了以新的价值观念及实现人的全面发展的基本途径。

### 2. 体现新课程标准的改革要求

《标准》在前言部分就强调课程从学生的学习兴趣、生活经验和认识水平出发，倡导体验、实践、参与、合作与交流的学习方式和任务型的教学途径，发展学生的综合语言运用能力，使语言学习的过程成为学生形成积极的情感态度、主动思维和大胆实践、提高跨文化意识和形成自主学习能力的过程。[①]"主题—探究—评价"英语活动课教学模式就是以主题学习作为具体的任务，让学生在教师的指导下通过自己的努力和亲身体验，主动获取知识或信息，应用知识或信息去完成任务，并以展示与交流成果的方式来体现教学的成效，有助于落实新课程标准的要求。

### 3. 学习论基础——建构主义的学习观

建构主义认为，学习应当是积极的、建构性的、累积性的、目标指引的，同时也是诊断性和反思性的。20世纪初对建构主义思想做出重要贡献并将其应用于儿童的学习与发展的杜威就认为，真正的理解是与事物怎样动作及事情怎样做有关的，理解在本质上是联系动作的，因此，教育基于行动。与杜威同时代的苏联著名心理学家维果茨基（L. S. Vygotsky）提出了以"活动"概念为基础的建构主义学习观，他认为学习并不是内蕴于知识之中的，而是通过"活动"社会地构成，又通过"内化"心理地构成的。因此，他所强调的"活动性学习"是以语言、逻辑、符号、概念三类"工具"为媒介的社会交往活动。

### 4. 心理学基础——需要、兴趣、活动

中学生血气方刚、活力充沛，学习兴趣与范围逐步扩大、分化，正处在思想开始形成的阶段，他们的观察力、想象力、有意注意和抽象思维能力有显著的发展，他们的情感也往往表现出高度的兴奋性和特有的热情，喜欢群体活动，他们的道德感和自我意识也与日俱增，他们爱说、爱动，自我表现欲和参

---

[①] 中华人民共和国教育部：《全日制义务教育普通高级中学英语课程标准》，北京师范大学出版社2001版。

与意识强烈。因此，英语活动课应抓住学生的这些年龄特点和心理特征，为学生创造条件，提供英语实践和活动的机会，激发学生学习英语的兴趣，满足他们用英语进行交际的需要，展现他们的活力与热情。这正是他们学习英语的真正动力。

**5. 语言学基础——语言习得和语言生成规律**

人类主要通过语言相互交流。毋庸置疑，我们出生时体内就有发声器官，但并非天生就有语言能力，语言能力必须通过某种方式习得。语言的习得是在有意义的自然语言交流中产生的。在大量试验的基础上，Krashen 提出了语言的输入定理，其主要论点是：通过理解那些比学生们目前的语言程度稍高一个层次的语言输入，学生们会自然地不断进步。关于语言输入，Long 也提出了重要的观点：①成功的语言习得，不管是第一语言还是第二语言，都依赖于可被理解的语言输入。②可被理解的语言输入量越大，语言习得的效果也越好。③无法理解的语言输入不可能产生语言习得。美国语言学家 Seliger 也通过试验证明：学生的实际语言表现与他们的语法知识是无关的，对语言能力产生更直接影响的是语言的习得。而我国传统的英语教学一直强调的是语言的学习，而忽略了语言的习得，我们对这种状况必须加以改观。

人类的语言还具有生成效能。美国语言学家乔姆斯基（Chomsky）认为：人类语言可以用有限的手段生成无限的句子。这就是说，任何语言的句子都是无限的，而语言规则却是有限的。应用一套有限的规则可以生成无限数目的句子，这正是语言创造性的表现。对于有限规则的无限运用这种语言的创造性，语言学家一般称之为语言的生成性。语言的生成特性为人们创造性地运用语言提供了可能。对于中学生而言，他们已经掌握了一定数量的英语词汇和语法规则，可用以描写各式各样的事物和现象，可以表达丰富多样的感情与思想，可以创造性地学习并掌握运用英语的规律。

基于上述因素，教师在开展英语活动课教学中应牢固树立学本观念，充分尊重学生的需要、愿望和自主学习的权力，激发学习的兴趣，积极为学生创设英语习得的理想环境，鼓励学生以多种活动方式探究、发现和掌握语言的生成规律。要尊重学生对英语课程丰富人文内涵的多元反应及独特体验，鼓励学生自主地、有创意地去感受、体验和理解英语作品，思他人之未思，悟他人之未悟；要鼓励学生有创意地表达，抒发对自然、社会、人生的独到见解，从而通过大量的英语实践活动，促进学生综合语言运用能力和创新能力的提高。这也正是构建"主题—探究—评价"英语活动课教学模式的根本目的所在。

## 三、"主题—探究—评价"英语活动课教学模式的基本特征

### 1. 教学情境的真实性和建构性

有效的英语学习活动，必须以一定的社会生活情境为背景，将语言知识作为工具，通过运用来理解。要改变以往英语活动课教学中存在的枯燥乏味的练习以及虚假热闹的游戏表演形式，必须通过设置真实或仿真实的学习情境，也就是说，活动的情境是正在发生或者能够发生的，活动的内容应有明确的主题，活动的形式应符合英语的文化特征，从而使学生理解英语知识在不同情境中的不同意义，促使学生去思考"真实的问题"。通过师生之间、生生之间的交流与合作，建构起对问题更深层的理解，在恰当地表达自己想法的同时，通过对语境的分析，准确、恰当、合理、有效地理解对方的思想。这是因为语境制约着语言的交流过程，如果离开语境这个载体，只通过言语形式本身就容易产生歧义。

### 2. 学生参与的自主性与广泛性

自主性指英语活动课程是根据学生的需要和兴趣开设的，或者是学生依据自己的需要和兴趣自主选择的，学生是活动的主体，教师起组织指导作用。广泛性是指活动要积极调动全体学生的积极性和主动性，尽可能让每个学生都有自我表现的机会，使每个学生在每一次活动中都有不同程度的提高。可以说，学生主动参与的广度与深度，是衡量活动效果的重要标志。

### 3. 教学目标的发展性与多元性

"学生的发展是英语课程的出发点和归宿。"[①] 英语活动课的教学目标主要有：①培养学习英语的兴趣，发展个性特长；②拓宽知识的广度与深度，加强实践，形成一定的综合语言运用能力，发展创造才能；③陶冶情操，丰富生活，愉悦身心，给学生"减负"；④热爱生活，适应社会，培养爱国精神，增强国际意识，为终身学习和发展打下良好的基础。

### 4. 教学内容的综合性和多样性

综合性是指英语活动应有明确的主题，结合学生已有的经验与现实生活的需要，遵循英语的文化特征，把听、说、读、写等多种技能与综合运用各学科的知识有机结合起来，知、能、智、德交融，学以致用，学生从中受到的教育是多方面的、综合的，对指导教师的要求也是多方面的、综合性的。多样性是

---

① 中华人民共和国教育部：《全日制义务教育普通高级中学英语课程标准》，北京师范大学出版社2001年版，第2页。

指英语活动的内容与形式要因地制宜，因校制宜，因人而异，灵活多样。

### 5. 教学过程的实践性和体验性

英语活动课就是英语的实践课，重在能力的培养。教师通过组织富有创新性的活动把枯燥的知识趣味化，抽象的知识具体化，书本的知识实践化，让学生全方位、多层次地"动"起来，使学生在动脑、动手、动口的操作活动中亲身体验语言文字的运用，掌握从不同角度观察、思考和解决问题的方法，敢于标新立异，提高实践能力和创新能力。

### 6. 师生关系的平等性、互动性

英语活动课要真正让学生动起来，就需要创设一种轻松愉快的气氛和民主平等的人际关系。师生之间、生生之间需要互相尊重，团结合作，不强迫、不指责、不嘲讽，给学生一种心理安全感，确保学生思想和行为的自由，发展和创造的自由。应强化师生互动式的活动。这里的互动，一是指教师与学生的互动，要根据学生的兴趣与需要，设计调整活动的方式，做到因材施教；二是指学生之间的互动，生生间的合作学习，讨论交流，扩大获取信息的渠道，互相启发思维，达到互相促进的作用，提高互动的质量。

### 7. 教学评价的全程性与整合性

"主题—探究—评价"英语活动课教学模式，是作为一种基于情境学习和情境认知的"登山型"教学模式。以大的主题（山）为中心，准备了若干学习的途径（登山道），学习者可以自己选择道路、方法，按照自己的速度去探究（登山）。随着一步步的攀登，能够不断开拓视野，过后还可以进行反思与评价（回味攀登途中的某种经验）。可见这是一种不仅注重学习结果而且更加注重学习过程的多元化、个性化的课程设计，强调教学要开展与学生学习过程相一致的全面的评估，亦即在活动过程中学生对问题解决以及对所学知识意义建构的程度本身就反映了活动的效果。换句话说，就是要让学生成为评价的主体，将评价贯穿于英语活动课教学的全过程，评价要促进教师更好地调整与改进自己的教学。总之，这是一种整合教与学、个人与集体的全程性评价。

## 第三节 模式的实施过程及课例点评

### 一、"主题—探究—评价"英语活动课教学模式的实施原则

#### 1. 情感激励与认知教育相结合

在英语活动课的教学中应处处体现出情感激励的力量。英语活动课是师生

共同创造和共同发展的舞台，教师应在教学中不断追求更新更高的境界，以自己的高度责任感和创造力感染学生。老师以新、奇、趣的方式，努力创设一个轻松、活泼、和谐、民主的英语学习情境和氛围，把英语学习渗透到学生的日常生活、休息、娱乐等各个角落中去，让学生在不知不觉中进入角色，充分感受到教学的民主和师生平等，受到激励，尝试成功，形成良好的激发学生不断创新的环境。

### 2. 主体探究与教师引导相结合

"主题—探究—评价"英语活动课教学模式，是一种开放的教学模式，让学生运用已学到的英语知识和技能、方法来解决实际问题，"教、学、做"合一，在动脑、动手、动口活动中，培养学生的英语表达能力、思维能力和动手能力，从而学会学习、学会创造；而教师在活动中的指导作用在于，要准确地把握学生的英语基础、年龄特征、心理特点、态度情感，合理利用各种教学环境和资源，组建活动小组，制订活动计划，选择活动主题，检查活动的进展、指引探究路经以及总结活动经验等，把教与学有机地融为一体。

### 3. 室内活动与室外活动相结合

英语活动课程的内容和形式是广泛而又丰富的，课内课外、校内校外、家庭社会、观察分析、动手操作、亲身体验、发明创造、野外考察等都可以是学生开展活动的场所。教师要善于利用各种教学资源和条件，引导学生利用课余时间深入生活，深入社会，为学生的自主探究和创造提供更为广阔和更为真实的发展空间。

### 4. 面向全体与分层指导相结合

活动课既要面向全体学生，在活动中要照顾到每一个学生，又要针对不同学生在认知、心理上的差异，提出不同的要求，采用不同的方法，使因材施教的原则得到落实。比如，在解决问题中让学生自主学习或分组合作探究，对于"迷路"的学生，只给"指南针"，让学生自己去体验成功；在讨论中重视学生的自我评价；给学生布置不同的作业等，使每个学生都在创新能力的发展中取得进展。

### 5. 教会应用与教会创新相结合

把主题学习引入英语活动课，设计一些能启迪智慧并带有挑战性的问题，激发学生的学习兴趣和创新意识，引导学生自主探讨研究，从而使学生在掌握知识的同时，培养解决问题的能力，表达思想感情，展现聪明才智，在指导学生应用英语进行交际的过程中也发展了学生的创新能力和创新品质。

## 二、"主题—探究—评价"英语活动课教学模式的实施过程

### 1. 确立以培养学生创新精神和实践能力为基本价值取向的英语活动课教学目标

"主题—探究—评价"英语活动课教学模式,总的目的是为学生创造语言实践的机会和环境,激发学习兴趣,开阔视野,拓宽知识面,发展特长,培养学生综合英语运用能力和创新能力,全面提高学生的素质。就每一次具体活动来说,针对每一次不同的主题,采用不同的具体教学模式,应该有不同的侧重点和更具体的活动目的。比如开展"Lovely Guangzhou—My Home"活动,其目的主要是让学生通过参观、调查、收集资料等各种方式更加了解广州的名胜古迹、风土人情、市政建设等的特点,在具体活动操作中提高学生综合运用英语的能力,更加激发起热爱广州进而热爱祖国的情感。又诸如开展英语演讲,主要是锻炼学生的英语表达能力和良好的心理品质等。

### 2. 精心设计主题,创新活动方式

主题学习(thematic learning)是现代教育的重要学习方式,也是学生自主研究探索与创新的一种重要形式。学生围绕一个主题,通过观察研究学习如何分析和处理有关的信息、综合概括主题的特征和本质。任何一个简单的主题,只要是学生所熟悉的,或正在认识的,都可能激发他们创新的热情。教师可以直接给出学生感兴趣的主题,这是学生学会探究的起点。教师更要善于不断培养学生的问题意识,引导学生做生活的有心人,多角度、全方位地从家庭生活、社会生活、学校生活、学习生活中自主选择活动主题进行深入的思考探究。当然,主题的选择要切合学生的年龄特点和英语学习的能力,不能过高于或过低于学生的现有水平,要让学生始终处于一种努力一跳便可"摘桃子"的状态,激发学生的探究意识。主题的选择在低年级尽量体现"浅""近"的特点,贴近学生的日常生活,如"I Shake Hands with Autumn"(见教学实例Ⅰ);而高年级则突出"广",以启发学生从不同角度提出小主题,给学生以充分的选择和创造空间,如"Doing Press Clippings"(见教学实例Ⅱ)。

不同的活动主题需要采取与之相适应的灵活多变的活动形式。如组织英语短剧表演,可以是课文短剧,如 *On the Train*,*Doctor Gold Smith*,*Thomas Edison*;也可以是根据课文编写的短剧或学生自编、自导、自演的短剧,如 *Little Red Riding Hood*,充分发挥学生的表演才能,锻炼学生的英语实践能力和创新能力,强化他们学习的兴趣。此外,组织英语角、英美佳作选读、英美概况介绍、英语演讲比赛、英语歌曲学唱、英语应用文入门、英语剪报制作、英语报

刊选读、英语社会实践、英语故事会、英语晚会等都是中学生喜闻乐见的活动形式，为学生提供了多种实践英语的机会和场所。课堂教学中所学到的知识在这里可以得到巩固与强化，英语课堂教学中的不足与短缺，在活动课中可以得到弥补。

### 3. 创设问题环境，激活创新意识

学生选定了主题后，教师就应该为学生创设或模拟真实的交际情景，因为任何一种活动课程的实施总是以现实的、学生自己的活动为情境去获取感性经验、即时信息、相关理性知识及情感体验的。由于中国学生学习英语缺乏社会大环境的支持，创设活动情景便成为进行语言交际活动的必要条件。教师只有将教学活动设计成一个真实或模拟真实的场景，为学生创建一种开放的、和谐的、积极互动的语言活动氛围，才能让学生愉快地融入英语学习的环境之中，才能使学生知晓英语词汇、短语、句子或对话运用的特殊场景，感受语言学习的贴切真实。这是因为情景在活动中替代汉语作为中介进行英语知识讲解和言语操练，加速英语与客观事物建立直接联系，增强了学生直接用英语进行思考的习惯的培养。同时，学生在充满情趣的情景里更能产生表情达意的愿望和需求，学习在不同的情景中扮演不同的角色，学习使用各种场合所需要的恰当的语言，在大量的言语实践活动中获得初步运用英语进行交际的能力和创新能力。

### 4. 将主题分解成有目标的"小主题"，通过讨论与探究，引导和激励学生有创意地表达主题

选定主题后，将主题分解成多个小主题，这是化整为零的办法。然后学生分成小组，每个小组都有自己的小课题，以保证每个学生都参与到活动中，由学生收集资料，分析和整理有关信息，根据主题做多种可能的思考和探究。教师应把学生要学习的内容巧妙地转化为问题情境，给学生以充足的探究时间和空间以及丰富的学习资料，鼓励学生学会从书刊、电视、互联网、图书馆等各种渠道获取信息，激励学生独立思考、自主地表达思想，用英语进行思维活动，将学生在英语课堂教学中掌握的语言知识应用到主题的探究之中。要鼓励学生多角度思考问题，不囿于固定的现成的解决问题的方法，敢于提出新的构想，敢于标新立异，在主题表达方面力求选材新、立意新、角度新、形式新、语言新，充分展示学生的个性与创意。

### 5. 评价反馈激励，成果展示交流，促进学生创新品质的发展

及时的反馈具有导向、激励的功能，因此，在活动中要加强评价意识，让学生按既定的活动目标进行自主评价，评价自己或同学在整个活动过程的表现

和收获，这是师生交流、生生交流中不可缺少的环节。通过评价，为学生今后的学习提供依据，让学生切实体验活动的成果，体验成功的喜悦，从而激励学生英语学习的热情，强化参与活动的积极性，收到"以评促学"的效果。在成果展示交流环节，把学生的作品、活动的成绩予以公布，让成果来说明情况。比如可以将毕业班同学制作的剪报编辑成册互相交流，而且可以将其作为毕业的礼物送给学生。开展学生自评，让学生谈收获，谈感受，提高学生评议的能力。开展相互评议，指师生之间、生生之间互相评价。在评价中，大家发扬民主，真诚相助，共同回顾和分享活动的经验，达到共同促进、共同提高的目标，从而进一步提高学生参与英语活动的积极性、主动性和创造性。

附两个教学实例

教学实例 I

Theme: I Shake Hands with Autumn

Students: Twenty students from an English extracurricular group.

Teacher: Zhimei Zhang

Subject: English Activities

1. Purpose of activity

(1) To perceive fall and comprehend the characteristics of fall through activities in the open air.

(2) To help the students develop frequent observational habits and love nature.

(3) To help the students improve their ability to express English and to be creative.

2. Activity preparation

(1) To organize an outing so that the students can observe the changes in nature when autumn is coming.

(2) To find materials and pictures about fall such as ripe plants, yellow leaves, rubicund hawthorns and so on, and pictures of information which is not easy gained such as an autumnal mountain, autumnal ocean, etc.

(3) To collect literary information about autumn including essays, poems, prose and so on. You can get such kind of information from libraries or internet.

### 3. Activity procedure

Step 1 Comparing

To compare datum in order to find the most accurate portrayal autumn. The teacher brings the students into a deep understanding of autumn. Grouping and communication are important. When comparing whose material is best fit to describe autumn, each student should show the collected materials and explain why they chose these particular items.

Step 2 Speaking

Each group can choose a delegate who will sum up the collected datum to present the autumnal characteristics. Try to describe systematically and clearly the change of humans and nature in autumn.

Step 3 Reading

Each group can choose a delegate to read the best poems and prose which has been collected before. Let the students taste the author's passion about the fall, thus learning how to express their feeling through literature.

Step 4 Group discussion

After summarizing the collected datum, everyone should express one's own thinking about autumn to other classmates. Such as "Do you like autumn?" "Why?"

Step 5 Writing

Everyone should share the essays, poems, pictures, and prose with each other and write down their understanding and sentiment about autumn in order to help the students to love nature and learn to express this love by using literary methods to observe and understand nature.

### 4. Students assignment

(A) Why Do Leaves Change Color in Autumn?

There are many materials such as chlorophyll, carotene, xanthophyll, anthocyanin in leaves. They show different colors, such as orange, snuff color and red. A carrot is very pretty because it contains saffron yellow. Also, leaves are green because they contain mostly chlorophyll. In the fall, leaves of hardwood turn yellow because the chlorophyll has been broken, thus the remaining causes the yellow color. In addition, maple leaves give out a deep red color because there is more anthocyanin than chlorophyll. This is also why the leaves of gingko show hyacinth.

(B) Lovely Autumn

Autumn is a bumper harvest season.

Rice is ripe. Golden rice paddy stretches to the horizon. When an autumn wind blows through, golden rice wave rolls in the fields.

A patch of persimmon trees show red color over the mountain, even as the apples and the red bananas.

In the grape garden, all kinds of colorful grapes hanging over grape trees look like many bunches of pearls.

Autumn often brings pleasure and happiness to us. How beautiful autumn is!


Teacher's simple remark

Autumn is beautiful, charming, rich and colorful. But we can taste the beauty of fall no other than we walk up to it.

Through taking part in the topical activity of "I shake hands with autumn", the students have a chance to go into nature, which will enrich their understanding and passion about both autumn and nature.

At this time, the students studying in nature may attract their desire to use English and free their imagination.


教学实例 II

Theme: Doing Press Clippings

Students: Fifteen students from an English extracurricular group

Teacher: Zhimei Zhang

Subject: English Activities

### 1. Purpose of activity

(1) To open up the students' knowledge horizon and develop their reading interest through doing press clippings.

(2) To train and enhance the students' all-around ability through reading, clipping, affixing, concluding, cleaning up, designing and so on.

(3) To inspire the students' reading interest in English, develop better reading habits and train their ability to obtain knowledge by themselves through doing clippings.

## 2. Activity preparation

(1) The students should collect suited and self-subscribed English newspapers and magazines and know the content of the article well.

(2) Preparing a pair of scissors, ruler, pen, marker, watercolor pen, glue, paper and some other tools.

## 3. Activity Process

Step 1　Reading papers and magazines

Under the teacher's guidance, the students should rapidly read the collected newspapers and magazines and find the useful or interesting articles. And the discovered articles should be marked or simply noted. The note should contain the theme, author, name of the press, date and location. They should also classify the noted content according to the differences among subjects. Knowledge is important for searches and references in the course of noting.

Step 2　Establishing topic

Based on the facts, newspapers and magazines the students find, the teacher should practically select one or more topics of press clippings for the students to choose, or a student also can establish a meaningful topic by himself according to his own newspaper and magazine.

Step 3　Selecting and designing a topic

After establishing a topic, the students should read in detail the first selected materials according to the selected topic again. Through this, the students can better understand the exact content and themes of each article. They will also seek out some proper articles to design and organize together on a blank sheet of paper according to type and size of paper. Sometimes sprinkling some vignettes on the blank area will make the press clipping appear more normative, perfect and beautiful.

Step 4　Clipping

The students should trim the article so that it is suitable for the blank area. It is necessary to cut straight and remain blank area on the sheet.

Step 5　Affixing

The clipped papers should be affixed firmly and beautifully on the sheet according to the design of the whole page.

Step 6　Communication, exhibition, and appraising through comparison

All press clippings should be intercommunicated in class. Then the best works will be selected and affixed on the blackboard or wall. Lastly, all press clippings should be shown in class, then the excellent works will be selected and the authors encouraged.

### 4. Activity explanation

To do an English press clipping is not only to cut down, sum up, sort and clear up the helpful articles and affix them on sheet, but also to use English to think and create.

In the course of doing clipping, reading, concluding, sorting, affixing and design all are blended together. To the students, doing press clippings can add to their reading quantity, develop their working, thinking and designing ability, inspire their English reading interest, and enrich their knowledge about science and culture.

The newspapers and periodicals to be clipped will be out of date and gathered or subscribed by the students themselves as well as dated with a short message.

Sometimes the teacher needs to guide the students on how to clip properly. For instance, when frontal and reversed content on a piece of paper are both useful, it is very good to keep them in entirety. Tell the students to place the press clippings in the shade and keep them air-dried. The best way is to put something heavy and straight on their surface to prevent wrinkling.

At the end of the activity, the teacher should lead the students to talk about the importance of doing the press clipping on time. Request them to do a plan of their press clipping. This will help them establish a good habit to do their press clipping. Truly, doing English press clippings are an effective way to promote the students to read more English books and newspapers and to develop good reading habits. It will also establish a stable foundation for further English study.

### 5. A brief introduction to a press clipping by the students

(1) Theme: Smoking Is Harmful

(2) Contents:

i. Smoking leads to cancer.

ii. Smoking is harmful to memory.

iii. Smoking is the reason for forest conflagration in Indonesia in 1998.

iv. According to the recent research, drug use usually begins with smoking.

v. In recent years, the number of young boys and girls who smoke has increased rapidly.

ⅵ. Review: Are young girls who smoke fashionable?

ⅶ. Recently in Beijing a regulation has been established that status that college students who smoke can't apply for a stipend.

ⅷ. In Guangzhou city, it is prohibited to smoke in public.

ⅸ. Indirect smoking is more harmful than direct smoking.

(3) A cartoon: One fellow with smoke in his mouth is walking slowly toward a coffin.

(4) Free thinking: There is a sentence "A single spark can set the prairie ablaze", beside the news "Forest conflagration in Indonesia in 1998".

(5) All kinds of vignettes.

(6) Author's opinion about smoking.

(7) Teacher's simple remark: It is a wonderful press clipping and I enjoy reading it.

### 6. Activity comment

Through the case above, it is clear that students' doing press clippings is a very helpful way to enhance their self-consciousness, creativity and practical ability.

At the same time, doing English press clippings can help students enlarge their English knowledge spectrum and further develop research study habits.

Therefore, it can be presumed that doing English press clippings will be an important teaching method in the future.

## 第四节　英语活动课教学模式点评

实践证明，英语活动课的开展有利于拓宽学生的知识，激发学生的兴趣，陶冶学生的情操，培养学生的创新精神和实践能力，但同时，英语活动课的设计、组织与实施是一项创造性的劳动，它需要教师付出巨大的、不懈的艰苦劳动。不同的活动内容有不同的活动形式；同一内容，也可以创造出多种不同形式的活动；而不同的活动又需要使用与之相适应的教学模式，才能得到事半功倍的活动效果。因此，英语活动课应精心设计，精益求精，与时俱进，不断创新。英语活动课的教学模式更是一块有待开发的领域，需要广大教师积极加入，大胆尝试探索，在培养学生创新精神和实践能力方面做出更大的贡献，使英语活动课在实施素质教育的过程中发挥更积极的作用。

# 第八章 "自主、互动、创造"的英语课堂教学模式的实验研究*

## 第一节 研究问题的提出

在以知识经济为主导的21世纪,现代科技的高速发展,以及新的科技革命,带来了人才的竞争和一系列深刻的社会变革。因此,如何培养具有高度自觉能动性和创造性的人才,越来越受到世界各国的普遍关注。社会的发展雄辩地说明:现代社会要求现代教育培养现代人,而"现代人"最根本的特征就是高扬人的主体性。因而,通过教育培养主体性强的个人是社会现代化的客观要求。发展主体性教育已成为国际教育发展的总主题、总目标。同时,随着网上教育的产生,终身教育转向终身学习,人的学习的自主性、能动性、选择性和创造性更大了,全世界都在更加鼓励和提倡独立思考和创新,鼓励和提倡个性的全面发展。世界性的研讨会探讨21世纪的人应掌握三张"教育通行证":一是学术性的通行证;二是职业性的通行证;三是事业心和开拓能力的通行证。这三张通行证所反映的中心主题就是人的主体性发展。因此,尊重学生的主体地位,把发展学生的主体性作为重要的教育目标具有战略意义。

我国的现代化建设决不是孤立于世界之外的。随着市场经济在我国经济生活中的主导地位的逐步确立,社会要求直接参与社会生活的人具有人格的相对独立性和行为的自主性,因而要求进行以人的素质社会化和个性化为目标的素质教育,在身体素质、文化素质、思想品德素质和心理素质全面提高的基础上,让学生学会学习、学会做人和学会发展。

随着素质教育改革的不断深入,我们可以清醒地认识到素质教育最重要的特征就是以学生为主体。近几年来,主体教育理论的研究和无数实践成果都证明了这样几点:第一,主体性是学生作为人的本质特性,在学生身上潜伏着主

---

\* 本文原发表于《中学英语课型与教学模式研究》(新世纪出版社2003年版)。本文获广州市教育局广州市中小学、中等职业学校第二阶段教学设计与实施活动的优秀成果一等奖(获奖时间:2002年10月)。

体性的天赋，它需要良好的教育来开发和发展，才有可能获得积极主动的、全面充分的发展。就这个意义而言，以学生为主体的教育实质上是抓住了素质教育的本质。第二，学生的主体地位得到尊重，学生的主体性才有发展的可能性，才有可能培养出能力强、品德优、人格健全、个性表现力强的学生。这些既可以从群体检查与评估中看出来，也可以从典型的个案中看出来。所以，抓主体性教育就是抓住了学生素质发展的主要矛盾，就能促进或带动学生素质的全面提高。第三，主体性发展不仅与学生整体素质提高关系密切，而且与学生的学习感受、学习态度密切相关。主体性发展好的学生，其学习积极性高，学习方法得当，效率也高，这些学生都不感到学习负担重，相反，他们能充分利用业余时间给自己增加感兴趣的学习内容。他们视学习为快乐，乐于学习，善于学习。因此，通过主体性教育有助于解决学生学习负担过重的问题。第四，主体教育是对现行人才培养模式的一种改革，由教育思想观念、教育教学策略、教育教学技术手段等构成的整体的主体教育是一种新的人才培养模式。它体现了以人为本的现代教育思想，符合素质教育的基本原则和目标要求，是全面推进素质教育的有益实践。

英语教学作为教育链的一环，不仅是让学生学习文化科学知识、获取世界信息、进行国际交往的重要手段，同时是培养学生全面发展的基本素质和创新精神的重要战场，不仅具有与语文教育同等的人文性，而且具有跨文化的人文性。在面向现代化、面向世界、面向未来的教育中学会英语，不但令学生多了一双眼睛、一对耳朵、一条舌头，甚至还多了一个头脑，具有更为特殊的重要作用。而且英语不同于其他基础学科，它是一门实践课，其语言技能是需要通过学生个人的实践活动才能培养和提高的。因此，它的教学效果应以学生的学习效果为依据，而学习效果在很大程度上取决于学生的主观能动性和创造性。认知心理学认为：英语学习的过程就是新旧语言知识不断结合的过程，也就是语言能力从理论知识转化成自动应用的过程。而这种结合与转化都必须通过学生自身的活动才能得以实现。因而，英语教学的首要任务是"学"而不是"教"，英国语言教学大师 Micheal West 曾经说过："外语是学会的，不是教会的。"这句至理名言足以说明学生在学习外语中的主体地位的重要性。

但是，中学英语教学受传统教育思想的消极影响和束缚，仍然处在偏向知识传授、偏向分数评价、课堂负担重的误区中。剖析课堂教学的病理症结，会发现有以下几点：①重教师的教，轻学生的学；②重知识的掌握，轻能力的培养；③重知识的讲解，轻知识的操练和运用；④重死记硬背，轻理解意义和灵活运用；⑤重书面能力，轻口语交际能力的培养；⑥重书本，轻情景，内容呆板,缺乏趣味性;⑦重统一要求,轻个性发展;⑧重全班集体活动,轻个人和小组活动;⑨重少数学生,轻大多数学生;⑩重批评罚抄,轻合作愉快的氛围;⑪重分数升学,轻素质培养;⑫学生消极被动学习,缺乏学习积极主动性和创造性。因此,英语教学至今仍处于"高消耗、重负担、低效率"的困境之中,即使是不少应试技能极好的学生,虽然在考试中能考出令人惊喜的高分,但一到交际应用,常常听不懂也说不出,学习成果变成"聋哑英语"。大多数学生负担过重的问题一直没有解决好,厌学问题也是一个"老大难",这些问题的存在表明学生在许多情况下还未成为真正的主体。因而,尝试以学生为主体的英语教学成为我国广大英语教师不断实践与探索的问题。

自20世纪90年代中期以来,随着主体性教育实验研究的开展,在英语教学领域中开始有了对主体性教学模式的探索,这段时期的研究成果主要包括以下几种:①课堂教学的方法,如激发兴趣、因材施教、MET教学、交际法等;②课堂教学模式,如整体教学、愉快教学、开放性戏剧教育、双重活动法、情景·结构·规则·交际法、张思中教学法等;③教材改革,如JEFC教材;④考试改革及学习策略研究等。这些成果实现了在教学观念、教学方法和教学模式等方面的转变,并使之成为外语教学发展的趋势。然而,与主体性教育在其他基础学科的研究相比,英语学科在这方面的研究显得较为薄弱,表现在"以学生为主体"的教学原则更多地被看成教学技巧的问题,"如何学好"在很多时候让位于"如何教好"。因此,相关的论文和实验报告极少,而且对教学过程中发挥学生主体地位的方法描写是不系统、不全面的,使用的是简单思辨性的办法,随意性很大。孙小英对(1995—2000)我国主要两种中小学外语教学期刊中的全部675篇文章做了统计,其中189篇属于语言知识,其他的486篇文章中,利用统计数据的占11.9%,随意罗列数据的占6.8%,不依赖数据的占81.3%。[①] 这些研究结果难以使人信服,更无法把中国特色的外语教学经验推出去与世界同行切磋。而且,到目前为止,针对英语教学中师生的主体性发展水平还没有建立科学的教学目标体系和评价指标体系。因此,如何在评价标准的确立中,既保持基本的英语教学需要,又能充分体现主体性教育实验的特色,成为迫切需要解决的问题。

在国外,以学生为主体的外语教学模式历来受到美国、日本、俄罗斯以及

---

① 孙小英:《我国基础英语教学研究现状的调查与分析》,载《中小学外语教学》1999年第4期。

许多欧洲国家的重视。近年来,国际知名英语教学专家 Alan Maley 在他所编写的"牛津英语教师宝库"丛书中介绍了 20 世纪 90 年代以来国际上英语教学与研究领域的重要成果,他们都把在英语教学中发展学生的自主性、能动性、创造性,促进学生的主体性发展以及教学过程的民主化、个性化放在首位。Colin Campbell 和 Hanna Kryszewska 所著的 *Learner-Based Teaching* 一书系统详尽地介绍了发展学生主体性的教学思想和教学活动,强调学生的主体性,学生的主体地位在英语教学中获得了更为自觉的关注,在教学评价中更多地听取了学生的声音。该书有实证性研究,也有数据,有统计,有分析。这些理论和实践的成果为开展我国基础英语教学中的主体性教学研究提供了宝贵的经验和研究方法的指导。

鉴于上述理论和实践的思考,本章试图通过以学生为主体的英语教学为切入点开展"自主、互动、创造"的课堂教学模式的实验研究,以主体性教育思想和素质教育理论为指导,在教学活动中树立学生是言语活动的主体地位的思想,充分调动学生学习的积极主动性,发展学生的主体性,建立英语教学中学生主体性发展的评价指标体系,通过评价,摒弃不利于学生主体性发展的消极观念和做法,完善教学的组织形式,提高教学质量,发展学生的主体性,使他们在日益发展的现代社会中发挥积极主动的作用,成为具有高度责任感和创新能力的公民和人才。在研究方法方面,采用了教育测量、教育实验、教育评价等科研方法,设计、实施并完成了相应的教育实验,用科学的方法收集数据,然后进行统计分析,并验证理论假设。

## 第二节 "自主、互动、创造"的英语课堂教学模式探索

主体性教育具有鲜明的时代价值取向,它是我国当前推进素质教育的现实选择。它不仅着眼于学生眼前的发展,更着眼于学生未来的发展,力争把学生培养成为主动适应社会发展需要的社会主体。如何把主体性教育繁多的概念演绎转变为广大教育实践者的切实行动,当务之急是教师对主体性教育理论进行再创造和发挥,创造适合自己教学风格和学生实际的教学模式,从而从根本上解决教学理论与教学实践之间严重脱节的问题,丰富和发展教学理论,更好地指导教学实践,提高教学质量。

## 一、关于教学模式的初步认识

### （一）基本概念

"模式"作为理论与实践中介的操作框架，被广泛运用于各种体制和各种行业的改革。《国际教育百科全书》中对"模式"有这样的说明："对任何一个领域都有一个过程。在鉴别出影响特定结果的变量，或提出与特定问题有关的定义、解释和预示的假设之后，当变量或假设的内在联系得到系统的阐述时，就需要把变量合并成为一个假设的模式。"[①] 查有梁认为模式是："一种重要的科学操作和思维的方法，是沟通实践与理论之间的桥梁。"[②] 高文主编的《现代教学的模式化研究》一书指出："在科学研究中，人们常将模式看成对某一过程或某一系统的简化与微缩式表征，以帮助人们能形象地把握某些难以直接观察或过于抽象复杂的事物。"[③] 从英语的词义看，"模式"有两个词：model 和 pattern。牛津大学出版社 1997 年出版的《牛津高级英汉双解词典》对 model 的释义是 "system used as a basis for a copy"，汉译为"模式"。pattern 的释义是 "way in which sth. happens, moves, develops or is arranged"，汉译为"模式；方式；样式"。以上说明与定义尽管从不同角度描述了模式的本质与特征，但显得有些繁复和不一定符合我们的思考习惯。我们不妨将"模式"解释为反映某一系统运动方式的一种程式化结构。

模式多种多样，比如在社会科学、人文科学领域中经常用"文化模式""教育模式""经济模式"……在教育领域中，教育包含了教学，而任何教学都具有教育性，显然，教学模式是一种狭义的教育模式。

"教学模式"（model of teaching）一词最初由美国学者乔伊斯和韦尔（B. Joyce & M. Weil）等提出，1972 年，两人出版了《教学模式》一书，系统地介绍了 22 种教学模式，并用较为规范的形式主义进行分类研究和阐述，"试图系统地探讨教育目的、教学策略、课程设计和教材以及社会和心理理论之间的相互影响的、以设法考察一系列可以使教师行为模式化的各种可供选择的类型"。[④]后来美国教育家、心理学家安德鲁斯和古德森把教学模式界定为：

---

[①④] 吴立岗：《教学的原理、模式和活动》，广西教育出版社 1998 年版。
[②] 查有梁：《教育建模》，广西教育出版社 1998 年版。
[③] 高文：《现代教学的模式化研究》，广西教育出版社 2000 年版。

"一组综合性成分,这些成分能用来规定完成有效的教学任务中的各种活动和功能的序列。"① 这是从教学结构的范畴来鉴定的。从理论上看,人们可以利用教学模式将教学活动或过程化解为某些关键要素或成分,并借助其简化的、微缩的方式研究与探讨有关现象。

我国最近几年才逐渐对教学模式进行了研究(尽管以前做过大量的相关的研究),并在教学实践的基础上产生了各种教学模式。学者吴立岗定义教学模式为:"依据教学思想和教学规律而形成的在教学过程中必须遵循的比较稳固的教学程序及其方法的策略体系,包括教学过程中诸要素的组合方式、教学程序及其相应的策略。"② 笔者认为这种观点比较切合教学的实际,因为从实践的角度来看,教学模式是将教学方法、教学手段、教学组织形式融为一体的综合体系,它可以使教师明确先做什么、后做什么,先怎么做、后怎么做等一系列具体问题,把比较抽象的理论转化为具体的操作性策略。

### (二) 教学模式的要素

吴立岗认为一个完整的教学模式,应含有以下6个要素:

(1) 教学思想或教学理论。这是教学模式所赖以形成的基础。

(2) 教学目标。它是教学模式的核心因素,决定着模式的操作程序、师生活动的比例及评价的标准等。

(3) 操作的程序。也就是教与学的步骤。

(4) 师生的角色。也就是师生在教学过程中的地位。

(5) 教学策略。即教学过程中教师和学生所采用的教与学的方式、方法、手段与管理措施的总和。

(6) 评价。这是控制论的反馈原理在教学中的应用。由于不同的教学模式有不同的教学目标、使用的操作程序不同,评价的方法和标准也不尽相同。

## 二、构建"自主、互动、创造"的英语课堂教学模式初探

### (一)"自主、互动、创造"的英语课堂教学模式的概念

基于前面对教学模式的初步认识,我们把"自主、互动、创造"的英语教学模式界定为:以主体教育理论为指导,以发展学生主体性为目标,以教学

---

①② 吴立岗:《教学的原理、模式和活动》,广西教育出版社1998年版。

过程中的自主、互动、创造活动为基本特点，在教师教的活动和学生学的活动中凸显学生在课堂的主体地位。其结构框架如下。

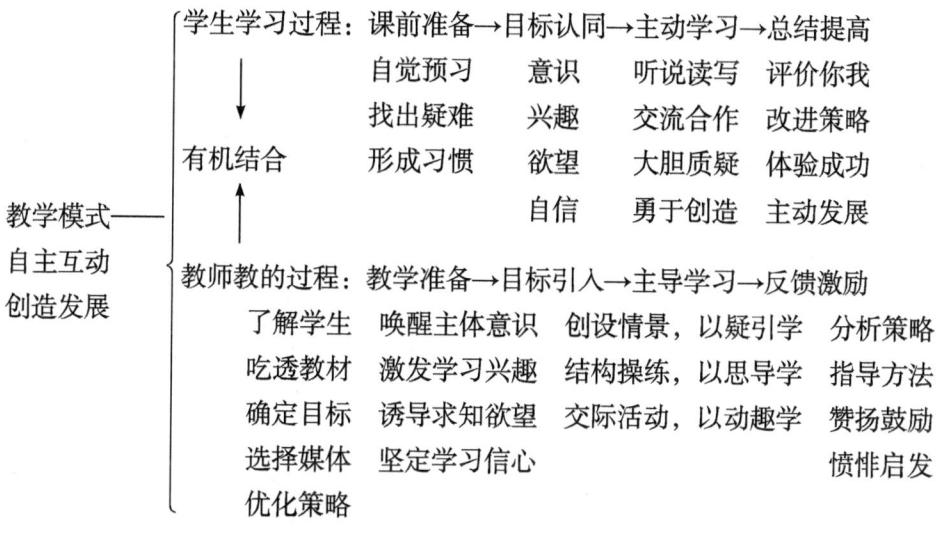

## （二）"自主、互动、创造"的英语课堂教学模式的理论依据

### 1. 主体教育理论

主体教育理论认为，学生是具体的活生生的、有丰富个性的、不断发展的认识主体，是具有主观能动性的独立个体和群体。主体性是作为主体的本质属性，是主体在同客体的相互作用中表现出来的能动性，既包括了对客观世界的自觉能动的掌握，也包括了对客观世界的自觉能动的创造。"自主性、主动性、创造性，是学生主体性的内在规定性。"① "实践是人特有的存在方式。"② 主体性是实践主体的个性。学生的主体性，在活动中生成，在活动中表现，在活动中发展。应坚持活动的客观性、目的性、群体性及创造性。个体在群体交往中得到发展，通过合作与交往，促进学生主体性发展。主体性发展水平，一方面表现为主体意识，另一方面表现为主体能力，具有外在的表现特征。

主体教育强调"从肯定人在社会历史发展中的主体地位与人在自身发展中的主体地位出发，探讨和阐明教育的主体性，充分发挥教育在促进人的全面发展中的积极的能动作用"③。主体教育的目标是使每一个学生的思想素质、

---

① 北师大教育系、安阳市人民大道小学联合实验组：《小学生主体性发展实验与指标体系的建立测评研究》，载《教育研究》1994 年第 12 期。
② 《马克思恩格斯全集》第 26 卷（上），人民出版社 1982 年版，第 2 页。
③ 王道俊：《关于教育的主体性问题》，载《教育理论与实践》1996 年第 5 期。

文化素质、心理素质、身体素质和劳动素质得到和谐的发展,核心是培养受教育者的"个体素质的主体性品质"[①]。可见,主体教育倡导尊重受教育者的人格,确立受教育者在教育过程中的主体地位,注重发展学生的自我教育能力。它的兴起既是对重知识传授、教师权威,忽视学生能力培养、学生主体性发挥的极端化教育的反叛,也是对弘扬人的价值、关注主体精神、发挥主体潜能、满足个体需要这一时代发展主旋律的必然回应。

可见,主体教育解决的是人的构成的哲学层面的分析,研究的是人的良好素质的全面构建。主体教育关于尊重学生主体地位的思想,关于促进学生个性自由发展的思想,关于发展自主性、主动性和创造性的思想,使素质教育有了一个更高的目标定位,提供素质教育以新的教育价值观念及实现人的全面发展的基本途径。

**2. 两块理论基石**

(1) 哲学基石:马克思主义关于人的全面发展学说。

马克思认为:"人在本质上是主动的、能动的,儿童是有个性的认识的主体,实践的主体,自我发展的主体,儿童成长发展的关键在于自身积极性的高低和主体意识的强弱"。[②] 马克思的观点充分肯定了学生在学习中的主体地位。同时,从内外因辩证关系来看,学生是学习的主体,是"内因",是学生学好的根据;教师的教是"外因",是学生学好的一个极重要的条件。教师"教"这个外因要通过"学"这个内因起作用。由此看来,教学过程中的教与学是辩证统一的关系,越是充分发挥教师的主导作用,就越能保证提升学生的主动性、积极性和创造性;学生越是充分发挥主动性、积极性和创造性,教师的主导作用越能真正有效的得到体现。所以在教学过程中只有充分发挥教师教的积极性和学生学的积极性,并使教与学之间积极配合、协调一致,才能解决好教学过程中的诸多矛盾,全面完成教学目标。

(2) 心理学基石:需要、兴趣、活动。

需要是有机体、个体和群体对其生存与发展条件所表现出来的依赖状态,是个体和社会的客观需求在人脑中的反映,是个人的心理活动与行为的基本动力。心理学家马斯洛曾把人的需要分成基本需要(包括生理、安全、爱与隶属、尊重等)和衍生需要(如自我实现)。需要的层次越高,主体在实现需要后的感觉就越完美,对主体的情绪、认识与活动的影响就越大。学生主体的学

---

① 王道俊:《关于教育的主体性问题》,载《教育理论与实践》1996 年第 6 期。
② 《马克思恩格斯全集》第 26 卷(上),人民出版社 1982 年版,第 2 页。

习一般表现出两种需求。

首先要满足主体心理发展的需求。在学习上有问题的学生，其"问题"实质是心理发展得不到满足而表现出的一种行为障碍。这种行为障碍有两种表现：其一是学习的内容与方式使其原有图式难以同化，形成学习障碍，导致学习心理的扭曲；其二是学习的要求与管理忽视个性长处，挫伤了渴望学习的心理。两种现象导致了学生在学习上获得发展的心理需求得不到满足，便从学习以外的活动内容寻找发展的机会，但由于其生活经验不足，受限于心理发展水平，他们必然出现"问题"。不难理解，学生的问题，或有问题的学生，与其主体学习需求的缺失有直接关系。

主体学习的另一种需求是实现自身个体学习向社会需求的转化。这种需求表现在学习的过程中，是对其积极主动参与的肯定。学生积极主动参与是个性倾向的一种表达，是责任感和义务感的一种流露。通过参与去享受在集体中的权利，体会自己在集体中的地位，得到他人的关心和认可，从而学会关心、学会自我调控、学会处理人际关系，通过参与，将学到的知识运用于实践，体会知识的社会价值，从而确定学习及自我的社会价值。

兴趣是人们力求认识某种事物或从事某项活动的意识倾向，表现为人们对某种事物、某项活动的选择性态度和积极的情绪反应。兴趣可使人集中注意力、产生愉快紧张的心理状态，对认识与活动产生积极影响。因此，J. 皮亚杰把兴趣说成是"能量的调节者"[1]。潘菽主编的《教育心理学》认为兴趣是学习动机中最现实、最活跃的成分。俄国教育家乌申斯基更直接地指出："没有丝毫兴趣的强制性学习，将会扼杀学生探求真理的欲望。"[2] 可见积极的兴趣对掌握知识、促进个性的发展起重要的作用。

活动是指主体与客体世界相互作用的过程，是主体有目的地影响客体以满足自身需要的过程。对活动可作多侧面的划分，最基本的主要依据心理学进行划分，即外部活动和内部活动。所谓外部活动，主要是指实物性的操作活动、感性的实践活动。内部活动主要指内部心理与观念活动，主要包括知、情、意三个方面。这两类活动在人的认识和发展中起着十分重要的作用。正如皮亚杰所说："儿童学习的最根本途径是活动，活动是联系主客体的桥梁，是认识发展的直接源泉。"[3]

英语课堂教学活动既具有人类一般活动的特征，更具有自己丰富的内涵和规定。首先，从表现形式来讲，内部活动有别于那种凭记忆、主要是机械记忆

---

[1][2][3] 袁锐锷：《外国教育史纲》，广东高等教育出版社1989年版，第50-52页。

和理解的活动，而更强调主动、积极的思维和想象，发现和创造的成分；外部活动也不仅仅是模仿和重复，被动地进行刺激—反应—强化的枯燥乏味的机械性操练，本质的、处于支配地位的是主动的、创造性的言语交际活动。因此需要有意识的注意思维的投入等。其次，从学生总体活动来分析，它不同于传统英语教学中学生的被动活动，以认知为主的片面、单一的活动，而是强调观念活动与实践活动相统一的完整的活动，是学生主体主动的、有思维积极参与的、观念与行动相统一的、充满创造精神的、能满足学生多方面发展需要的多样性活动。学生只有充分理解自己是学习活动的主人，才能调动学习的积极主动性，才能把消极被动接受知识转化为积极主动地接收和运用语言知识。

显然，教师要充分尊重学生的需要、愿望和自主学习的权力，激发学生学习的兴趣，将英语教学活动组织成一个在教师激励和指导下学生自主学习、互动学习、创造学习的过程，以真正确立学生在英语教学过程中的主体地位，充分发挥英语教学在促进人的主体性发展中的积极的能动作用。这也正是构建"自主、互动、创造"的英语课堂教学模式的根本目的所在。

### （三）"自主、互动、创造"的英语课堂教学模式的特征

**1. 体现以教师为主导、学生为主体辩证统一的教学思想**

在教学过程中，以教师为主导、学生为主体是现代教育理论中的重要原则之一，而教师的指导作用与学生的主体作用是相互影响、相互制约的辩证统一关系，如果我们在教学中忽视某一方面或者片面强调某一方都是不可取的。该模式要求教师根据英语教学大纲的内容，理解和熟悉教材，了解学生的需要，合理安排教学内容、设计教学活动，选择现代化的教学媒体把教学内容活化为实际情景，吸引学生积极参与到教学活动中，组织学生开展师生之间、生生之间的多向交流，使他们自主地、主动地、创造性地投入到学习之中，通过教师的启发、诱导、调动、激励等手段，引导学生发挥主体作用，最终实现教为主导，学为主体的统一。

**2. 确立以促进学生主体性发展为核心的教学目标**

主体性是学生作为人的发展的核心部分，是一切素质发展的基础。主体性的发展需要通过主体的活动。而学生要成为学习活动的主体，必须具备两个基本条件：首先必须具备较强的主体意识，其中最重要的是要具有学习的需要及动机，即学生必须对学习活动本身及学习所要达到的目标有强烈的兴趣，缺乏学习兴趣与学习动机的学生不能成为学习的主体，因此也无法体现其主体性。其次，学生还必须具有学习的能力及自主学习的可能性。就英语学科而言，学

生必须具备按照认知对象存在的方式认识、把握以至改变对象所需要的英语背景知识,以及使新旧知识相互关联的学习策略,还必须具备学习的情感与意志,它们作为主体能力的能量因素控制与调节着主体与客体之间的相互作用,并最终促成主体活动目标的实现。缺乏相应的主体能力的学生,就不具备学习活动的内在可能性,就不可能发展主体性。正是由于兴趣、意志、情感等心理因素在促进学生主体性发展中起着极其重要的作用,所以在确立"自主、互动、创造"的英语课堂教学目标的时候,教学的每一个环节,都要从学生心灵健康成长的角度、以发展上述心理因素为主要内容提出要求,以培养和激发学生的学习兴趣、动机、信心、参与心理、合群心理为重点培养主体意识,以提高自觉自理能力、改进学习方法与策略、养成良好的态度和坚强的意志等为重点发展学生的主体能力,最终促进学生的主体性发展。

### 3. 模式的操作步骤符合学生主体性发展的内在逻辑

首先在课前准备阶段强调培养学生良好的学习习惯,启发学生的自觉自主意识,让他们意识到:学习是自己的事,别人不能替代,学习要主动,不能坐等,力所能及的事情要自己做。而相应的教师的教则是了解学生的学习基础、思想状况、个性特点、对学习的需求等,然后深入钻研教材,挖掘教材中所蕴含的智力价值和审美价值,并把它们和学生的发展联系起来,在此基础上制订符合学生实际需要的、有利于学生主体性发展的教学目标。这一环节要重点培养学生的自主性。

在学生学习的"目标认同"阶段,从学生的主体意识、学习兴趣与求知欲、自信心等的培养出发,表现了一种心向的发展,体现出自立选择的特点;而相应的教师的教是创造出学生产生这种心向的氛围,教师教的这个环节被称为"目标引入",突出培养学生的主动性。

学生具备了主动学习的心理,就进入了学习过程的关键环节"主动学习"。教师充分利用现代化的电教手段创设语言情景,揭示语义以加深听觉、视觉、动觉等感知印象,提出思考的问题,以疑引学,让学生在语言情境中主动进行听、说、读、写有意义的语言活动;然后在语言活动的基础上抽出典型的语言结构进行操练,句型操练要情景化、意义化和交际化,可以是听力反应、句型转换、对话操练等形式,启发学生积极思考,在积累语言材料和句型结构的基础上归纳出语法规则,从而认知和内化语法规则,培养用英语思维的能力;接下来是教师指导学生尽可能地把已掌握的语言知识和技能运用于生动活泼、相互合作的言语交际活动,并在此基础上自己认识新事物,获得新知识,自己探索和提出有价值的新问题、新见解,比如在形象思维、灵活多变的训练中提高语用能力，在开放的想象中发展创造性思维等。这个环节充分体现师生多向交流、合作互动、创造和生生多向交流、创造的特点，不仅是智力的交锋过程，更是自主意识、参与精神、合作精神、竞争意识、创造精神等发展的过程。

学生学习的最后一个环节是"总结提高"，这是学生在课堂教学中对知识和心理升华的阶段。首先是愉快地评价自我，学会接受老师和同学的评价，辩证地看待自己的长处与不足。其次是进一步分析和把握知识结构，逐步学会分析自己掌握知识的思路和方法，改进学习的策略，提高自我意识的水平，体会学习的成功，找出自己的"生长点"。而促成这一过程的是教师的"反馈激励"，这需要教师在知识的上、下位关系上启发引导学生悟出"联系点"，引导学生对自己的认知特点、学习方法进行回顾，从中体会自己成功的经验以及错误的原因，激励学生主动发展。在这一环节上，要求老师以前面各个环节发现的问题为例，将迁移成功的同学设为典型，以赞扬鼓励为手段，引起学生的反思，使学生对老师有"指点迷津"的感觉，同时产生一种"愤悱启发"的体验。

**4. 重新确立师生在课堂教学中的三个最基本关系**

（1）服务关系。传统的教学思想是学生的学习服从于教师的教学方法，而教师的教学过程只依赖于知识的逻辑过程。这在实质上忽视了学生学习的主体地位，形成教师为知识服务，学生为教师服务的关系。教师教学不适应学生需要，于是产生了"差生"阴影。长期以来，师生在教学中是学生为老师讲课服务，还是教师为学生发展服务的"难题"，在实践中并未得到解决。该模式明确了在教学上学生的学决定老师的教，是老师适应学生，而不是学生适应老师。学生学习模式依据学生心理系统的组织特点，根据解决问题的思维过程和学生心理发展的需求的有机结合而组织。

（2）知识、内容上的关系。传统教学思想认为，在知识内容上教师是已知方，学生是未知方；教师传授，学生接受；学生掌握了知识即教师完成了教学任务。该模式则表现为教师以知识为工具，以学生主动获取知识的过程为依托，实现教师在学生心理发展上的指导作用，促进学生主体性的发展。学生则通过掌握知识的过程去发展自己的思维，学会探求真理，与人合作的品质。知识作为师生之间的媒介，不仅仅是授受关系的中介，而且升华为启发学生学会主动驾驭自己而取得个人成就的一种标志。在这方面，该模式继承了以往教学突出知识掌握的教学思想，同时将是否掌握知识纳入学生心理其他因素发展的标志。这就赋予学习以新的内涵，为学生的终身学习和创造能力奠定了基础。

（3）情感关系。教师为学生展示自己创造了条件，学生获得的是自立能力和对未来的自信。学习的过程使学生充分地享受或占有自由的一种机智和权利，获得了"创造"的体验，学生的心理走向健康成熟，主体性得到发展。这种过程中的师生情感，彻底改变了"教师绝对权威""教师居高临下"状态下建立起来的感情。学生与教师平等，学生不需要以"顺从"表示自己对老师的尊重。在独立人格基础上建立的感情，才是真诚的。

### 5. 学生主动学习的教学策略与方法

要使学生积极主动地参与学习，关键在于教师采用促进学生主动学习的教学策略与方法。总结近年来国内外有关主体性教学的经验，结合笔者的教学实际，行之有效的教学策略和方法主要有：①学生的主动参与。作为英语教师，在课堂教学中要努力为学生提供主动参与的时间和空间。教师通过引导学生积极主动参与，为学生提供自我表现的机会，还学生学习的主动权，拓展学生的发展空间，使学生掌握英语基础知识和基本技能，形成独立获取知识、创造性地运用知识解决现实问题的能力，同时形成良好的个性。②合作学习。以学生为主体的英语教学非常关注课堂教学中体现出来的群体间人际关系和交往活动，积极建立群体间合作学习的关系，师生共同构建学习主体，在充分尊重人格的基础上，通过多样、丰富的交往形式，有意识地培养学生学会"倾听、交流、协作、分享"的合作意识和交往技能。③学生自主学习及尊重差异。通过学生自我选择、自我监控、自我调节逐步形成自我学习的能力；同时在课堂教学中区别指导，分层教学，使学生实现有差异的发展。④鼓励创新。创造性是主体性的最高表现，应鼓励学生质疑问题的精神和行为，努力挖掘学生的创造潜能，并创造条件使学生经常体验到创造的乐趣。

### 6. 实施以促进学生主体性发展为目标的教学评价

长期以来，由于受应试教育的影响，课堂教学以学生掌握知识为根本目的，因此造成课堂教学评价又以学生掌握知识为归宿，学生学习活动的过程却是一个"被人遗忘的角落"。这种认识上的局限性产生了诸如分数"挂帅"，学生处于被评价的被动状态，评价不能有效地发挥促进教学的作用，常常挫伤学生学习的积极性等种种问题。因此，本模式试图以学生学习活动过程为评价的主要内容，以促进学生的主体性发展为目标实施对传统课堂教学评价的改革。体现这种改革的主要思路有以下三点。

（1）让学生成为评价的主体。要改变传统的教学评价中教师为中心的倾向，使评价成为促进学生主体意识开发、自主学习能力提高、自我系统完善的活动。使学生在评价中学会为自己的学习主动承担责任，并为改进学习效果积极地努力。为此，英语课堂教学的评价要成为学生广泛参与的过程，要重视学生的自我评价。对学生进行个别化评价，不仅要注意学生学到了哪些知识，更要关心他们在获得知识的过程中对未来发展起奠基作用的那些主体意识和能力，如学习的兴趣、动机、参与意识、合作意识、创造能力等。

（2）将评价贯穿英语教学活动的全过程。评价不是消极地对教学结果进行测量和描述的活动，而应当积极地促进教学过程，成为使学生受到教育、加深对教学实际过程的认识以及改进教学工作的重要手段。为此，评价要关注教学过程，使评价在学生眼中不再是一张张令人发怵的"考卷"，也不再是教师严厉目光下的"监督劳动"，而是学生活动的过程、学习的过程、正确认识自己的过程，形成对英语教学策略与成效的共识，并共同谋求改进方向的过程，同时，也是教师鼓励学生个性发展的过程。教师应强化评价的形成性与激励性，从多方面肯定学生的进步，肯定学生的努力，肯定学生的发展可能，激励学生不断取得新的进步。这样，学生可以从中肯的他人评价和积极的自我评价中找回自己做人的自尊和自信，从而体验一个作为"自然人"在成长中的自由与快乐，从而实现主体性的不断发展。

（3）评价要促进教师更好地发挥主导作用。教好学生的前提是了解学生。如果一个教师对所教的每一个学生的学习活动都能做出全面的、具体的、系统的评价，那么他/她也就基本做到了"了解学生"。对老师而言，学生学习活动评价的结果是一种信息。评价得越科学，信息越准确；评价得越具体，信息量越大，反馈作用越强。此外，学生的学习活动是有规律的，教师可以从对学生学习活动的评价中获取信息，一方面可以帮助教师管理学生的学习活动，使之朝着更有规律、更有利于学生发展的方向发展；另一方面可以帮助教师随时调整和改进自己的教学，使"教"与"学"更有机地融合在一起，从而更好地发挥主导作用。

## 第三节 "自主、互动、创造"的英语课堂教学模式的实验

### 一、实验背景

广州市第某某中学办学条件差，生源不强，师资力量不足，教育质量不尽如人意，学校声誉也偏低。究其原因，教师队伍青黄不接，生源、设备、场地条件十分薄弱。这些固然是阻碍前进的不利因素，但主观上的薄弱环节更不容

忽视；管理不够科学，教师缺乏教育科研的理论、意识和方法，较多采用注入式和强迫处罚等方式进行教学，造成学生有厌学情绪，学生学习被动，后进面大。这些都不利于学生发展，使教学质量的提高举步维艰。"加大改革力度，尽快把教学质量搞上去"已成为工作中刻不容缓的主题。

立足于现代教学的高度，针对学校教学中存在的弊端，学校从 1998 年开始，提出了"构建主体教育模式，全面推进素质教育"的整体改革方案。本实验配合学校的整体改革，尝试通过构建"自主、互动、创造"的英语主体性课堂教学模式，培养学生的主体意识，让学生意识到自己是全面发展的主体，意识到自己在教学过程中的主体地位、主体责任、主体力量、主体需要和主体活动，发展学生的主体能力，让学生能主动驾驭学习、驾驭教材、驾驭活动、驾驭世界，具有崭新的精神面貌，成为具有能动性、自主性和创造性的人才。

## 二、实验的变量

自变量："自主、互动、创造"的英语课堂教学模式。
因变量：学生的主体性。

## 三、实验的假设

使用"自主、互动、创造"的英语课堂教学模式比常规的教学方法更有利于促进学生的主体性发展，更有利于提高教学质量。

## 四、实验的对象

本实验采用自然实验法，选取初三 1 班为实验班，采用"自主、互动、创造"的英语课堂教学模式进行教学。本实验自 2001 年 9 月至 2002 年 6 月结束，为期一年。

## 五、实验的工具

（一）学生主体性发展的评估表

评估表方式，简明、评估项目条例清楚。赋予分值进行量的评估。实验一开始就印发给学生，让他们掌握学习和评价的主动权。该评估表依照学生学习活动的一般规律将评价的内容分为学习程序、学习方法、学习品行三个方面，试图通过学习程序的评价着重培养学生自主学习的主体意识，通过学习方法、学习态度、学习意志等的评价促进学生主体能力的发展。这三方面的评价内容从逻辑关系上说，不是互相分立的，而是互有交叉的，是"你中有我，我中有你"的关系，只是为了操作方便才从不同角度分别进行评价。该评价要经过长期的观察，参与平时课堂上学生自评和互评的情况做好记录，还可以通过家长座谈会、家长意见表、班主任/科任老师评价等了解多方面的情况，确保评价结果的可靠性。需要说明的是，各项指标以及指标分配权数，由主管教学的领导和有丰富经验的教师采用专家意见平均法确定。具体评价内容和方法见表1至表4。

表1 学生学习程序评价量表（XHP4-1-C）

| 二级指标 | 权重 | 三级指标 | 权重 | 等级 | 分数 | 合计 |
|---|---|---|---|---|---|---|
| 预习 | 0.2 | 经常预习 | 0.5 | | | |
| | | 有重点 | 0.3 | | | |
| | | 有方法 | 0.2 | | | |
| 上课 | 0.3 | 能抓住老师的讲课思路 | 0.3 | | | |
| | | 掌握本节课重点、解决预习中的难点和疑点 | 0.3 | | | |
| | | 耳、眼、手、口、心并用 | 0.4 | | | |
| 复习 | 0.15 | 及时，经常 | 0.5 | | | |
| | | 有目的，有计划，有重点，有措施 | 0.5 | | | |
| 作业 | 0.15 | 先看书复习，后做作业 | 0.25 | | | |
| | | 及时、独立完成 | 0.5 | | | |
| | | 对照老师批改，订正错题 | 0.25 | | | |
| 应试 | 0.1 | 精神饱满，有信心 | 0.2 | | | |
| | | 审题、答题、复查有序有法 | 0.4 | | | |
| | | 守纪 | 0.2 | | | |
| | | 试后认真核对答案 | 0.2 | | | |
| 总结 | 0.1 | 经常做阶段或专题（专项）总结 | 1.0 | | | |
| 评语 | | 教师评定、学生自评 | | | | |

表2 学生学习方法评价量表（XHP4-2-F）

| 二级指标 | 权重 | 三级指标 | 权重 | 等级 | 分数 | 合计 |
|---|---|---|---|---|---|---|
| 重视计划 | 0.3 | 目的、任务、措施明确，合适 | 0.4 | | | |
| | | 按计划学习 | 0.4 | | | |
| | | 有自查、自结 | 0.2 | | | |
| 安排时间 | 0.2 | 基本上与学校一致 | 0.2 | | | |
| | | 符合自身特点 | 0.2 | | | |
| | | 有规律性 | 0.3 | | | |
| | | 没有浪费时间 | 0.3 | | | |
| 追求效率 | 0.3 | 有效率意识 | 0.5 | | | |
| | | 掌握高效率学习的一些方法 | 0.5 | | | |
| 注意调查 | 0.2 | 学习时间调整 | 0.2 | | | |
| | | 学习内容调整 | 0.3 | | | |
| | | 学习心态（情绪）调整 | 0.5 | | | |
| 评语 | | 教师评定、学生自评 | | | | |

表3 学生学习品行评价量表（XHP4-3-P）

| 二级指标 | 权重 | 三级指标 | 权重 | 四级指标 | 权重 | 等级 | 分数 | 合计 |
|---|---|---|---|---|---|---|---|---|
| 学习态度 | 0.5 | 主动的精神 | 0.3 | 有志向 | 0.2 | | | |
| | | | | 有良好的主动学习习惯 | 0.8 | | | |
| | | 争先的意识 | 0.1 | 不甘落后 | 0.5 | | | |
| | | | | 不满足现状 | 0.5 | | | |
| | | 勤奋的劲头 | 0.2 | 以学为乐 | 0.2 | | | |
| | | | | 保证每天按计划学习 | 0.5 | | | |
| | | | | 抓紧一切可学时机 | 0.3 | | | |
| | | 认真的品质 | 0.2 | 不马虎 | 0.4 | | | |
| | | | | 不虚假 | 0.2 | | | |
| | | | | 求甚解 | 0.4 | | | |
| | | 互助的风格 | 0.1 | 向他人学习 | 0.3 | | | |
| | | | | 乐于助人 | 0.4 | | | |
| | | | | 关心集体 | 0.3 | | | |
| | | 创新的勇气 | 0.1 | 求新、求异的创新意识 | 0.3 | | | |
| | | | | 多角度思考和解决问题的创新思维 | 0.4 | | | |
| | | | | 角色表演等动手实践能力 | 0.3 | | | |
| 学习意志 | 0.5 | 注意力 | 0.3 | 在预习、听课、复习、做作业等学习活动中专心致志，没有心不在焉或一心二用的情况 | 1.0 | | | |
| | | 坚持力 | 0.2 | 上课、自习或在家学习时，善始善终，坚持到底 | 1.0 | | | |
| | | 抗挫力 | 0.2 | 不怕失败 | 0.5 | | | |
| | | | | 在逆境中不屈服 | 0.5 | | | |
| | | 自信心 | 0.3 | 从没有放弃自己的想法 | 0.2 | | | |
| | | | | 勇于并善于表现自己 | 0.5 | | | |
| | | | | 经常鼓励自己 | 0.3 | | | |
| 评语 | | 教师评定、学生自评 | | | | | | |

表4　学生主体性发展评估总表（XHP4-4-Z）

| 一级指标 | 权重 | 二级指标 | 合计 | 权重分 | 等级 |
|---|---|---|---|---|---|
| 学习程序 | 0.2 | 预习 | | | |
| | | 上课 | | | |
| | | 复习 | | | |
| | | 作业 | | | |
| | | 应试 | | | |
| | | 总结 | | | |
| 学习方法 | 0.2 | 重视计划 | | | |
| | | 安排时间 | | | |
| | | 追求效率 | | | |
| | | 注意调整 | | | |
| 学习品行 | 学习态度 0.3 | 主动的精神 | | | |
| | | 争先的意识 | | | |
| | | 勤奋的劲头 | | | |
| | | 认真的品质 | | | |
| | | 互助的风格 | | | |
| | | 创新的勇气 | | | |
| | 学习意志 0.3 | 注意力 | | | |
| | | 坚持力 | | | |
| | | 抗挫力 | | | |
| | | 自信心 | | | |
| 评语 | | 教师评定、学生自评 | | | |

说明：

（1）评价量表共4份。第一份是学习程序评价，即 XHP4-1-C；第二份是学习方法评价，即 XHP4-2-F；第三份是学习品行评价，即 XHP4-3-P；第四份是学生学习活动总评价，即 XHP4-4-Z。其中 X、H、P 分别为"学习""活动""评价" 3 个汉字拼音首字母大写，C、F、P、Z 分别为"程序""方法""品行""总评" 4 个汉字拼音首字母大写。

（2）表中"等级"分 A、B、C、D、E 五个等级。C 为中等，分值是 70～79 分；B 为中上等，分值是 80～89 分；A 为上等，分值是 90～100 分；D 为中下等，分值是 60～69 分；E 为下等，分值是 59 分以下。

(3) 评价时，学习程序和学习方法评价从三级指标开始，学习品行评价从四级指标开始。先看具体指标项，如认为该项做得一般，则划为 C 等，从 70～79 分取值；如认为很好，则划为 A 等，从 90～100 分取值，以此类推。然后再按权重计分。

## （二）学生主体性发展水平调查问卷

为了进一步观测学生的主体性发展水平，我们参考北京师范大学教育系与河南安阳市人民大道小学联合实验组建立的小学生主体性发展指标体系[①]，将主体性按自主性、主动性、创造性三个特质分类，每个特质各按意识与行为分为 10 个分析单元，在广泛征求有相关经验的英语教师意见的基础上，结合学生在英语课堂教学中的日常行为表现编制了一套英语课堂教学中学生主体性发展情况调查问卷，共 38 题（见附录 1）。然后进行了试测指标的筛选。采用预试方法，在初一、初二、初三每个年级随机抽出一个班共 150 名学生进行了预试，在问卷施测基础上对收集的数据进行了统计处理，一是计算各题的鉴别力指数，进行区分度分析；二是进行信度分析。

### 1. 区分度分析

所谓区分度，是指测验项目对所测量的心理特征的区分程度或鉴别力，它是鉴别题目质量的重要依据。由于测验为二值记分，采用鉴别指数法（即以两个极端组通过率的差异作为区分度的指标）计算，选用的 38 个题目的区分度分析见表 5。

表 5　试题区分度

| 题号 | 1 | 2 | 3 | 4 | 5 | 6 | 7 | 8 |
|---|---|---|---|---|---|---|---|---|
| 区分度 | 0.41 | 0.59 | 0.06 | 0.28 | 0.74 | 0.29 | 0.74 | 0.44 |
| 题号 | 9 | 10 | 11 | 12 | 13 | 14 | 15 | 16 |
| 区分度 | 0.54 | 0.18 | 0.28 | 0.22 | 0.57 | 0.37 | 0.62 | 0.5 |
| 题号 | 17 | 18 | 19 | 20 | 21 | 22 | 23 | 24 |
| 区分度 | 0.64 | 0.71 | 0.69 | 0.20 | 0.64 | 0.68 | 0.5 | 0.22 |
| 题号 | 25 | 26 | 27 | 28 | 29 | 30 | 31 | 32 |
| 区分度 | 0.29 | 0.74 | 0.57 | 0.66 | 0.56 | 0.65 | 0.26 | 0.61 |
| 题号 | 33 | 34 | 35 | 36 | 37 | 38 | | |
| 区分度 | 0.54 | 0.46 | 0.55 | 0.68 | 0.79 | 0.58 | | |

---

① 戴忠恒：《心理与教育测量》，华东师范大学出版社 1987 年版。

美国的伊贝尔（L. Ebel）提出评价试题的区分度指标为：区分度的值在 0.40 以上的题目为优良题，0.30～0.39 之间的题目为较好，0.20～0.29 之间的题目尚可，0.19 以下的题目需淘汰。[①] 由表可见，区分度在 0.40 以上的题目有 26 个，占 68.4%，即绝大多数题目为优良题；属于较好的题目有 1 题，占 2.6%；属于尚可有 8 题，占 21%；属于不合格有 2 题，占 5.30%，即第 3 题、第 10 题的区分度在 0.19 以下，区分度很小，因此在正式使用时将这两道题删去。

### 2. 信度分析

信度指的是测量的一致性程度，即受试者在测验中的稳定水平。计算信度有多种方法，在此采用内在一致性系数来估算，具体使用库德-理查森（Kuder-Richardson）公式 21（KR-21）。

$$r = \frac{ks_x^2 - \bar{x}(k-\bar{x})}{(k-1)s_x}$$

式中 k 为构成测验的题目数，$\bar{x}$ 为测验总分的平均数，$s_x^2$ 为测验总分的变异数。计算得到 $r=0.81$ 可见，该测试题目的内部一致性系数较大，说明这是一个同质性信度好的测验。

## 六、实验的效果

### （一）学生的主体性得到了较好的发展

（1）根据学生主体性发展评估总表中的一级指标，评价结果统计如表 5、表 7 所示。

表 5　实验前后教师对学生主体性发展的评估

| 项目 | 实验前 | 实验后 | 显著性检验 | 评价 |
|---|---|---|---|---|
| 学习程序 | $\bar{x}=60.2$<br>$s=24.0$ | $\bar{x}=70.6$<br>$s=27.0$ | $t=2.10$ | 显著提高 |
| 学习方法 | $\bar{x}=58.5$<br>$s=22.0$ | $\bar{x}=67.3$<br>$s=23.0$ | $t=2.01$ | 显著提高 |

---

① 参见北师大教育系、安阳市人民大道小学联合实验组：《小学生主体发展实验与指标体系的建立测评研究》，载《教育研究》1994.12

续上表

| 项目 | 实验前 | 实验后 | 显著性检验 | 评价 |
|---|---|---|---|---|
| 学习品行 | $\bar{x}=56.6$<br>$s=20.2$ | $\bar{x}=65.7$<br>$s=25.1$ | $t=2.00$ | 显著提高 |
| 总　评 | $\bar{x}=57.8$<br>$s=21.3$ | $\bar{x}=67.0$<br>$s=25.0$ | $t=2.04$ | 显著提高 |

表7　实验前后学生对主体性发展情况的自评

| 项目 | 实验前 | 实验后 | 显著性检验 | 评价 |
|---|---|---|---|---|
| 学习程序 | $\bar{x}=71.7$<br>$s=32.3$ | $\bar{x}=82.8$<br>$s=25.1$ | $t=1.98$ | 显著提高 |
| 学习方法 | $\bar{x}=62.6$<br>$s=14.8$ | $\bar{x}=77.6$<br>$s=40.2$ | $t=2.56$ | 显著提高 |
| 学习品行 | $\bar{x}=65.0$<br>$s=19.4$ | $\bar{x}=73.8$<br>$s=23.3$ | $t=2.12$ | 显著提高 |
| 总　评 | $\bar{x}=65.8$<br>$s=21.1$ | $\bar{x}=76.4$<br>$s=27.0$ | $t=2.25$ | 显著提高 |

由此可见，无论是教师评定，还是学生自评，其结果都表明学生的主体性水平得到了较好的发展。具体表现在学习活动的各个环节，包括预习、上课、复习、作业、应试、总结，绝大多数学生基本上都能做到有计划、有安排、有方法、有总结，自主学习的意识和自觉自理的能力比实验前大大提高。同时，在学习方法方面得到了改进，更多的学生重视计划、合理安排时间、追求高效率的学习方法和注意调整学习情绪，学生的参与意识、合作意识、创新能力等得到了发展，学习的意志力不断增强，这一切都表明学生的主体能力得到了发展。

（2）根据学生主体性发展水平调查问卷对实验班进行问卷调查，问卷共36个陈述句。只要求学生答"是"或"否"，每答一个"是"得1分，各题得分之和为学生主体性发展水平分。满分为36分，统计结果如表8所示。

表8 实验前后学生主体性发展水平对照表

|  | 人数 | 平均分 | 标准差 |
|---|---|---|---|
| 实验前 | 54 | 16.44 | 9.88 |
| 实验后 | 54 | 20.30 | 9.289 |
| 显著性检验 $t = 2.097 > 1.96$ ||||

由表8可见，前后测验的平均分数存在显著的差异，即说明通过实验，学生整体的主体性得到了明显的发展。

## （二）学生主体性的发展促进了英语学习成绩的提高

实验前后学生成绩对比见表9。

表9 实验前后学生英语成绩对比

|  | 人数 | 平均分 | 标准差 | 年级名次 | 13校名次 |
|---|---|---|---|---|---|
| 前测（协作组统一命题考试） | 54 | 83.6 | 22.1 | 2 | 7 |
| 后测（广州市2000年升学考试） | 54 | 88 | 37.8 | 1 | 3 |
| 备注 | 实验班所在年级共四个班，初中入学时按测试成绩均匀分班，各班之间学生的入学基础、智力水平、人数、年龄、性别相似。前测试题的编制依照后测试题的命题要求制定了双向细目表，由协作组富有经验的教师完成。 |||||

为了纵向比较实验班英语成绩在实验前后的变化，对表8中两次测验进行两个相关总体的平均数检验。采用 $t$ 检验的步骤如下：

（1）提出统计假设：设 $\mu_D = \mu_2 - \mu_1$，$D_i = X_{2i} - X_{1i}$

$H_0: \mu_D = 0$；$H_1: \mu_D \neq 0$

其中 $\mu_D$ 为前后测平均分之差，$D_i$ 为学生 $i$ 前后测平均分之差的平均数，$\mu_1$ 为前测平均分，$\mu_2$ 为后测平均分，$X_{2i}$ 为考生 $i$ 在后测中得分，$X_{1i}$ 为考生 $i$ 在前测中得分。

（2）检验统计量为：

$$t = \frac{\overline{D}}{S_D / \sqrt{n}}$$

由样本分数得：$\overline{D} = 88 - 83.6 = 4.4$

$S_D = 12.656$

$\therefore t = \dfrac{4.4}{12.656/\sqrt{54}} = 2.56$

查 $t_{0.025(53)} = 2.01$，$\therefore |t| > t_{0.025(53)}$，拒绝 $H_0$。故实验后的英语成绩有显著的进步。

而且从表9可以看出实验班在年级和协作组中的名次都有进步，从显著进步的趋势看，我们有理由相信，长期进行主体教育实验会明显提高学生的英语成绩。

### （三）实验结果的动态描述

随着实验措施的逐步实施和慢慢深入，实验班的学习气氛有了很大的好转。具体表现在课堂专心听讲，积极参与的学生多了，自习课向巡堂老师提问的学生多了，缺交或抄袭作业的现象明显减少了，学生学习的主动性、自觉性较以前有了较大提高，绝大多数学生能自觉完成老师布置的学习任务，表现出良好的学习态度。实验结束后，师生座谈会上针对"你对英语课感兴趣的程度"这样一个问题问卷调查，比较感兴趣的人数占61%，一般的占24.2%，比较不感兴趣的占14.8%，可见大多数学生对英语课是持欢迎态度的。他们普遍认为新模式与原有的教学模式相比，最大的特点是课堂上实践活动形式多样，提升了学习英语的趣味性。学生的英语语言水平有了较大的提高，辨音能力正确率由51%提高到76%（由13校联考试题中统计出来），能听懂基本上没有生词的英语国家人士录音的材料，语速为每分钟100～110个词，正确率达到70%以上。而且在经常性的课堂实践活动中，语言使用的机会多了，学生之间的互动也多了，不少学生对自己的学习状况感到不满足，主动要求老师介绍学习方法，想通过改进学习方法不断提高学习效果。更为可喜的是，学生的创造能力表现出良好的发展趋势，全班同学都能较为流利地进行课前值日报告，70%以上的学生能改编课文进行角色表演，有半数以上学生能根据非完整性的情景或图画进行想象和创造。他们还经常学唱英语歌，有的学生还自编自演英文短剧并在学校表演。可见学生创新意识增强，求新、求异、求变化，动手实践能力也有了较大的发展。这些都有力地说明学生的主体性得到了良好的发展。

### （四）部分同行教师的评价

为探讨模式的实操性及同行教师的可接受性，在非实验班进行了一次全校的公开课，内容是九年义务教育三年制初级中学英语第二册 Lesson 95。采用体现主体性教学目标的课堂教学评估表（见附录2）。先后请同科组教师及学校领导进行课堂教学评估，该公开课被评为学校青年教师教学技能比赛第一名。

## 七、讨论

（1）"自主、互动、创造"的英语教学模式将学生的主体性发展融入教学环节之中，符合主体教育与学科教育的统一性，该模式达到了优化课堂教学结构的目的，对学生的主体性发展以及学习成绩的提高都有显著的效果。实验过程中，教学管理部门、教师和学生的反映都是积极的、肯定的，实验的初步数据也证实了这一点。我们可以得出结论，实验结果证实了实验假说。

（2）实验教师体会到，先进的教育理论指导下的教育实验对教育的发展有着重要的促进作用，教育科研可以有效地提高教学质量，创造性的工作可以使人体会到一种职业享受。学校不仅是学生发展的场所，而且也是教师"继续社会化"的场所。教师只有不断地学习先进的教育理论，不断地向学生学习，才能在实践中不断自我完善，不断创新和发展，才有可能真正主导学生的学习，真正确立学生的主体地位。

（3）实验所采用的教学模式决不意味着否定和抛弃常规教学。只是从比较来看，主体性教学更全面、更先进，常规教学需要更新，不能彻底抛弃。在某些方面，例如在使学生牢固、系统地掌握英语基础知识方面，常规教学有很强的效力。所以，提倡吸收常规教学的优点。

（4）教学模式的改革意味着开放、进取、创新，随时准备接受新事物、新观念以及新的行为方式。只有教学价值观、教学目标、教学内容、教学评价由单一转向多元化，才能突出学生的主体地位，只有由过去的"唯知"转向完善学生的内心世界，才能真正发挥学生的主体作用。

（5）人的主体性发展是个复杂的过程，它涉及多重因素的影响。在学校教育中，必须优化影响学生主体性素质发展的教育因素，比如优化物质环境、文化环境、人际环境及其社会环境，开办家长学校，进而优化学生家庭育人环境，形成教育的合力。

**附录**1
英语课堂教学中学生主体性发展情况调查问卷
说明：本调查作研究用，不需记名，请如实打"√"或"×"。
（　）1. 我经常预习要学的英语功课。
（　）2. 我能及时复习所学的单词、词组、句型和课文。

（　）3．我自觉遵守课堂纪律及考试规则。

（　）4．作业发下后，我能对照老师的批改更正错误。

（　）5．我经常做单元或专题英语学习小结。

（　）6．无论是上课、自习还是在家学习时，我都能善始善终。

（　）7．我能制订阶段性的英语学习计划并付诸行动。

（　）8．我每天合理安排英语学习的时间。

（　）9．我根据自己的需要不断调整和追求高效率的学习方法。

（　）10．我独立完成英语作业。

（　）11．英语考试时，我精神饱满，充满信心。

（　）12．考试时我注意认真审题、答题和检查。

（　）13．上课时我力求掌握本节课的重点，解决预习中的难点和疑点。

（　）14．我对自己通过努力获得的成绩感到满意。

（　）15．最能促使我努力学习英语的因素是学习的成功感。

（　）16．上课时，我能抓住老师的讲课思路。

（　）17．我经常在上课时举手回答问题。

（　）18．遇到自己有把握的问题我会举手回答。

（　）19．遇到有挑战性的问题我会举手回答。

（　）20．我有丰富的英语课外知识。

（　）21．上课时，我主动用英语与同伴交谈。

（　）22．我敢于大胆表达英语角色。

（　）23．我积极参加小组讨论和小组之间的比赛。

（　）24．遇到不懂的问题时，我会查找字典或参考书。

（　）25．遇到不懂的问题时，我经常请教老师或同学。

（　）26．我觉得对学习英语有兴趣。

（　）27．我乐意帮助英语学习有困难的同学。

（　）28．我主动协助老师管理英语课堂纪律。

（　）29．和同学一起表演时，我欣赏其表演并给予客观的评价。

（　）30．我欣赏自己表演的角色并从中受到教益，提高交际能力。

（　）31．如果答错问题或角色表演时做得不够好，我总是鼓励自己下次加倍努力。

（　）32．通过角色表演，在全班同学面前发言不再感到害怕。

（　）33．上课时有不同于老师或其他同学的见解，我会当场说出来。

（　）34．我能根据老师创设的情景，或者给出的关键词、短语组成对话。

（　）35．我能根据图画进行想象，完成对话或情景。

（　）36．我能表演根据课文改编的短剧。

（　）37．我坚持写英语作文或日记。

（　）38．我经常参加英语课外活动或英语角。

附录2

### 英语课堂教学水平评估记录表

班级_____　　任课教师_____　　时间_____

| 评估类目 | 评估要素 | 评估等级 | | | |
|---|---|---|---|---|---|
| | | 优 | 良 | 中 | 差 |
| 1．教学目标 15 | 体现主体性发展要求 | 8 | 6 | 4 | 2 |
| | 符合大纲要求 | 7 | 5 | 3 | 1 |
| 2．教学内容 15 | 合理的知识结构、突出重点、深浅适度 | 8 | 7 | 6 | 5 |
| | 联系社会实际和学生生活实际 | 7 | 6 | 5 | 4 |
| 3．教学策略与方法 20 | 学生主动参与学习的有效度 | 7 | 5 | 3 | 1 |
| | 学生合作学习与探讨的实效性 | 7 | 5 | 3 | 1 |
| | 学生自主学习及差异发展 | 6 | 4.5 | 3 | 1.5 |
| 4．教学能力 20 | 密度适当，条理清楚，时间安排合理，应变能力强 | 7 | 5 | 4 | 2 |
| | 现代教学技术手段设计应用适时适度，操作规范熟练 | 5 | 4 | 3 | 2 |
| | 语音语调规范，词汇语法正确，教态自然亲切，板书规范正确 | 8 | 6 | 5 | 4 |
| 5．教学效果 20 | 学生获得的基础知识扎实 | 5 | 4 | 3 | 2 |
| | 学生善于思考，发言有独到见解 | 5 | 4 | 3 | 2 |
| | 学生的参与活动面广 | 5 | 4 | 3 | 2 |
| | 课堂气氛活跃，师生关系融洽和谐 | 5 | 4 | 3 | 2 |
| 6．教学特色 10 | 有教改创新 | 6 | 4.5 | 3 | 1.5 |
| | 有独特良好的教学风格 | 4 | 3 | 2 | 1 |
| 总　评 | 等级 | 优 | 良 | 中 | 差 |
| | 总分 | 100—88 | 87—73 | 72—46 | 45以下 |

# 第九章　学习·收获·反思·感悟[*]
## ——漫谈赴英国伯明翰大学的"Teacher-Training"

不知不觉中，2个月的培训匆匆过去了。从初到英国时的新奇、开口说英语的谨慎、饮食起居的烦琐、为完成作业的熬夜，到课堂上自信地与英国老师探讨问题，与来自世界各地的人用英语自由交谈以及最终通过考试拿到证书的欣喜，短短的8个星期，我有过欢乐，有过疲劳，更多的是收获和思考。而所有的一切将是我人生旅途中的最难忘的经历，也将开启我教育教学生涯中新的篇章。

## 一、学习

### （一）我们的培训班

我们这个班的全称叫"广州市中学英语骨干教师'1+2'培训班"，这是由广州市教育局举办，广州市教育评估和教师继续教育指导中心组织的培训项目。培训项目分两部分完成：2006年9月3日—29日在广东外语外贸大学进行一个月的国内培训，10月7日—12月3日在英国伯明翰大学进行为期两个月的培训，所以叫作"1+2"培训班。国内培训采用全脱产方式，为出国培训做好预备；国外培训主要通过与当地教师共同开展教学实践的形式，学习研讨英语教学理论和教学方法，系统地提高英语教师的英语教学能力和水平。本次培训有22名来自广州市各中学的科长、骨干教师和各区教研员参加。由于培训团所有成员都是第一次来到英国，为此，我们在国内就进行了周密筹划，在组织上、思想上和物质上做足准备。在国内培训期间建立了班委，由广州市教研室何琳老师担任班长，海珠区教育发展中心张志梅老师担任学习委员。到英国后，我们进一步加强了组织领导，在团长何琳老师的带领下，又将22人分成5组，每组选一人任组长，负责联络、沟通、学习、安全等工作。从团长到各小组长，积极性很高，责任感很强，特别是何琳老师以身作则，对各团员

---

[*] 本文于2007年1月在英国驻广州领事馆新年文化交流活动中分享。

关怀备至，做了大量细致的工作。比如对身体不舒服的学员非常关心，对这次学习培训及时进行总结，对回国途中的注意事项、可能出现的问题进行提醒，周密部署各项工作。学员之间也互相关心，互相照顾，显示了空前的团结和协调配合，使培训团真正成为一个团结友爱、步调一致、具有良好精神面貌的好集体，在异国他乡留下了难忘的回忆，也得到了伯明翰大学老师的高度赞扬。

（二）英国伯明翰大学

伯明翰大学创建于1900年，是英国最好最大的大学之一，其优异的教学和科研成果在世界各地均享有极高的声誉。伯明翰大学现有在校学生1.9万人，其中博士及硕士研究生约6000人；我国著名地质学家李四光，以及香港特区前行政长官董建华均毕业于该校。在2000年《时代》周刊排行榜上，学校综合排名第13位。伯明翰大学同时又是由全球21所知名大学组成的国际基础研究中心协会的会员。伯明翰大学在以下领域提供广泛的学位课程：艺术、商业、教育、工程、法律、医药、科学和社会科学。大学以其高水平的教学和研究而著称。2万多名学生中有1000多名来自120多个国家，使这里真正充满了国际氛围。

伯明翰大学对在中国开展和建立教学及研究持有积极的态度，已经与中国多所著名大学建立紧密联系，包括北京大学、复旦大学、武汉大学、南京大学、中国科技大学、中国人民大学、哈尔滨工业大学等。该大学与英国政府及各阶层有广泛的合作。

伯明翰市是广州市的友好城市，地处英格兰的心脏地带，人口300多万，历史上的富庶和发展与19世纪的工业革命密不可分。各种交通工具更是四通八达。无论搭乘飞机、火车还是汽车，都可以方便抵达伯明翰。许多海外留学生都趁在校期间去世界各地旅行，因为伯明翰机场与阿姆斯特丹、巴黎、法兰克福等大都市都有直达航班。从伯明翰乘火车去伦敦只需1小时40分钟。伯明翰是英国第二大城市。在这里，可以找到所有欧洲大都市都拥有的文化、运动和娱乐等设施。

（三）课程设置情况

经过市教育局与英国伯明翰大学的交流，我们培训班的课程设置及参观考察内容都经过了精心的设置，一方面有利于提高中国英语教师的英语语言水平和教学水平，另一方面使参加培训的教师们能更加广泛地了解英国的历史、文化、社会、语言、文学、生活习俗等。

（四）培训总体安排

开课时间如下：星期一、二、四：9：15—11：15 ；Break；11：45—1：15；Lunch；14：15—16：15。星期三到学校 Observation；星期五：9：15—11：15；休息；11：45—12：45；下午自由活动。

第1周

周一 欢迎会 课程介绍 Survival English 1：如何介绍 办理学生证及计算机卡 英语水平测试 参观校园

周二 计算机上机培训 参观图书馆 伯明翰大学历史介绍

周三 伯明翰市中心参观 Survival English 2

周四 生活在英国 Survival English 3 参观中学的安排

周五 Survival English 4－5：表达观点、购物、去银行

第2－7周

周一 英语的发展 教学法 少年儿童的英语教学

周二 英语的发展 教学研究方法 教学大纲设计与评价 参观图书馆 伯明翰大学历史介绍

周三 全天下学校听课与调研

周四 英语的发展 学校听课与调研反馈 英语教学技能

周五 英语的发展 英语语音

第8周

周一 英语的发展 Teaching preparation 1－2

周二 英语的发展 Peer teaching 1－2

周三 Teaching assessments 1－3

周四 考试

周五 课程评估 课堂游戏 告别午餐

（五）课程培训的主要内容

A. Language Development 语言水平提高，授课教师：Richard

听力和口语 英语习惯用语 文章阅读 英语媒体 写作技巧

英国社会和文化 英国背景 英国社会 英国社会阶层 英国教育体系

B. Teaching Approaches 教学理论与方法：授课教师：Rick

英语教学理论的发展史

英语教学的主要流派介绍：Direct method/ Grammar-translation/ Suggestopedia/ The Natural Approach/ Community language learning/ PPP/ Communicative Approach/ lexical Approach/ Dogme, /Eclectic Approach/ ARC/ Task-based Approach/ The Silent Way/ TPR/ Audiolingual/

C. Teaching of Skills 教学技能　授课教师：Rick

词汇/语音/语法/阅读/听力/写作教学

课堂气氛控制与提高

课程计划与提纲设计

教学游戏应用

教学中的计算机技术及网络应用

综合教学能力

教学测试与评价

D. Teacher as Researcher 教师的教科研　授课教师：Rick

动机

多元智能 1. Bodily-kinaesthetic 2. Interpersonal 3. Intrapersonal 4. Linguistic 5. Logical-Mathematical 6. Musical 7. Naturalist 8. Spatial

学习风格

E. Teaching Young learners 少年儿童的英语教学　授课教师：Rick

学习策略

语言学习与习得

音乐在教学中的应用

录像在教学中的应用

戏剧在教学中的应用

F. Syllabus Design & Assessment 教学大纲与教学评价　授课教师：Rick

大纲设计

评价理论

评价方法——定性评价与定量评价，形成性评价与终结性评价

G. Pronunciation 英语语音　授课教师：Dave

H. Teaching Observation 教学考察　授课教师：Eleanor

I. 每周三在伯明翰大学的主校园会举行面向国际学生的与英语语言学相关的讲座，讲座内容包括英语文学、语言学和外语教学领域最新的研究和应用。

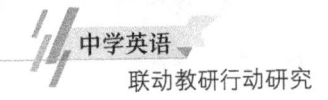

J. 对受培训教师的评估

从课程开始到培训结束都对培训教师进行面试、笔试，上课期间的行为表现以及个人作业及小组作业都纳入评估的范围。上课期间指导老师会对学生进行个人单独辅导；对学生英语水平提供反馈，并对其英语提高提出必要的建议。

K. 到学校考察

全班 22 人分成几个小组，每组 2—3 人，分别到中学进行深度教育考察，每逢周三到一所学校一天。另外，全班还集体参观了一所幼儿园，通过与学校校长、副校长、校长助理、科组长、老师及学生的座谈，听取介绍，讨论问题，观摩上课，交换上课，互相评课，感受校园文化，加深了对英国教育及学校管理的了解。

L. 社会活动

伯明翰大学在课程学习期间为我们安排了丰富的社会活动和参观考察项目，我们可以在星期五下午或者周末外出游览。在晚上及其他业余时间，学校还组织了游览伯明翰运河及参观当地人的家，并且为运动爱好者组织体育活动，比如打乒乓球、羽毛球等。我们上课的地方叫 Selly Oak，我们的教学楼叫 Elmfield House，那里有个国际学生课间休息的地方叫 Common Room 或者 Coffee Room，也是一个发布各种信息的地方，如学校科系部门的负责人介绍、学生团体机构招新、校园活动介绍，愿意参加什么活动就在什么活动的通知上面签名。大家手里拿着咖啡，辨认着各个广告，不亦乐乎。伯明翰大学里的学生非常多样化，来自不同国家、不同年龄的人穿梭在校园中，都是好奇地四处张望，见面互相打个招呼，排着队冲茶或者咖啡，在微波炉里加热食物，然后找个位子坐下来吃，气氛热闹又友好。为满足广州教师全方位了解英国的需要，课程期间校方专门组织我们到英国多处代表性地区参观，体验生活。具体行程安排如下。

| Date | Weekday | Sites/activities | Definition | Feedback |
| --- | --- | --- | --- | --- |
| 19/Oct | Thursday | International meal at Selly Oak | Sharing your national meal with others | |
| 20/Oct | Friday | Sports | Badminton and football | |
| 21/Oct | Saturday | Bath | Daytrip | |
| 22/Oct | Sunday | Warwick Castle | Daytrip | |

续上表

| Date | Weekday | Sites/activities | Definition | Feedback |
|---|---|---|---|---|
| 24/Oct | Tuesday | Canal side walk | 6pm | |
| 27/Oct | Friday | Scotland | Two days' trip | |
| | | | | |
| 2/Nov | Thursday | Cinema trip | 7pm | |
| 3/Nov | Friday | Jam house | 8pm dance | |
| 4/Nov | Saturday | Oxford | Daytrip | |
| 5/Nov | Sunday | | Daytrip | |
| | | | | |
| 8/Nov | Wednesday | Theatre | Opera | Book in advance |
| 10/Nov | Friday | Sports/shopping | Active | |
| 11/Nov | Saturday | Whales | Two-day-trip | |
| 12/Nov | Sunday | Millennium point | Civil trip | |
| 14/Nov | Tuesday | Symphony | Czech Orchestra | |
| 15/Nov | Wednesday | Football live | Pub life is there! | |
| 16/Nov | Thursday | Concert | Guitar | |
| 18/Nov | Saturday | Cambridge | Daytrip | |
| 19/Nov | Sunday | York | Daytrip | |
| | | | | |
| 25/Nov | Saturday | London | Two-day-trip | |
| 26/Nov | Sunday | London | | |
| 26/Nov | Sunday | Concert | 7pm | |
| | | | | |
| 28/Nov | Tuesday | Ballet | 7pm | Book in advance |
| 29/Nov | Wednesday | Stratford | 7pm | |
| 1/Dec | Friday | German market | Afternoon | |
| 2/Dec | Saturday | No arrangement | Whole day | Free |
| 3/Dec | Sunday | Airport | China | Home |

## 二、收获

### (一) 来自课程

**1. 提高了英语语言能力**

听力的提高是最为突出的。记得在途中,我们经过曼彻斯特,一下飞机,就有伯明翰大学的 Heriate 小姐前来接待我们。因为她是伯明翰本地人,语速很快,带有比较明显的地方口音,我当时听她的讲话听得很辛苦,基本上是丈二和尚摸不着脑袋,而且我问同班同学,听得懂的好像也不多。现在我能够轻松听懂 Heriate 的讲话,后来又与一些当地的居民接触,包括双双毕业于牛津大学的 Johnson 和 Jill 夫妇、会计师 Mike、教法语的 Allan,还有坐轮椅的 David,等等,我跟他们都能够很自然地沟通,并且深入探讨了很多问题。我们公共厨房里有德国人、法国人、津巴布韦人。刚开始,大家都不太讲话,后来就无所不谈了。这些都说明听力是大大提高了的。

口语方面也进步比较大,我在参加培训前不太愿意开口,生怕说错了,贻笑大方。现在总算迈出了这一步,敢于说英语,不怕别人笑话,这种方式没表达清楚,就换一种方式。其实英语老师本来的语言根底不错,关键就在于克服胆怯的心理。事实上,我在学习期间,基本上不存在口语交流的障碍,流利的英语还经常得到外国朋友的称赞。

泛读能力提高较为明显,差不多平均每周都有 1000～3000 字的书写作业。每个作业都有参考书籍、刊物及网站,因此快速阅读是必须的,否则跟不上。现在一本英文书翻下来,大致讲什么内容,是否有自己需要的章节,我都能够很快识别出来,还能特别注意英语句式的工整、用词的考究、结构的清晰。写得好的英文句子和中文诗歌一样韵味无穷。

写作进步也非常大。来英国前我习惯写中文的文章,自己的中文文化背景知识和写作能力还不错,但是纯英语的论文还没有写过一篇。在英学习时则要完成很多的作业,都是以论文或报告的方式上交,哪怕是写个教案,也要交待背景、教学目标、教材来源及其选择依据、教学方法、教学过程、学生分析、方法改进,等等,于是要写的东西就多了。而且,英国老师对学生自己的见解是十分在意的,有一套相当成熟的衡量标准,加之我自己也十分珍惜这样难得的学习机会,不敢有丝毫懈怠,心里总有一种信念,要努力提高语言应用能力,一定坚持写出自己的观点。也正是在高强度的授课、作业、考试,以及生活交流中,我们的语言水平在不知不觉中提高了,对一些词语的使用环境、感情色彩、多义理解了解得更为清楚。下面是在培训结束后的作文考试中老师给我的评价。

Timed Essay Feedback

| Name | Accuracy | Comp & Vocab | Org & Coh | Com & Style | Con & Anal | Overall |
|---|---|---|---|---|---|---|
| Rainbow | A (73) | A (74) | A (75) | A (74) | A (74) | A (74) |

Comment
This is an extremely well written essay that shows a sound awareness of current thought about the teaching of grammar. You cover a number of points in a clear, accurate and well organized way. Many thanks and best wishes for the future.

从写作的内容到形式，从文章组织到整体的连贯，从词汇到语法以及整个行文老师都给了 A 级，而且给了非常肯定的评语，我也为自己在英文写作方面的进步感到特别高兴。

### 2. 更新了教育观念，拓展了国际视野

我在教学第一线工作了十多年，虽然积累了较为丰富的经验，但知识老化和知识结构不合理的问题依然存在，此次学习使自己在教学理论和教育观念上得到了最大的补充。如最新的语言学理论、语用学理论、心理语言学理论，最新的语言教学方法，各种语言教学活动包括音乐、戏剧、游戏、故事、电影、录像、角色扮演、唱歌等的使用，肢体语言在语言教学中重要性等。这一切都为我开辟了新视野，使我不断反省以往的教学思想，不仅更新了知识、充实了结构，也对当今英语教育理论与实践发展的趋势有了更明晰的把握。这对我将来的教研工作有着重大的指导作用。

开放的授课和学习环境培养了学生活跃的思想和多样性的思维，但这并不是英国式教育的全部。另一方面，严格、完善、务实的制度环境也强化了按章办事的理念。从入学开始，学校的相关部门，比如图书馆、教学管理、国际学生服务、学生联合会、住宿管理等，事无巨细，都会有详尽的条款规定，比如图书馆书籍的借阅使用、作业的上交、体育场馆的使用等。总之，学习期间可能涉及的一切设备设施，都能在各项制度中找到说明，遇到问题也会被告知去哪里寻求帮助，因为学校认为这是校方的责任所在。相反，怎么安排自己的学习和生活则是学生自己的事情，学校绝不会干涉。开放与严谨、务实与认真，构成了学校生活的主导原则，这也是英国社会的一个缩影。

### 3. 学习了贯穿西方先进的语言教学法

英国老师的教学更侧重培养学生的创新思维和发散思维，注重学生学习积

极性的培养和调动。教学是启发式的，没有固定的教科书。课堂上老师开始一个主题之后，首先让同学们进行积极的讨论，开启思路，畅所欲言。或者分组讨论，再让各个小组进行总结发言。最后，他再给出个人倾向性的观点。这种教学方式，充分激发了每个人的参与性和能动性，汇集了集体的智慧，也交流了思想，开阔了每个人的视野。老师授课的言谈举止中，处处体现出尊重学生、启发学生的理念。他们对学生们提出的问题，从不轻易说"yes"或"no"，而是鼓励、肯定、分析、讨论，给学生充分的展示空间，锻炼提高学生的交流能力。而且各个教室的墙面布置也透着浓厚的创新意识，给学生留下广阔的空间，供学生发挥其独特的想象力，提倡个性张扬。在每门课程学习的开始、中间，到最后，学校都通过问卷调查的方式收集学生对课程内容、课程的有用性和难易程度、授课老师的表现、课程改进等各方面的看法和意见，从而确定今后的改进方法和措施。他们这种注重实际能力培养、尊重学生个性、充分挖掘学生潜力的方法，确实值得我们借鉴。

### 4. 领略到了高素质的英国教师的风采

为我们上课的老师主要有 Rick、Richard、Dave、Eleanor，负责活动安排的主要是 Jon、Tim 和 Heriate，这几位老师多才多艺，都非常敬业并且活力充沛。最受欢迎的两位老师应当数 Rick 和 Richard，他们在教学中善于通过幽默的语言、轻松的话题、有亲和力的表达营造和谐的气氛；善于设计有趣的情景或有挑战性的任务调动激发学生参与的意愿；同时善于引导分享、智谋挑战与总结激励。在 Rick 的课堂上，他示范了 10 多种生动活泼的教学活动，其中的戏剧表演以及通过音乐学习英语的方法令人赞叹不已，收到了奇特的效果，给大家留下了特别深刻的印象。Rick 的吉他和钢琴弹奏得很棒，他每逢星期四中午 1：30—2：10 都利用休息时间教我们这些学生学英语歌。他的歌声，还有他的吉他和钢琴演奏次次都让我陶醉。在在这些老师身上，可以看出他们有丰富的文化底蕴、渊博的知识、儒雅的学者风范，他们钻研教学的能力很强，教学风格各异，有着各自独特的个性，让我强烈地感觉到：出色的外语教师不仅应是博学的学者，还应是出色的演员、导演等。而且我觉得要做一个有幽默感的老师，幽默是教师人格魅力的展示。教师要拥有健康的身心、强健的体魄、优雅的仪表、好听的口音、幽默的个性、愉悦的心情，才能做一个成功快乐的老师，所有这些都如"随风潜入夜，润物细无声"那样影响着我，让我从心理上思想上对教师这个职业的理解得到洗礼和升华。

最难忘的是 12 月 1 日，也是上课的最后一天，我们大家和老师们一起玩游戏，一起欢乐，依依惜别。Rick 还特地为我们创作了一首叫作 *The Wild Rov-*

er 的新歌，以非常幽默的语言反映我们在伯明翰大学的学习和生活，歌词如下：

The Wild Rover

Well you've been in Brum now for quite a long time
And been working so hard, it's such a crime
You now need a holiday, a break don't you know
So now you're returning, back to Guangzhou

And it's no, no never, no no never no more
Will you be a student, of EISU no more (Chorus)

Rick taught you reflections and methodology
You looked in the mirror, discussed PPP
You read lots of handouts, then lots and lots more
Now your bags are too heavy, to lift off the floor

From Rich you had language development
But most of the time, you didn't know what he meant
You got into groups and did lots of jigsaws
And at the end of the lesson, you'd cry out 'no more'!

With Dave you learnt how to say lots of things
Like 'marvellous' and 'fabulous', and 'really lovely rings'
You voiced and you didn't, formed short vowels and long
But despite lots of practice, you still can't speak Brum

Well weekly on Wednesdays, you'd go into school
You thought you'd left school behind, but that was the rule
But then on a Thursday, as if that wasn't enough
Eleanor would make you discuss lots of stuff

So it's goodbye to Chelwood, to room 211
To terrible food from the microwave oven

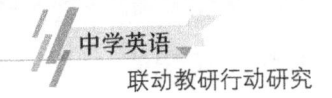

To weather that changes three times in one day
To times you get lost and can't find your way

You've been to Stratford and London, and even to Wales
Spent far too much money in markets and sales
But now you're returning to your families
We hope they remember you, please don't forget me

当时 Rick 一边弹着吉他一边唱，Richard 也一起唱，然后师生同唱，情感交融达到顶峰。转眼间，我们就要与沿路陪伴我们的可敬可亲的老师们挥手告别了，我有千万个舍不得，舍不得那些新朋友，舍不得各位老师们，更舍不得他们的谆谆教诲……各位老师对我来说，虽然相处的时间很短暂，但是却带给我们一节节深刻而有趣的课，陪伴着我们在教学道路上成长。他们是我们的良师益友。我想我会永远记住这一刻，永远珍惜彼此的友谊。

**5. 加强了交流，增进了友谊**

除了从老师们的传授中学到、领悟到很多东西，在课堂中，在作为学生的我们在思想碰撞、交流中也相互学到了很多。感谢这次培训带给我们一个同龄人相聚的机会。在自主、合作、探究的课堂上，老师们让我们小组合作讨论提出问题、解决问题。而在小组合作中，我们不仅增进了友谊，而且在交流中得到一些启发。"他山之石，可以攻玉。"在倾听彼此的回答中，我有时候得到的不仅是对工作方法的学习，还引发了不少对生活的深刻思考。从周围的同学中，我学到很多东西，有思想、方法、观点的交流，从而达到资源的共享。也就是说，师生互动，生生互动，心灵撞击心灵，语言呼唤语言。

此外，每逢星期三晚上我都去参加伯明翰当地的一个 Global Coffee，实际上是一个类似英语角的活动，使我有机会接触到来自不同国家、有着不同文化背景的同学。在与他们的交往过程中，让我感受到东西方文化的不同，例如大家在礼仪、文化、价值观、发展观、生活方式、民俗习惯等方面都存在差异。通过与当地人的交往我发现，英国普通百姓对中国的了解是很少的，知道广州的人很少，但是现在随着中国经济的日益强大，他们愿意甚至渴望了解中国。为了让更多的外国友人了解中国，所以我也时常向他们介绍中国的历史、文化、教育以及中国在各个领域所取得的伟大成就，成为传播祖国文化的使者。

**（二）来自学校**

英国教育制度享誉全球。这不仅因为英国有健全的高等教育体系，其中学教育也颇具特色。我被安排到伯明翰郊区的 St. John Wall School 中学进行考察，那是一所基督教教会资助的学校，校园很小，只有一栋教学楼加上不标准的运动场，如果在广州也应该称得上是所麻雀学校。该校教学设备比较简陋，学生主要来自非洲和亚洲，还有部分来自波兰和伊拉克。我在这所学校里参观考察了 6 个星期，主要是广泛地听课、观摩，协助该校老师教学和管理学生，利用可能的机会介绍中国，尤其是广州，采访该校的领导、老师、学生等。通过在那里进行深入细致的观察和学习，我受益匪浅。

### 1. 关于英国的课堂教学

在访问 St. John Wall School 期间，我听过 Mr. Darren Gallagher 的信息技术课和英语课、Mr. Newman 的科学课、Anna 小姐及 Marinda 小姐的法语课、Katherine 小姐的西班牙语课、来自香港 Mianne 小姐的粤语课、Mr. Stanton 先生的数学课，还有 2 节戏剧表演课，前前后后听了 16 节课。我所看到和经历的课堂教学几乎都可用这句话来概括：以学生为中心，以活动为手段，以开发思维为目的。不管哪一门学科，老师都可能把它组织成一堂以学生为中心的活动课。很少有老师一人讲授到底的情况。课堂上很少见到同学们一排排整整齐齐地坐着。他们的教室布置也很别致，老师用的小黑板只有一小块，全部的墙面都贴满了与教学课程有关的内容，有学生写的文章、诗歌、明信片、图片和单词卡等，也有对孩子的表彰和一些行为规范，还有一些生活常识。所有的老师对学生都是那么的和蔼可亲，老师们常用的语言是：I'd like you to do…Could you please…课堂气氛轻松融洽，内容简单明了，没有固定的课本，但老师给每个学生准备了本节课有关的学习资料。老师上课类似谈话聊天，精讲多练，腾出大量的时间给学生自学，学生做练习很独立和诚实，没有抄袭现象。例如，Mr. Stanton 的数学课，从头到尾都是学生自己做练习，下课前，老师给出正确答案，让全班学生自己检查，然后让全班学生起立，接着说：答对 10 题的坐下，答对 9 题的坐下……最后一个学生只答对了 1 题，所以他最后坐下，但老师和同学们没有嘲讽他。在该校的图书馆，每次都能够见到 Mr. Flemous，还有教波兰语的 Polina 小姐在单独辅导几个英语跟不上班里其他人的学生。老师们说要一直辅导这些孩子，直到他们能够赶上同班同学为止。英国教育的人文化、人性化和个性化真的值得我们借鉴。

### 2. 关于英国中学的考试体制

我采访了该校英语系主任 Mr. Darren Gallagher，了解到英国中学的考试体制。

英国中学学制为七年，初中五年，高中两年。每个学校都有严格的考试制度。考试课目可以根据各校自己规定的课程而定，也可以按教育部门的规定而设。英国教育部门规定，中学的必考课目有英语、数学、科学（包括物理、化学、生物）、第二外语（法文或德文）等。

初中考高中的考试叫 GCSE，要求比较严。但为了减轻学生的压力和负担，考试重点几乎不包括前三年所学的内容，主要是后两年所学的课程。英国的中学虽然开设体育课，但不用考试，学生们冬天去游泳，夏季练跑步。除英国教育部门规定的考试课目外，该校还规定，学生必须选择一门常识课并参加考试，一般是历史课或地理课。

初中升高中要考英语、数学、科学（物理、化学、生物）、法语、历史、电脑、地理等，由英国教育部门统一命题，在规定的时间举行全国统考。学生可以参照英国教育部门指定的复习大纲进行复习，复习大纲分 A、B 两类，但差别不大。

高中一年级的考试称为 AS，二年级的考试称为 A level。考试科目有英语（语言、文学）、数学（数学、高等数学）、生物、化学、经济等课程。选修课有古英语、音乐、历史、地理等。学生选修的课目也要考试，但有例外，如日语。该校目前还将汉语列为选修课。

英国中学考试的特点是，为培养中学生独立思考的能力，许多课都要考论文，如历史课论文成绩占 40%，其他知识占 60%。数学课也要考论文。论文一般采取开卷式，老师提前把题目告诉学生，字数在 2500 左右。

英国中学的考试评分标准分为 A-star, A, B, C, D, E, F, G, U。A-star 最好，相当于中国的 100 分；U 相当于零分。与国内中学不同的是，考试前学校给学生两周时间回家自己复习。

### 3. 关于英国青少年的家庭教育问题

我在 St. John Wall School 中学进行考察期间，与该校主管学生行为规范的 Helena 女士有比较多的合作，从她那里我了解到他们中学的青少年家庭教育问题。虽然英国和中国的国情不同，但是他们在家庭教育方面存在的问题也不少。

（1）单亲家庭。目前，英国的离婚率比较高，所以生活在单亲家庭的青少年也不少。在 St. John Wall School，一个班里来自完整家庭的学生大约占学生总数的 50%，大约有 80% 的单亲家庭是由离婚或者分居造成的。单亲家庭一般都面临比较严重的经济困难。在英国，它是继失业者、领取养老金者之后的最贫困者。不仅如此，那些来自单亲家庭的孩子往往学习成绩差，心理问题和情感方面的障碍也比较多。

（2）代沟问题。代沟问题也是一个比较严重的问题。父母和子女在一些问题上常常持有不同的看法，这些问题不仅涉及服装式样和发型之类的小事，还涉及升学、交朋友、就业等大事。许多未成年子女向父母要求更多的自由和自主权，有的甚至辍学，离家出走，吸烟甚至吸毒，很多父母不知道如何处理这样的问题，常常为他们和子女之间的矛盾所困扰。

（3）青春期教育。孩子们进入青春期后同父母发生冲突在英国家庭中特别常见，孩子不愿意受到父母的干涉，而吸烟、酗酒之类的事情让父母感到非常棘手。为了与孩子们沟通，达成和解，许多父母只好去读一些专业方面的书籍，听一些有关子女教育方面的讲座，并且参加关于青少年问题的专门课程的学习，以此来增长知识，寻求解决问题的办法。

（三）来自见闻

1. **英国的环境**

我们所到之处，有着清新的空气、洁净的街道、葱郁的树丛、遍地的花草。晴天时碧空万里，蓝天下到处是绿色的草地和参天古树，随手任拍一张都是一幅美丽的风景画。这里树林里到处是小动物在蹦蹦跳跳，小溪中的野鸭和天鹅在自由地嬉戏，自然环境保护得非常完好，给我留下了深刻的印象。相对中国而言，英国的历史并不长，但英国到处都是博物馆和古建筑。在繁华的城市中，常常能见到被保护得很好的城墙、码头、教堂等。古老与现代相得益彰、和谐共存。人们心情轻松、享受生活、讲求个性、注重实效，这种积极的生活方式也同样感染着每一个外来人。很多地方都有体育场馆，跑步的人处处可见，锻炼身体真正体现在众多群众性、自愿性、爱好型体育活动中。

2. **英国的法律法规**

英国的法律法规建设也让人啧啧称奇，其完备性、及时性、动态性、效用性和透明性体现在生活的许多细节中。以环境法为例，与环境相关的法律不下三四十部，法规有两百多篇，涉及到环境的每一个领域。英国只发现了一例外来鹦鹉感染禽流感，但是预防、监测、应急处理等法规就马上出台了。至于一部法规根据实际中出现的新情况一年内修改几次进行更新的情况比比皆是。法规出台后，有许多部门来监督执行，并面向社会通报情况，让法规不是停留在书面上，而是落到实处。同时，关于法规所涉及问题需要的表格、指导性文件、办事程序、负责部门等，在网上可以直接查到和下载，每隔一段时间公布统计信息，使得全社会都来参与、都来监督、都来遵守。作为一个高度发达的法制社会，这里不管是个人还是组织都需要严格遵守法律，而且社会诚信度较高。这一切让人感觉生活非常简单和愉悦。

### 3. 英国的信息与标志

在英国,各类基础信息丰富、全面、翔实的程度令人羡慕,无论是公众服务还是专业应用都很容易通过网络找到相应层次的信息、服务机构和联系人员,极大方便了应用和服务。当然,其资源和信息并非一朝一夕得来的,政府重视积累并常年累月的坚持是关键所在。信息的标识也有许多可取之处。比如,邮政编码是个人的重要信息,如同家庭电话号码一样需要一定程度的保密,因为根据邮政编码可以在网络上迅速定位到家庭地址以及航空影像。再比如,伦敦地铁四通八达,盘根错节,其复杂程度只要乘坐过的人都会有深刻的印象。但是,任何一个只认识几个基本英语单词的人,都能快速地找到要去乘坐地铁的通道和方向,因为标识十分简洁、醒目。身处信息时代,在英国,衣食住行等一切问题,除非必须本人到场,都可以通过网络搞定。以旅游为例,从目的地选取、宾馆预订到车船票购买等系列事宜都可以身在家中,通过一张银行卡、一台上网电脑轻轻松松完成。你甚至可以将到达某个城市火车站或飞机场后如何前往预订宾馆的路线图打印出来。现代通信和网络技术在英国社会的广泛应用并不排斥一个个简单明了的指路牌或导游图出现在大大小小城市的街头,这些路牌或导游地图设置在重要的路口或游客容易迷路的地方,设身处地从陌生人需求的角度出发,极大地方便了来自世界各地的游人。另一方面,能够简单处理的事情在这里绝不会复杂化。这从电子邮件的使用中可见一斑。无论是相互通信还是会议安排、通知通告都是通过电子邮件来办理,并具有类似正式文件的权威功效,作用远远超过电话。英国人对实质内容的重视远远大于形式,不管是什么会议,简单地介绍后马上切入主题,而对演讲或报告后的问题和讨论也是热烈异常,用时会非常多。

## 三、反思

### (一) 关于教育——让学生享受课堂

回想在伯明翰大学学习期间的每一天,每个课堂无不传出阵阵欢声笑语。大家愉快地学习,愉快地回答问题,愉快地做作业,愉快地写论文,满意地完成培训课程的学习。我们的学习始终处于一种自由、开放、创新的氛围中。教学的每个环节无不渗透着创新的精神,外教在我们身上采取的是"广种薄收"的方法,大量的"输入",有限的"输出",使每个学生都处于爱学习、渴望学习的状态。而反思我们的教育,太注重结果,使学生和教师都背上了沉重的负担。学习不是一种快乐，一种补充，一种兴趣，而是必需要承受的重任。长此以久，教师的教只是一种机械工作，而不是人性的发挥、对大自然的探求、对人类真情的交流。国内的教育体系与英国的教育体系不同，我们要面对的是大班教学，如何把英国先进的教学理念灵活地运用到课堂中去，还需要我们不断地探索、研究。

### （二）关于新课程的实施——要有全面的认识

在到英国学习之前，我一直认为英国的课程改革应是走在世界各国的前面，通过考察，却发现事实并非如此。虽然英国在20世纪90年代已经制定了新的课程标准，也编了一些新的教科书，但他们的教学方法还是比较传统的。我们看到，英国教师的课堂教学大都以讲授、讨论为主，辅之以活动，尤其是英语、数学、历史、地理等科目，很多课室虽建有多媒体，但是教师使用得并不多。一些校长和老师认为，面向新世纪的挑战，教育必须更新观念，改革课程的设置和教材内容以及教学方法，但是，对优秀的文化传统和有效的教学方式不能轻易放弃。我们很赞同他们的观点，目前，我国一些地区、一些学校在宣传新课改的时候并不是很客观，存在一些误解。基础教育涉及面广，课程改革是一个非常庞大的系统工程，推进步骤既要积极，又要稳妥。目前，我们实施新课程有操之过急的现象，对新课程的实质的理解有些偏差。从这种切身体会出发，我们建议各级教育管理部门和学校多创造机会，让更多的老师到国外参观考察，开阔眼界，走有中国特色的教育改革之路。

### （三）关于环境教育——从一点一滴抓起

环保意识已经深入到每一个英国人的骨子里。公共场所无人喧哗；汽车主动给行人让路；购物、上车主动排队；见面互致问候；不随地扔脏物，吐痰；房前屋后种植鲜花；自觉遵守各项法律法规等。除了感慨英国秀丽安闲的风景外，让我印象深刻的就是遍布各地的博物馆，从一场战争到一条小船，英国人都用他们独特的方式——博物馆予以纪念，而且绝大部分是免费的。

## 四、感悟

三个月的培训时间很短，不知不觉间就过去了。
老师的教育总是有限的，我们要在不断的实践中逐步成熟。
我们未来的路还很长，我们要学习的东西还很多，我们的责任重大！
学习不是目的，学以致用才是目标所在。

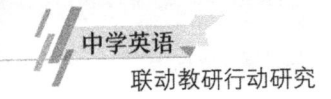

用所学的新知识、新本领,为广州教育事业做出贡献,才是学习的最终目标。

感悟很多,思考很多,收获很多……展望未来,让我们更加自信地迎接各种机遇和挑战!

# 第十章 2023年广州市初中学业水平考试英语试题评析及教学启示*

2023年广州市初中学业水平考试（以下简称"新中考"）英语试题基于《义务教育英语课程标准（2022年版）》的理念，对学生的知识掌握和能力素养提出新要求。应对新中考，师生都要把握新课标修订后考查的新趋势，实现教考衔接，有效备考。

## 一、基于新课标，体现立德树人的价值取向

《新课标》强调在主题语境、主题意义引领下学习语言知识和文化知识。2023年广州新中考的命题呈现出基于情境、追求本源、点多面广等特点，注重传递核心价值，引导学生形成适应未来社会发展的正确的世界观、价值观和人生观，落实立德树人根本任务。

语法选择题来源于中华经典成语故事"笨鸟先飞"，讲述了先天体弱的幼鸟通过坚强意志和刻苦锻炼最终成为第一只会飞的小鸟，鼓励学生勇于挑战逆境，自强不息。完形填空的语篇讲述鲸鱼救人的故事，引导学生关爱野生动物，倡导人类与自然和谐共生的理念。阅读理解A篇给需要帮助的青少年提供解决实际生活问题的建议，帮助他们克服困难，成长为独立、有自信心的个体。阅读理解B篇讲述的是新生交友的故事，也是每位青少年成长历程中都可能经历的故事。新生艾米在迎新破冰比赛中和队员们群策群力，最终虽然只拿到第二名，但收获了彼此的友谊。故事鼓励学生积极融入集体，倡导团队精神和合作意识。阅读理解C篇结合热点话题提出机器人外貌设计的思考和讨论，引导学生思考科技对社会的影响，并培养他们对新技术的理解和适应能力。阅读理解D篇介绍了过去词典的编撰过程：阅读文献，抄录词卡、卡片排序，定义词汇……一部大词典的编撰，常意味着编者数十载孜孜不倦的耕耘。学生做题时不但了解了历史，还领略了工匠精神，获得了一次职业启蒙。阅读填空的语篇强调了绿色思维、绿色建筑和可持续发展的重要性。它引发了关于环境

---

\* 本文收录于《点评广东中考试题 剖析中考动向》，西藏人民出版社2023年版，第8页。

保护、资源利用和空间规划的思考，引导学生以可持续的方式思考和行动，为构建一个更加可持续和健康的未来做出贡献。语篇填词介绍中国端午节，强调了传统文化的重要性、团队合作和年轻人的成长，鼓励年轻人弘扬中华传统文化，参与传统节日的庆祝活动，培养团队合作精神和积极进取的态度。

## 二、基于学业质量标准，体现与核心素养的有机结合

《新课标》指出学业质量是学生在完成课程阶段性学习后的学业成就表现，反映核心素养要求。学业质量标准是以核心素养为主要维度，结合课程内容，对学生学业成就具体表现特征的整体刻画。英语学业质量标准以学生在语言能力、文化意识、思维品质和学习能力等方面的核心素养及其学段目标为基础，结合英语课程的内容和学生英语学习的进阶情况，从学习结果的角度描述各学段学业成就的典型表现。2023年广州新中考英语试题体现了核心素养的考查重点。

试题将思维品质的考查融入到阅读填空中：第41题需要观察与辨析，理清上下文之间的因果关系；第42题需要归纳与推断，归纳首段的主要观点，同时推断与下文之间的关联；第43题需要观察与辨析，综合思考与多角度分析材料选择各个因素之间的关系；第44题需要批判与创新，从使用者的角度进行创新思考，绿色能源让人们感到更加舒适是观点，接着举例说明理由，例如，自然风为人们带来更清新的空气；第46题需要归纳与推断，能够提取、整理、概括下文的关键信息，主要内容、思想和观点。总之，各考点都会展现出学生的认知与思维水平，有助于考查其解决问题时的逻辑性、思辨力和创新度。

## 三、服务"双减"，加强了试题的开放性和创新性

在"双减"政策纵深推进的背景下，为了改变机械刷题的备考模式，2023年广州新中考英语加强了开放性和创新性，培养学生运用跨学科视角、创造性地解决问题的能力。

完成句子强调了学科整合与跨学科学习的重要性。首先提到了一群学生通过数学项目不仅提高了数学水平，还改善了飞镖技巧，并赢得了广东飞镖锦标赛，鼓励学生将不同学科的知识进行整合和应用，促进跨学科学习，从而在实际问题中提升综合能力。紧接着提到了作者喜欢的学科是美术，并思考如何利用数学知识更好地进行绘画，引导学生认识到数学在各个领域的应用价值，包

括艺术。最后表达了作者希望有一天自己的绘画作品能够在美术馆展示的愿望，鼓励学生树立追求梦想和奋斗目标的信念，通过跨学科学习努力实现自己的理想。

再来看书面表达的考查，情境为向交换生 Sam 介绍主题（theme）为"健康你和我"的志愿服务活动安排。一改往年的中文内容提示，本次使用的是 A 冒号 B 的全英语内容提示，除了提示了 Theme、Time、Place，关于 Activities、Purpose 都完全开放。从此类命题的趋向看，新中考命题视角更灵活，也尊重个性化与差异化，实际上给学生提供了更大的思维空间和展示平台。

## 四、启示

《新课标》背景下的新中考引导教学聚焦于培育和发展核心素养的育人模式，推进立德树人理念落地课堂，落实"双减"政策，提质增效。应对新中考，课堂教学要建立课堂所学和学生生活的关联，让学生多进行合作性探究、开放性思考和多元化问题解决。同时，课后作业也需要不断推陈出新，以引导学生适应探究式学习和新中考水平测试与选拔功能相关的要求。

# 第十一章 "实施过程性评价,发展英语核心素养"广州市高一英语市区联动教研活动简报[*]

在"高畦新雨足,布谷唤春耕"的时节,全市教育教学工作者们也耕耘不辍。2022年3月31日,广州市高一英语市区联动教研活动如期在线上进行。

主题:基于核心素养发展的教学评价理念,实施过程性英语教学评价。

对象:高一英语教师——教与研携手,学与思并肩。

形式:研讨课——课堂展风采,教研促成长。

## 一、准备阶段

本次教研活动全程得到广州市教研院镇祝桂老师的悉心指导。镇老师不仅从宏观上把关育人目标,而且从理论到实践指导本次活动的教学设计、课件和学案甚至海报通知的制作,尤其帮助参与的教师们进一步厘清了语法教学的思路和明确了教学重点。海珠区教研院张志梅老师首先建立三人组微信群,指导两位主讲老师一起研课,然后依靠中心组和学校的集体智慧,进行了教案、学案和课件的修改。

## 二、研讨交流

### (一)贴心的主持人

广州市为明学校的韦微老师用英语主持了本次教研活动,她精心制作海报通知和课件,给发言的老师们制作图文并茂的介绍,把视频和课件制做成超级链接。韦老师声音愉悦,言简意赅,整个过程如行云流水,又有满满的仪式感。

---

[*] 本活动由广州市教育研究院镇祝桂指导。本文由海珠外国语实验中学肖丽琴、海珠区教育发展研究院张志梅撰写,原发表于"广州市中学英语教研"微信公众号(2022-04-13)。

## （二）课例展示一

广州市第五中学的王丽老师展示听说课，教学内容是必修三第 3 单元的 Listening and Speaking，话题是"Talk about the origins of American food"（谈论美国食物的起源）。王老师设计了听前、听中、听后任务和"课堂学习过程评价表"，并针对不同任务中的活动进行了不同形式的过程性评价。如听前的任务完成以老师点评为主，老师对学生回答问题做口头点评；听中的判断和填空两个任务以自评或同学互评为主，老师点评为辅。在最后 Speaking 的环节，王老师升华了主题意义："如果我们一直对中国文化充满自信和骄傲，中国传统文化就有无限生命力，也会让世界更加美好。"

## （三）课例展示二

紧接着广州市第九十七中学周燕梨老师展示了本单元的语法课："省略"。周老师以学生阅读和表演两则对话作为导入，引出课题"省略"的定义和功能，接着让学生讨论和发现一段对话中的省略现象，加深对"省略"形式和功能的理解。她进而带领学生发现该语法在公共标识、新闻标题、日记、便条或非正式信件等语境中的其他功能，然后带着学生运用"省略"改写介绍三藩市的来信中的并列句、定语从句、状语从句。然后，放手让学生自己运用"省略"填句子，完成介绍广州特色的回信。最后，带领学生总结本课要点，课后完成"课堂学习过程评价表"。在上课过程中，周老师也会对学生的任务完成情况及时做出评价。

## （四）同伴点评

广州市第五中学钟仲嫦老师和广州市第九十七中学王浩生老师分别就这两堂课进行了点评。

钟仲嫦老师先概括了王丽老师的听说课三大特点：以终为始、情景创设、过程评价。然后条分缕析，指出过程性评价既有同伴互评，也有自评。然后，钟老师提出两个小建议：①让学生回答问题时说出完整的句子；②可用更为简化的自评表。

王浩生老师从《新课标》提倡的以语言运用为导向的"形式—意义—使用"三维动态语法观出发，分析主题意义引领下的高中英语语法教学应使学生在主题语境中体悟、分析、归纳和使用语法规则，培育学生的综合语言运用能力。而周燕梨老师的这堂语法课的四个步骤恰好与之一一对应。周老师在过程性评价方面按不同任务运用了不同的评价方式，如同伴互评、自我评价。王老师详细例析了周老师预设的四个教学目标如何逐一实现。王老师为评课还专门录制了点评视频，非常用心！

两位老师的评课既肯定了优点，也提出了建议，达到了同伴学习、共同提高的目的。

### （五）活动总结

海珠区教研员张志梅老师做了"聚焦核心素养和过程性评价的市区联动教研活动初探——以 Book 3 Unit 3 Diverse Cultures 听说课和语法课为例"为专题的总结发言。

张老师从三方面进行了分享：新挑战；我们的尝试；回顾与展望。

新挑战源自三点：市区联动教研新方式；基于核心素养发展的教学评价理念带来的新要求；过程性评价实施的可行性和实效性。

我们的尝试主要体现在四个方面，旨在发展师生的核心素养：

(1) 市、区、校融合的学习共同体，发展学习能力。

我们珍惜这次给老师们提供的锻炼机会和平台，激励老师们积极参与研究《新课标》、新教材、新评价、新改革，老师们的学习热情很高。

(2) 研究《新课标》，用好新教材，确定核心素养导向的教学设计，提高文化意识和思维品质。

基于对《新课标》的学习，我们以 Diverse Cultures 主题意义为引领，尝试使用体现《新课标》理念的动词如 help、facilitate、encourage、invite、lead、demonstrate 等来规范教学行为，使用 learn、understand、enjoy、improve、evaluate、reflect、assess 等体现核心素养为导向的学习目标。

(3) 依据《新课标》，对应教学目标，尝试实施过程性评价，提高思维品质。

周燕梨老师和王丽老师的教学设计在课标提供的案例基础上调整如下：把 Teacher's activities 改为 Teacher-Student activities；并且增加 Evaluation，尝试了包括 Self-evaluation, Peer-evaluation, T-S evaluation, Internet evaluation 等评价方式。

(4) 坚持多用英语做事，提高 Language Ability。

教研员带头，鼓励老师们一起用英语听课评课，主持、发言，写总结、全员参与集体备课，大家资源共享，减负增效，提高语言能力。

然后，张老师和同行们探讨如何做好关于过程性评价的问题，特别就学生自评后的结果反馈提出三个方面的建议：①教师要运用丰富的评价语言，让学生树立自信心；②创造民主、和谐、轻松的学习氛围；③教师要及时总结反馈，充分发挥评价的激励作用。然后就两节研讨课以无记名的问卷方式收集听课老师的反馈评价，为上课老师以及教研工作的改进提出宝贵建议。

## 三、结语

这次市区联动教研活动内容丰富翔实，进展顺利有序，全英主持、授课、点评和总结分析，有浓浓的英语氛围，线上互动讨论热烈，老师们认为市引领区校，形成了学习共同体并发展了共同体，引领教师专业成长，促进教师队伍建设，提升区域联动科研水平，对于每一位参与的老师来说，机会难得，意义重大，因此，我们也当不辱使命、不负众望！

"一缕春风舒碧叶，千丝细雨润青苗。"这次活动如春风化雨，让我们尝到了教研的幸福和乐趣，也是我们今后不断学习和进步的动力，这个过程才是最有意义的。期待广州英语教研之花结出更多丰硕成果！

# 第十二章　用英语推进中西文化交流互鉴*
## ——广州市海珠区初二英语教研活动简报

为了引导青少年建立与中华优秀传统文化的亲密关系，在对中华优秀传统文化的文化自觉和文化自信中走向世界，用英语讲好中国故事，推进中西文化交流互鉴，2023年6月1日，海珠区2022学年下学期第17周初二英语教研活动在广州市华海双语学校演艺厅进行。

本次教研活动全程得到广东外语外贸大学郑杰教授、广州市海珠区教育学会中学英语教学研究分会副会长张志梅教研员和广州市华海双语学校外籍教师Lukas的悉心指导，由广州市海珠外国语实验中学附属学校梁蕴娜老师主持。具体的流程如下：①课例展示，八年级下册Unit 7 The Unknown World-Reading（广州市为明学校刘志刚老师）；②课例展示，诗歌《天净沙·秋思》双语教学（华南师范大学附属中学陈颖园老师）；③专家点评，广州市华海双语学校外籍教师Lukas；④专家点评，广东外语外贸大学英文学院郑杰教授；⑤总结发言，广州市海珠区教育发展研究院张志梅教研员。

首先，来自广州市为明学校的刘志刚老师带来了八年级下册Unit 7 The Unknown World-Reading的教学展示课。刘老师首先引入与外星人相关的话题和观点，调动学生的相关背景知识，激发其学习兴趣。接下来，刘老师通过故事元素的"蛛网图"，启发学生根据图片和标题预测故事可能发生的内容，培养了学生的分析和预测能力。接下来，刘老师讲解课文内容，同时提出相关问题链，让学生融入课堂，还通过比较标题和深度思考任务，培养学生的批判性思维。在最后的输出部分，学生通过小组合作续写故事，发挥自己的想象力和培养团队合作的能力。本堂课的情感目标是告诉学生探索无止境，人类应该不断地创造可能。本堂课气氛和谐，师生互动良好，学生参与度高，教学效果良好。

接下来，广州市华南师范大学附属中学的陈颖园老师为我们带来了英语诗歌《天净沙·秋思》的双语教学展示课。陈老师首先展示了本节课的学习目

---

\* 本活动由广州市海珠区教育发展研究院张志梅指导。本文由广州市为明学校刘志刚撰写，原发表于"海珠教育学会"微信公众号（2023-06-25）。

标，让学生清晰地知道本节课的学习旅程。然后一步一步带领学生吟唱古诗，感受诗歌韵律之美，赏析诗歌意境，领悟作品内涵，获得良好情感体验。接下来，陈老师让学生掌握意象种类，运用比较和对比能力，对比《天净沙·秋思》与英语诗歌 Home Home Sweet Home 的写作特点。通过一步一步地构建，从意象、图片、情感、成诗，比较两首关于家的诗歌，让学生更深层次感受中西诗歌的独特性。本堂课内容新颖，师生互动良好，学生表现积极，发散思维性强，给人以美的享受。

第三位是来自华南师范大学附属中学海珠双语学校的外籍教师 Lukas，他对刘志刚老师的展示课进行了专家点评。

Lukas 指出：刘老师通过预测环节，让学生猜测故事内容，培养了学生的发散思维能力。通过开放性问题链的设置，引发学生多角度、多层次地思考。学生通过课堂讨论，可以学习其他同学的思维视角，开放性问题没有固定的答案，没有对错，体现了对于自由思考的认可和尊重。和谐的教学氛围让学生在轻松愉悦中学习和思考，达成启发思维、培养学习兴趣的目标。

第四位是来自广东外语外贸大学英文学院的郑杰教授，他对陈颖园老师的展示课做了专家点评。郑教授指出：陈老师的课对于诗歌教学是很好的尝试和开端，是跨文化交际和跨文化教学中一个重要的起点。诗歌教学通过发现不同文化中事物的概念不同，通过比较不同文化之间的差异，让学生领略到文化之间的差异。尊重不同，求同存异，取其精华，去其糟粕。郑教授还列举了中国文化和外国文化对于离家的情感的差异。他用三只小猪的故事说明外国文化中，三只小猪离家时候的独立和喜悦，给人以不同角度的思考与启迪，让人领略了不同文化下故事情感的差异。如此精彩的点评启发思考，让人收获良多。

最后，广州市海珠区教育学会中学英语教学研究分会副会长张志梅教研员做了题为"用英语推进中西文化交流互鉴与创新"的总结发言。张老师对标《新课标》，强调中华经典是中华优秀传统文化的重要载体，也是实施文化育人工程的核心内容。英语教师有责任弘扬中华优秀文化和世界上一切优秀的文化，今天通过跨学科融合教学，促使学生在自主、合作、探究的过程中，将汉语与英语诗歌在相互联系中融合，让各种思维观念在交流碰撞中融结，培养了学生的学习兴趣，增强了对中华优秀文化的自信心。今后我们将继续推广各种形式的文化交流，包括语言学习、文化融入以及协作项目，创建更加相互联系且和谐的世界，共同塑造更美好的未来。最后，张老师用一首自创的诗歌《挖呀挖》把两节展示课和专家点评的精髓都展示了出来。

### 挖呀挖

在未知的世界里，挖呀挖呀挖

寻外星人的踪影，探宇宙的谜

在马致远的秋思里，挖呀挖呀挖

品古诗的意境，悟诗人的情，

在 Sweet 的 Home 里，挖呀挖呀挖

比中西的文化，采中外的精华

在专家的点评里，挖呀挖呀挖

种人文课堂的种子，开实践的花

张老师智慧、优雅、和善和创新的风格，一直影响着每一位参会的老师，让老师们勇于在教学里尝试，保持谦谦之风。张老师还衷心感谢刘志刚和陈颖园两位老师的精彩课堂展示，感谢 Lukas 和郑杰教授的专家点评和精心指导，感谢华海双语学校对本次教研的大力支持，感谢中心组老师们的精心准备，感谢所有老师们的积极参与，最后祝大朋友和小朋友们儿童节快乐。

# Epilogue

On the path of English linkage teaching and research, we deeply feel a simple yet profound truth: one person may walk fast, but a group of people can go much further on this journey. When we gather wisdom and strength, united in the pursuit of the grand goal of education, each of us becomes a beacon, shining brightly in the darkness. We believe that the power of education does not solely come from classrooms and textbooks, but also from collaboration and sharing. When we intertwine experience, wisdom, and creativity, ordinary moments transform into magical sparks. Teamwork gives us infinite possibilities because each person's contribution is like a star, illuminating the unknown ahead.

Along this path, we have encountered challenges and difficulties, but it is the power of unity that enables us to overcome each obstacle. We support and assist each other, facing difficulties together. We contemplate with heart, interpret with love, and gain wisdom and growth from them. Each person is a part of the team, and each individual's efforts propel us forward. When we are closely united and trust each other, we transcend our personal limitations, blending into a stronger force. In this journey of English teaching and research, we not only achieve personal growth but also collective progress. We inspire each other, spreading love and hope, contributing our own strength to the cause of education.

Let us continue moving forward, gracefully dancing on the stage of English collaborative teaching and research, playing the harmonious and joyful melody of wisdom. Let us always maintain an open mindset, embracing the joy within and sharing the beauty of life with others. Let us remember our shared mission, infusing love and wisdom into every classroom, every research endeavor, igniting the spark in the hearts of every child. May they savor the beauty of language, develop diverse thinking, possess a global perspective, and the ability to engage in cross-cultural communication, stepping into a broader world!

# 后　　记

在英语联动教研的路上，我们深感一个朴素而伟大的真理：独行速，众行远。当我们汇聚智慧和力量，共同追求教育的宏伟目标时，每个人都成为一座灯塔，在黑暗中闪耀着光芒。我们相信，教育的力量不仅来自课堂和书本，更源自合作与分享。当我们将经验、智慧和创意交织在一起时，那些平凡的瞬间便化作了神奇的火花。团队合作让我们拥有了无限的可能性，因为每个人的贡献都如同一颗星星，点亮着未知的前方。

在这条道路上，我们曾遇到挑战和困难，但正是团结的力量让我们跨越了一个个障碍。我们相互支持、互帮互助，共同面对困难，我们用心去感悟，用爱去诠释，并从中获得智慧和成长。每个人都是团队的一部分，每个人的付出都推动着我们向前迈进，因为当我们紧密团结，彼此信任时，我们能够超越个人的局限，融汇成更强大的力量，使我们在英语教研的旅途中收获更多。我们不仅获得个人的成长，更获得共同的进步。我们互相激励，传播着爱与希望，为教育事业贡献力量。

让我们一起继续前行，在英语联动教研的舞台上翩然起舞，用智慧的旋律奏响和谐幸福的乐章。让我们永远保持开放的心态，乐享其中，与他人共同分享这份生命的融合之美。让我们铭记共同的使命，不断提升自己的精神境界，勠力同心，勇于担当，不负韶华，携手共进，倾心守护这片教育教研热土，将爱和智慧注入每一个课堂、每一次教研；点燃每个孩子心中的火花，让他们品味语言的美妙，发展多元思维，具备全球视野和跨文化交流的能力，走向更宽广的世界！

2023 年 10 月 16 号于广州